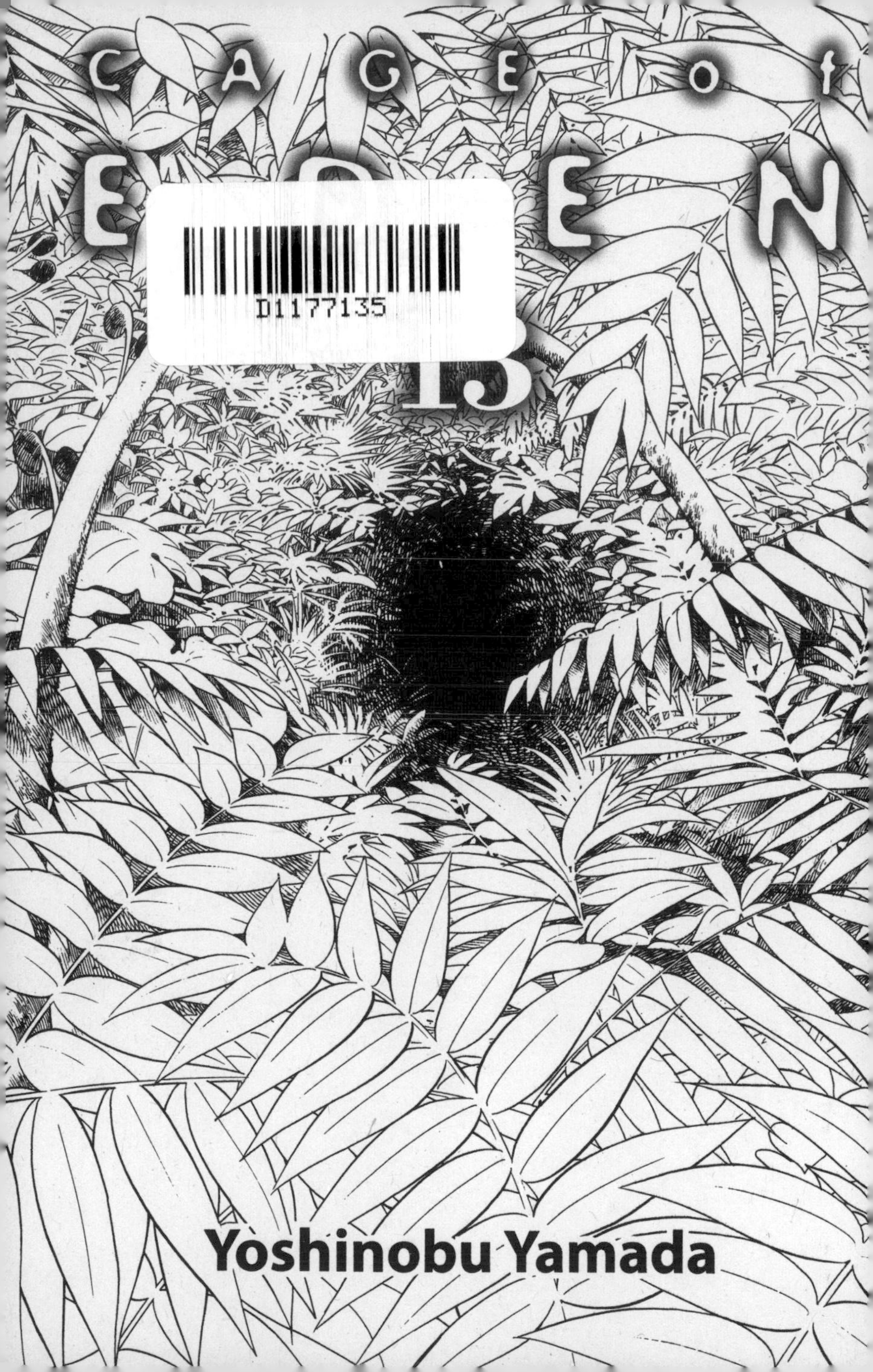
CAGE of
EDEN
13
Yoshinobu Yamada

CAGE of EDEN

CONTENTS

Chapter 104 A MYSTERIOUS LADY

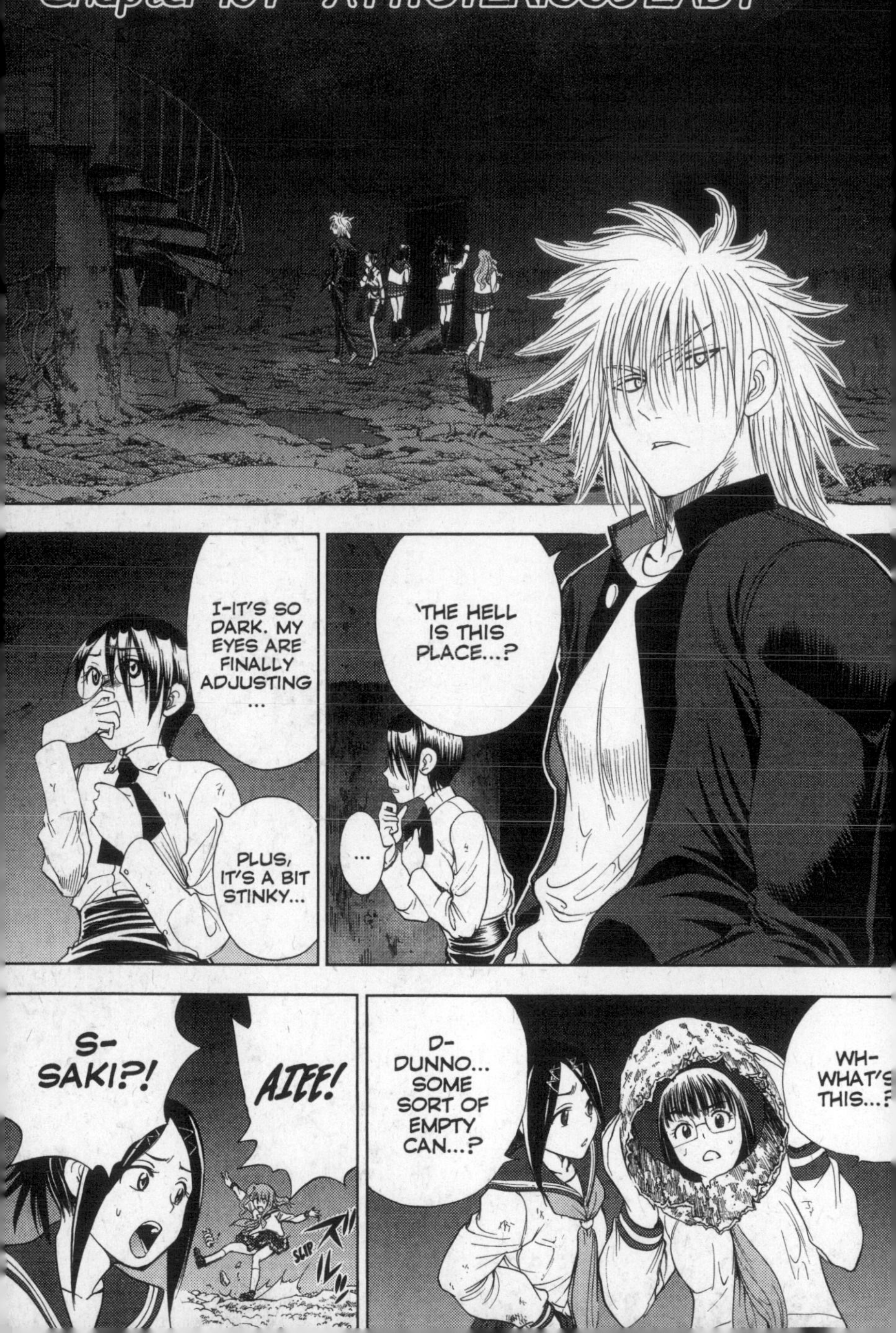
'THE HELL IS THIS PLACE...?
...
I-IT'S SO DARK. MY EYES ARE FINALLY ADJUSTING ...
PLUS, IT'S A BIT STINKY...
WH- WHAT'S THIS...?
D- DUNNO... SOME SORT OF EMPTY CAN...?
AIEE!
SLIP
S- SAKI?!

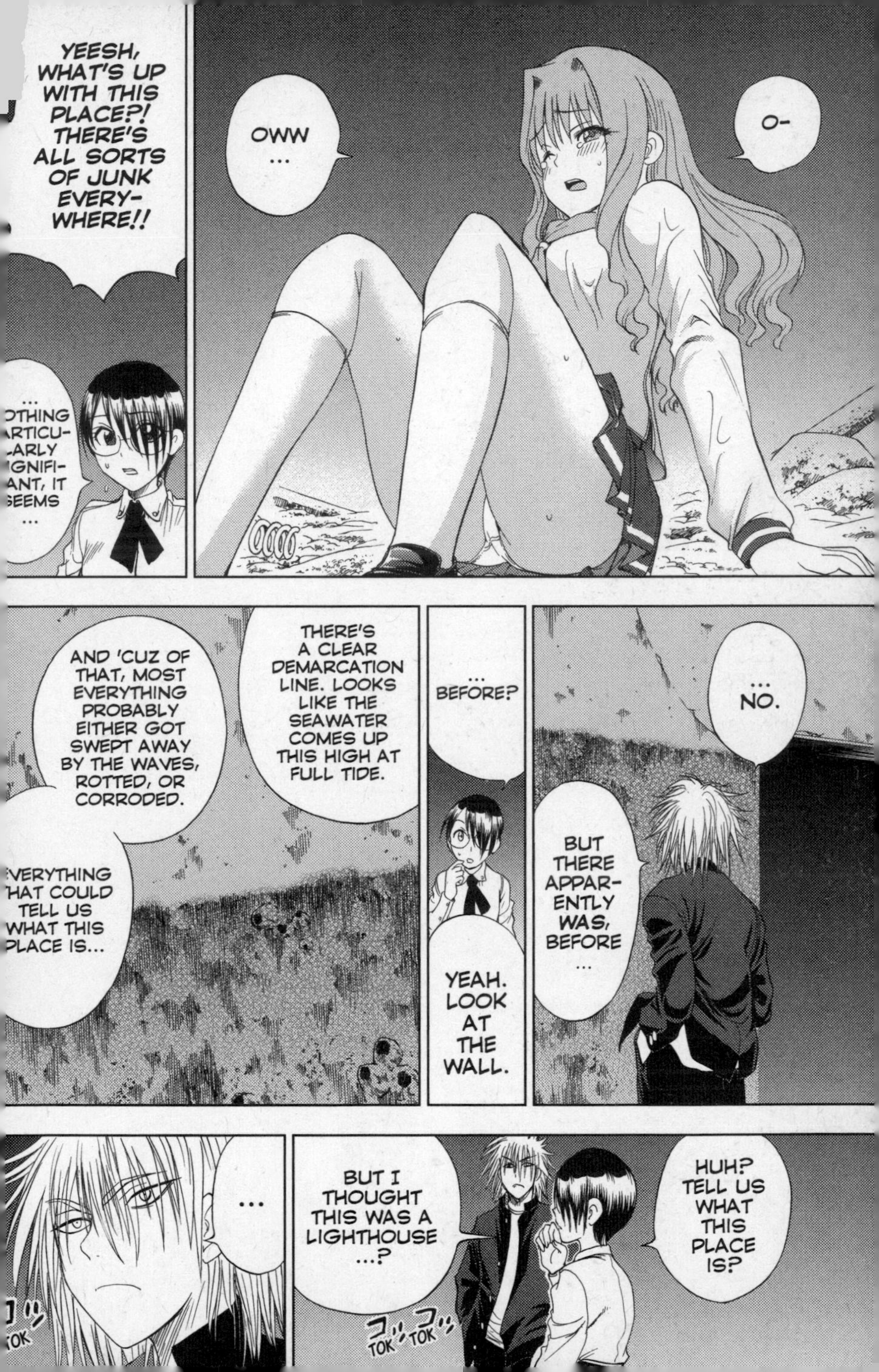
O-
OWW ...
YEESH, WHAT'S UP WITH THIS PLACE?! THERE'S ALL SORTS OF JUNK EVERY-WHERE!!
... OTHING ARTICU-LARLY IGNIFI-ANT, IT SEEMS ...
... NO.
BUT THERE APPAR-ENTLY WAS, BEFORE ...
... BEFORE?
YEAH. LOOK AT THE WALL.
THERE'S A CLEAR DEMARCATION LINE. LOOKS LIKE THE SEAWATER COMES UP THIS HIGH AT FULL TIDE.
AND 'CUZ OF THAT, MOST EVERYTHING PROBABLY EITHER GOT SWEPT AWAY BY THE WAVES, ROTTED, OR CORRODED.
EVERYTHING HAT COULD TELL US WHAT THIS PLACE IS...
HUH? TELL US WHAT THIS PLACE IS?
BUT I THOUGHT THIS WAS A LIGHTHOUSE ...?
TOK TOK
...
TOK

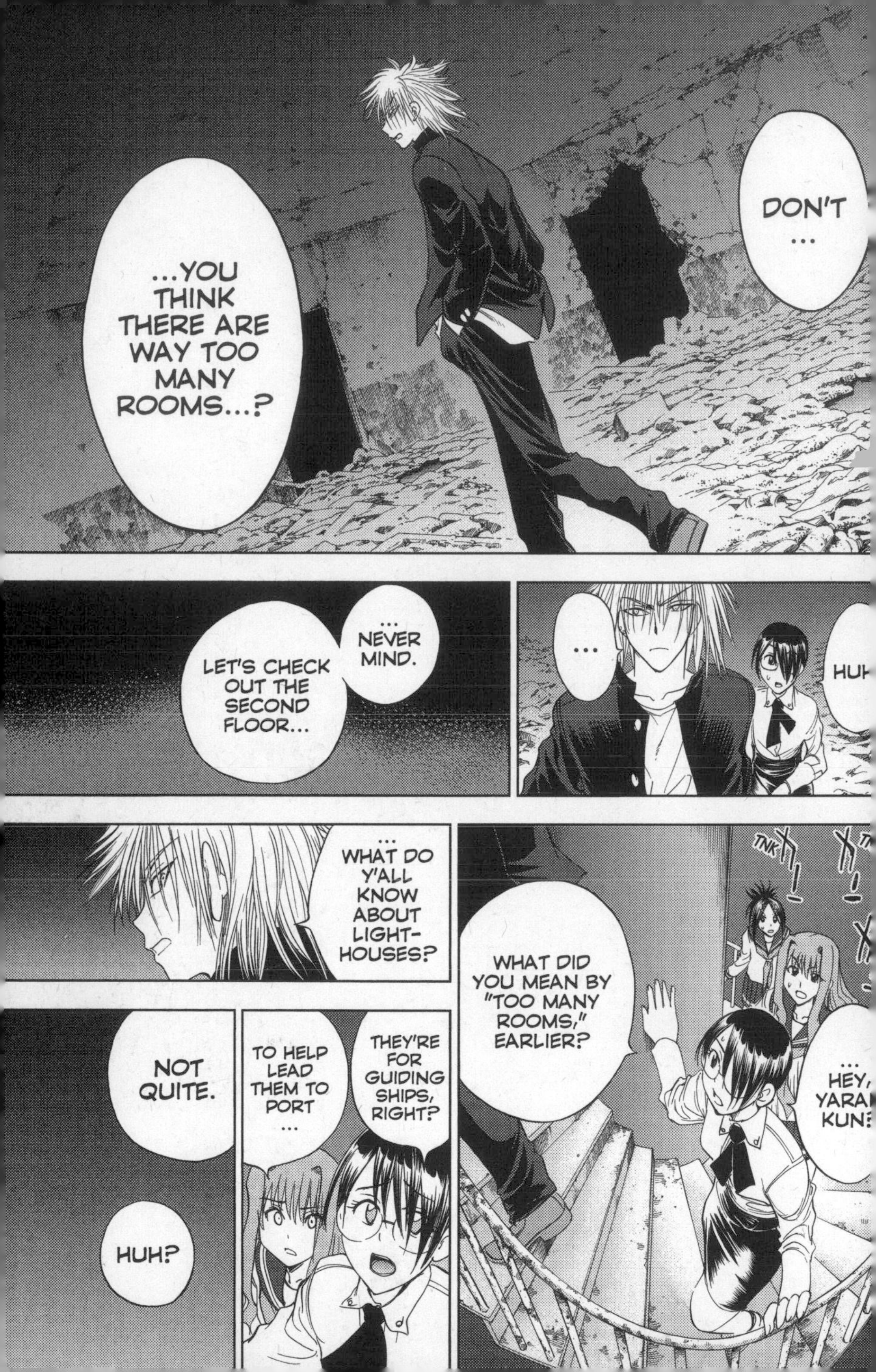
DON'T ...
...YOU THINK THERE ARE WAY TOO MANY ROOMS...?
HU
...
... NEVER MIND.
LET'S CHECK OUT THE SECOND FLOOR...
TNK
... HEY, YARA KUN?
WHAT DID YOU MEAN BY "TOO MANY ROOMS," EARLIER?
... WHAT DO Y'ALL KNOW ABOUT LIGHT-HOUSES?
THEY'RE FOR GUIDING SHIPS, RIGHT?
TO HELP LEAD THEM TO PORT ...
NOT QUITE.
HUH?

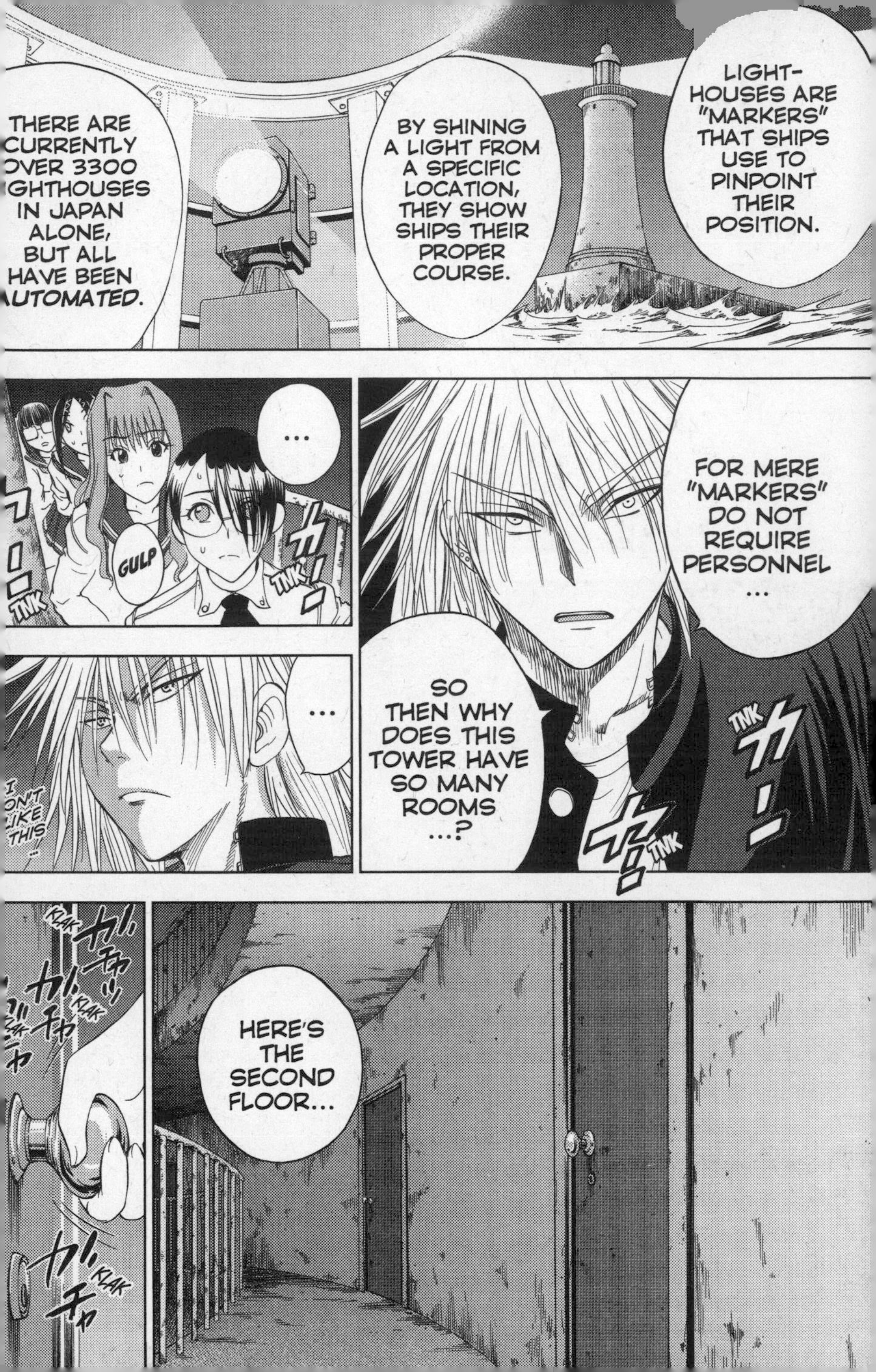
LIGHT-HOUSES ARE "MARKERS" THAT SHIPS USE TO PINPOINT THEIR POSITION.
BY SHINING A LIGHT FROM A SPECIFIC LOCATION, THEY SHOW SHIPS THEIR PROPER COURSE.
THERE ARE CURRENTLY OVER 3300 IGHTHOUSES IN JAPAN ALONE, BUT ALL HAVE BEEN UTOMATED.
FOR MERE "MARKERS" DO NOT REQUIRE PERSONNEL ...
SO THEN WHY DOES THIS TOWER HAVE SO MANY ROOMS ...?
TNK
TNK
...
GULP
TNK
TNK
...
I ON'T IKE THIS ...
HERE'S THE SECOND FLOOR...
KLAK
KLAK
KLAK
KLAK

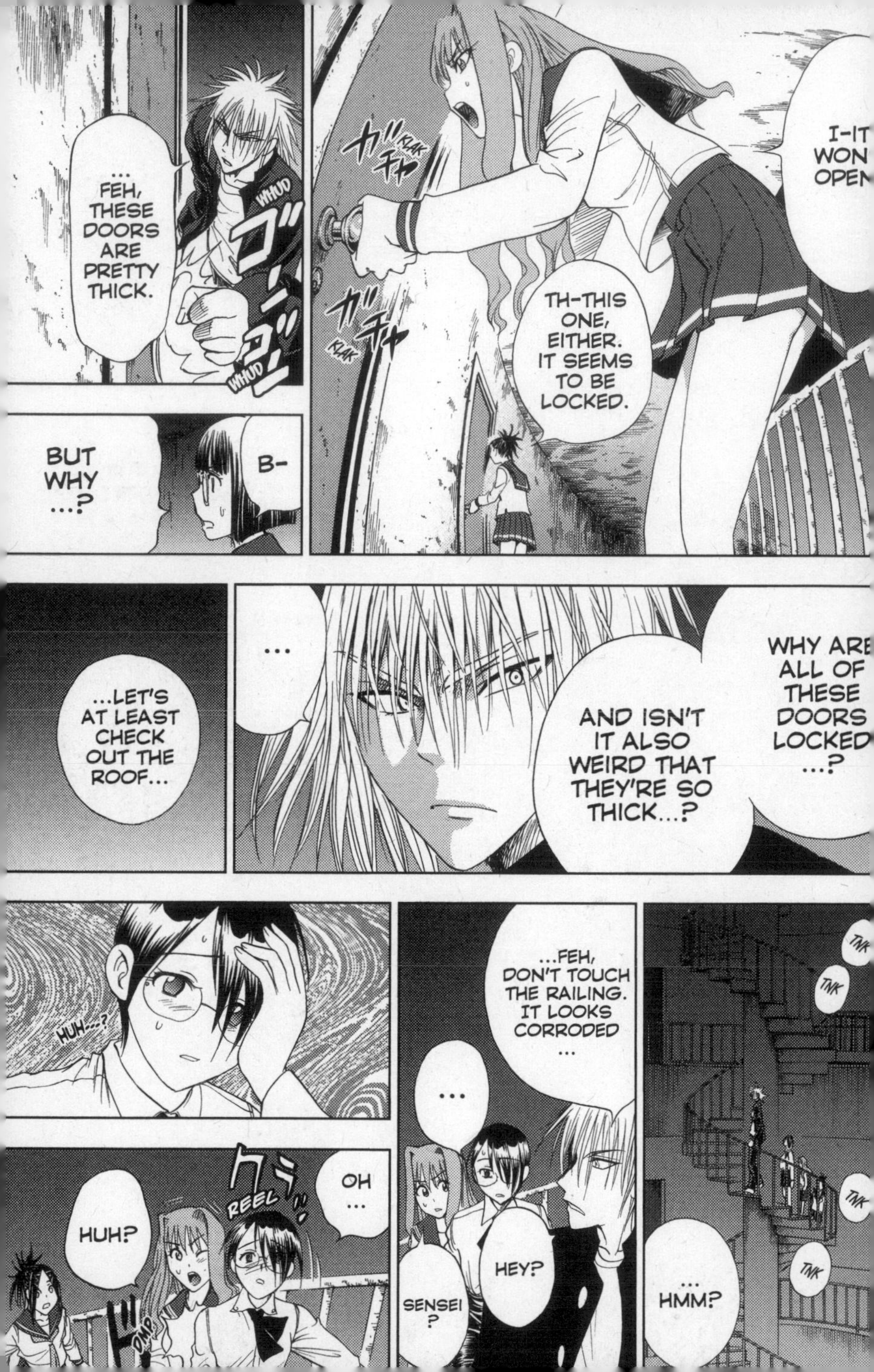
I-IT WON OPEN
KLAK
KLAK
TH-THIS ONE, EITHER. IT SEEMS TO BE LOCKED.
... FEH, THESE DOORS ARE PRETTY THICK.
WHUD
WHUD
B-
BUT WHY ...?
WHY ARE ALL OF THESE DOORS LOCKED ...?
AND ISN'T IT ALSO WEIRD THAT THEY'RE SO THICK...?
...
...LET'S AT LEAST CHECK OUT THE ROOF...
TNK
TNK
TNK
TNK
... HMM?
...FEH, DON'T TOUCH THE RAILING. IT LOOKS CORRODED ...
...
HEY?
SENSEI ?
HUH...?
OH ...
REEL
HUH?
THOMP

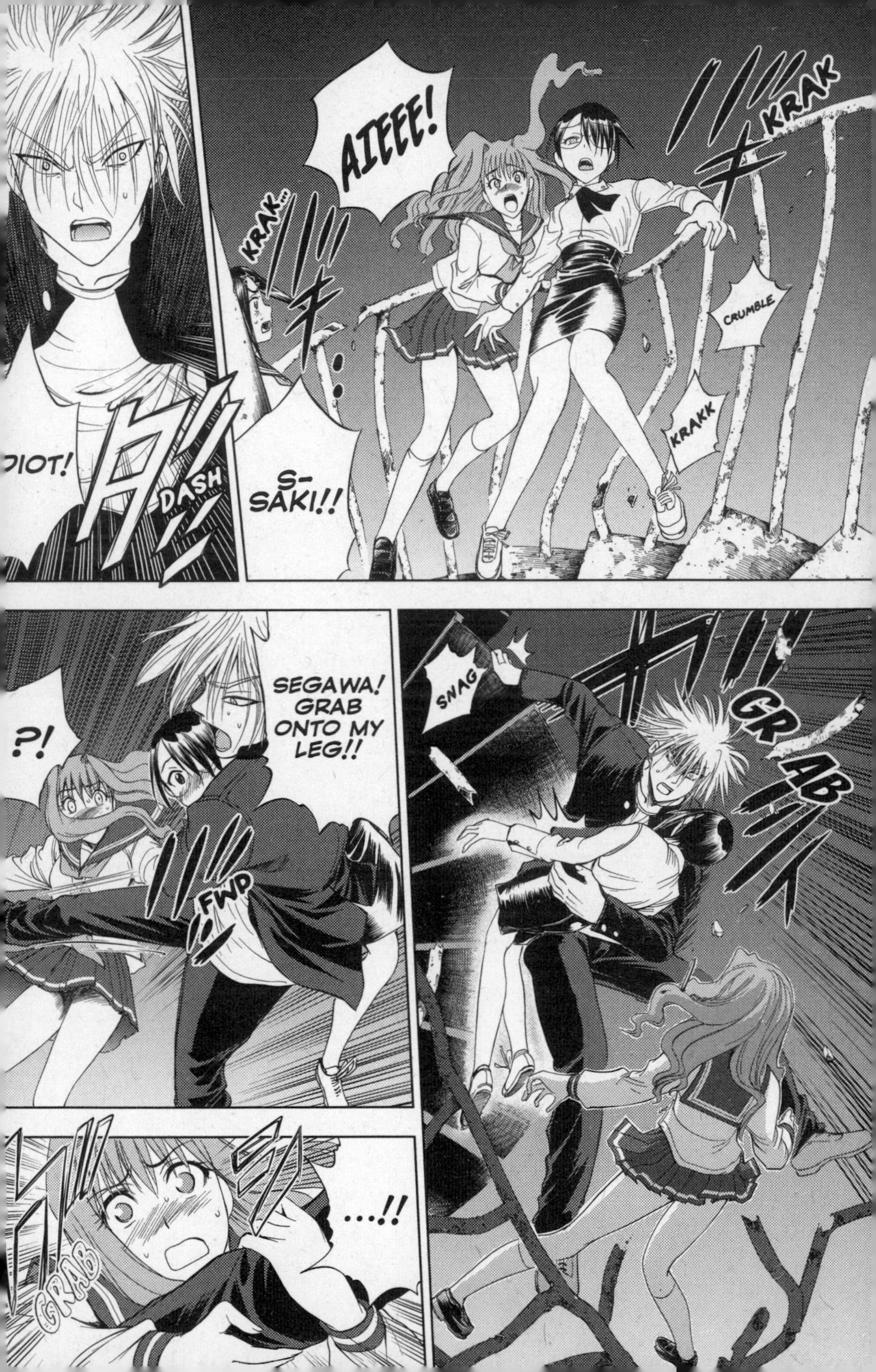
KRAK
AIEEE!
KRAK...
CRUMBLE
KRAKK
S-SAKI!!
DIOT!
DASH
GRAB
SNAG
SEGAWA! GRAB ONTO MY LEG!!
?!
FWP
...!!
GRAB

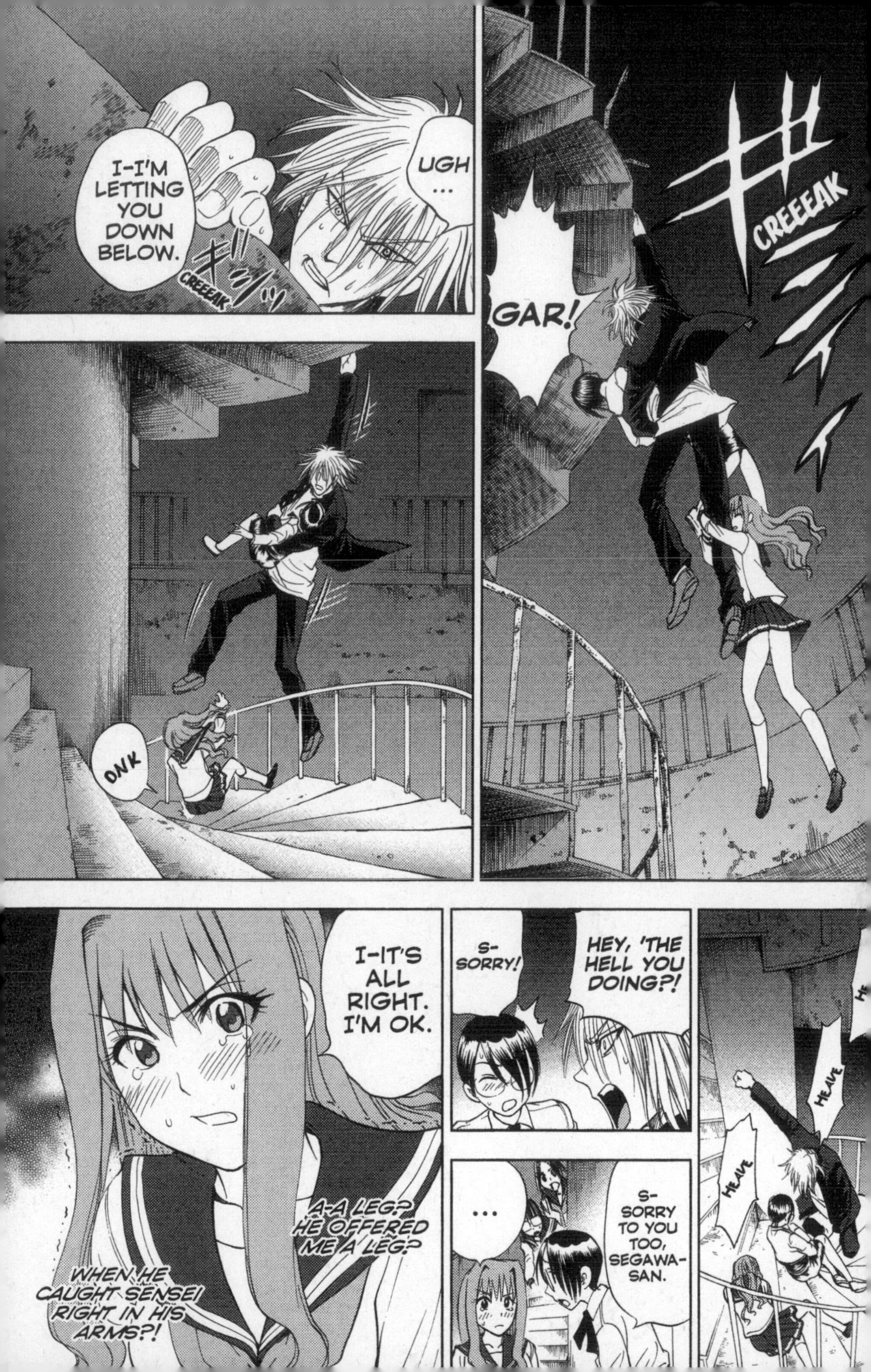
GAR!
CREEEAK
UGH ...
I-I'M LETTING YOU DOWN BELOW.
CREEEAK
ONK
HEAVE
HEAVE
HEY, 'THE HELL YOU DOING?!
S-SORRY!
S-SORRY TO YOU TOO, SEGAWA-SAN.
...
I-IT'S ALL RIGHT. I'M OK.
A-A LEG? HE OFFERED ME A LEG?
WHEN HE CAUGHT SENSEI RIGHT IN HIS ARMS?!

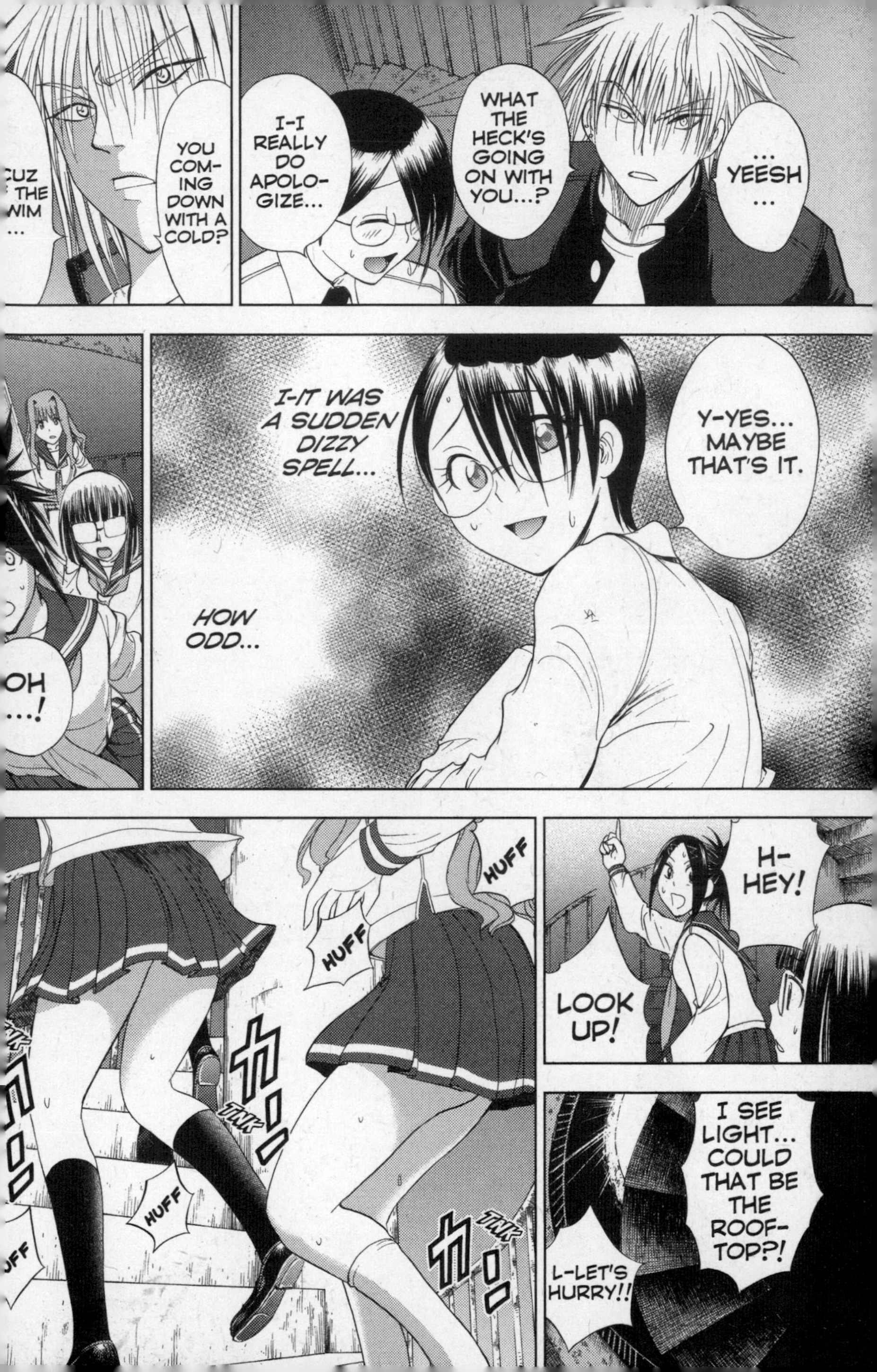
...YEESH...
WHAT THE HECK'S GOING ON WITH YOU...?
I-I REALLY DO APOLOGIZE...
YOU COMING DOWN WITH A COLD?
Y-YES... MAYBE THAT'S IT.
I-IT WAS A SUDDEN DIZZY SPELL...
HOW ODD...
OH ...!
H-HEY!
LOOK UP!
I SEE LIGHT... COULD THAT BE THE ROOFTOP?!
L-LET'S HURRY!!
HUFF
HUFF
TNK
HUFF
TNK
TNK

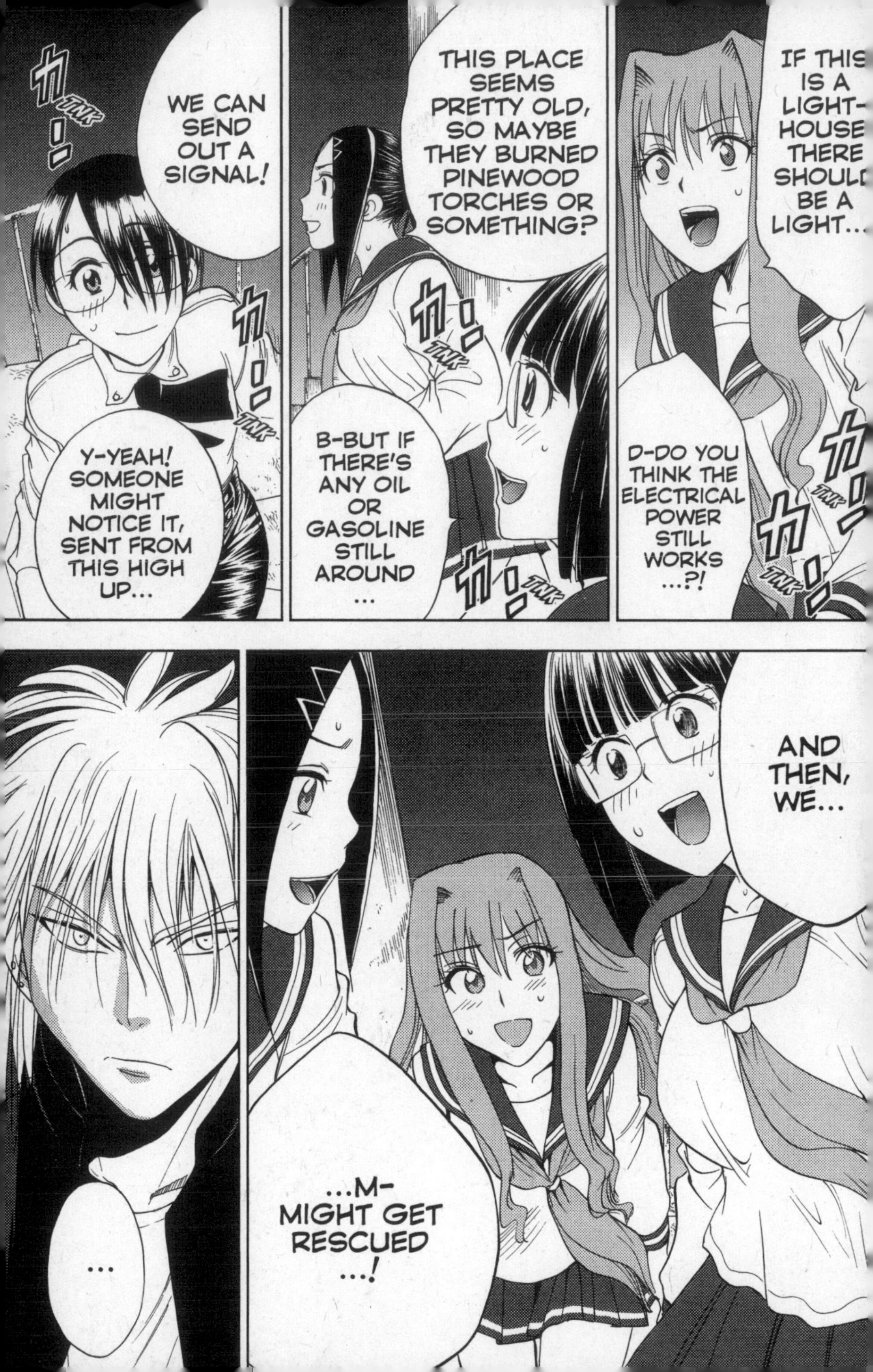
IF THIS IS A LIGHT-HOUSE THERE SHOULD BE A LIGHT...
D-DO YOU THINK THE ELECTRICAL POWER STILL WORKS ...?!
TNK
TNK
THIS PLACE SEEMS PRETTY OLD, SO MAYBE THEY BURNED PINEWOOD TORCHES OR SOMETHING?
TNK
B-BUT IF THERE'S ANY OIL OR GASOLINE STILL AROUND ...
TNK
WE CAN SEND OUT A SIGNAL!
TNK
TNK
Y-YEAH! SOMEONE MIGHT NOTICE IT, SENT FROM THIS HIGH UP...
AND THEN, WE...
...M-MIGHT GET RESCUED ...!
...

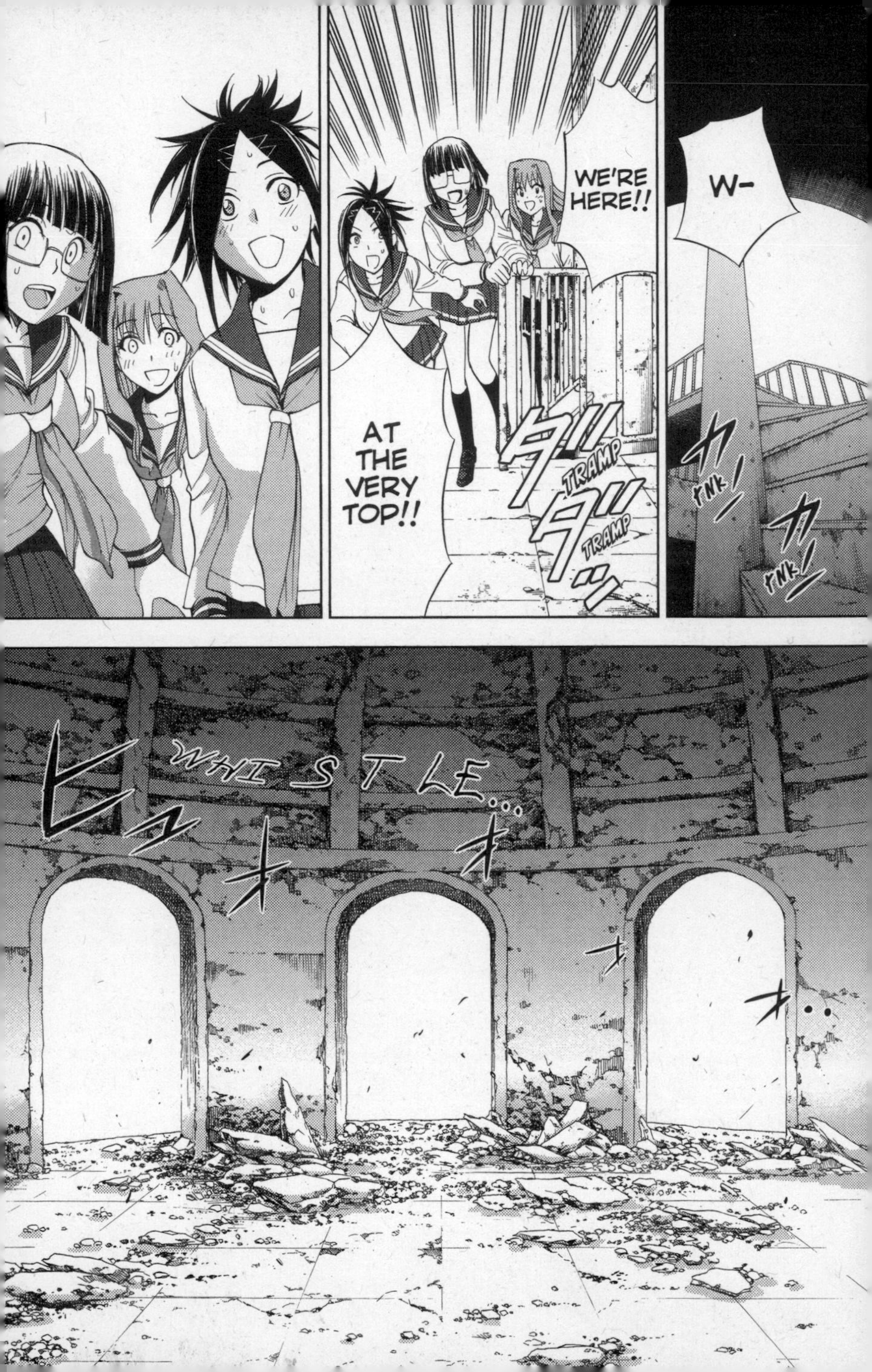
W-
TNK!
TNK!
WE'RE HERE!!
AT THE VERY TOP!!
TRAMP
TRAMP
WHISTLE...

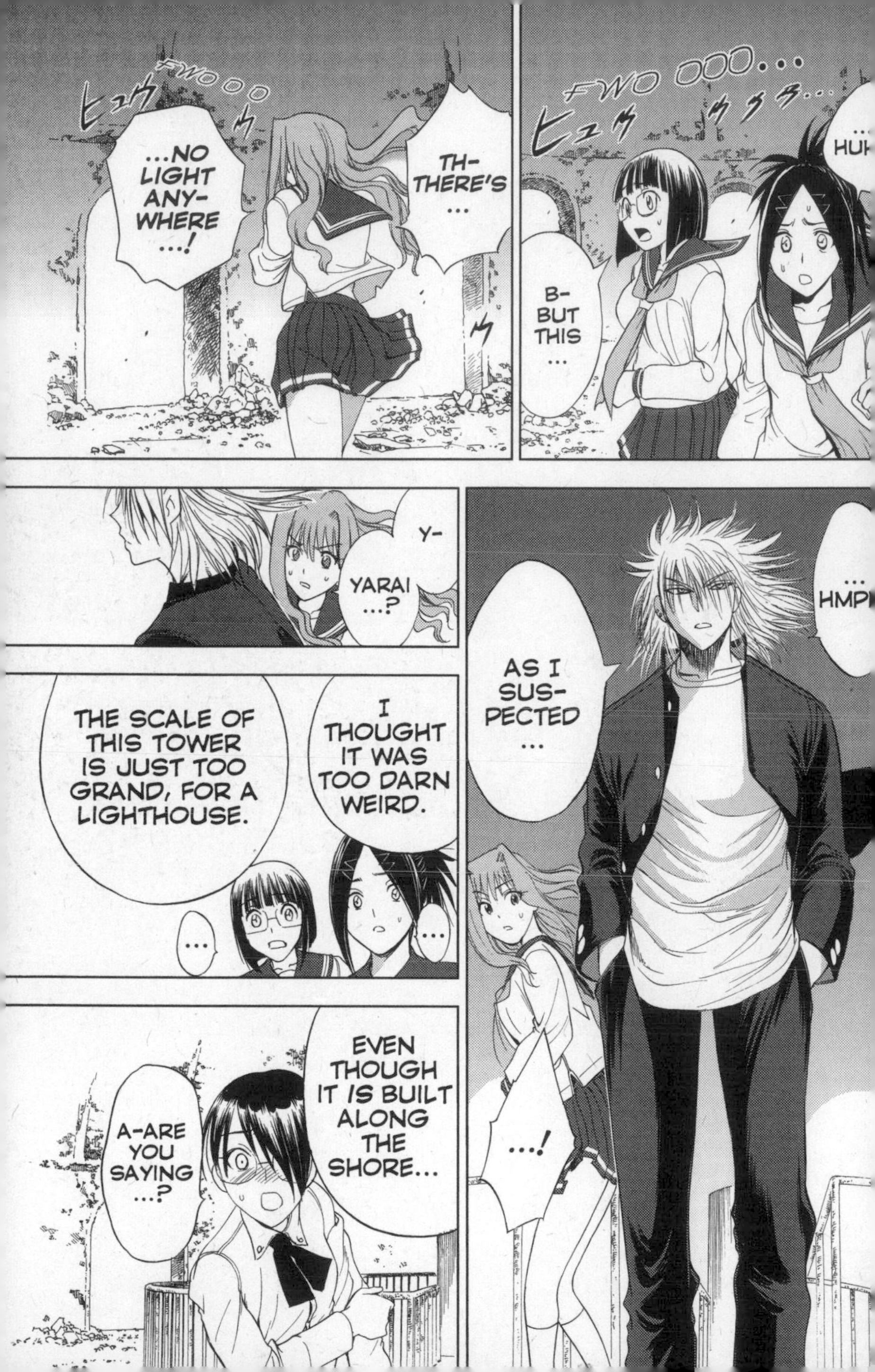
FWO OOO...
... HUH
B-BUT THIS ...
FWOOOO
TH-THERE'S ...
...NO LIGHT ANYWHERE ...!
... HMP
AS I SUSPECTED ...
...!
Y-YARAI ...?
I THOUGHT IT WAS TOO DARN WEIRD.
THE SCALE OF THIS TOWER IS JUST TOO GRAND, FOR A LIGHTHOUSE.
...
...
EVEN THOUGH IT IS BUILT ALONG THE SHORE...
A-ARE YOU SAYING ...?

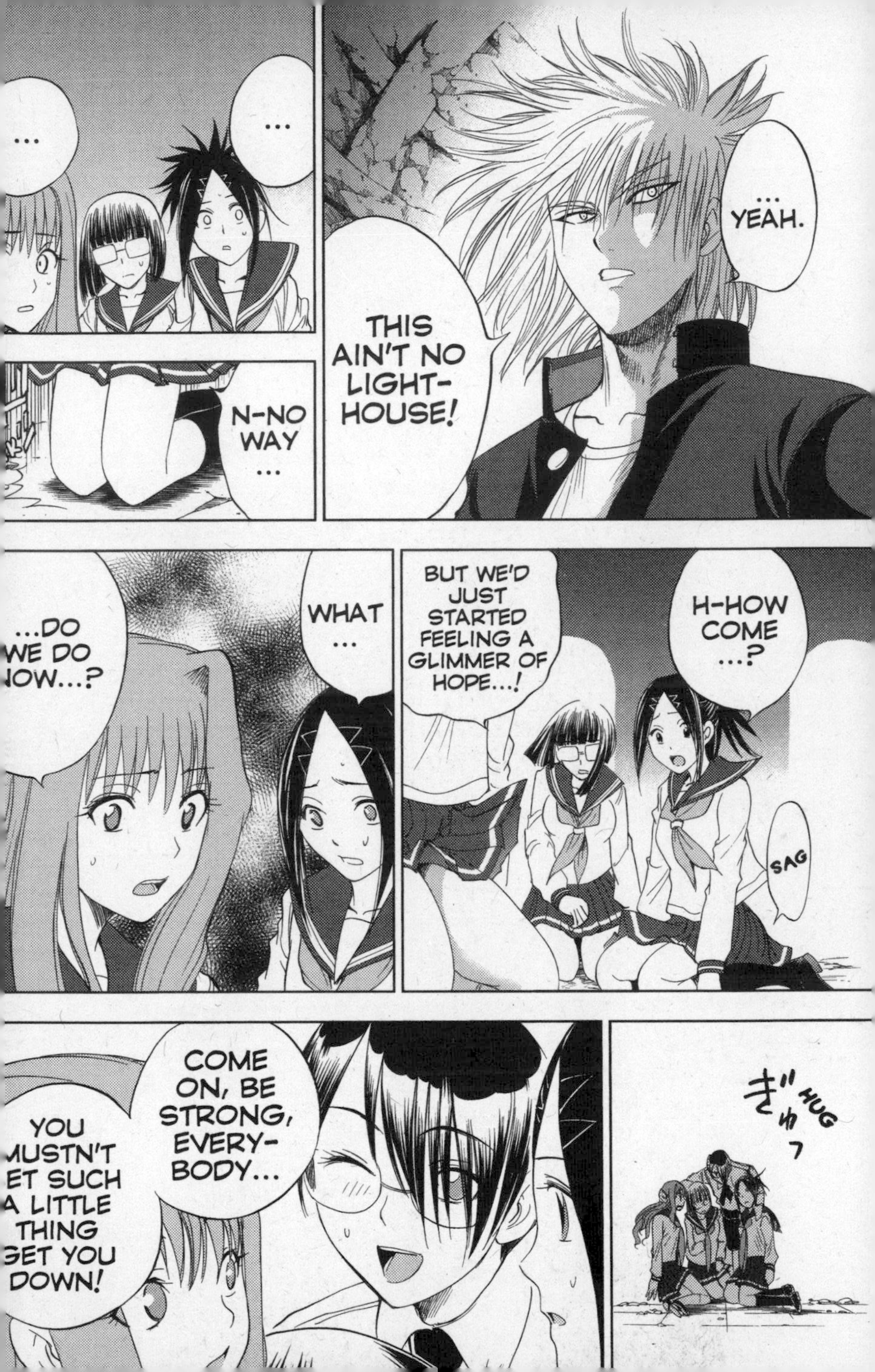
... YEAH.
THIS AIN'T NO LIGHT-HOUSE!
...
...
N-NO WAY ...
H-HOW COME ...?
BUT WE'D JUST STARTED FEELING A GLIMMER OF HOPE...!
SAG
WHAT ...
...DO WE DO NOW...?
ぎゅっ HUG
COME ON, BE STRONG, EVERY-BODY...
YOU MUSTN'T LET SUCH A LITTLE THING GET YOU DOWN!

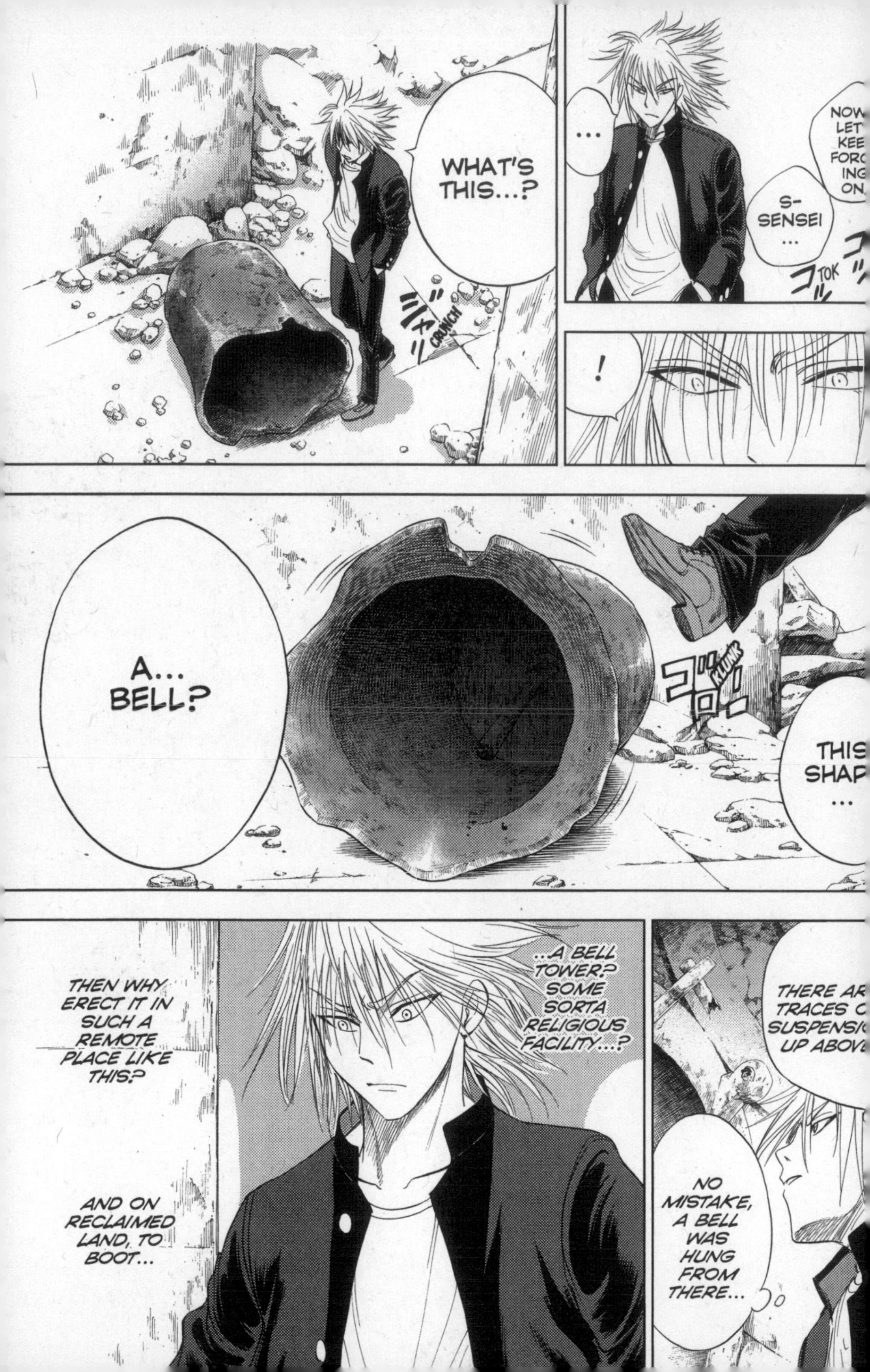
NOW LET KEE FORC ING ON
S-SENSEI ...
TOK
...
!
WHAT'S THIS...?
CRUNCH
THIS SHAP ...
KLUNK
A... BELL?
THERE AR TRACES O SUSPENSI UP ABOVE
NO MISTAKE, A BELL WAS HUNG FROM THERE...
...A BELL TOWER? SOME SORTA RELIGIOUS FACILITY...?
THEN WHY ERECT IT IN SUCH A REMOTE PLACE LIKE THIS?
AND ON RECLAIMED LAND, TO BOOT...

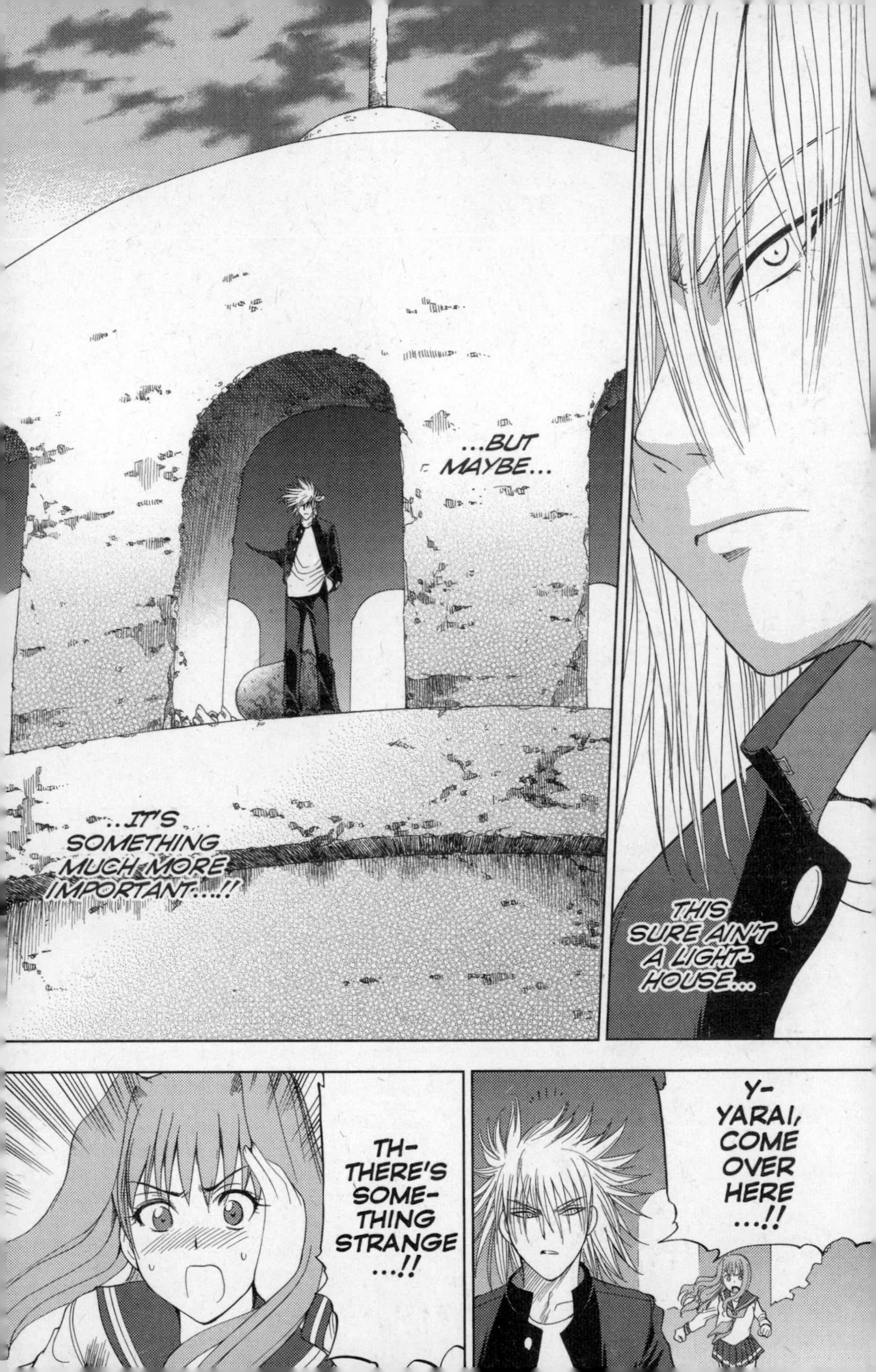
THIS SURE AIN'T A LIGHT-HOUSE...
...BUT MAYBE...
...IT'S SOMETHING MUCH MORE IMPORTANT...!!
Y-YARAI, COME OVER HERE ...!!
TH-THERE'S SOME-THING STRANGE ...!!

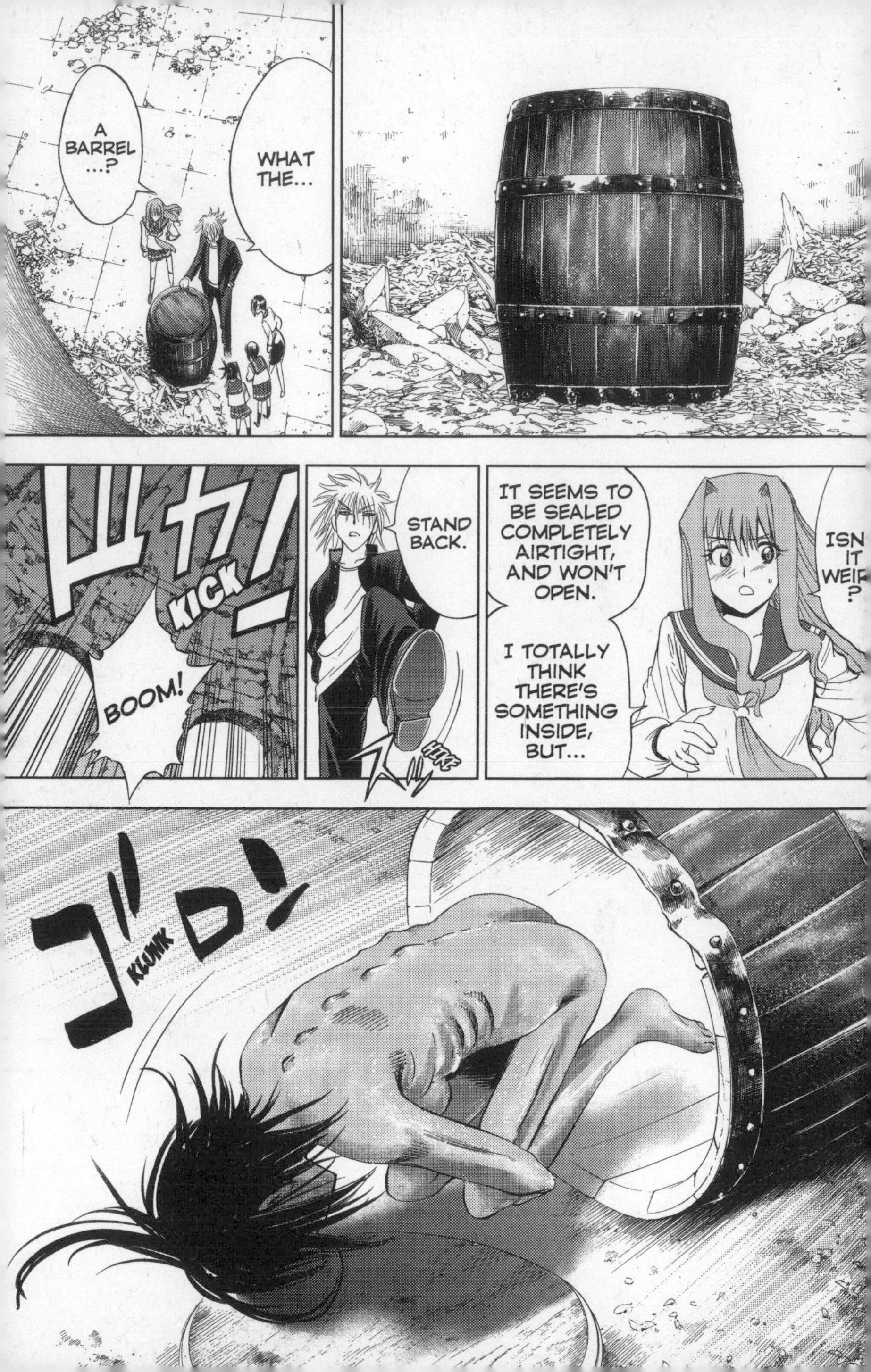
WHAT THE...
A BARREL ...?
ISN IT WEIR ?
IT SEEMS TO BE SEALED COMPLETELY AIRTIGHT, AND WON'T OPEN.
I TOTALLY THINK THERE'S SOMETHING INSIDE, BUT...
STAND BACK.
KICK
BOOM!
KLUNK

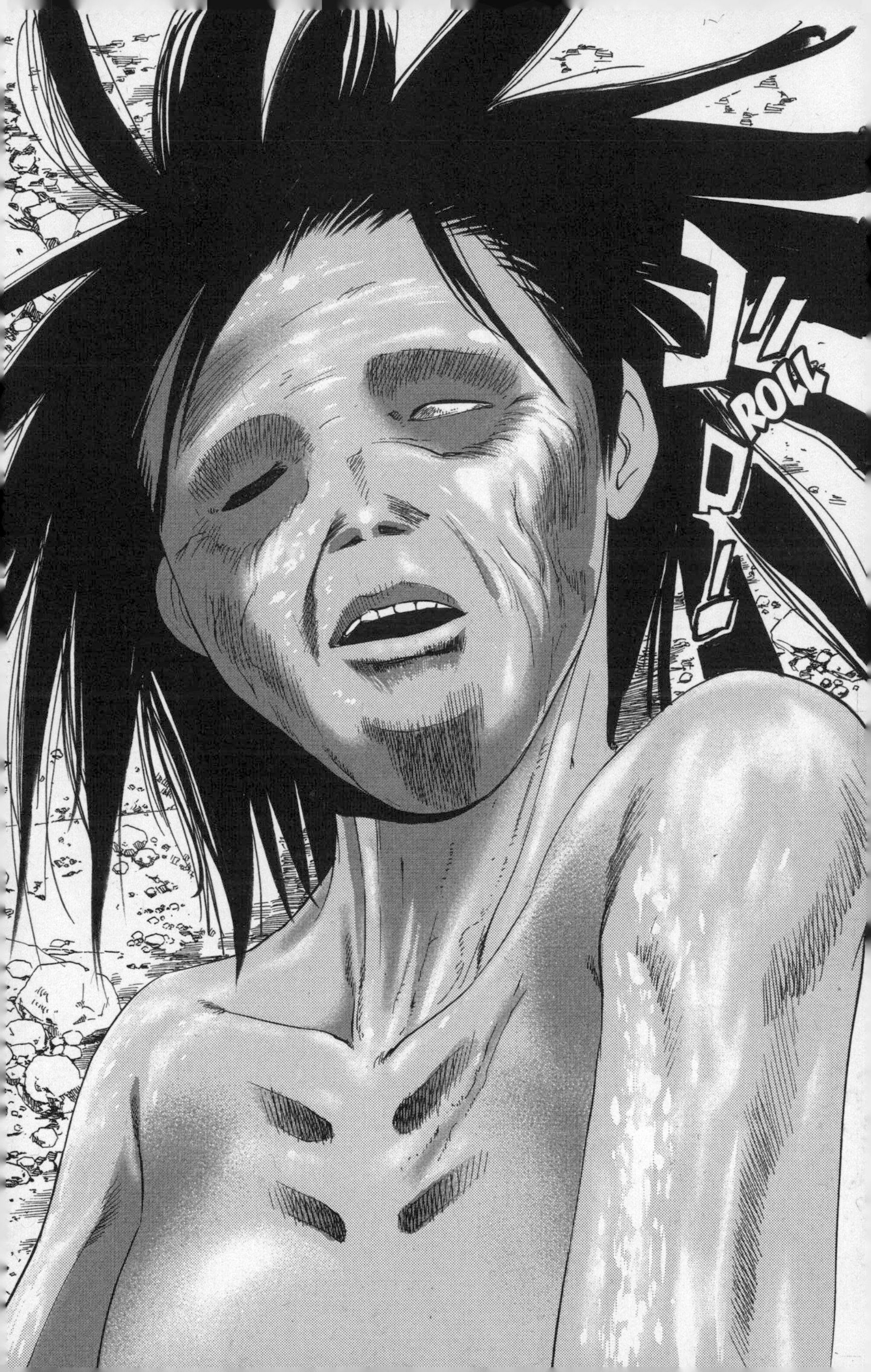
ROLL

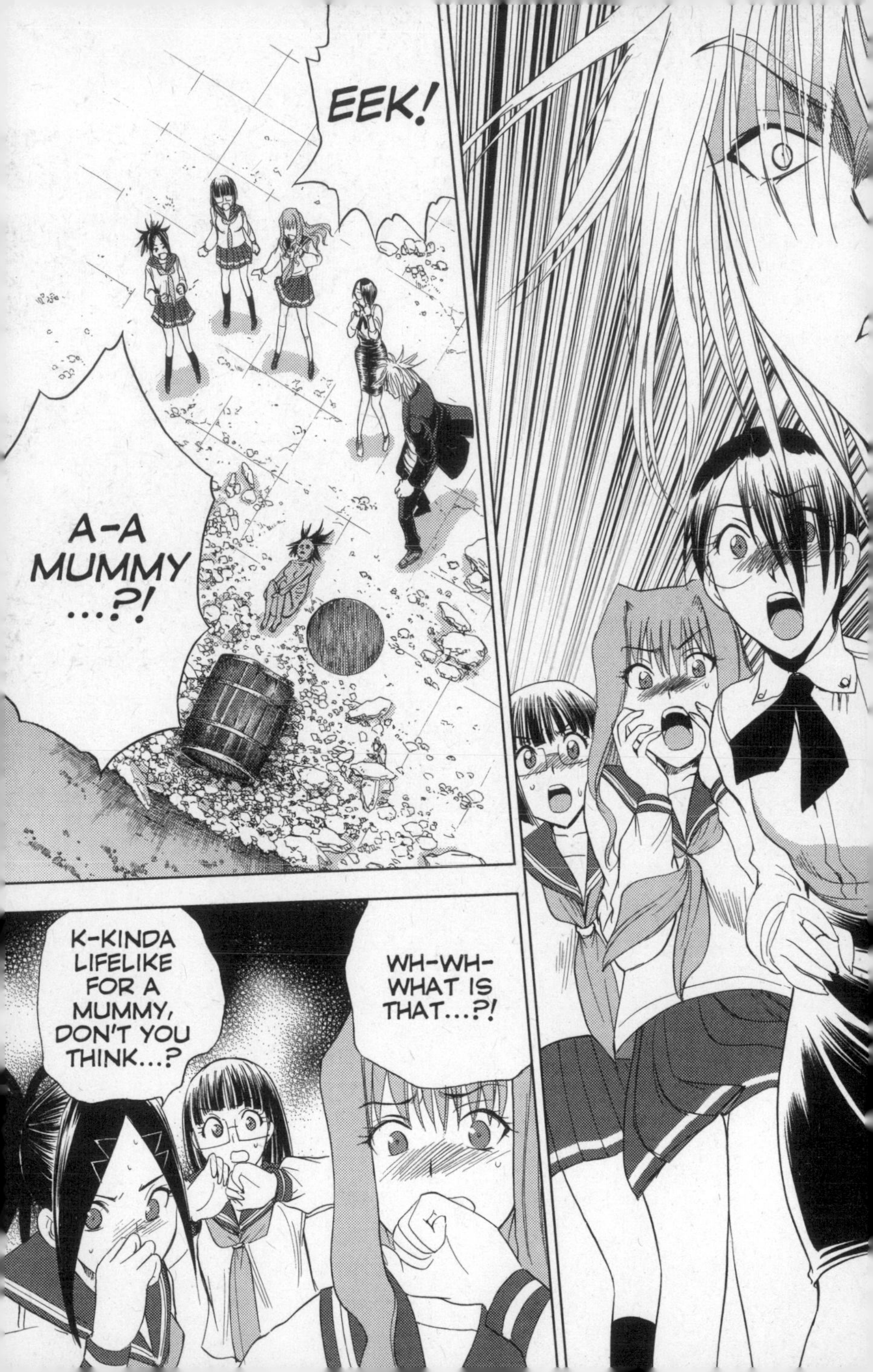
EEK!
A-A MUMMY ...?!
WH-WH-WHAT IS THAT...?!
K-KINDA LIFELIKE FOR A MUMMY, DON'T YOU THINK...?

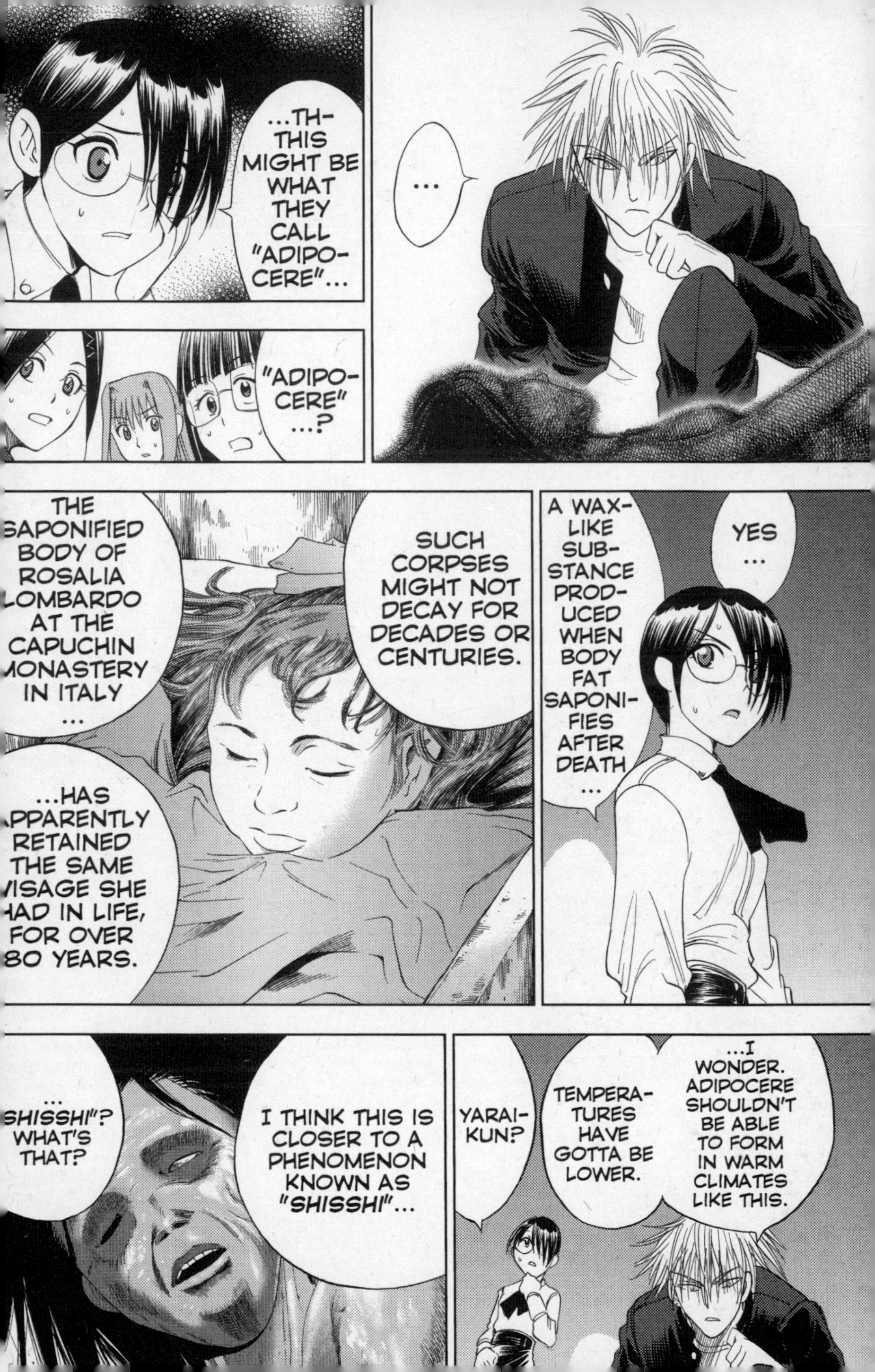
...
...TH-THIS MIGHT BE WHAT THEY CALL "ADIPOCERE"...
"ADIPOCERE" ...?
YES ...
A WAX-LIKE SUBSTANCE PRODUCED WHEN BODY FAT SAPONIFIES AFTER DEATH ...
SUCH CORPSES MIGHT NOT DECAY FOR DECADES OR CENTURIES.
THE SAPONIFIED BODY OF ROSALIA LOMBARDO AT THE CAPUCHIN MONASTERY IN ITALY ...
...HAS APPARENTLY RETAINED THE SAME VISAGE SHE HAD IN LIFE, FOR OVER 80 YEARS.
...I WONDER. ADIPOCERE SHOULDN'T BE ABLE TO FORM IN WARM CLIMATES LIKE THIS.
TEMPERATURES HAVE GOTTA BE LOWER.
YARAI-KUN?
I THINK THIS IS CLOSER TO A PHENOMENON KNOWN AS "SHISSHI"...
..."SHISSHI"? WHAT'S THAT?

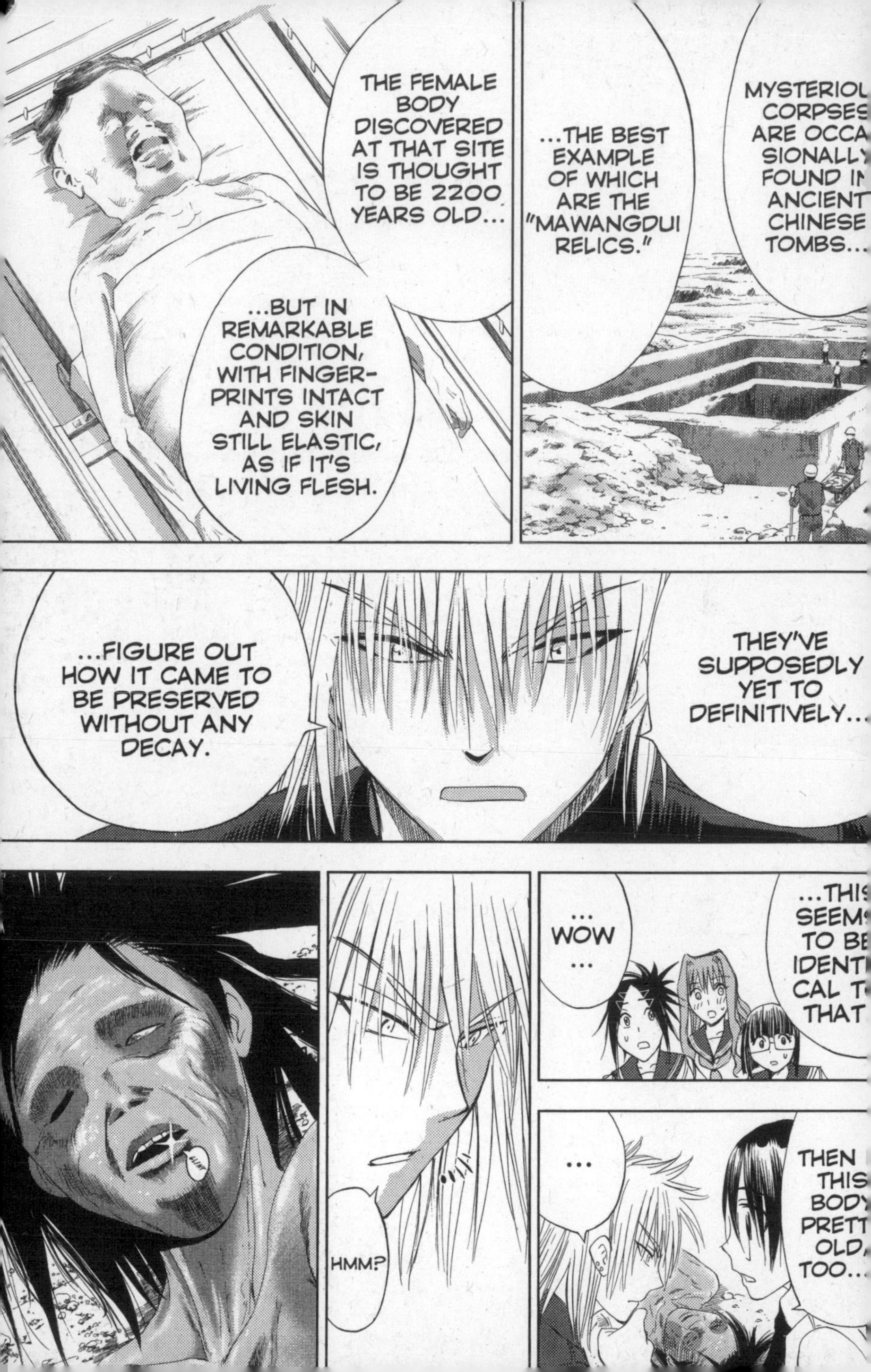
MYSTERIOU CORPSES ARE OCCA SIONALLY FOUND IN ANCIENT CHINESE TOMBS...
...THE BEST EXAMPLE OF WHICH ARE THE "MAWANGDUI RELICS."
THE FEMALE BODY DISCOVERED AT THAT SITE IS THOUGHT TO BE 2200 YEARS OLD...
...BUT IN REMARKABLE CONDITION, WITH FINGER-PRINTS INTACT AND SKIN STILL ELASTIC, AS IF IT'S LIVING FLESH.
THEY'VE SUPPOSEDLY YET TO DEFINITIVELY...
...FIGURE OUT HOW IT CAME TO BE PRESERVED WITHOUT ANY DECAY.
...THIS SEEM TO BE IDENT CAL T THAT
... WOW ...
THEN THIS BODY PRETT OLD, TOO...
...
HMM?

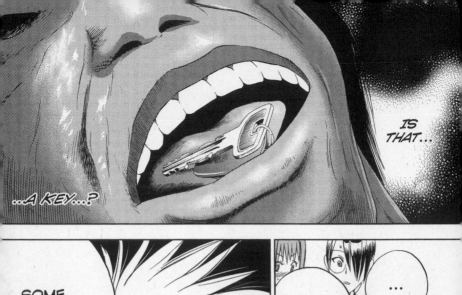

IS THAT...

...A KEY...?

SOME ROOM ON THE THIRD FLOOR, HUH....?

303...

...

CHAPTER 105 THE MAP

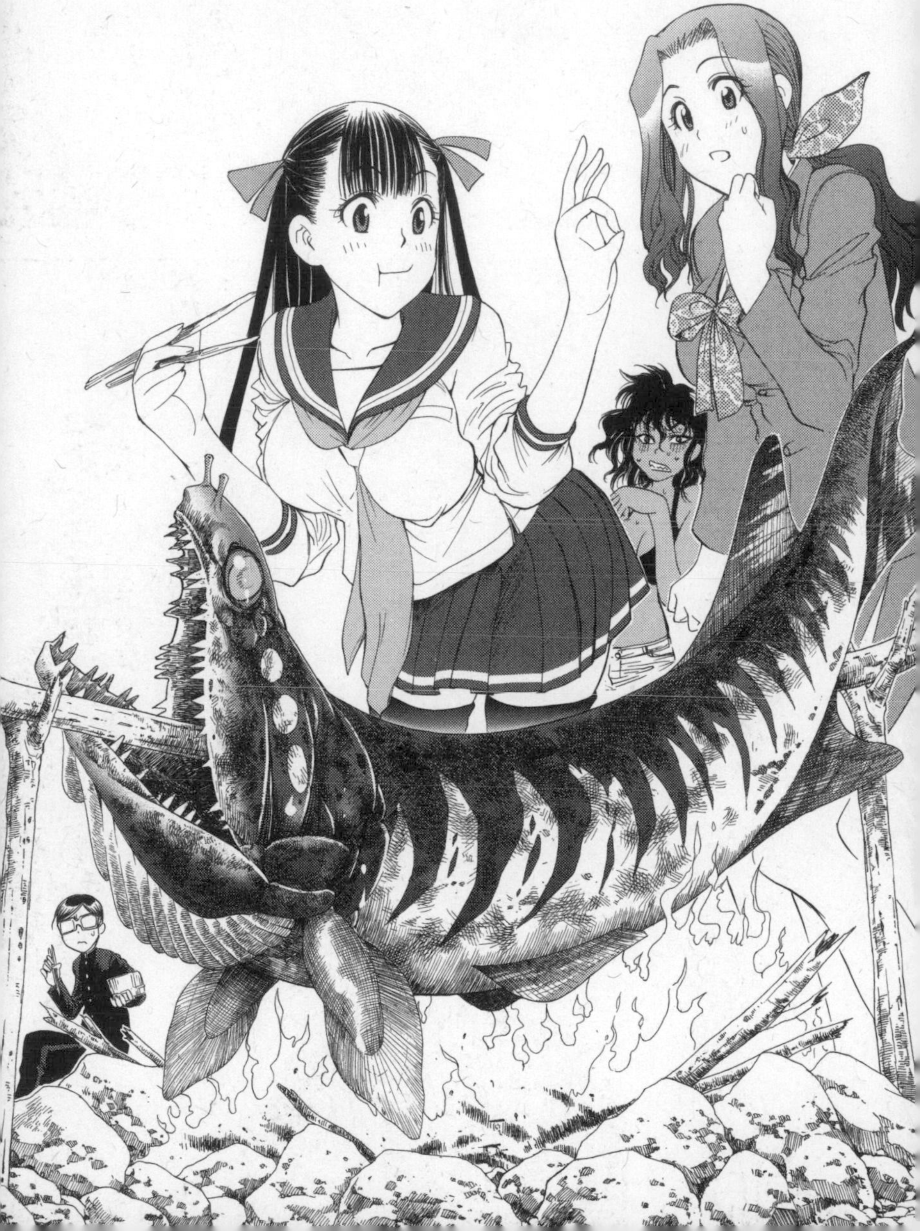

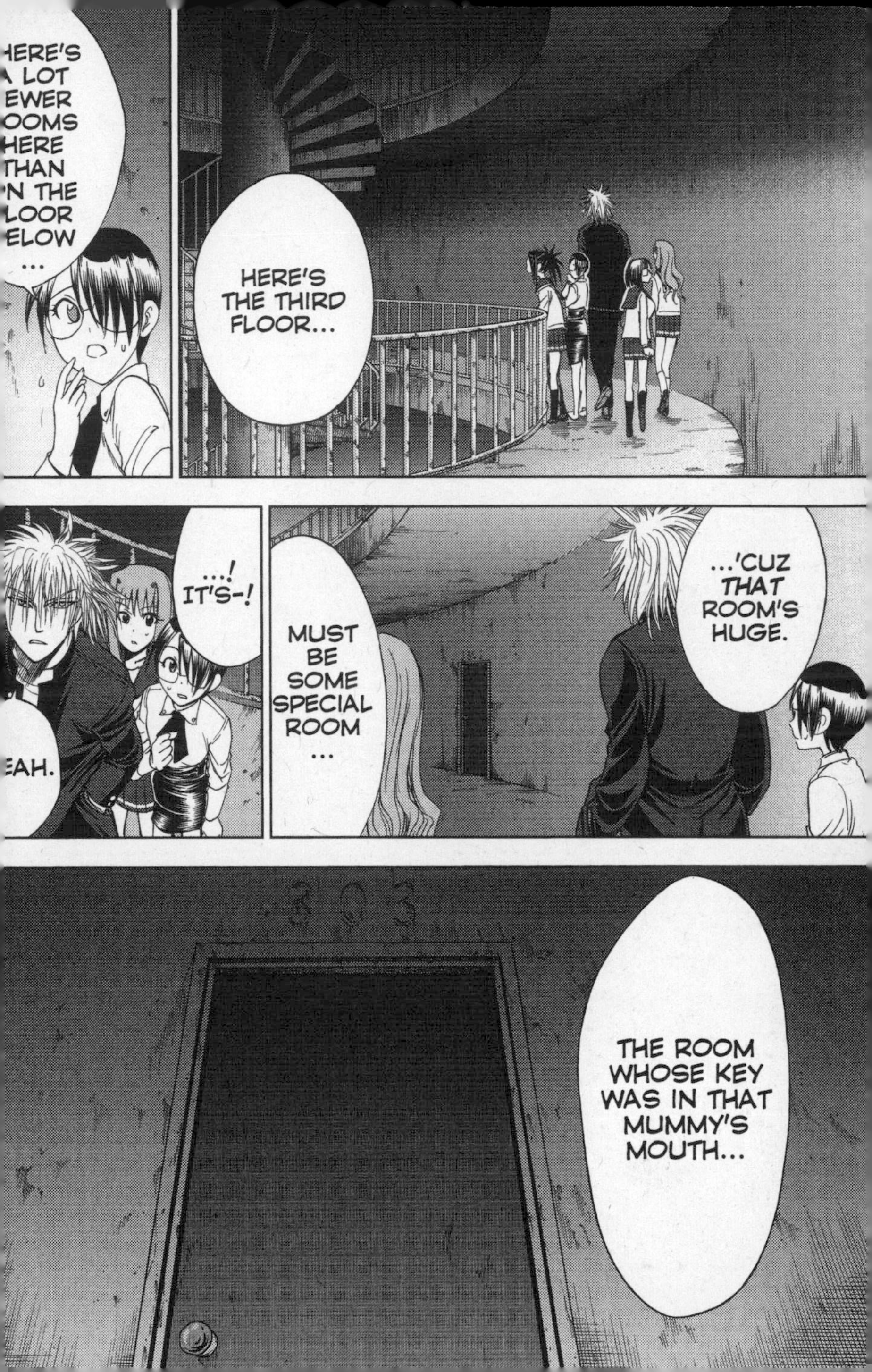
HERE'S THE THIRD FLOOR...
HERE'S A LOT EWER OOMS HERE THAN N THE LOOR ELOW ...
...'CUZ THAT ROOM'S HUGE.
MUST BE SOME SPECIAL ROOM ...
...! IT'S-!
EAH.
303
THE ROOM WHOSE KEY WAS IN THAT MUMMY'S MOUTH...

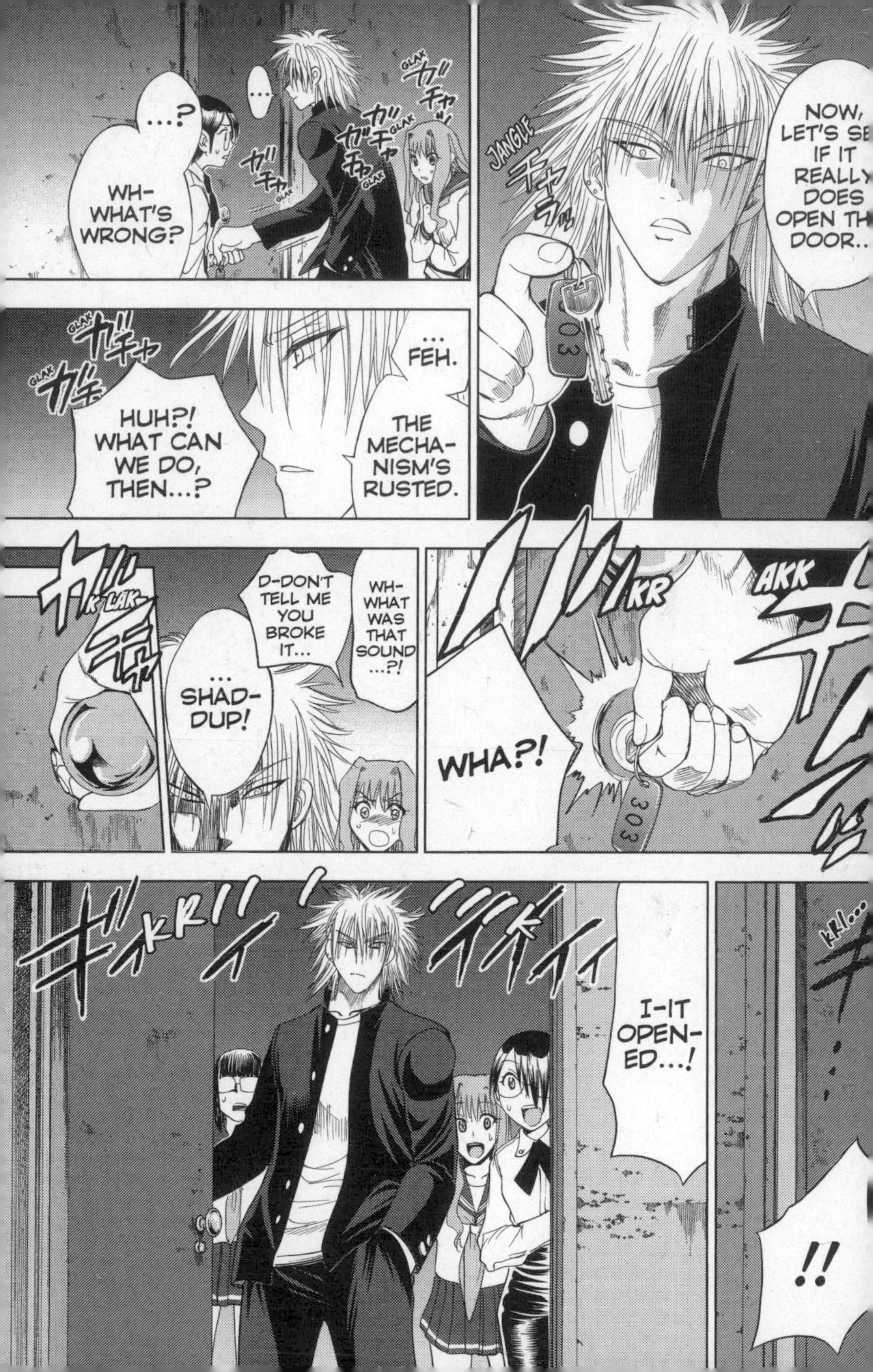
JANGLE
NOW, LET'S SE IF IT REALLY DOES OPEN TH DOOR..
GLAK
GLAK
GLAK
GLAK
...
...?
WH- WHAT'S WRONG?
GLAK
GLAK
... FEH.
THE MECHA- NISM'S RUSTED.
HUH?! WHAT CAN WE DO, THEN...?
KR
AKK
WHA?!
WH- WHAT WAS THAT SOUND ...?!
D-DON'T TELL ME YOU BROKE IT...
KLAK
... SHAD- DUP!
kri...
!!
I-IT OPEN- ED...!
KRII

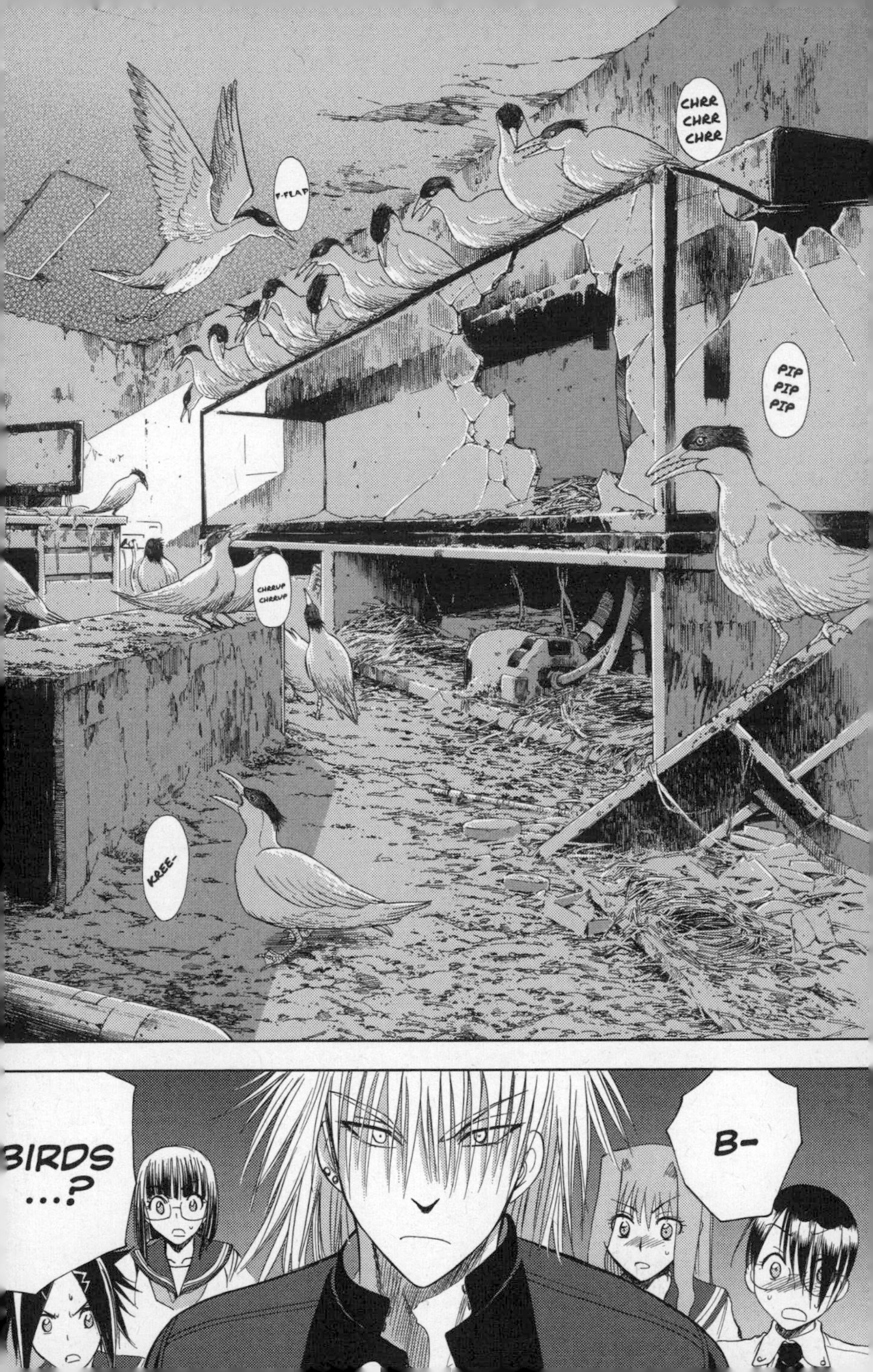
CHRR CHRR CHRR
F-FLAP
PIP PIP PIP
CHRRUP CHRRUP
KREE-
B-
BIRDS ...?

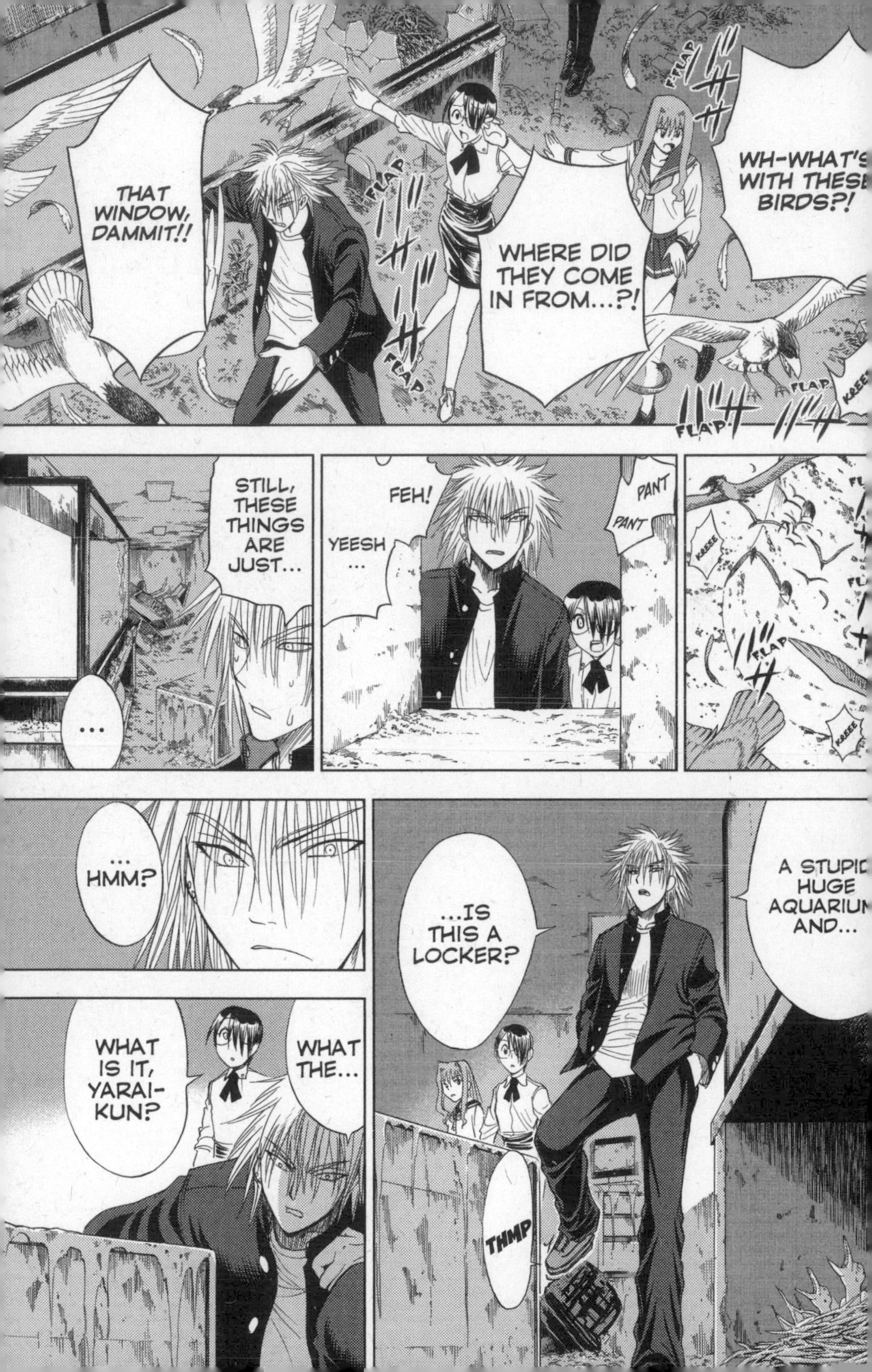

FLAP
WH-WHAT'S WITH THESE BIRDS?!
WHERE DID THEY COME IN FROM...?!
THAT WINDOW, DAMMIT!!
FLAP
FLAP
KREEE
FLAP
FLAP
FLAP
KREEE
KREEE
PANT PANT
FEH!
YEESH ...
STILL, THESE THINGS ARE JUST...
...
A STUPID HUGE AQUARIUM AND...
...IS THIS A LOCKER?
THMP
... HMM?
WHAT THE...
WHAT IS IT, YARAI-KUN?

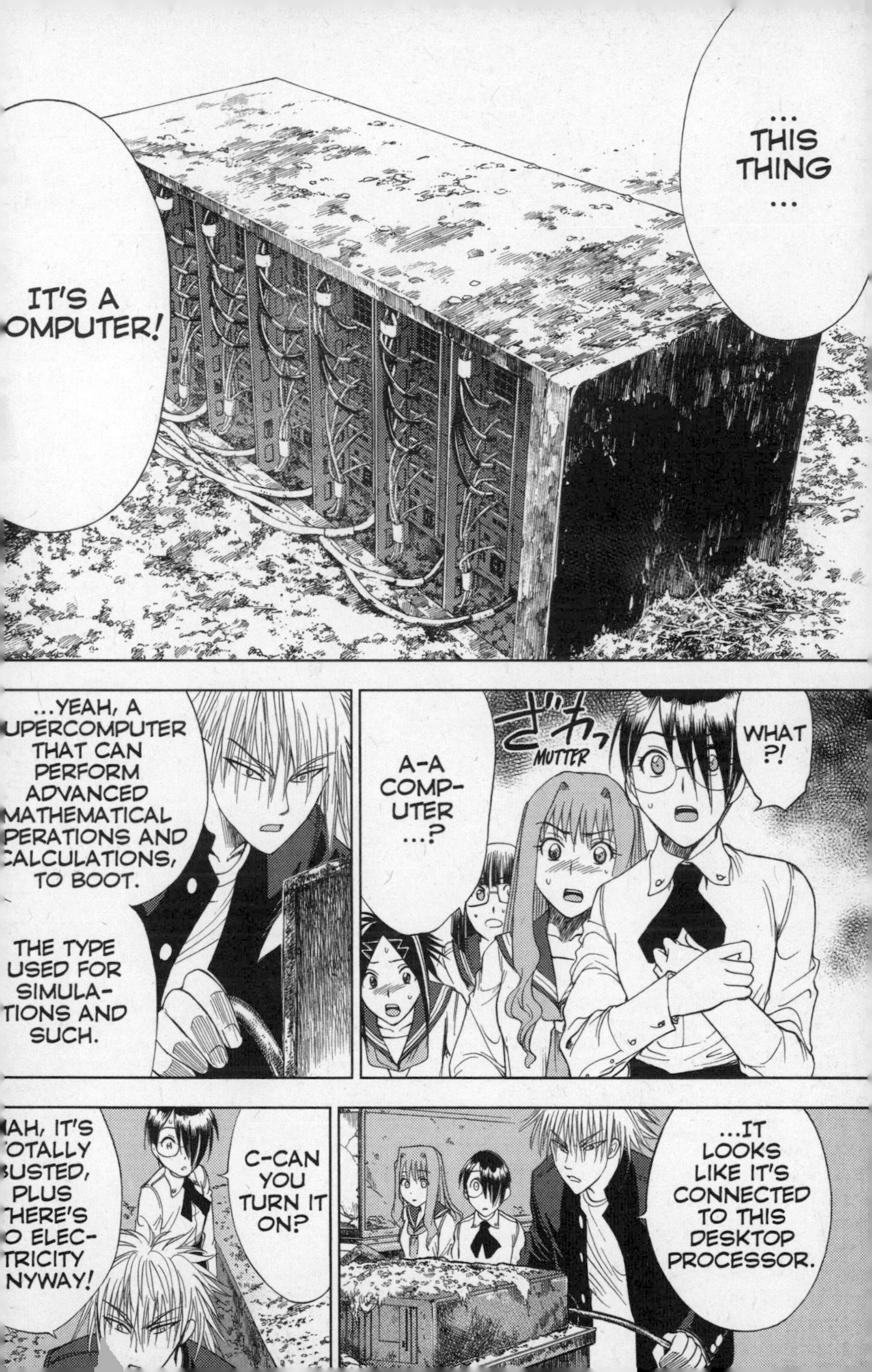
...THIS THING...
IT'S A OMPUTER!
WHAT ?!
ざわっ MUTTER
A-A COMP-UTER ...?
...YEAH, A UPERCOMPUTER THAT CAN PERFORM ADVANCED MATHEMATICAL PERATIONS AND ALCULATIONS, TO BOOT.
THE TYPE USED FOR SIMULA-TIONS AND SUCH.
...IT LOOKS LIKE IT'S CONNECTED TO THIS DESKTOP PROCESSOR.
C-CAN YOU TURN IT ON?
AH, IT'S OTALLY USTED, PLUS HERE'S O ELEC-TRICITY NYWAY!

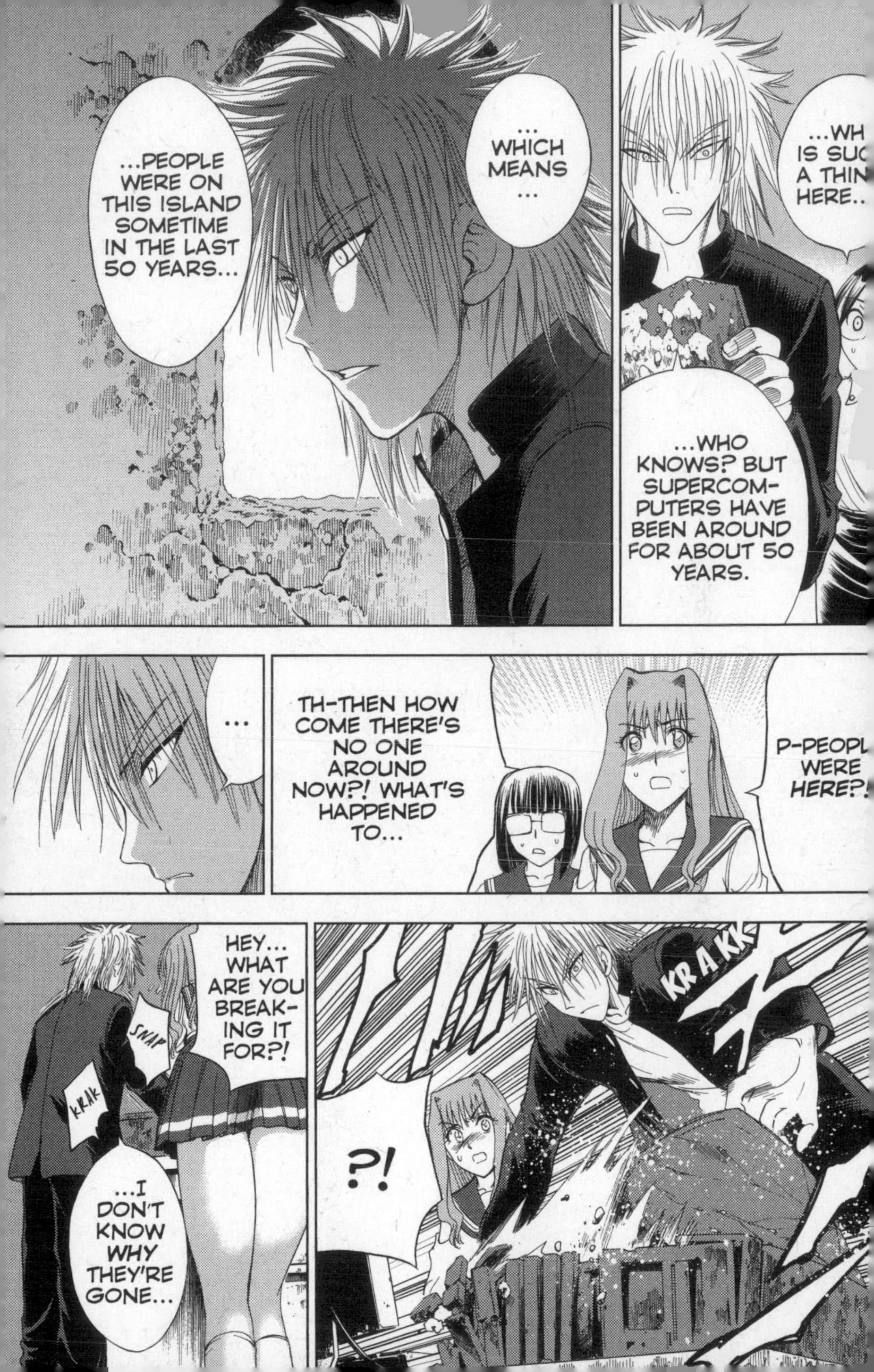
...WH IS SUC A THIN HERE..
...WHO KNOWS? BUT SUPERCOMPUTERS HAVE BEEN AROUND FOR ABOUT 50 YEARS.
...WHICH MEANS ...
...PEOPLE WERE ON THIS ISLAND SOMETIME IN THE LAST 50 YEARS...
P-PEOPL WERE HERE?!
TH-THEN HOW COME THERE'S NO ONE AROUND NOW?! WHAT'S HAPPENED TO...
...
KRAKK
?!
HEY... WHAT ARE YOU BREAKING IT FOR?!
SNAP
KRAK
...I DON'T KNOW WHY THEY'RE GONE...

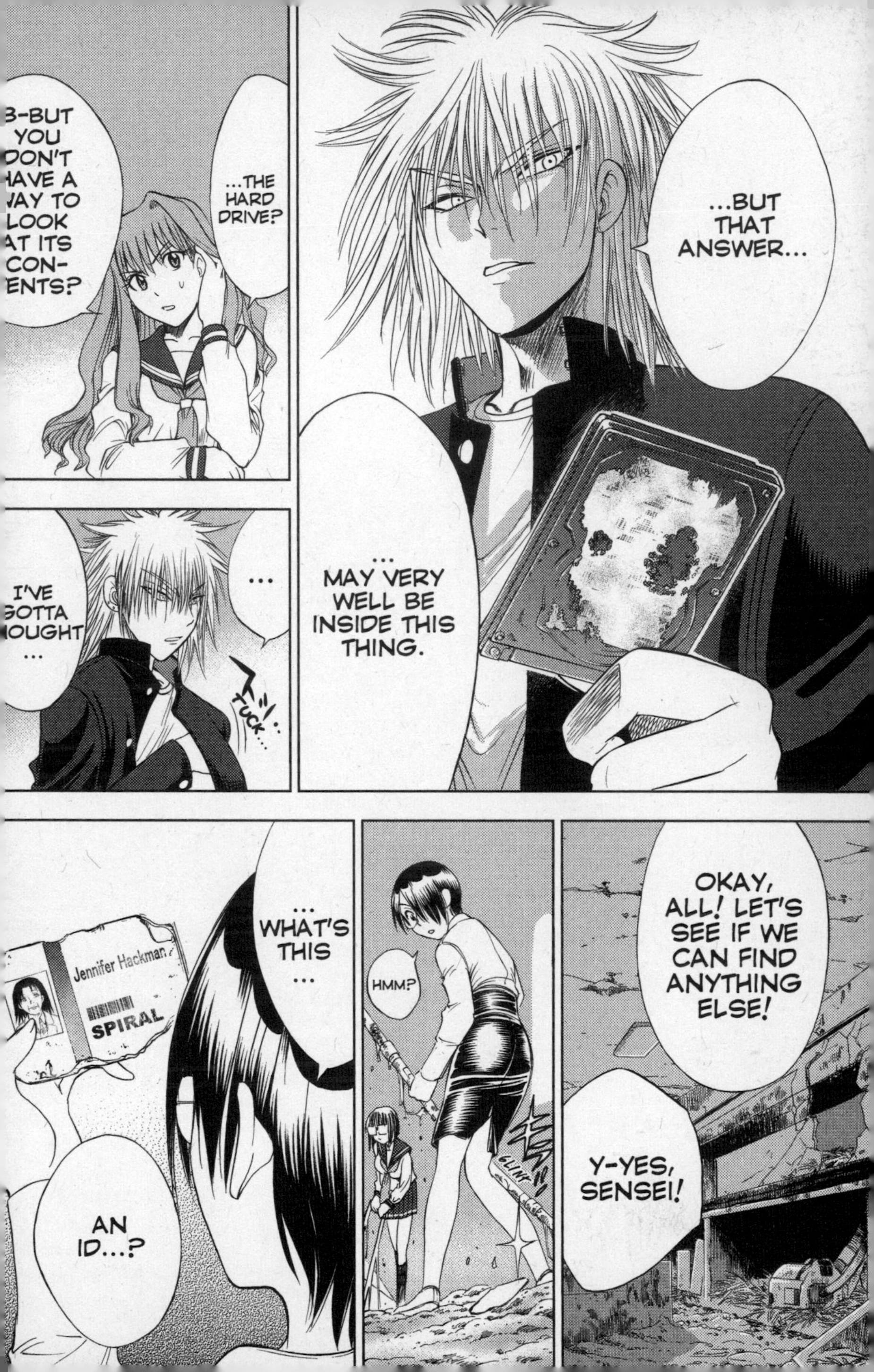
...BUT THAT ANSWER...
... MAY VERY WELL BE INSIDE THIS THING.
...THE HARD DRIVE?
B-BUT YOU DON'T HAVE A WAY TO LOOK AT ITS CON- TENTS?
...
I'VE GOTTA OUGHT ...
TUCK...
OKAY, ALL! LET'S SEE IF WE CAN FIND ANYTHING ELSE!
Y-YES, SENSEI!
HMM?
GLINT
... WHAT'S THIS ...
Jennifer Hackman
SPIRAL
AN ID...?

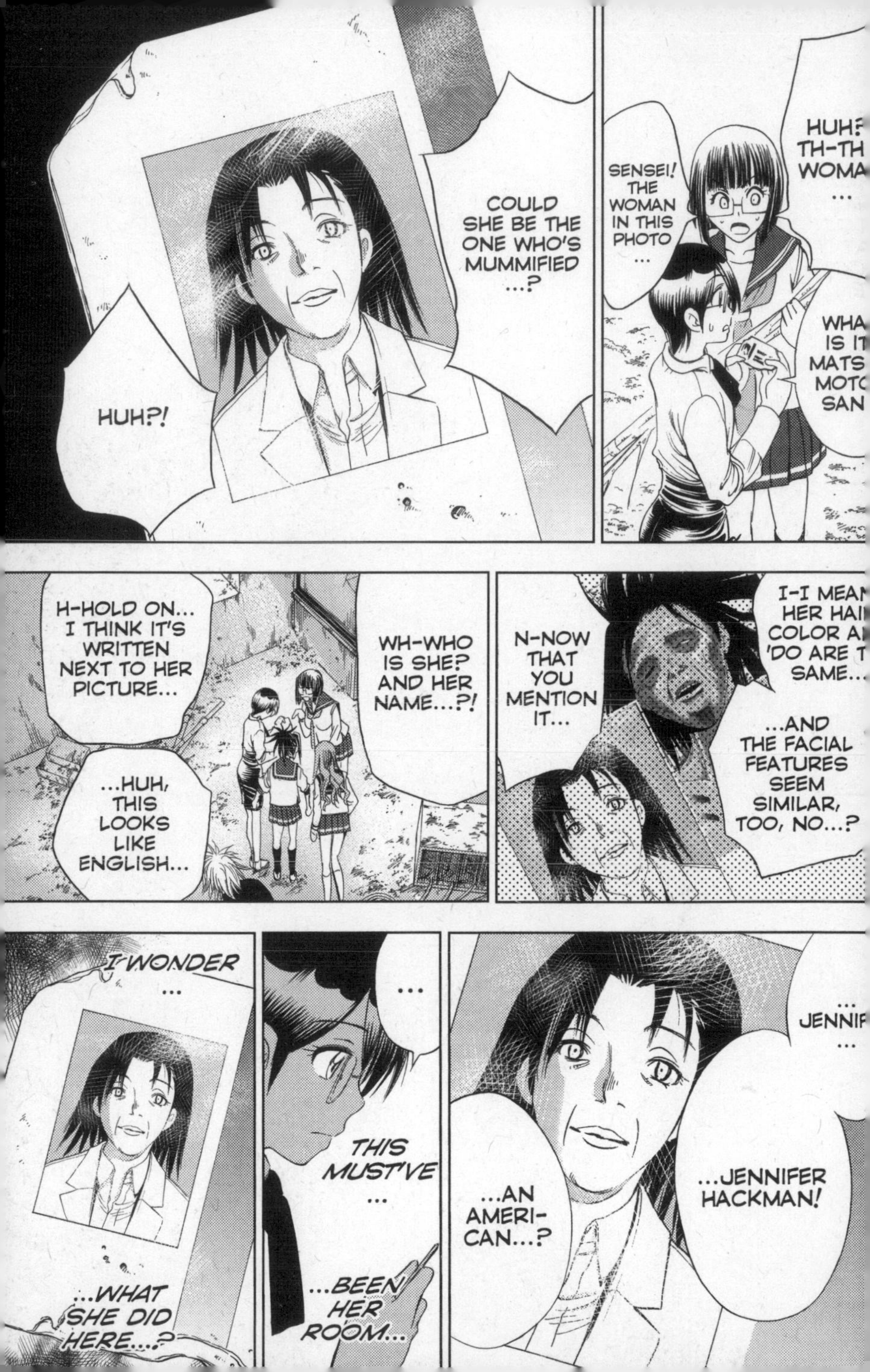
HUH?! TH-TH WOMA ...
SENSEI! THE WOMAN IN THIS PHOTO ...
WHA IS IT MATS MOTO SAN
COULD SHE BE THE ONE WHO'S MUMMIFIED ...?
HUH?!
I-I MEAN HER HAI COLOR A 'DO ARE T SAME...
N-NOW THAT YOU MENTION IT...
...AND THE FACIAL FEATURES SEEM SIMILAR, TOO, NO...?
WH-WHO IS SHE? AND HER NAME...?!
H-HOLD ON... I THINK IT'S WRITTEN NEXT TO HER PICTURE...
...HUH, THIS LOOKS LIKE ENGLISH...
... JENNIF ...
...JENNIFER HACKMAN!
...AN AMERI-CAN...?
...
THIS MUST'VE ...
...BEEN HER ROOM...
I WONDER ...
...WHAT SHE DID HERE...?

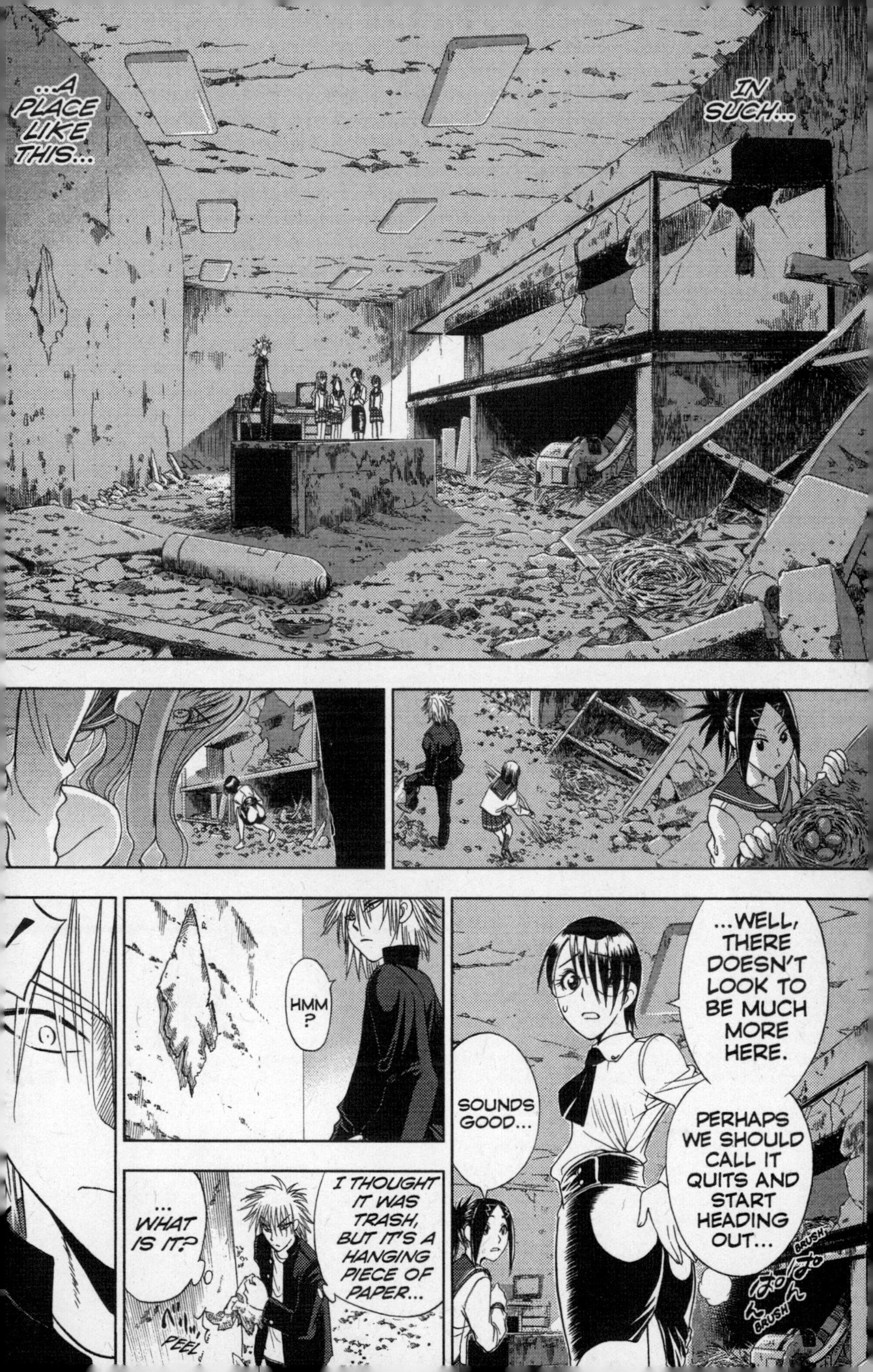
IN SUCH...
...A PLACE LIKE THIS...
...WELL, THERE DOESN'T LOOK TO BE MUCH MORE HERE.
PERHAPS WE SHOULD CALL IT QUITS AND START HEADING OUT...
BRUSH
BRUSH
SOUNDS GOOD...
HMM?
I THOUGHT IT WAS TRASH, BUT IT'S A HANGING PIECE OF PAPER...
...WHAT IS IT?
PEEL

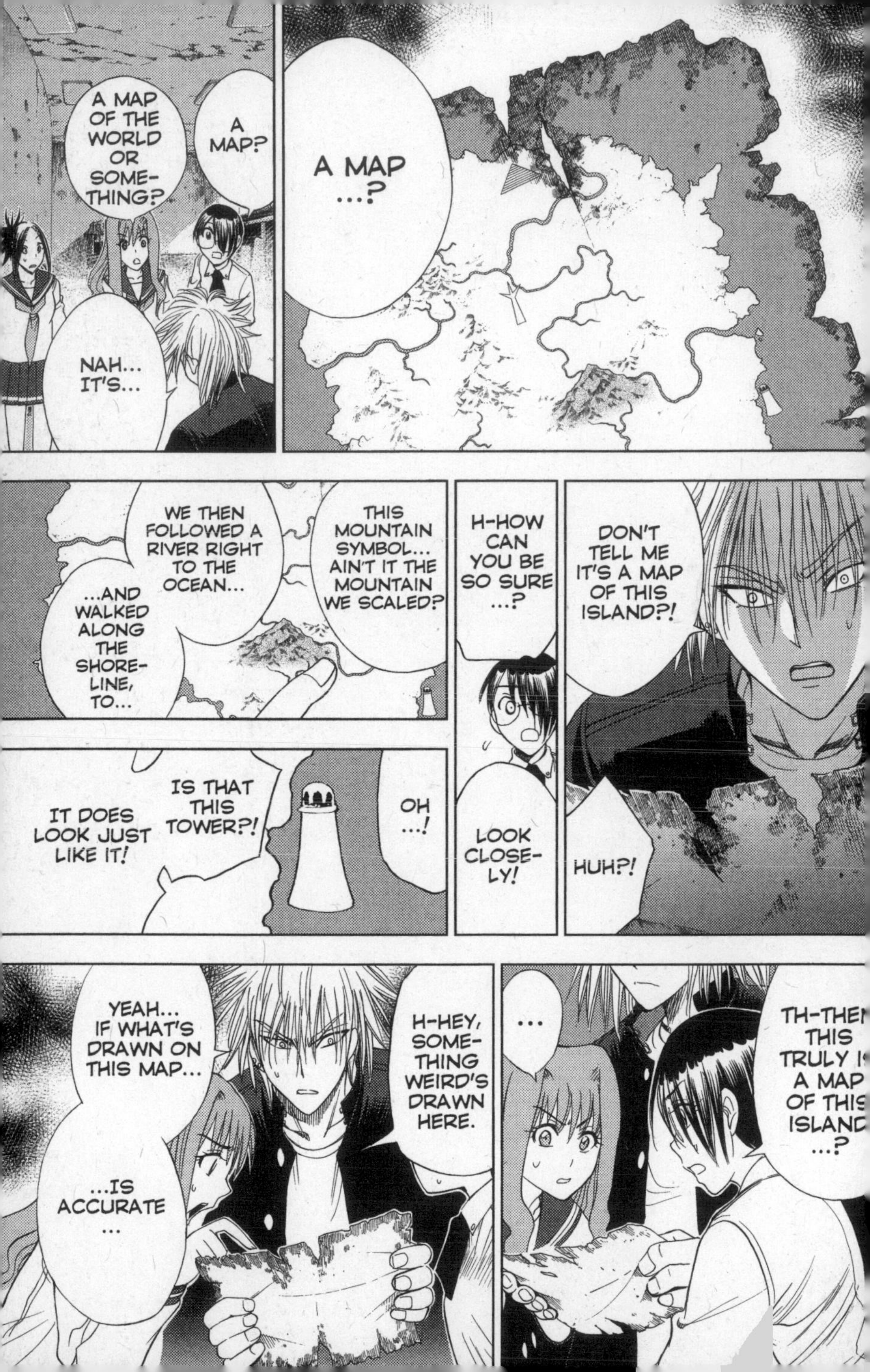
A MAP ...?
A MAP?
A MAP OF THE WORLD OR SOMETHING?
NAH... IT'S...
DON'T TELL ME IT'S A MAP OF THIS ISLAND?!
HUH?!
H-HOW CAN YOU BE SO SURE ...?
LOOK CLOSELY!
THIS MOUNTAIN SYMBOL... AIN'T IT THE MOUNTAIN WE SCALED?
WE THEN FOLLOWED A RIVER RIGHT TO THE OCEAN...
...AND WALKED ALONG THE SHORELINE, TO...
OH ...!
IS THAT THIS TOWER?!
IT DOES LOOK JUST LIKE IT!
TH-THEN THIS TRULY IS A MAP OF THIS ISLAND ...?
...
H-HEY, SOMETHING WEIRD'S DRAWN HERE.
YEAH... IF WHAT'S DRAWN ON THIS MAP...
...IS ACCURATE ...

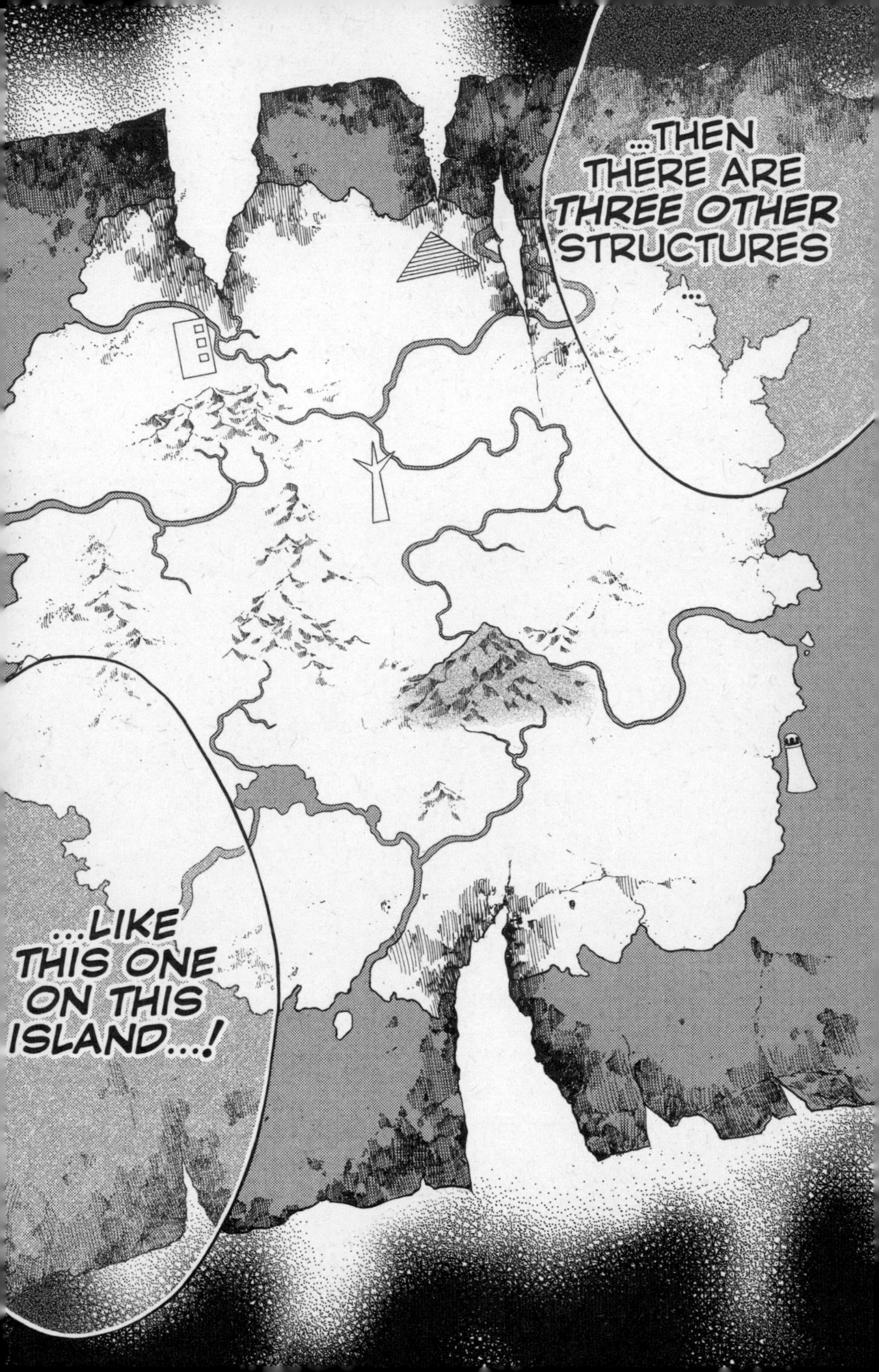
...THEN THERE ARE THREE OTHER STRUCTURES ...
...LIKE THIS ONE ON THIS ISLAND...!

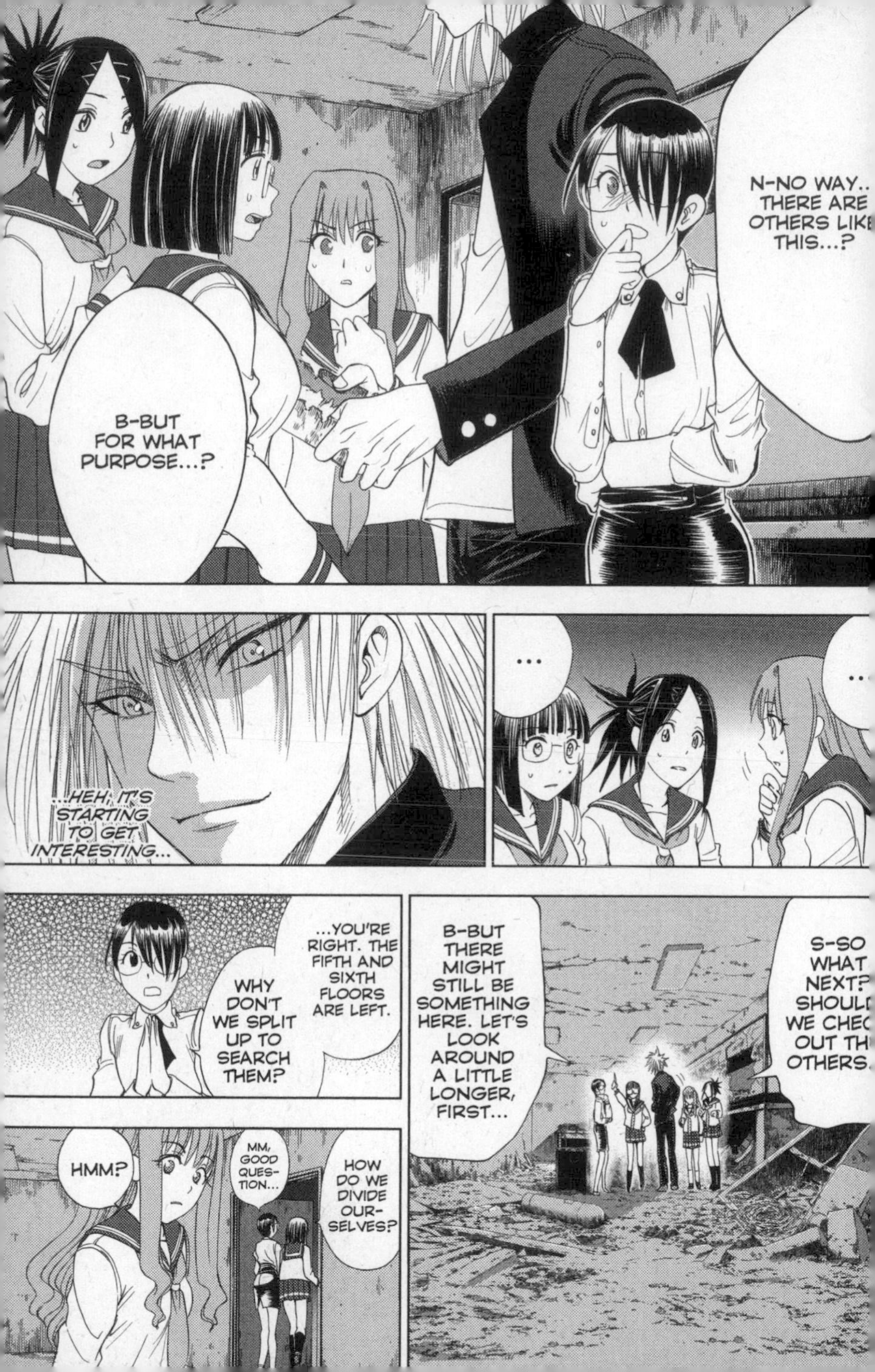
N-NO WAY.. THERE ARE OTHERS LIKE THIS...?
B-BUT FOR WHAT PURPOSE...?
...
...
...HEH, IT'S STARTING TO GET INTERESTING...
S-SO WHAT NEXT? SHOULD WE CHEC OUT TH OTHERS.
B-BUT THERE MIGHT STILL BE SOMETHING HERE. LET'S LOOK AROUND A LITTLE LONGER, FIRST...
...YOU'RE RIGHT. THE FIFTH AND SIXTH FLOORS ARE LEFT.
WHY DON'T WE SPLIT UP TO SEARCH THEM?
HOW DO WE DIVIDE OUR-SELVES?
MM, GOOD QUES-TION...
HMM?

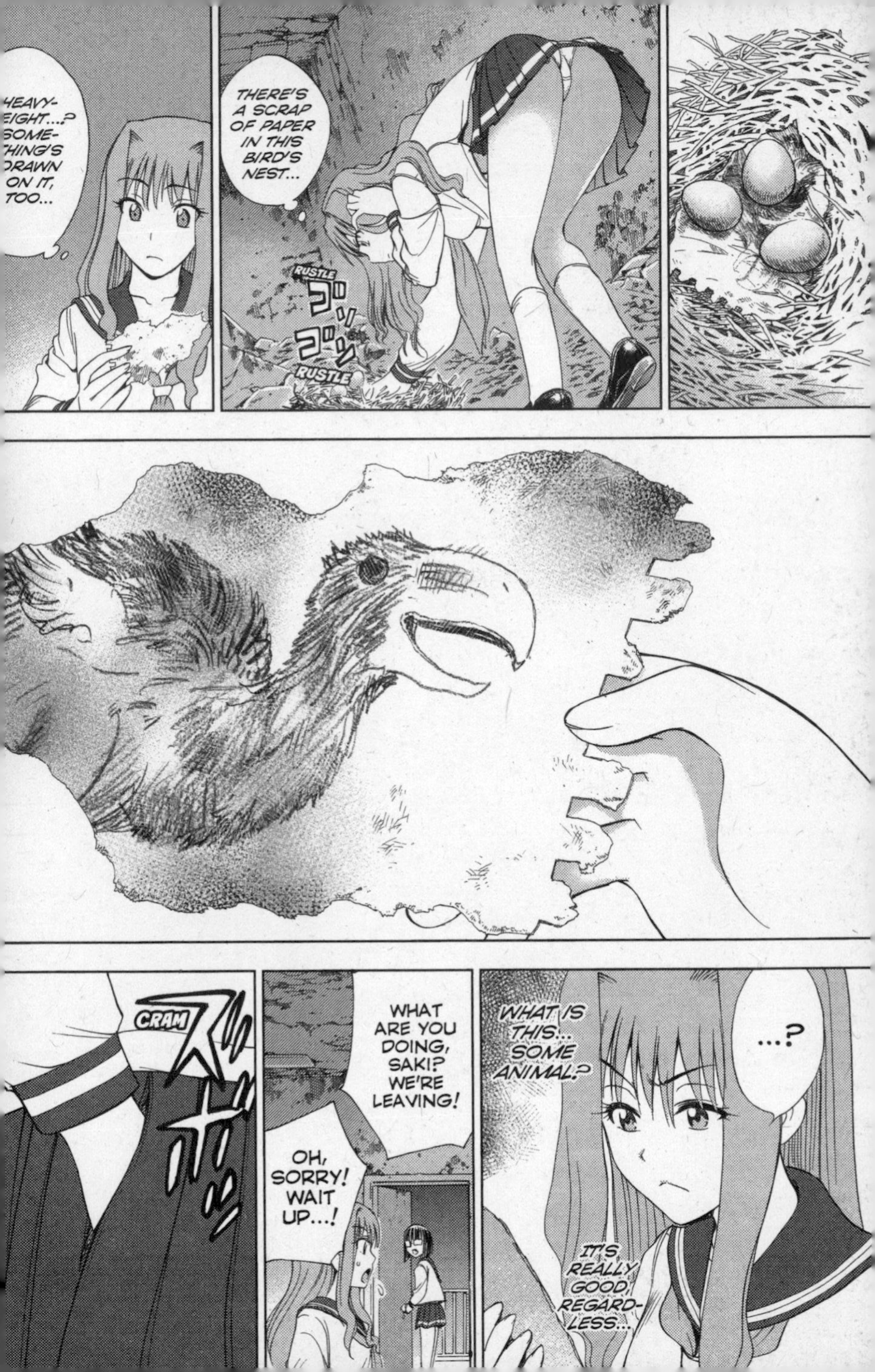
THERE'S A SCRAP OF PAPER IN THIS BIRD'S NEST...
RUSTLE
RUSTLE
HEAVY-EIGHT...? SOME-THING'S DRAWN ON IT, TOO...
...?
WHAT IS THIS... SOME ANIMAL?
IT'S REALLY GOOD, REGARDLESS...
WHAT ARE YOU DOING, SAKI? WE'RE LEAVING!
OH, SORRY! WAIT UP...!
CRAM

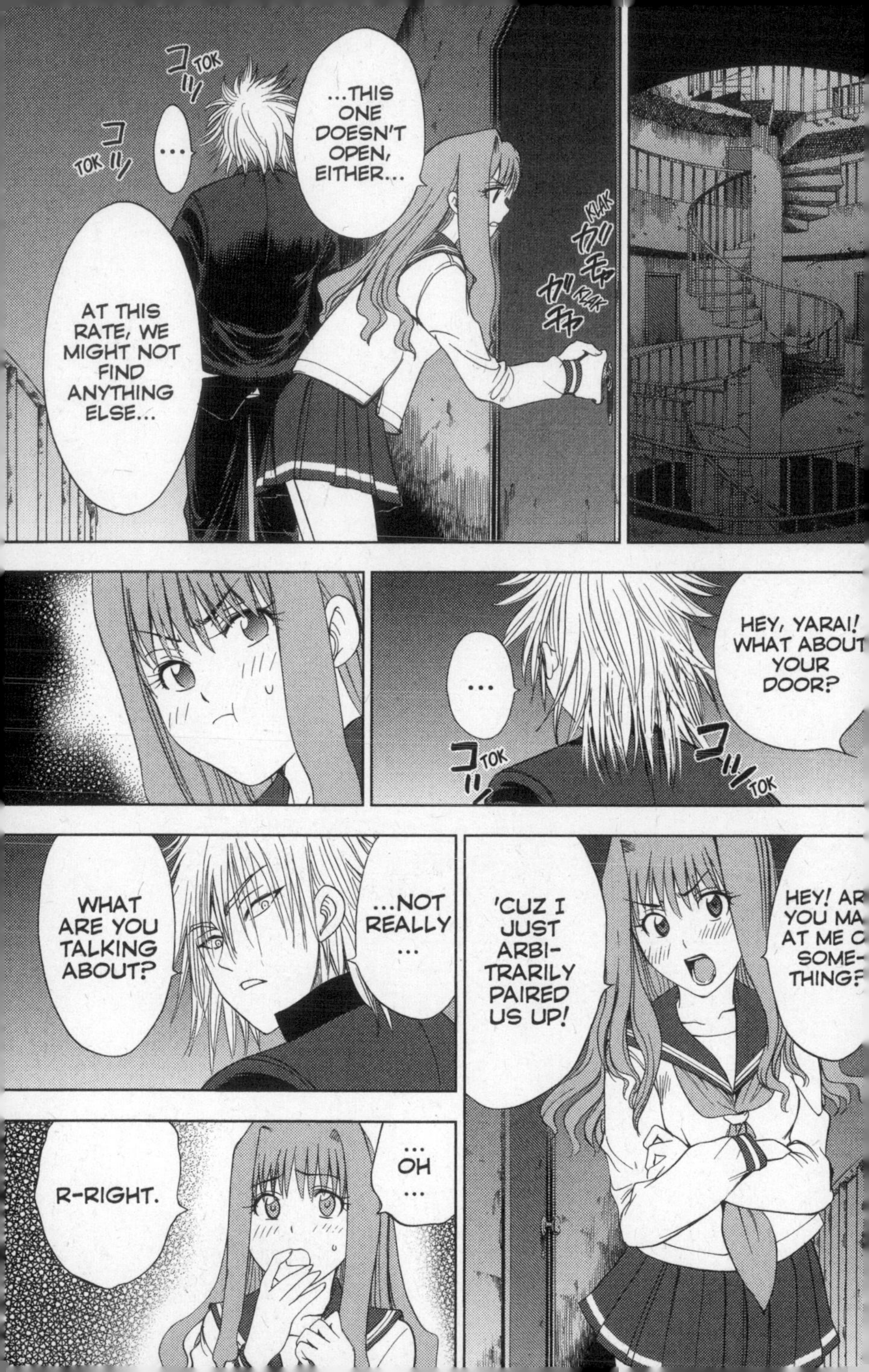
KLAK
KLAK
...THIS ONE DOESN'T OPEN, EITHER...
TOK
...
TOK
AT THIS RATE, WE MIGHT NOT FIND ANYTHING ELSE...
HEY, YARAI! WHAT ABOUT YOUR DOOR?
TOK
...
TOK
HEY! AR YOU MA AT ME O SOME-THING?
'CUZ I JUST ARBI-TRARILY PAIRED US UP!
...NOT REALLY ...
WHAT ARE YOU TALKING ABOUT?
... OH ...
R-RIGHT.

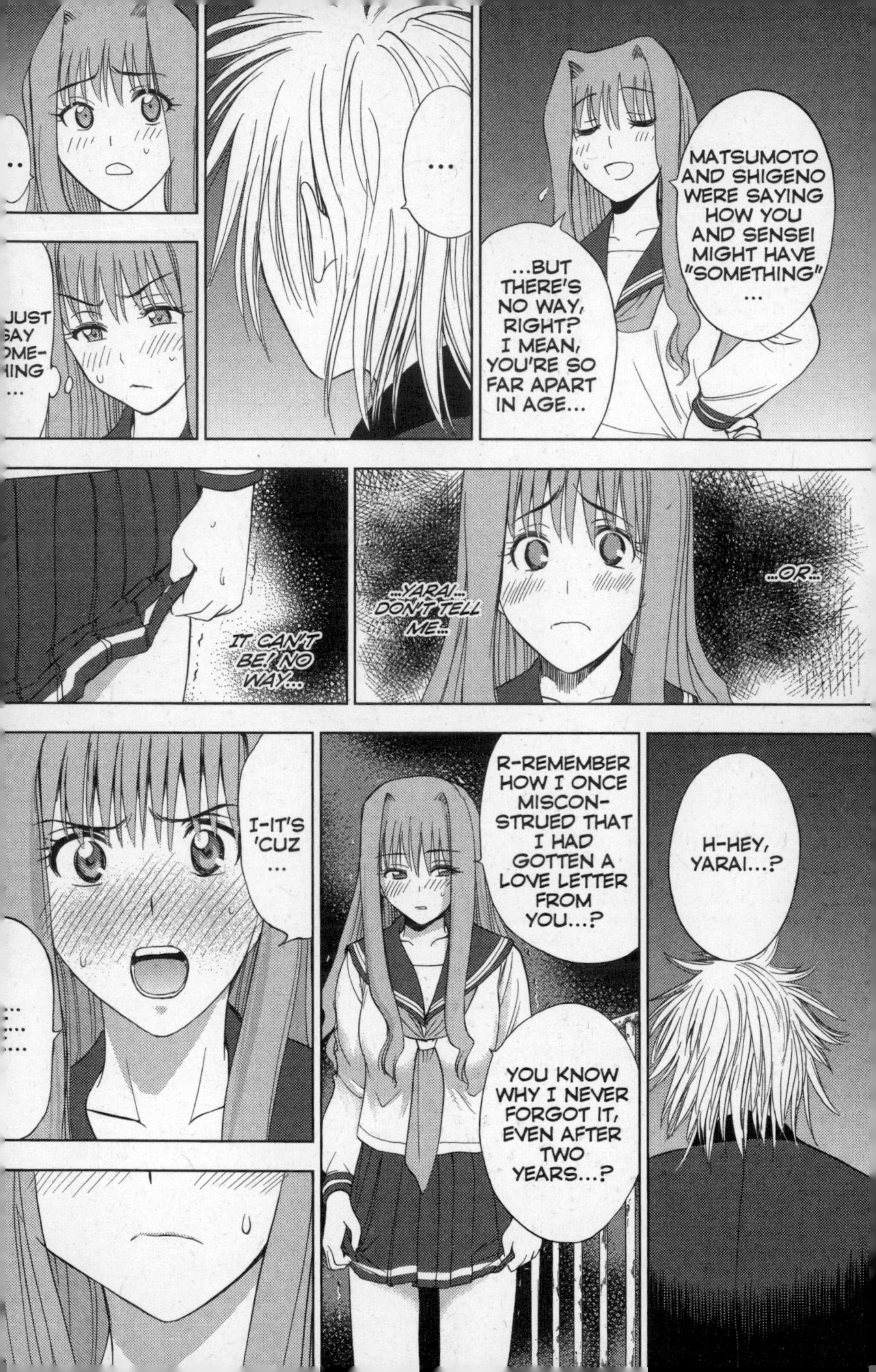
MATSUMOTO AND SHIGENO WERE SAYING HOW YOU AND SENSEI MIGHT HAVE "SOMETHING" ...
...BUT THERE'S NO WAY, RIGHT? I MEAN, YOU'RE SO FAR APART IN AGE...
...
...
JUST SAY OME- HING ...
...OR...
...YARAI... DON'T TELL ME...
IT CAN'T BE! NO WAY...
H-HEY, YARAI...?
R-REMEMBER HOW I ONCE MISCON- STRUED THAT I HAD GOTTEN A LOVE LETTER FROM YOU...?
YOU KNOW WHY I NEVER FORGOT IT, EVEN AFTER TWO YEARS...?
I-IT'S 'CUZ ...
... .

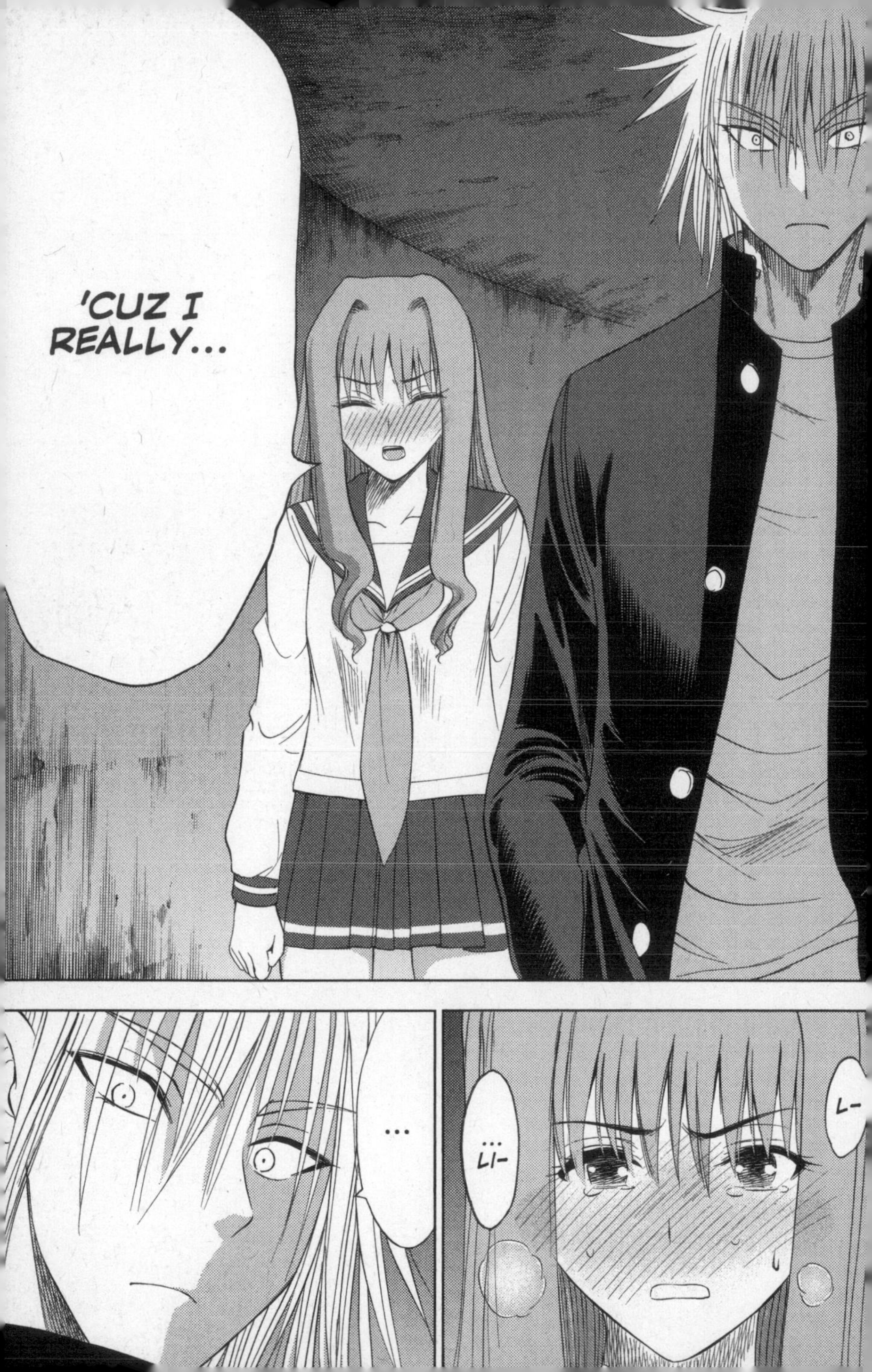
'CUZ I REALLY...
L-
...LI-
...

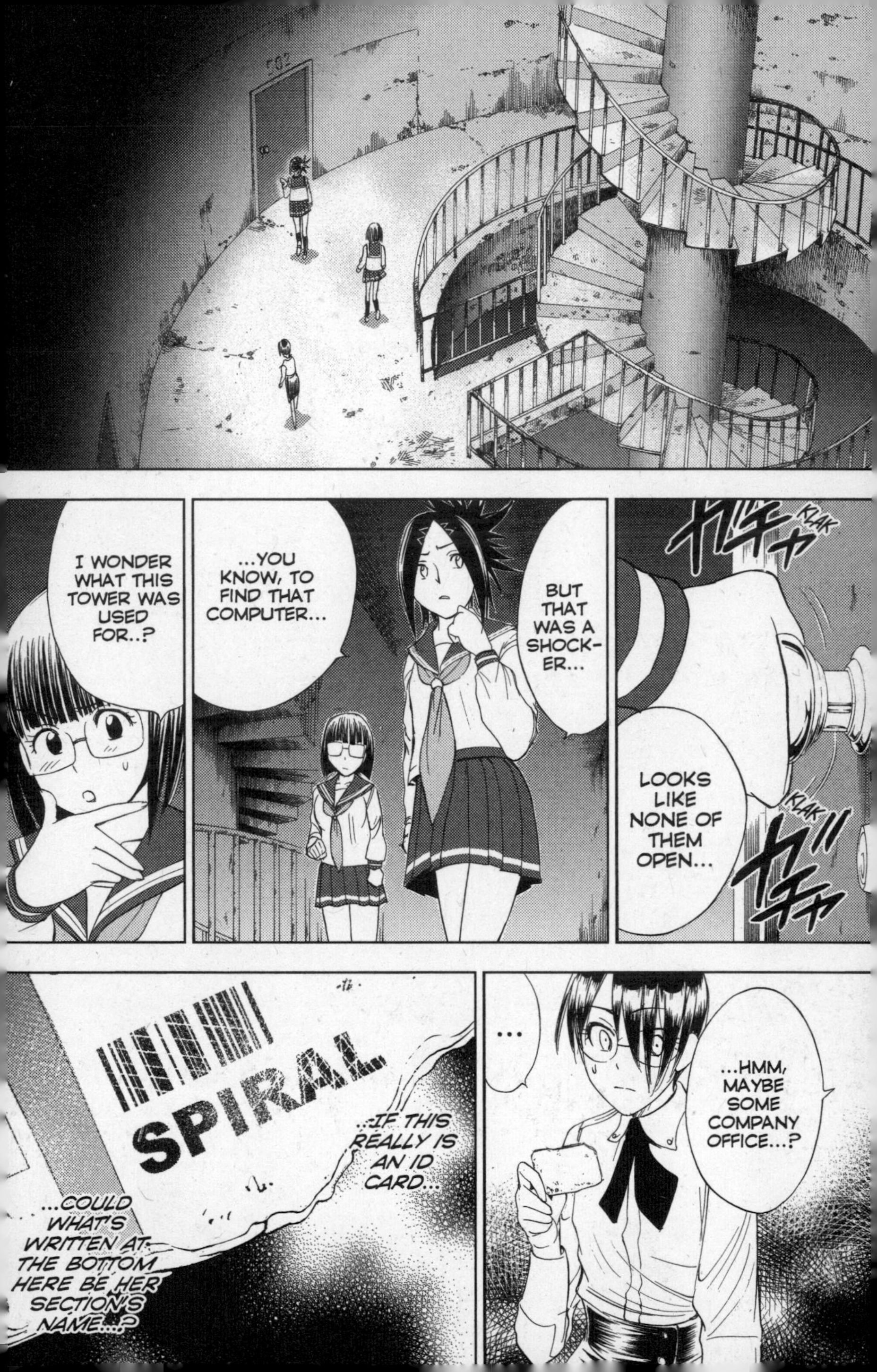
KLAK
LOOKS LIKE NONE OF THEM OPEN...
KLAK
BUT THAT WAS A SHOCKER...
...YOU KNOW, TO FIND THAT COMPUTER...
I WONDER WHAT THIS TOWER WAS USED FOR..?
...
...HMM, MAYBE SOME COMPANY OFFICE...?
SPIRAL
...IF THIS REALLY IS AN ID CARD...
...COULD WHAT'S WRITTEN AT THE BOTTOM HERE BE HER SECTION'S NAME...?

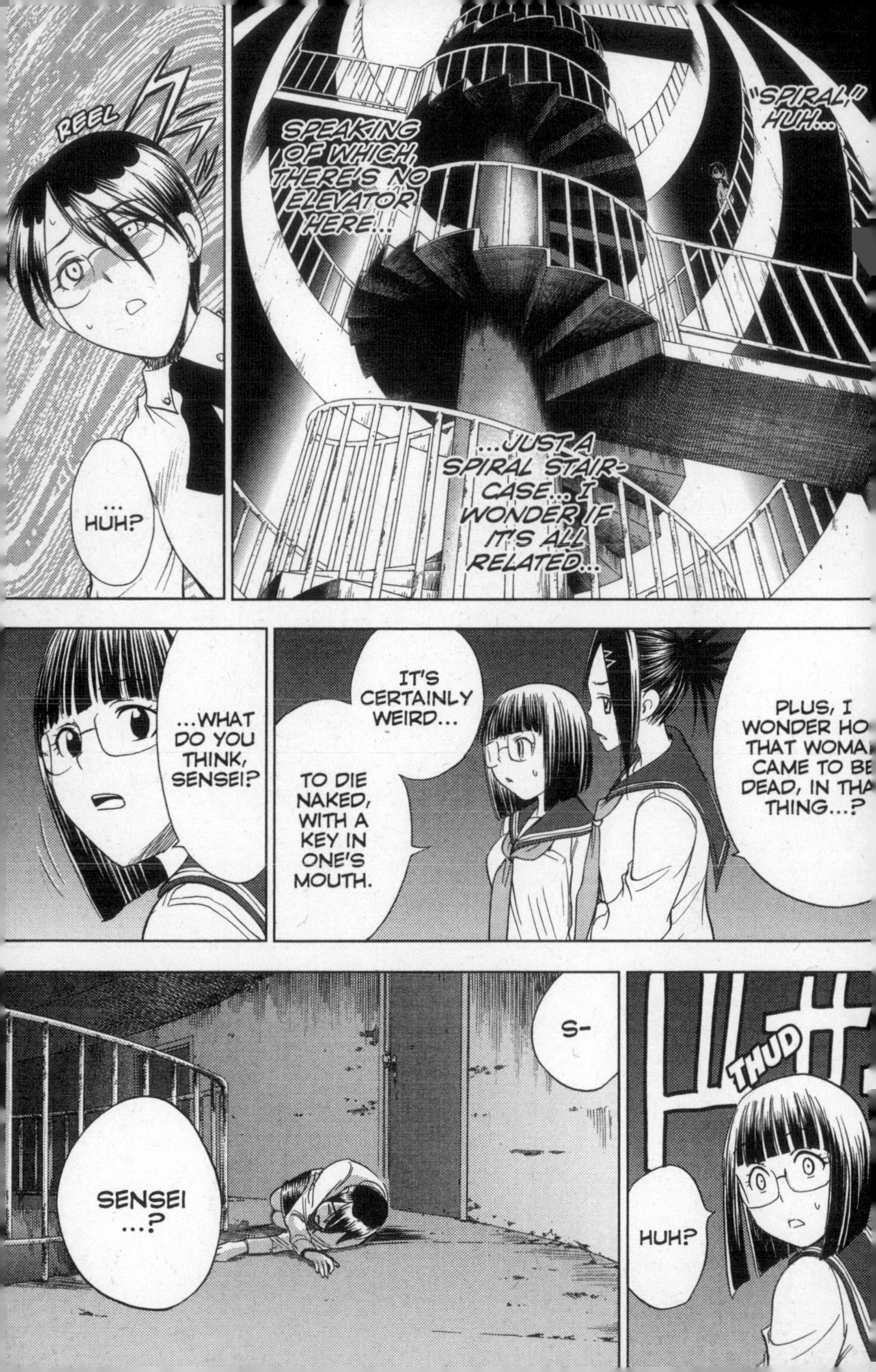
"SPIRAL," HUH...
SPEAKING OF WHICH, THERE'S NO ELEVATOR HERE...
...JUST A SPIRAL STAIR-CASE... I WONDER IF IT'S ALL RELATED...
REEL
... HUH?
PLUS, I WONDER HO THAT WOMA CAME TO BE DEAD, IN THA THING...?
IT'S CERTAINLY WEIRD...
TO DIE NAKED, WITH A KEY IN ONE'S MOUTH.
...WHAT DO YOU THINK, SENSEI?
THUD
HUH?
S-
SENSEI ...?

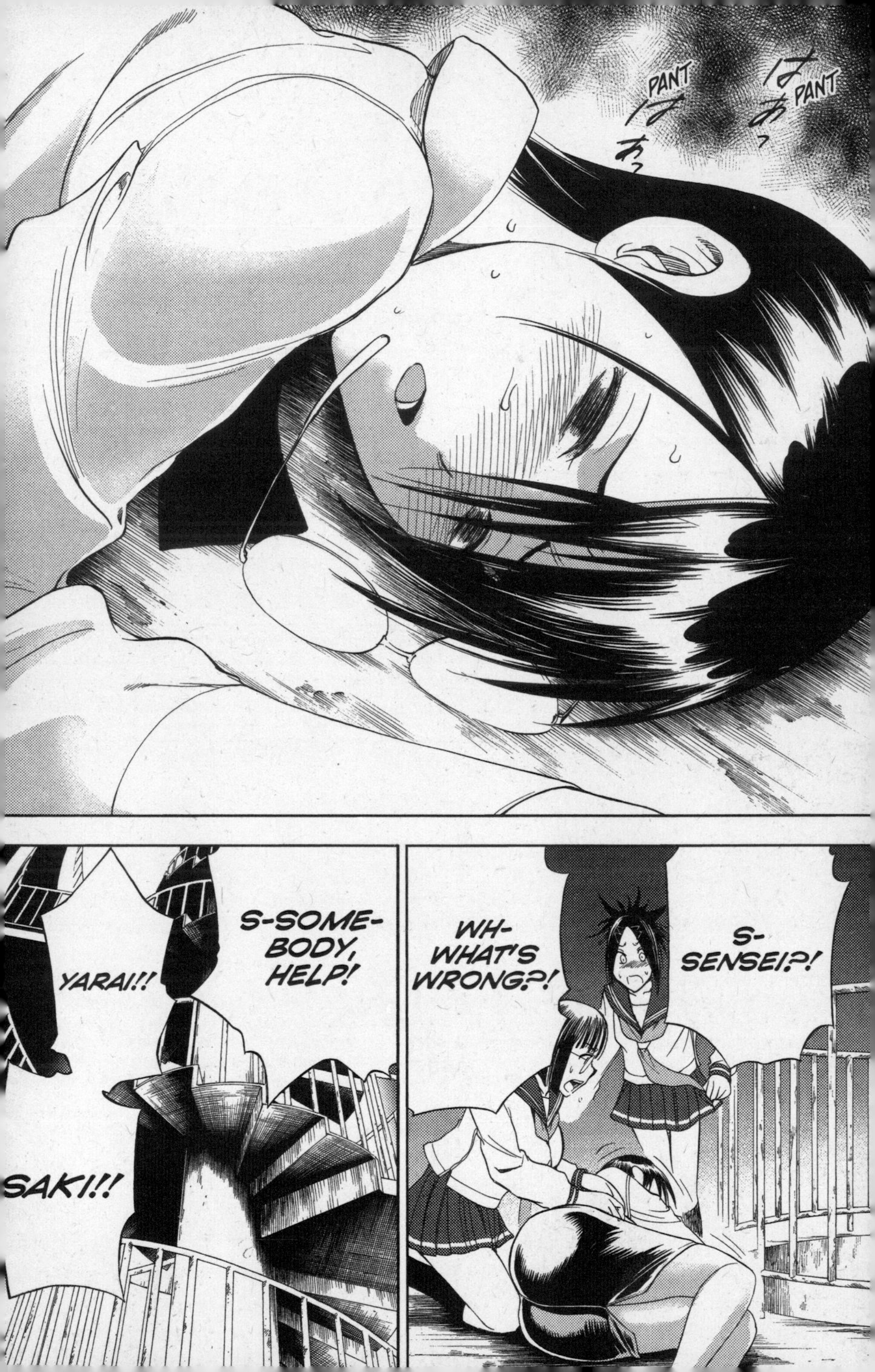

はあっ
PANT
はあっ
PANT
S-SENSEI!?!
WH-WHAT'S WRONG?!
S-SOMEBODY, HELP!
YARAI!!
SAKI!!

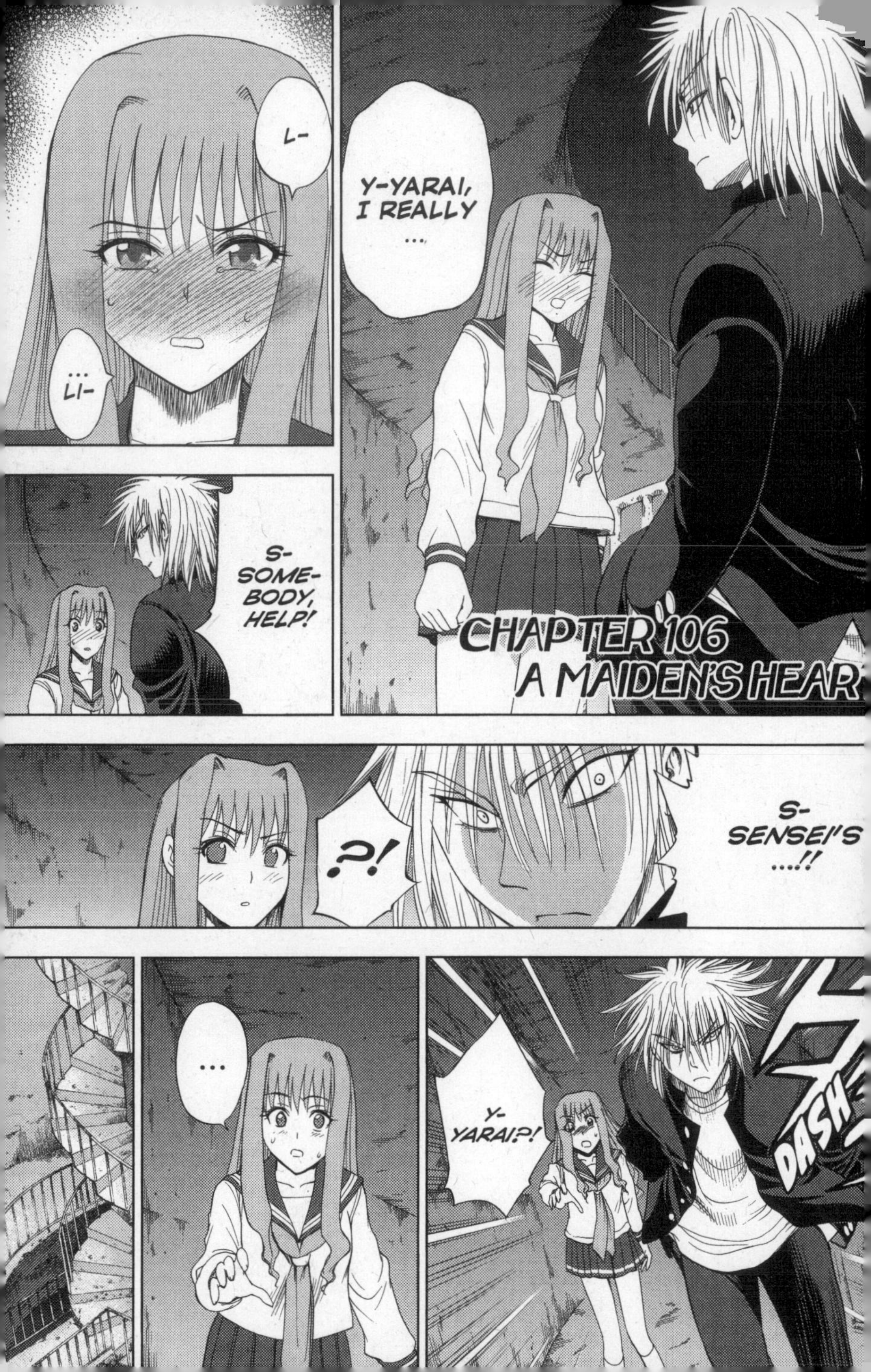
Y-YARAI, I REALLY ...
CHAPTER 106
A MAIDEN'S HEAR
L-
...LI-
S-SOMEBODY, HELP!
S-SENSEI'S ...!!
?!
DASH
Y-YARAI?!
...

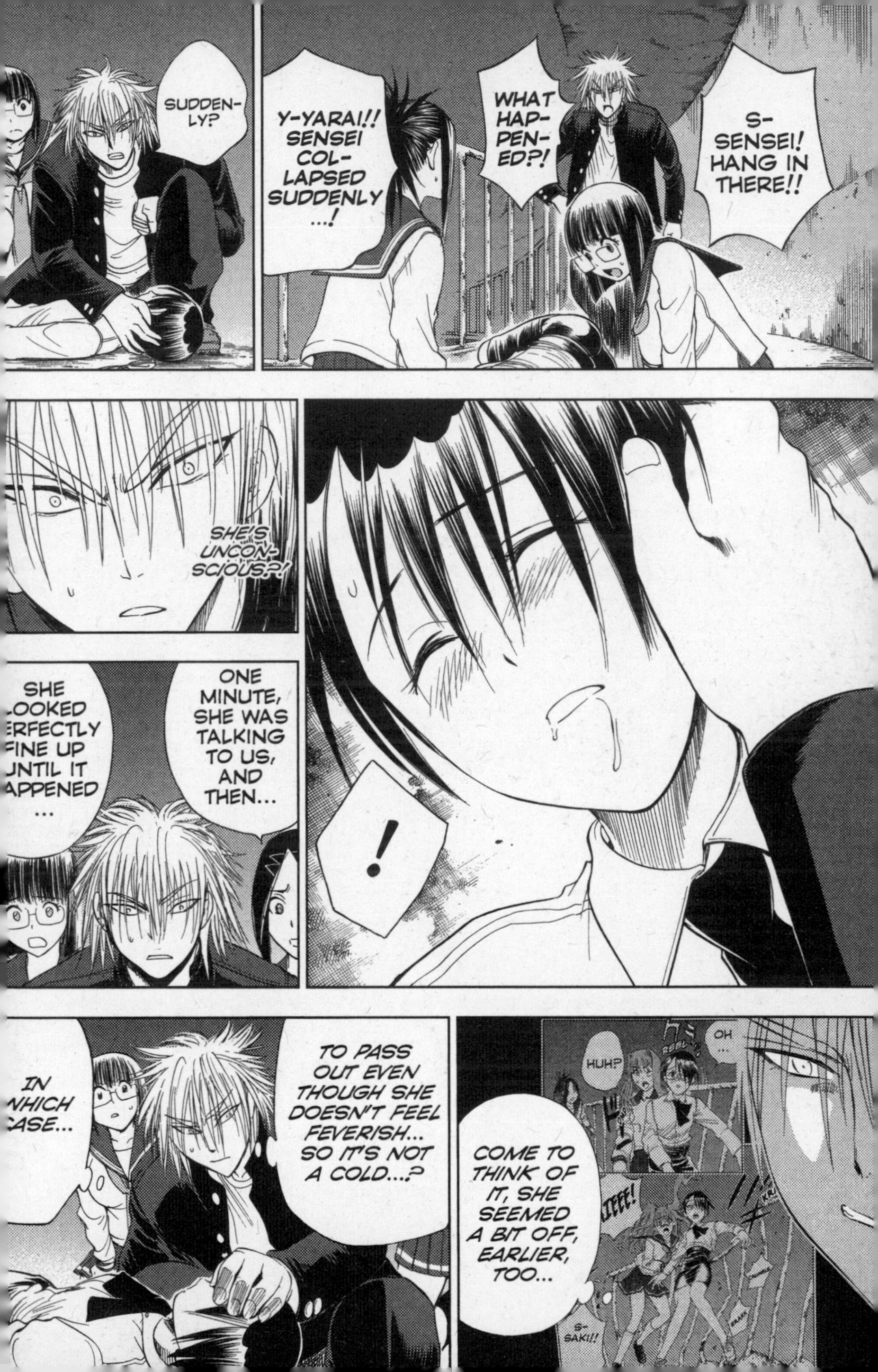
S-SENSEI! HANG IN THERE!!
WHAT HAP-PEN-ED?!
Y-YARAI!! SENSEI COL-LAPSED SUDDENLY...!
SUDDEN-LY?
!
SHE'S UNCON-SCIOUS?!
ONE MINUTE, SHE WAS TALKING TO US, AND THEN...
SHE LOOKED ERFECTLY FINE UP UNTIL IT APPENED ...
COME TO THINK OF IT, SHE SEEMED A BIT OFF, EARLIER, TOO...
OH...
HUH?
S-SAKI!!
TO PASS OUT EVEN THOUGH SHE DOESN'T FEEL FEVERISH... SO IT'S NOT A COLD...?
IN NHICH CASE...

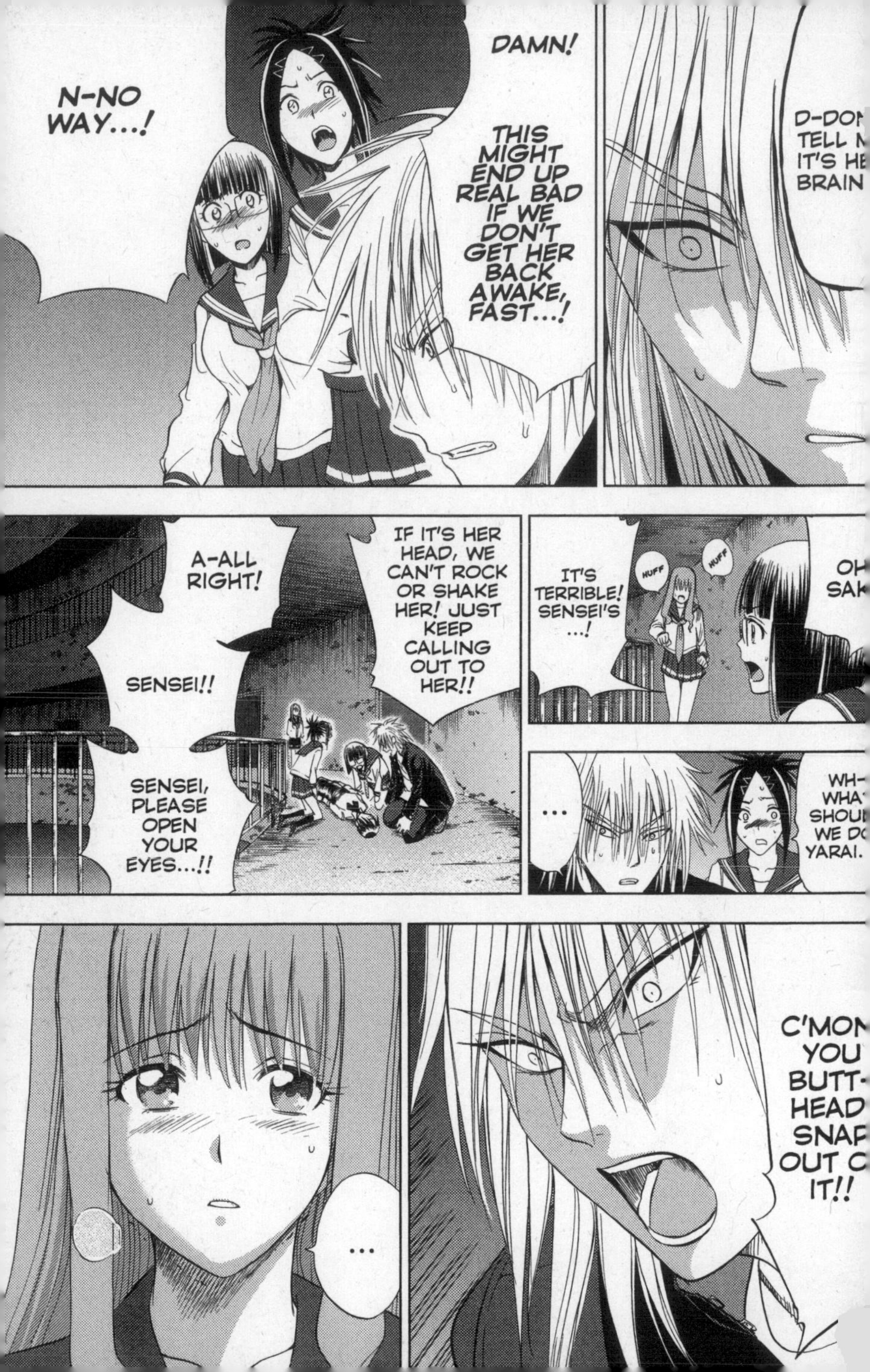
D-DON
TELL M
IT'S HE
BRAIN
DAMN!
THIS MIGHT END UP REAL BAD IF WE DON'T GET HER BACK AWAKE, FAST...!
N-NO WAY...!
OH
SAK
HUFF
HUFF
IT'S TERRIBLE! SENSEI'S ...!
WH- WHAT
SHOUL
WE DO
YARAI.
...
IF IT'S HER HEAD, WE CAN'T ROCK OR SHAKE HER! JUST KEEP CALLING OUT TO HER!!
A-ALL RIGHT!
SENSEI!!
SENSEI, PLEASE OPEN YOUR EYES...!!
C'MON
YOU
BUTT-
HEAD
SNAP
OUT O
IT!!
...

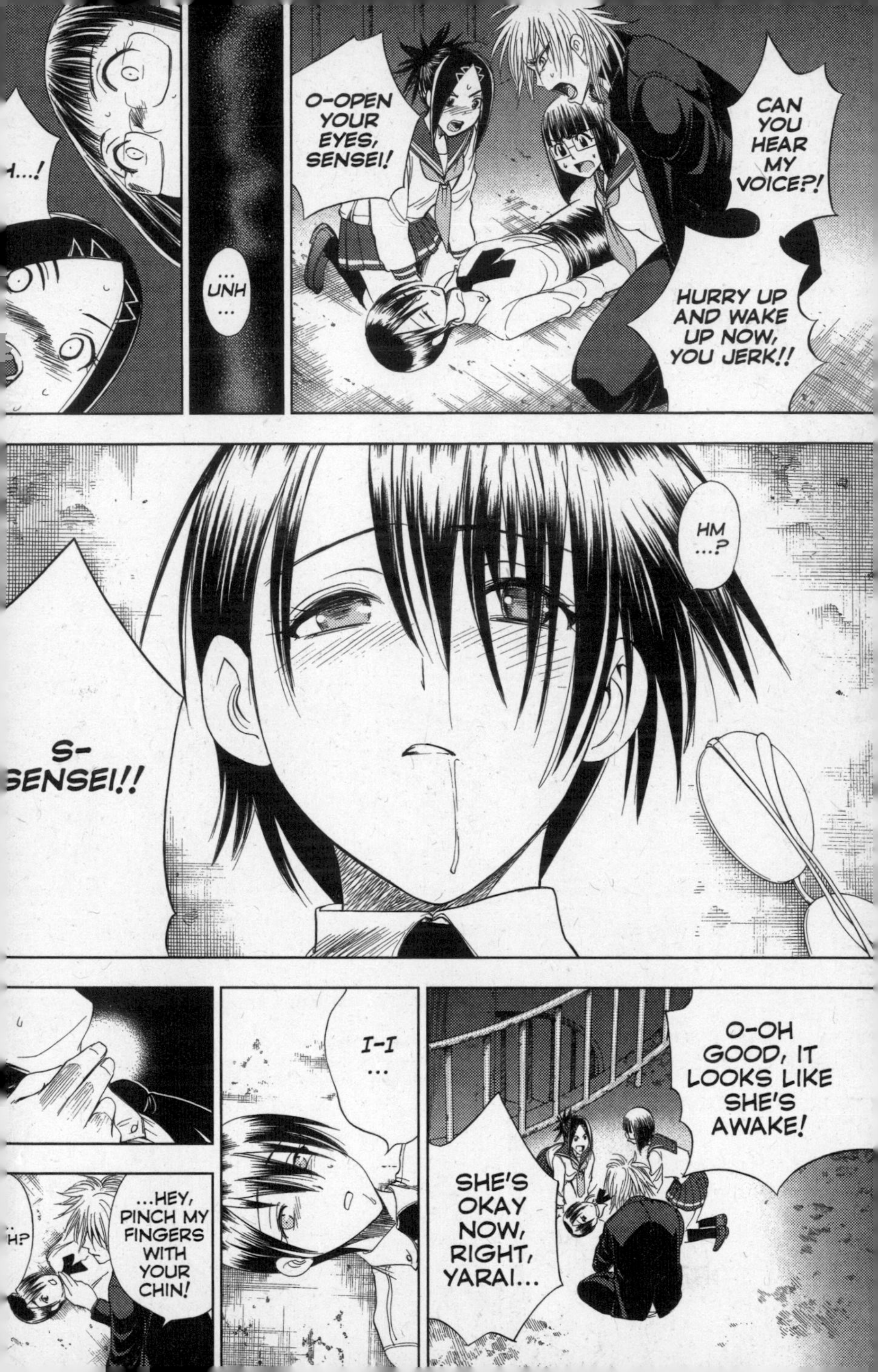
CAN YOU HEAR MY VOICE?!
O-OPEN YOUR EYES, SENSEI!
HURRY UP AND WAKE UP NOW, YOU JERK!!
... UNH ...
H...!
HM ...?
S-SENSEI!!
O-OH GOOD, IT LOOKS LIKE SHE'S AWAKE!
SHE'S OKAY NOW, RIGHT, YARAI...
I-I ...
...HEY, PINCH MY FINGERS WITH YOUR CHIN!
H?

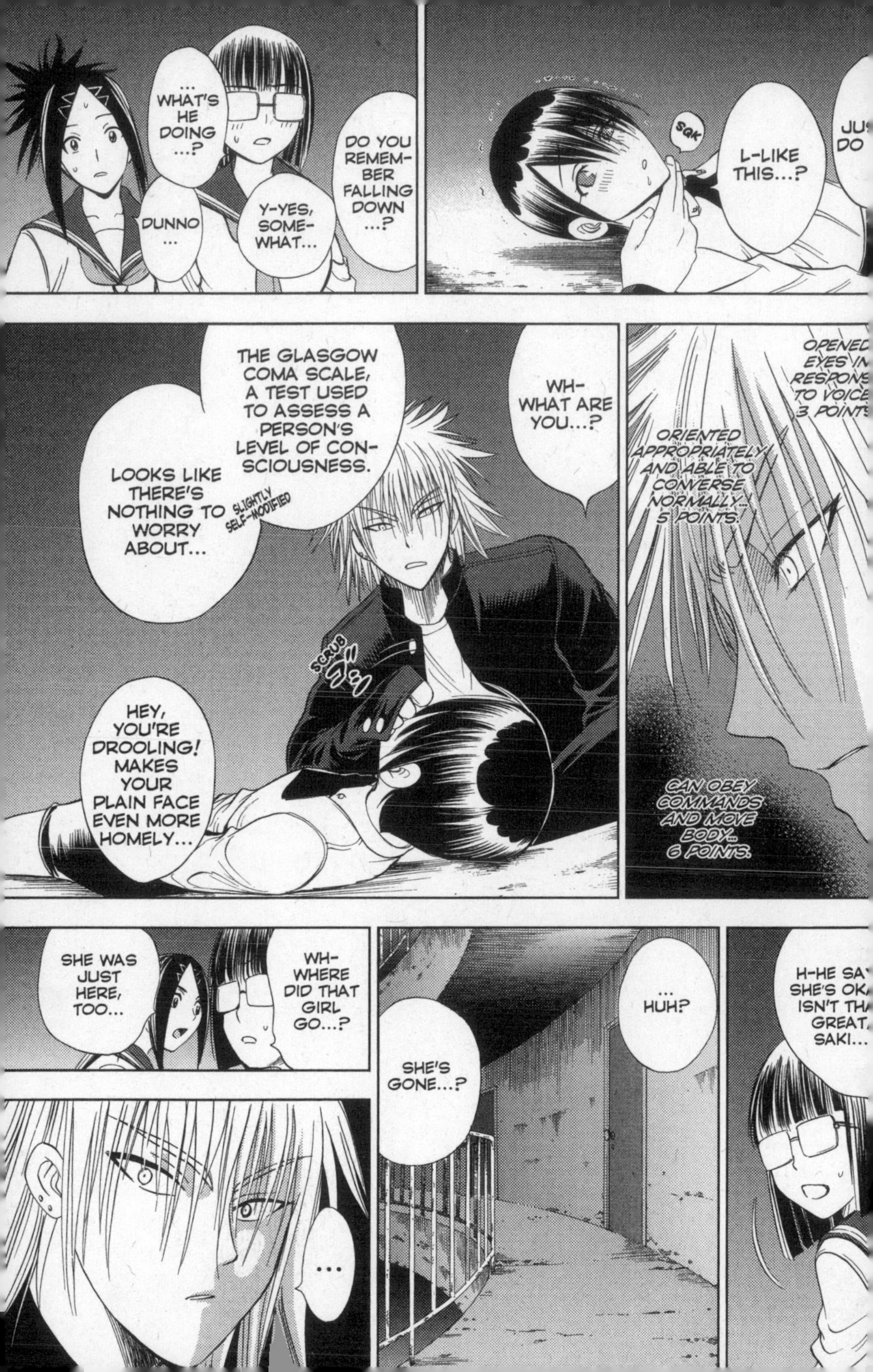
JUS DO
SQK
L-LIKE THIS...?
DO YOU REMEMBER FALLING DOWN...?
Y-YES, SOMEWHAT...
...WHAT'S HE DOING...?
DUNNO...
OPENED EYES IN RESPONS TO VOICE 3 POINTS
ORIENTED APPROPRIATELY AND ABLE TO CONVERSE NORMALLY... 5 POINTS.
CAN OBEY COMMANDS AND MOVE BODY... 6 POINTS.
WH- WHAT ARE YOU...?
THE GLASGOW COMA SCALE, A TEST USED TO ASSESS A PERSON'S LEVEL OF CONSCIOUSNESS.
LOOKS LIKE THERE'S NOTHING TO WORRY ABOUT...
SLIGHTLY SELF-MODIFIED
SCRUB
HEY, YOU'RE DROOLING! MAKES YOUR PLAIN FACE EVEN MORE HOMELY...
H-HE SAY SHE'S OKA ISN'T THA GREAT, SAKI...
...HUH?
SHE'S GONE...?
WH- WHERE DID THAT GIRL GO...?
SHE WAS JUST HERE, TOO...
...

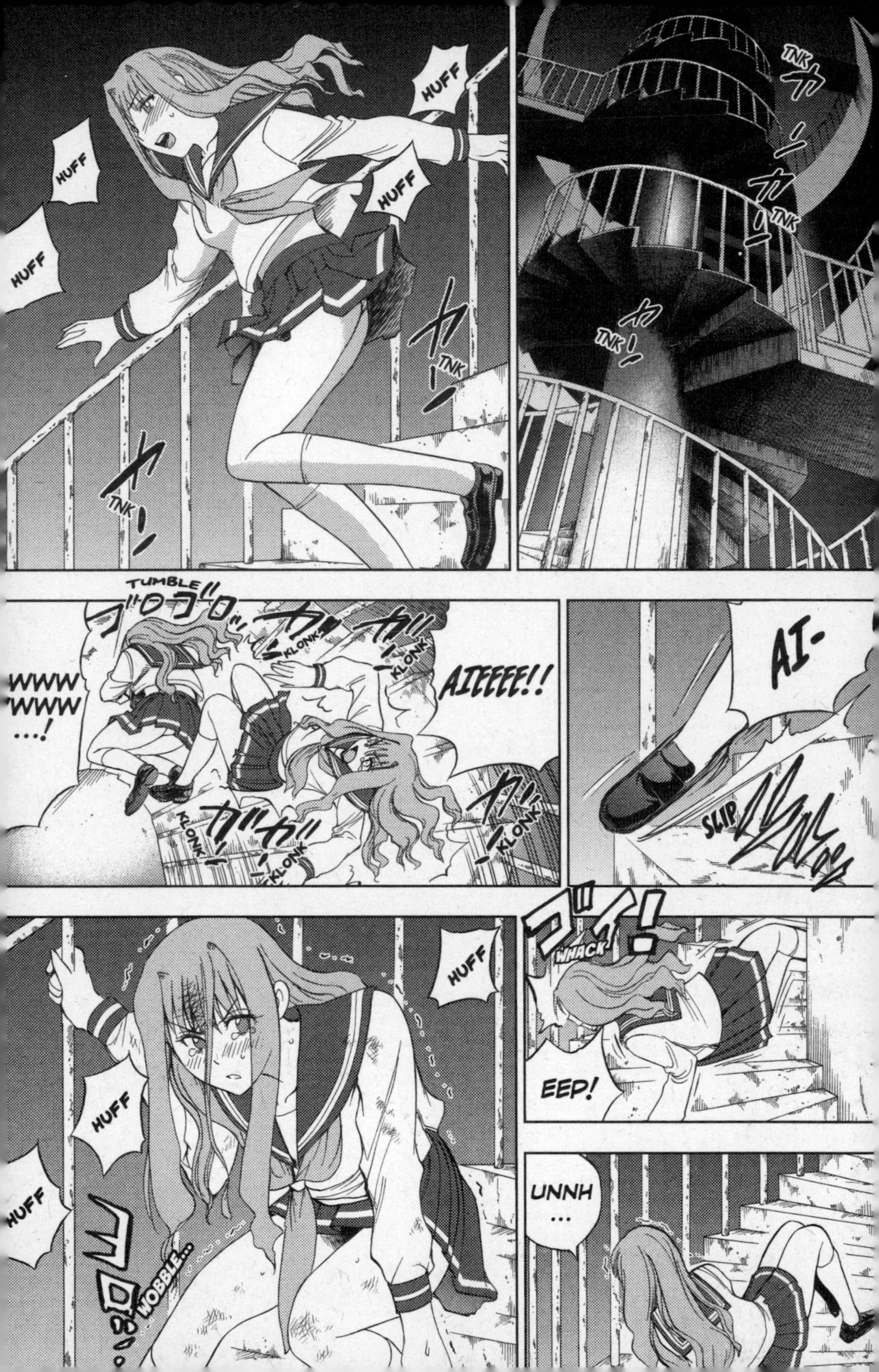
TNK
TNK
TNK
HUFF
HUFF
HUFF
HUFF
TNK
TNK
AI-
SLIP
TUMBLE!!
KLONK
KLONK
AIEEEE!!
WWWWWW...!
KLONK
KLONK
KLONK
WHACK
EEP!
UNNH ...
HUFF
HUFF
HUFF
WOBBLE...

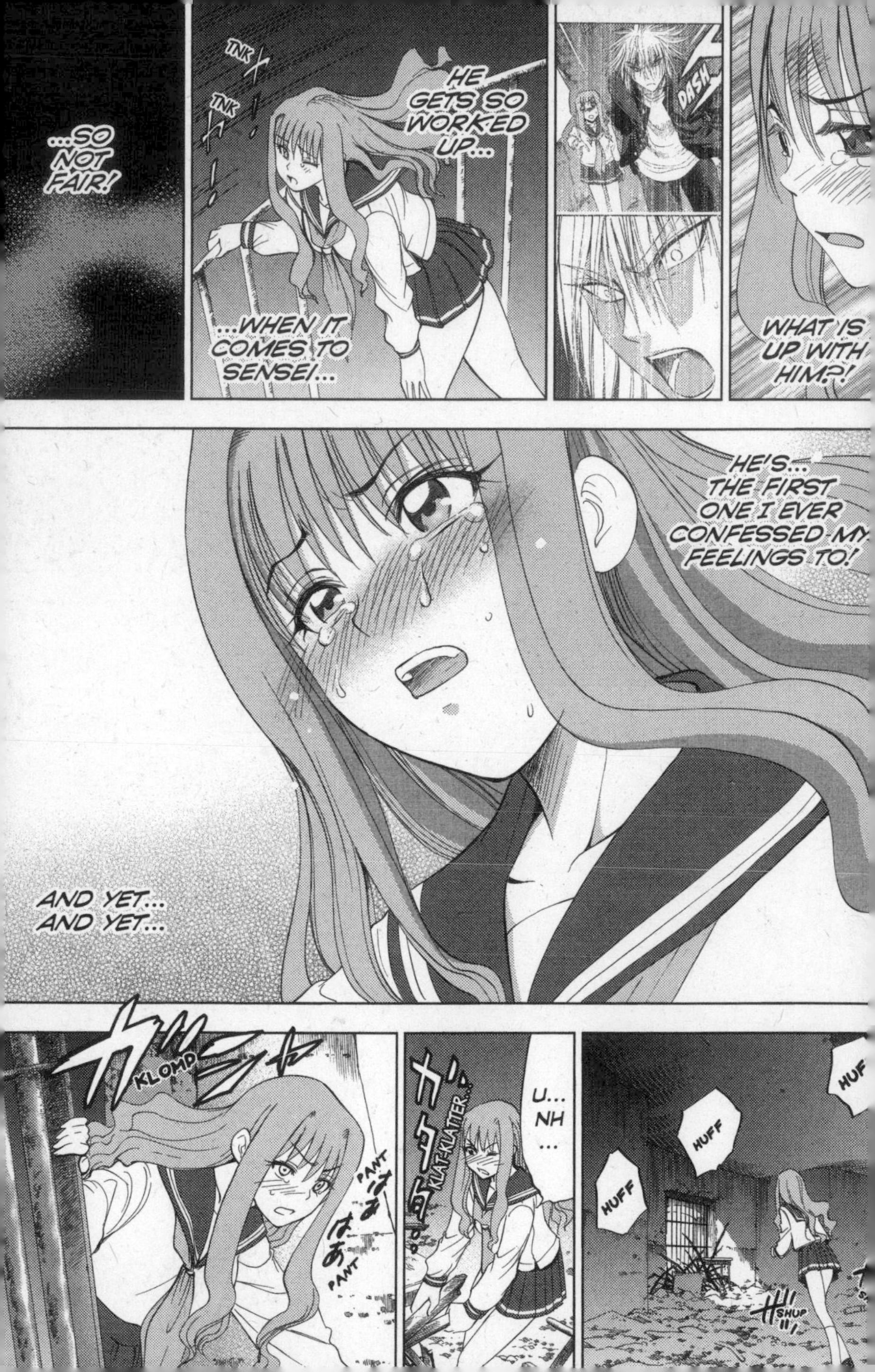
WHAT IS UP WITH HIM?!
DASH
HE GETS SO WORKED UP...
TNK
TNK
...WHEN IT COMES TO SENSEI...
...SO NOT FAIR!
HE'S... THE FIRST ONE I EVER CONFESSED MY FEELINGS TO!
AND YET... AND YET...
HUF
HUFF
HUFF
SHUP
U... NH ...
KLAT-KLATTER
KLOMP
PANT
PANT

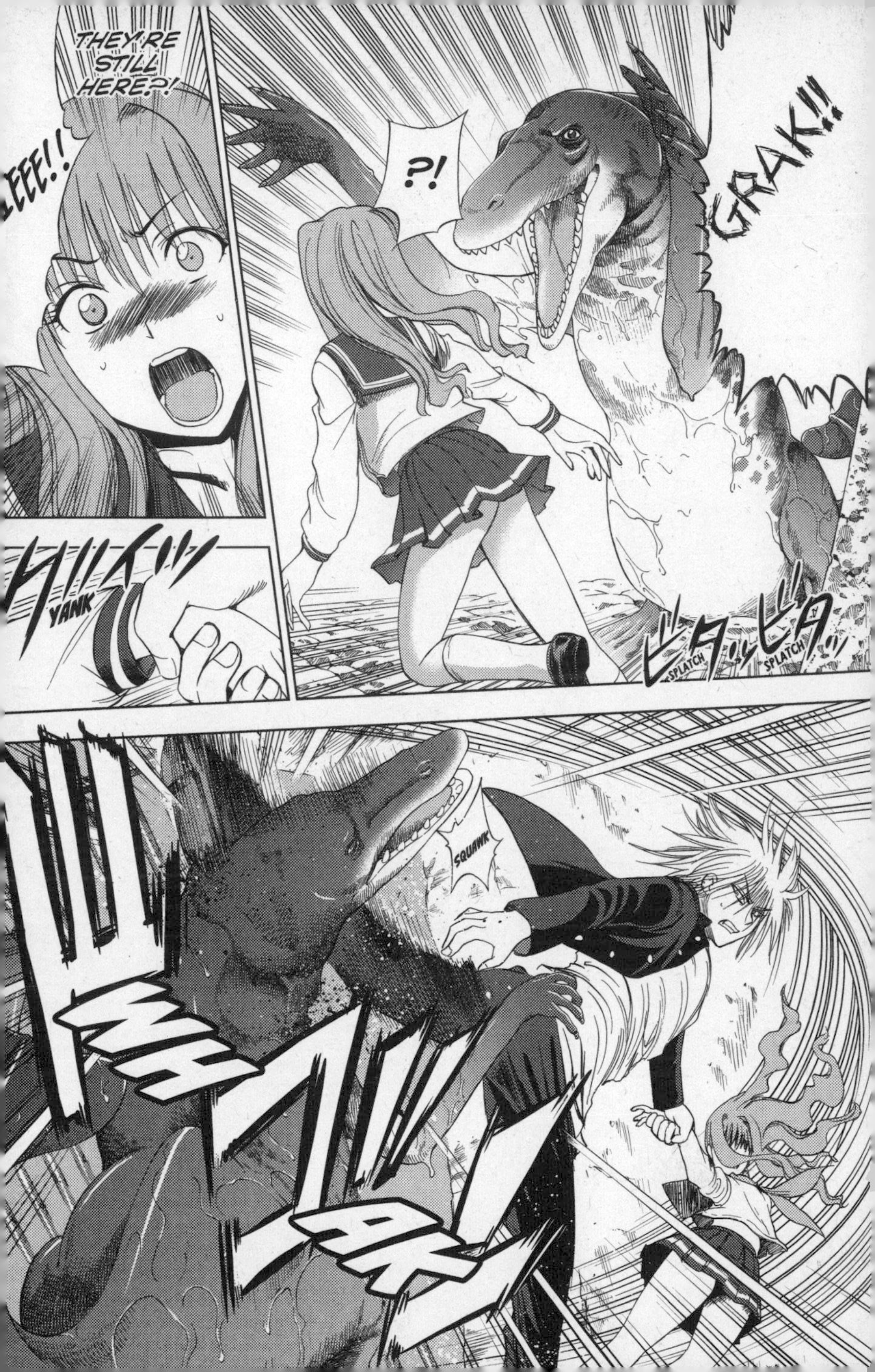

?!
GRAK!!
SPLATCH
SPLATCH
THEY'RE STILL HERE?!
EEEE!!
YANK
SQUAWK
WHAK!!

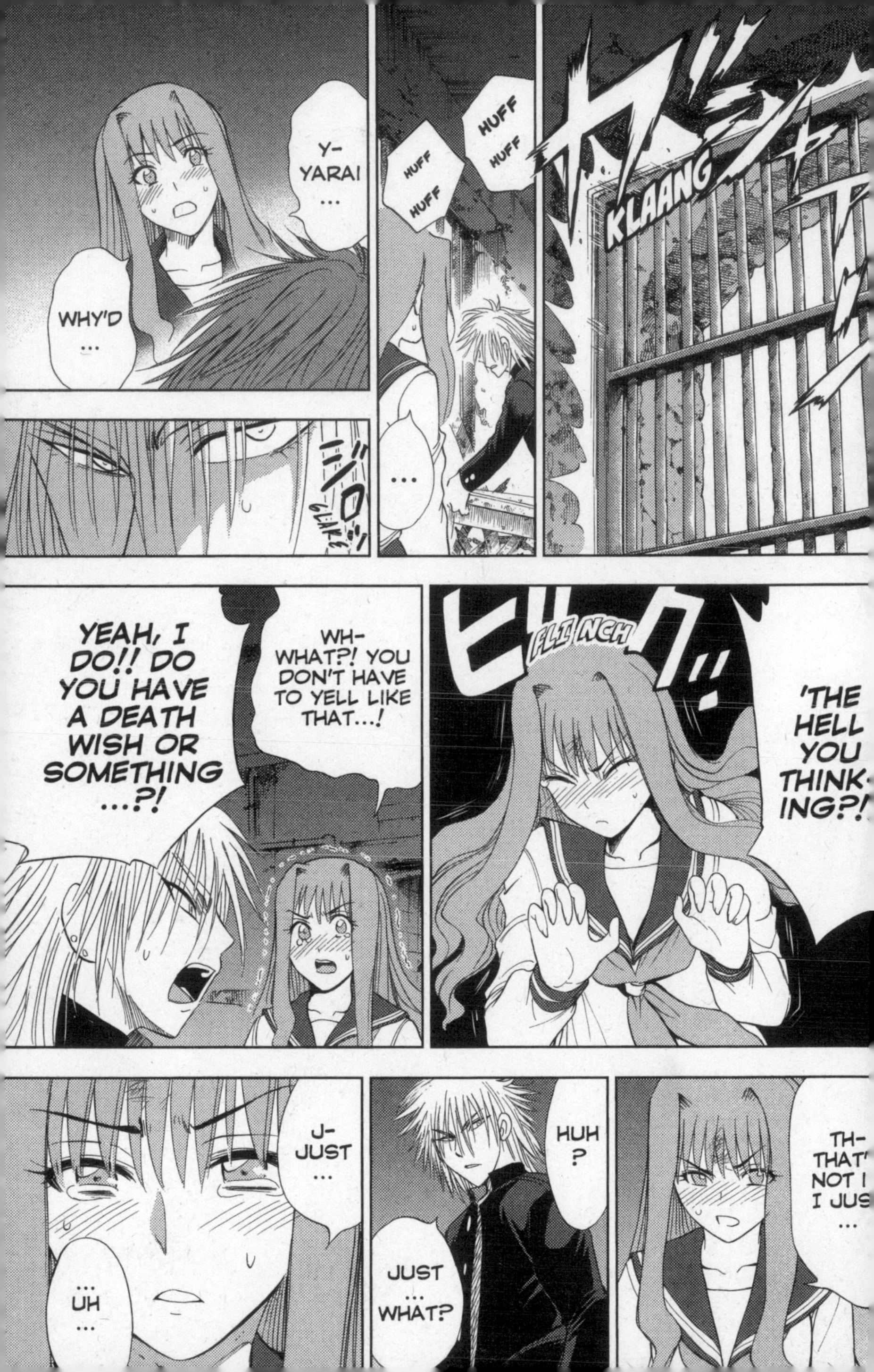
KLAANG
HUFF HUFF
HUFF HUFF
...
Y-YARAI ...
WHY'D ...
GLARE
FLINCH
'THE HELL YOU THINKING?!
WH-WHAT?! YOU DON'T HAVE TO YELL LIKE THAT...!
YEAH, I DO!! DO YOU HAVE A DEATH WISH OR SOMETHING ...?!
TH-THAT' NOT I I JUS ...
HUH ?
JUST ... WHAT?
J-JUST ...
... UH ...

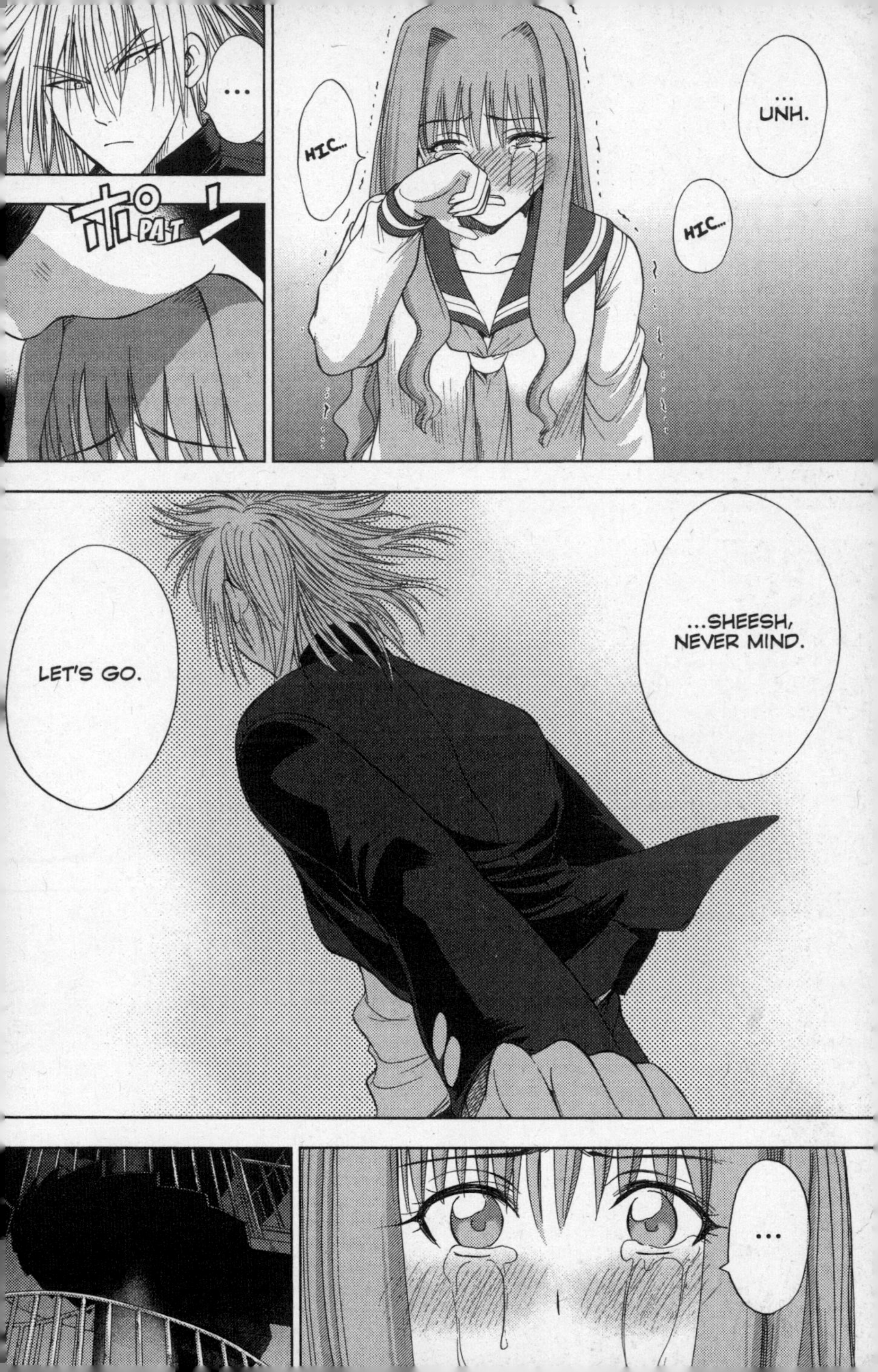

...UNH.
HIC...
HIC...
...
ポン
PAT
...SHEESH, NEVER MIND.
LET'S GO.
...

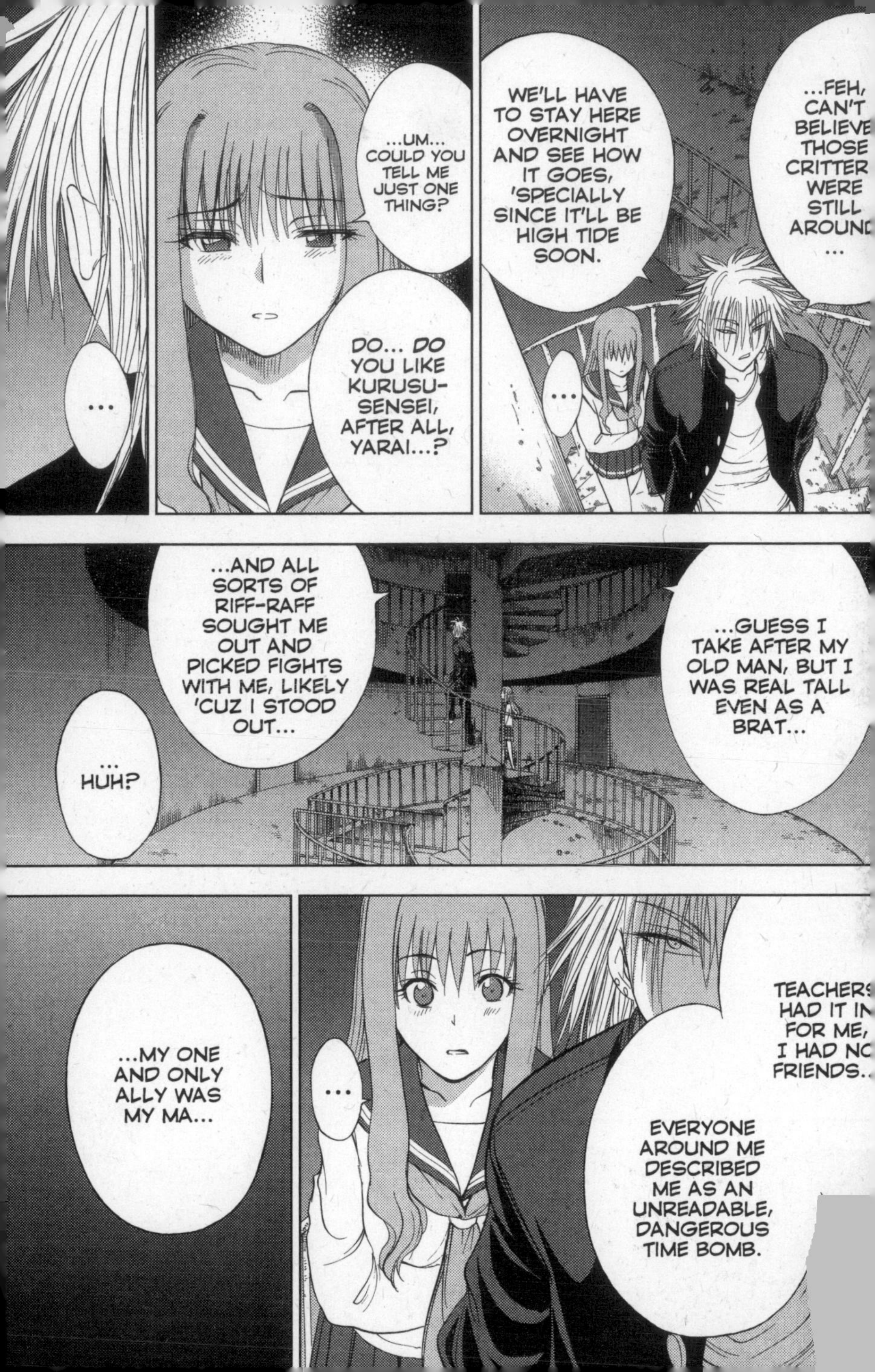
...FEH, CAN'T BELIEVE THOSE CRITTER WERE STILL AROUND...
WE'LL HAVE TO STAY HERE OVERNIGHT AND SEE HOW IT GOES, 'SPECIALLY SINCE IT'LL BE HIGH TIDE SOON.
...
...UM... COULD YOU TELL ME JUST ONE THING?
DO... DO YOU LIKE KURUSU-SENSEI, AFTER ALL, YARAI...?
...
...GUESS I TAKE AFTER MY OLD MAN, BUT I WAS REAL TALL EVEN AS A BRAT...
...AND ALL SORTS OF RIFF-RAFF SOUGHT ME OUT AND PICKED FIGHTS WITH ME, LIKELY 'CUZ I STOOD OUT...
... HUH?
TEACHERS HAD IT IN FOR ME, I HAD NO FRIENDS...
EVERYONE AROUND ME DESCRIBED ME AS AN UNREADABLE, DANGEROUS TIME BOMB.
...
...MY ONE AND ONLY ALLY WAS MY MA...

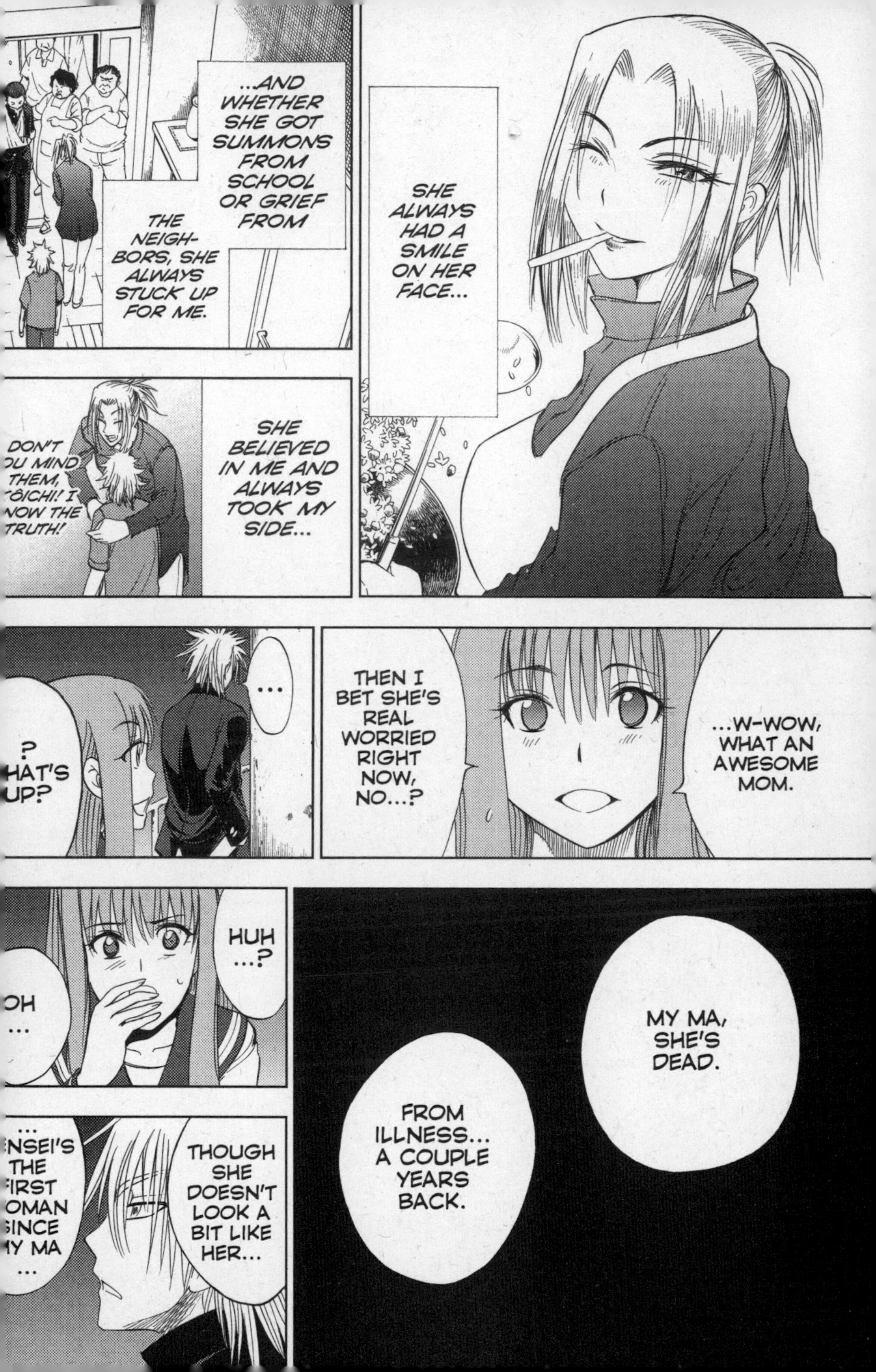
SHE ALWAYS HAD A SMILE ON HER FACE...
...AND WHETHER SHE GOT SUMMONS FROM SCHOOL OR GRIEF FROM
THE NEIGH-BORS, SHE ALWAYS STUCK UP FOR ME.
SHE BELIEVED IN ME AND ALWAYS TOOK MY SIDE...
DON'T OU MIND THEM, ŌICHI! I NOW THE TRUTH!
...W-WOW, WHAT AN AWESOME MOM.
THEN I BET SHE'S REAL WORRIED RIGHT NOW, NO...?
...
? HAT'S UP?
MY MA, SHE'S DEAD.
FROM ILLNESS... A COUPLE YEARS BACK.
HUH ...?
OH ...
THOUGH SHE DOESN'T LOOK A BIT LIKE HER...
... ENSEI'S THE FIRST OMAN SINCE MY MA ...

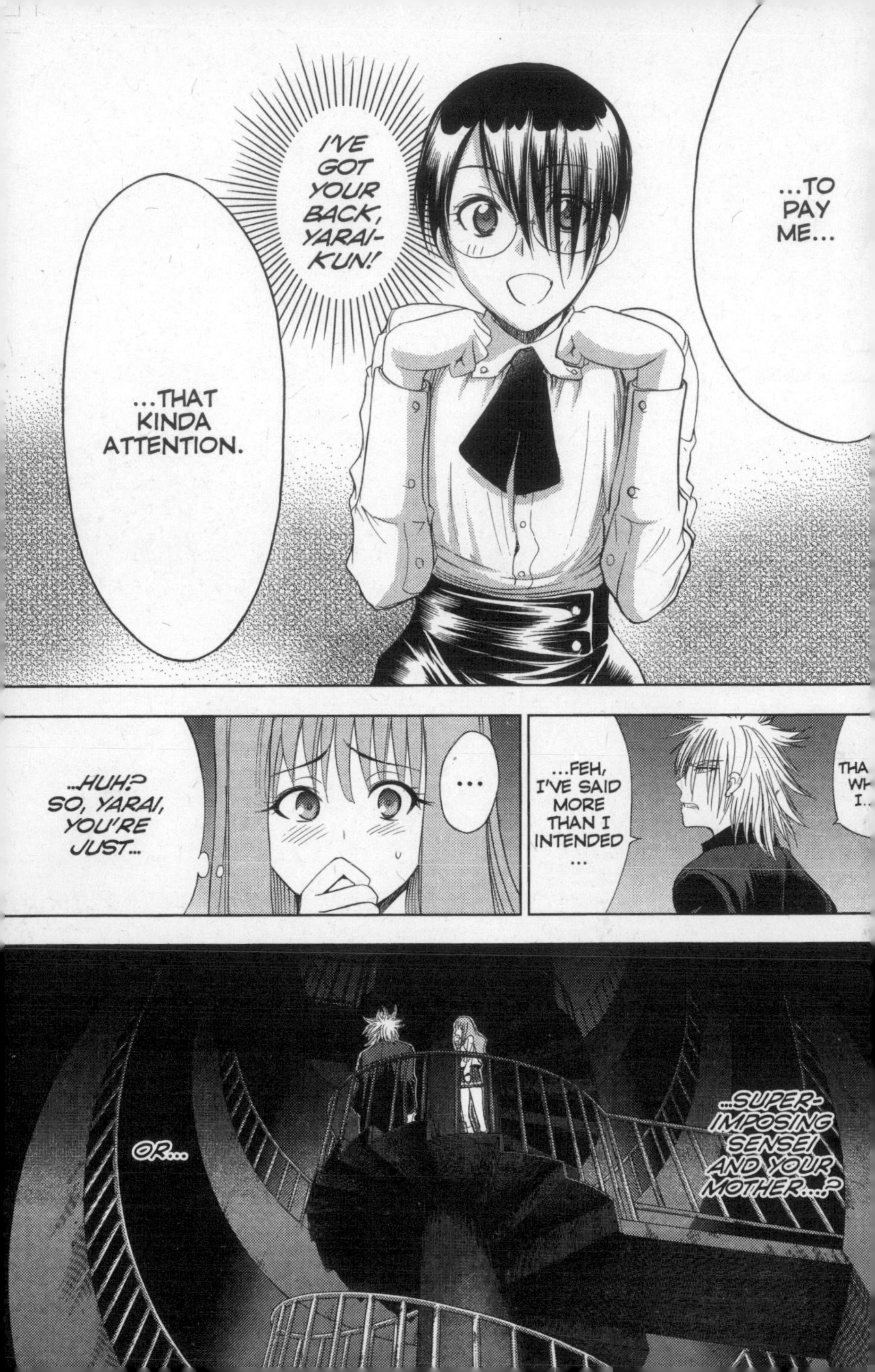
...TO PAY ME...
I'VE GOT YOUR BACK, YARAI-KUN!
...THAT KINDA ATTENTION.
THA WH I..
...FEH, I'VE SAID MORE THAN I INTENDED ...
...
...HUH? SO, YARAI, YOU'RE JUST...
...SUPER-IMPOSING SENSEI AND YOUR MOTHER...?
OR...

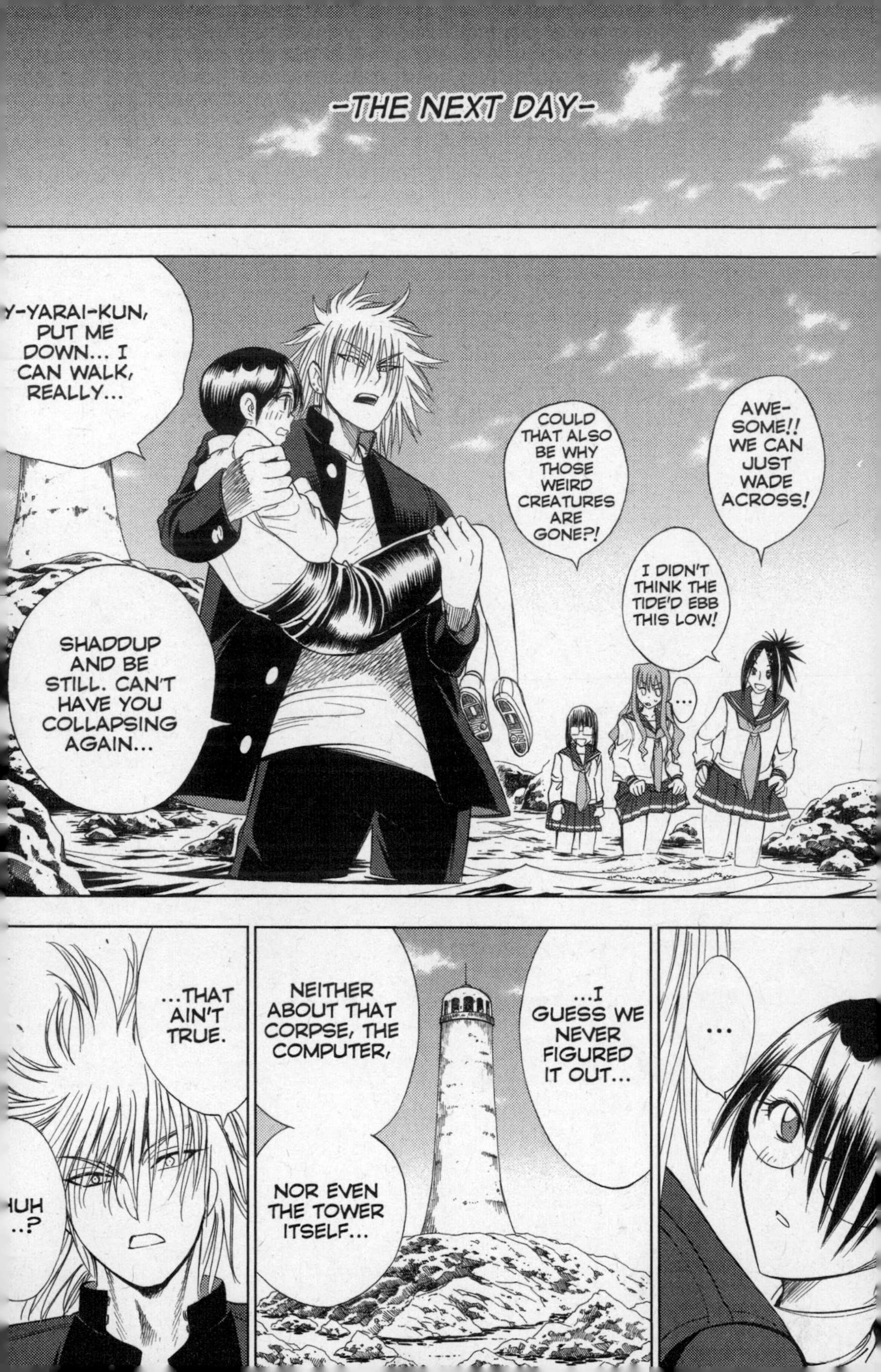
-THE NEXT DAY-
AWE-SOME!! WE CAN JUST WADE ACROSS!
COULD THAT ALSO BE WHY THOSE WEIRD CREATURES ARE GONE?!
I DIDN'T THINK THE TIDE'D EBB THIS LOW!
...
Y-YARAI-KUN, PUT ME DOWN... I CAN WALK, REALLY...
SHADDUP AND BE STILL. CAN'T HAVE YOU COLLAPSING AGAIN...
...
...I GUESS WE NEVER FIGURED IT OUT...
NEITHER ABOUT THAT CORPSE, THE COMPUTER,
NOR EVEN THE TOWER ITSELF...
...THAT AIN'T TRUE.
HUH ..?

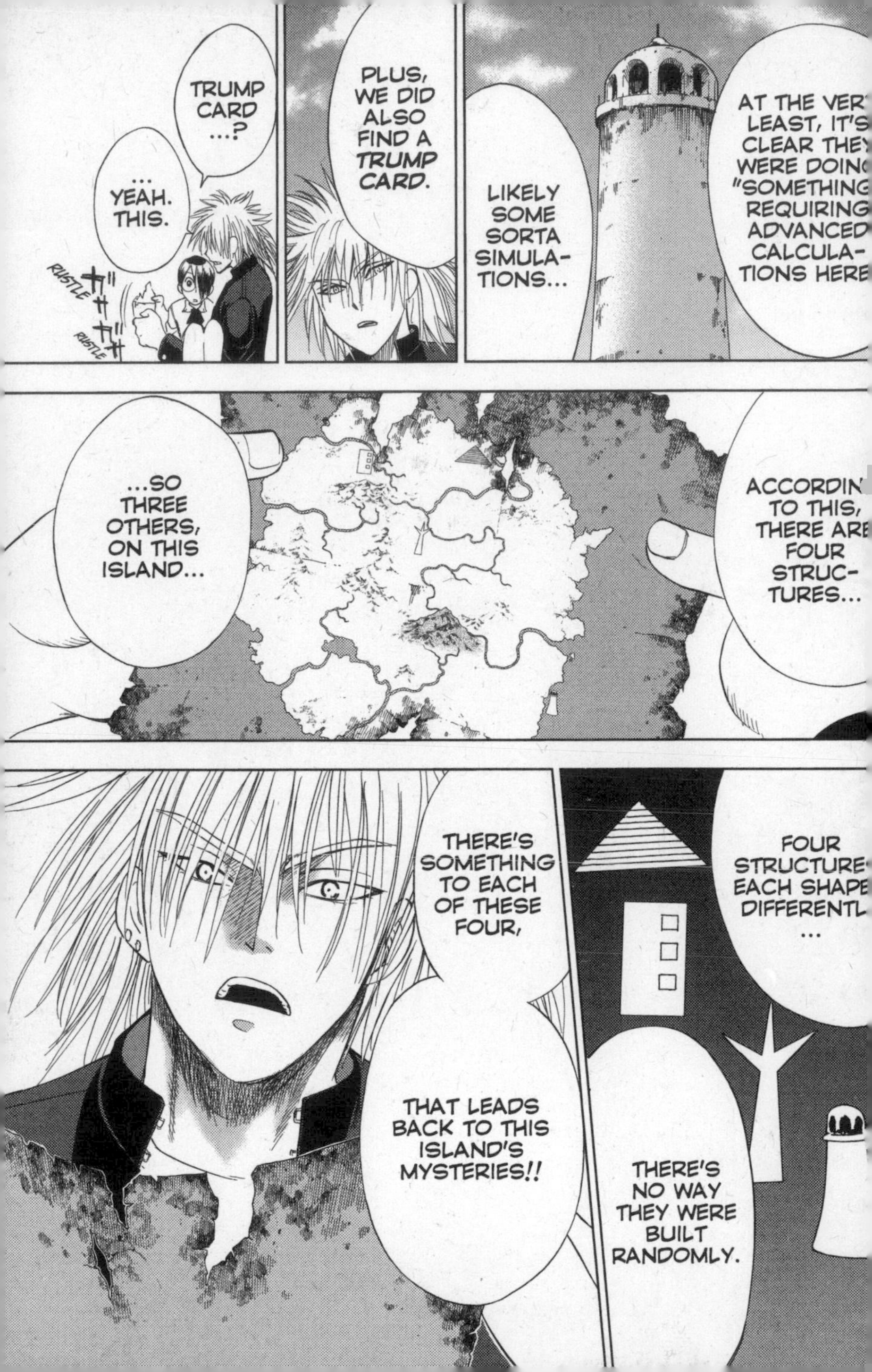
AT THE VERY LEAST, IT'S CLEAR THEY WERE DOING "SOMETHING REQUIRING ADVANCED CALCULA-TIONS HERE"
LIKELY SOME SORTA SIMULA-TIONS...
PLUS, WE DID ALSO FIND A TRUMP CARD.
TRUMP CARD ...?
... YEAH. THIS.
RUSTLE
RUSTLE
ACCORDIN TO THIS, THERE ARE FOUR STRUC-TURES...
...SO THREE OTHERS, ON THIS ISLAND...
FOUR STRUCTURES EACH SHAPE DIFFERENTL ...
THERE'S NO WAY THEY WERE BUILT RANDOMLY.
THERE'S SOMETHING TO EACH OF THESE FOUR,
THAT LEADS BACK TO THIS ISLAND'S MYSTERIES!!

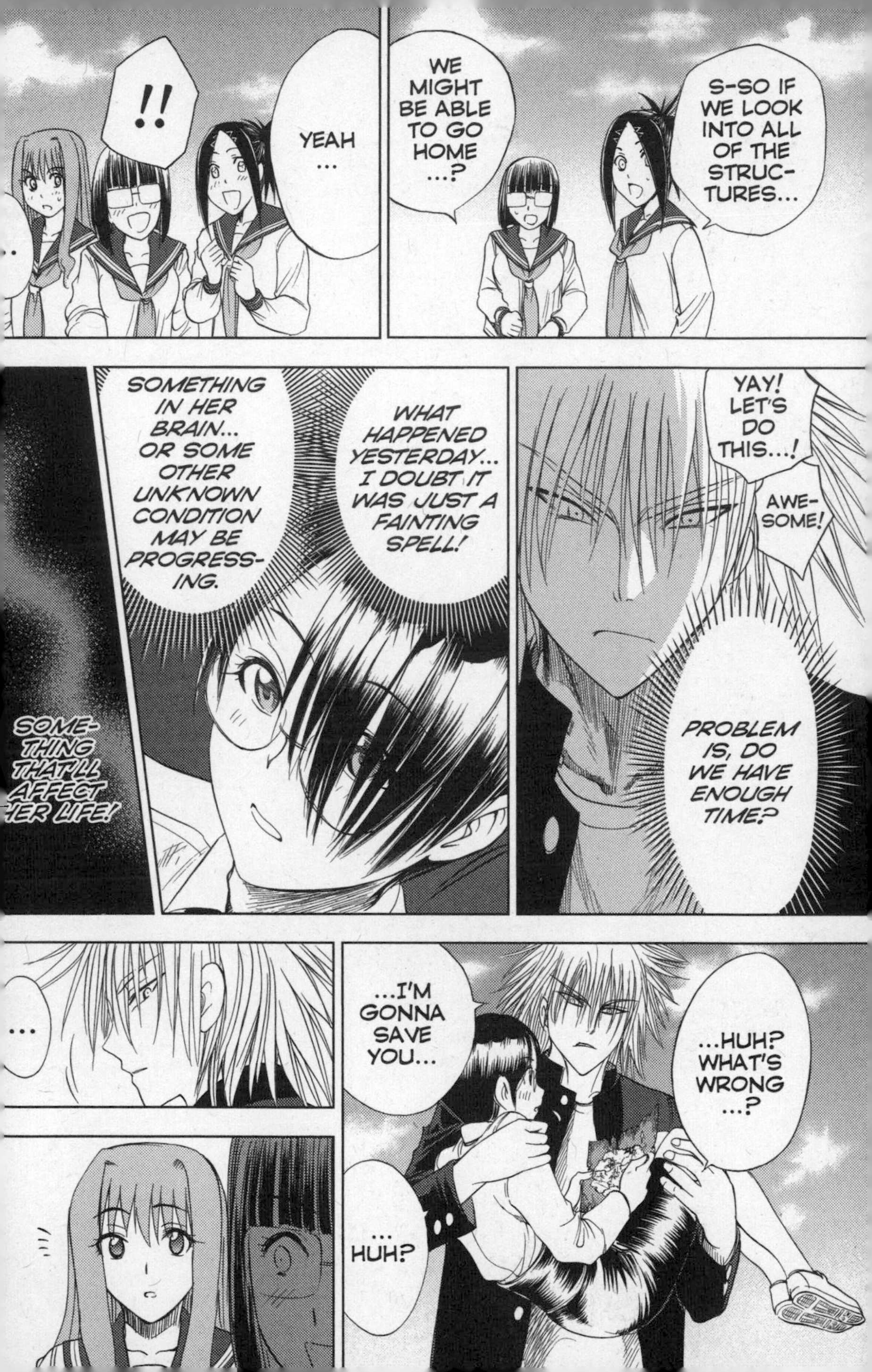
S-SO IF WE LOOK INTO ALL OF THE STRUC-TURES...
WE MIGHT BE ABLE TO GO HOME ...?
YEAH ...
!!
...
YAY! LET'S DO THIS...!
AWE-SOME!
PROBLEM IS, DO WE HAVE ENOUGH TIME?
WHAT HAPPENED YESTERDAY... I DOUBT IT WAS JUST A FAINTING SPELL!
SOMETHING IN HER BRAIN... OR SOME OTHER UNKNOWN CONDITION MAY BE PROGRESS-ING.
SOME-THING THAT'LL AFFECT HER LIFE!
...I'M GONNA SAVE YOU...
...HUH? WHAT'S WRONG ...?
... HUH?
...

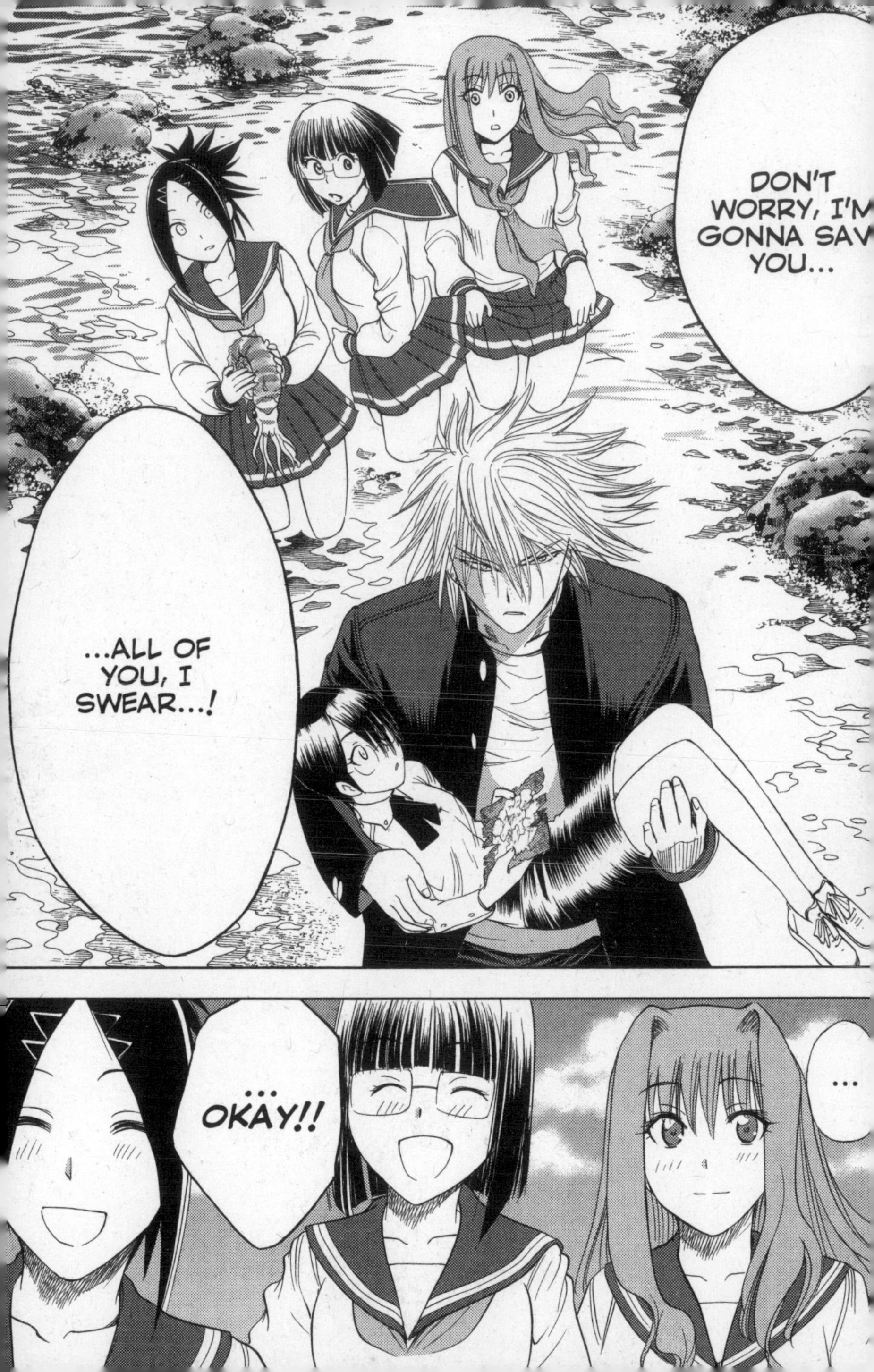
DON'T WORRY, I'M GONNA SAV YOU...
...ALL OF YOU, I SWEAR...!
...
...OKAY!!

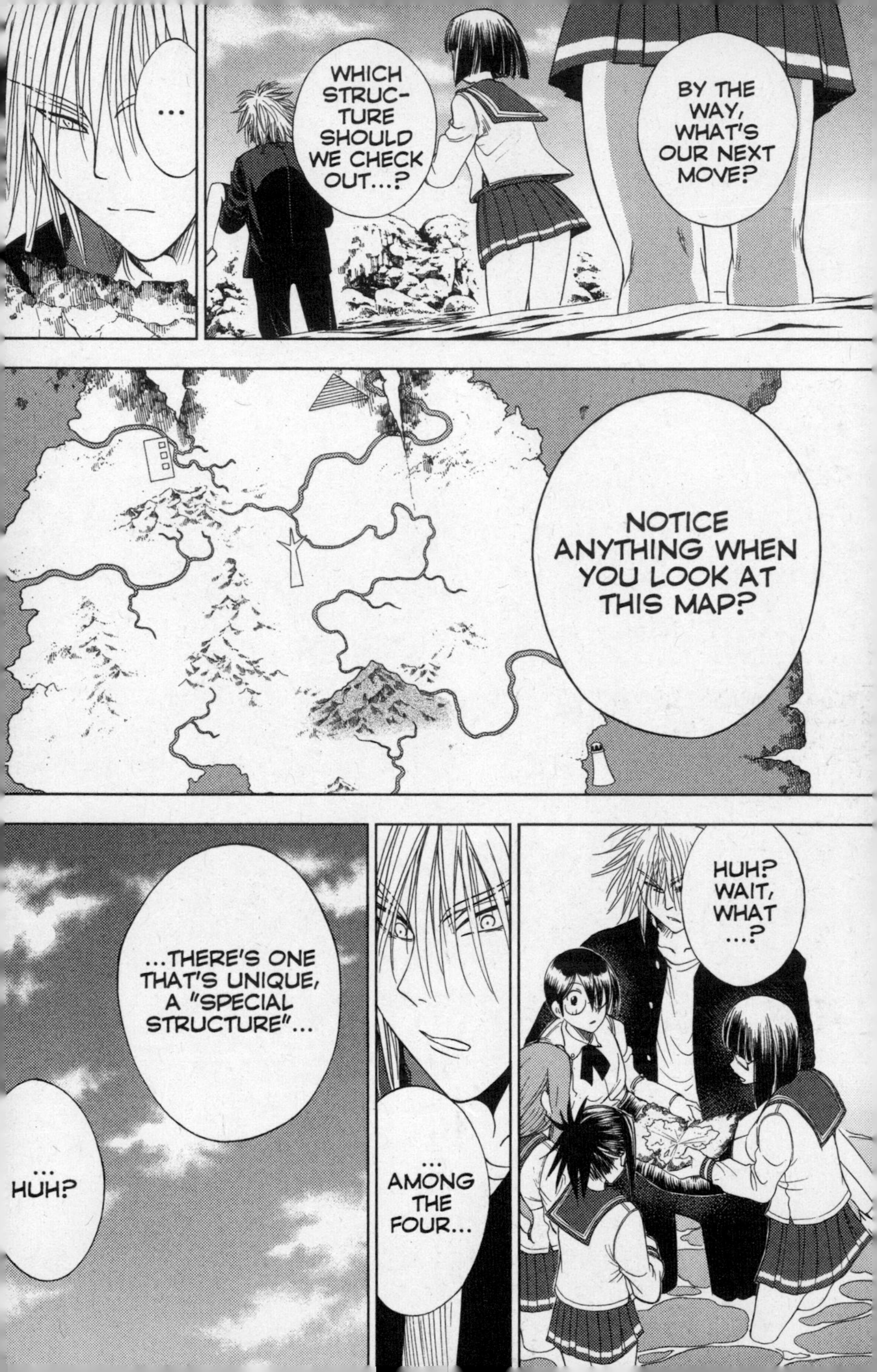
BY THE WAY, WHAT'S OUR NEXT MOVE?
WHICH STRUC-TURE SHOULD WE CHECK OUT...?
...
NOTICE ANYTHING WHEN YOU LOOK AT THIS MAP?
HUH? WAIT, WHAT ...?
... AMONG THE FOUR...
...THERE'S ONE THAT'S UNIQUE, A "SPECIAL STRUCTURE"...
... HUH?

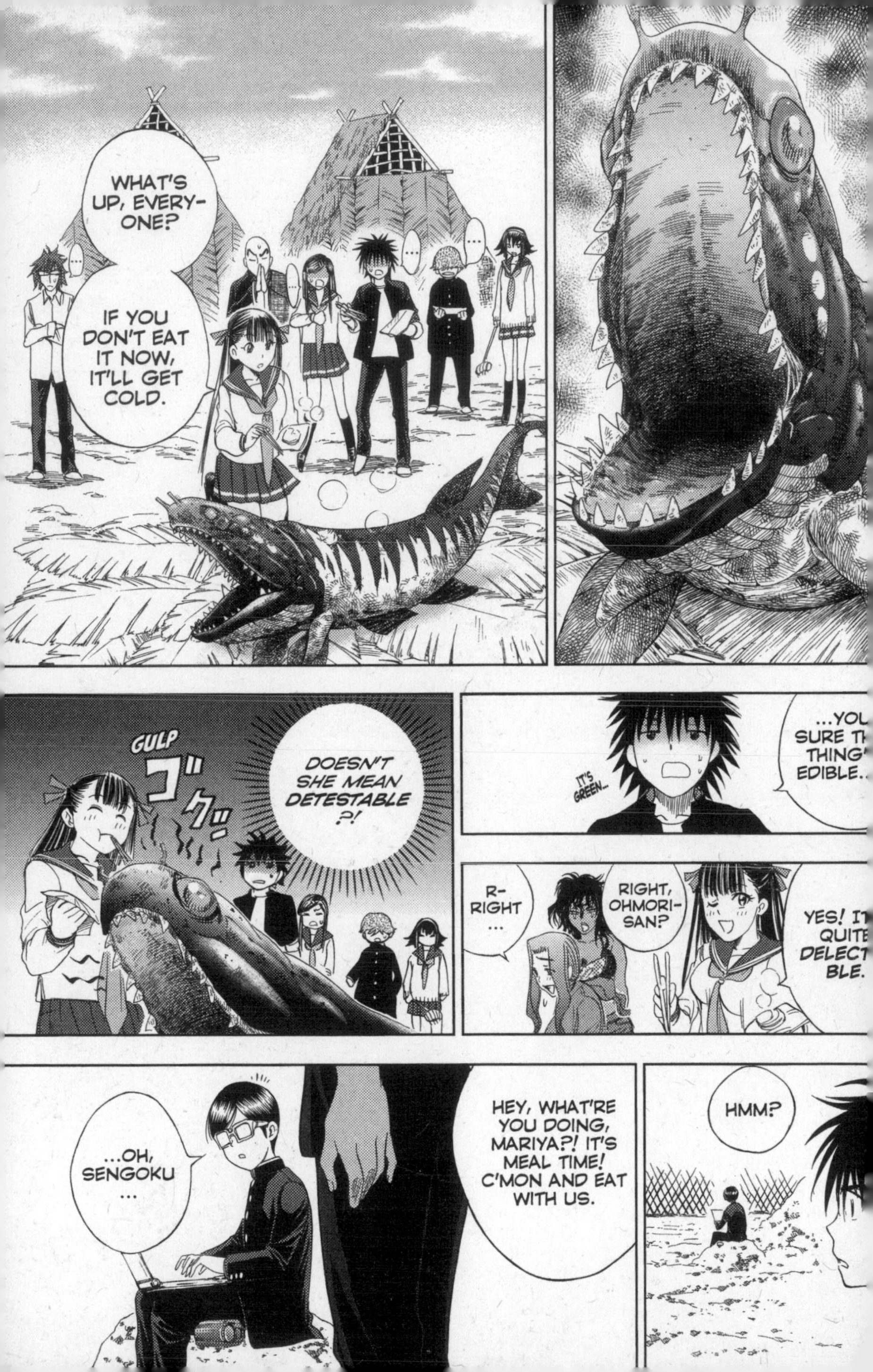
...
...
...
...
...
WHAT'S UP, EVERY-ONE?
IF YOU DON'T EAT IT NOW, IT'LL GET COLD.
...YOU SURE TH THING' EDIBLE..
IT'S GREEN...
YES! IT QUITE DELECT BLE.
RIGHT, OHMORI-SAN?
R-RIGHT ...
DOESN'T SHE MEAN DETESTABLE ?!
GULP
ゴクッ
HMM?
HEY, WHAT'RE YOU DOING, MARIYA?! IT'S MEAL TIME! C'MON AND EAT WITH US.
...OH, SENGOKU ...

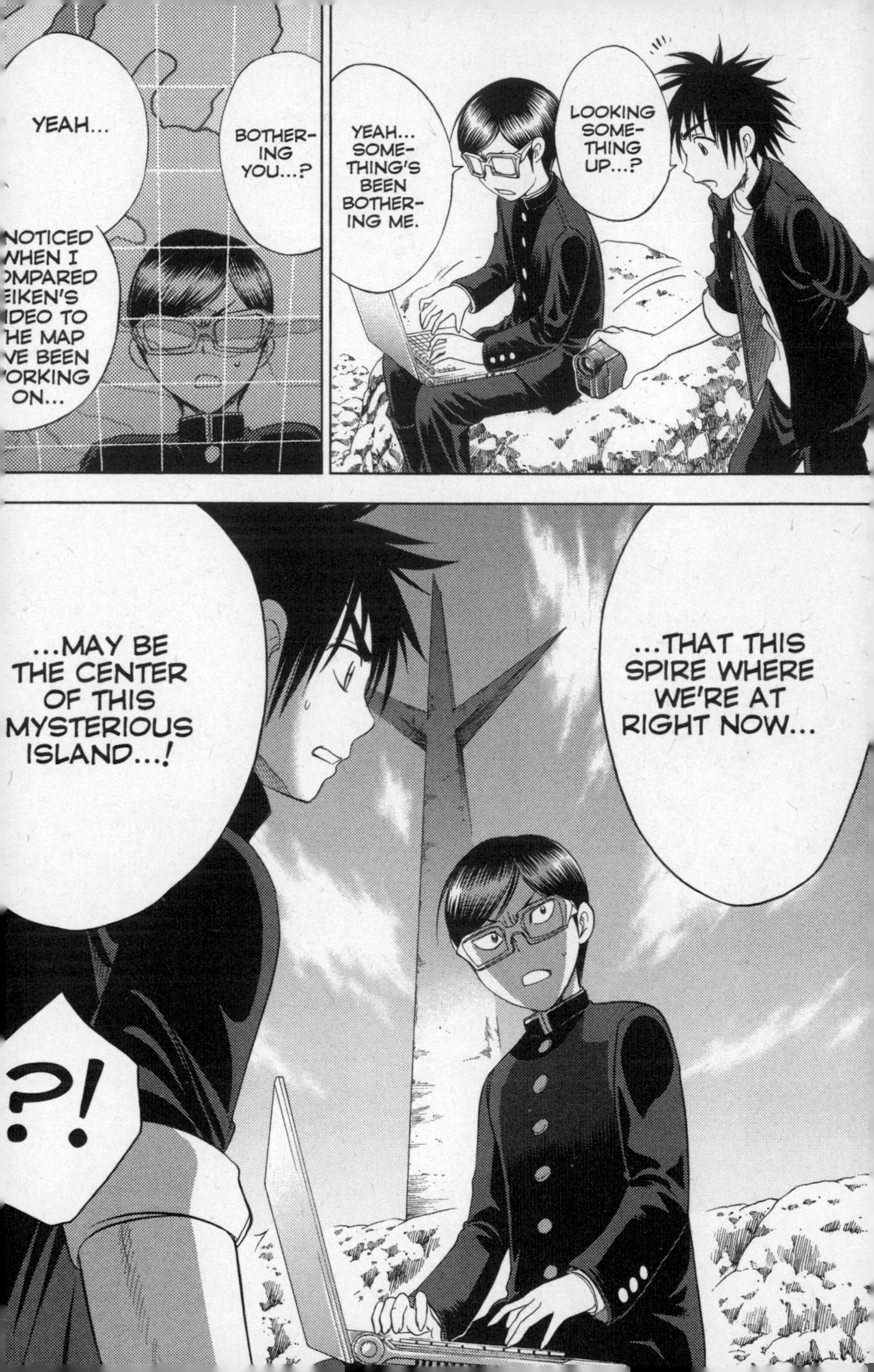
LOOKING SOMETHING UP...?
YEAH... SOMETHING'S BEEN BOTHERING ME.
BOTHERING YOU...?
YEAH...
NOTICED WHEN I OMPARED EIKEN'S IDEO TO HE MAP VE BEEN ORKING ON...
...THAT THIS SPIRE WHERE WE'RE AT RIGHT NOW...
...MAY BE THE CENTER OF THIS MYSTERIOUS ISLAND...!
?!

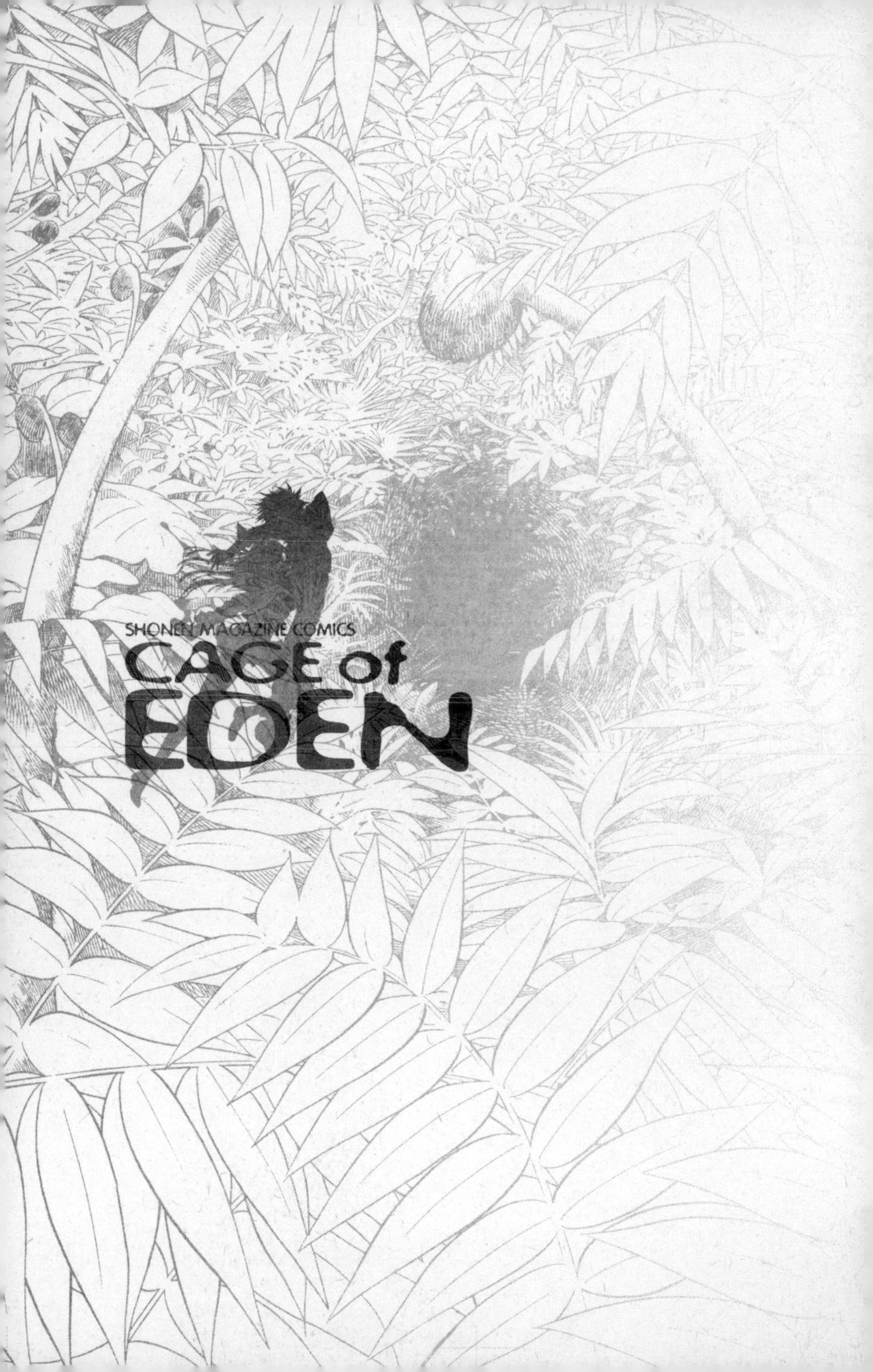
SHONEN MAGAZINE COMICS
CAGE of EDEN

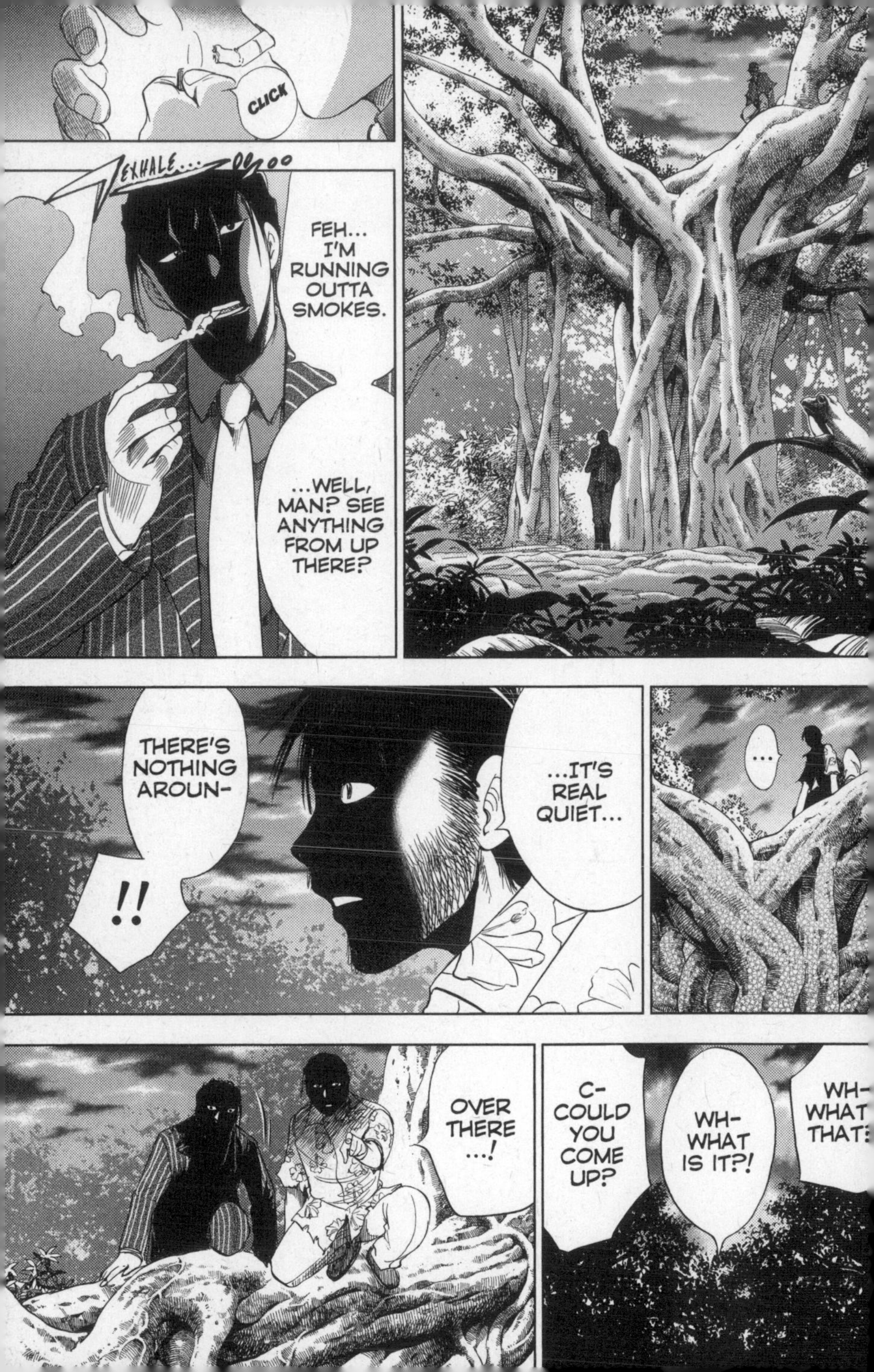

CLICK
EXHALE...
FEH... I'M RUNNING OUTTA SMOKES.
...WELL, MAN? SEE ANYTHING FROM UP THERE?
...
...IT'S REAL QUIET...
THERE'S NOTHING AROUN-
!!
WH- WHAT THAT
WH- WHAT IS IT?!
C- COULD YOU COME UP?
OVER THERE ...!

I-I'LL BE DARNED...

!!

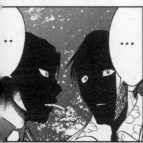

...　...

...

NO MISTAKE ...

IT'S THE TOWER...!!

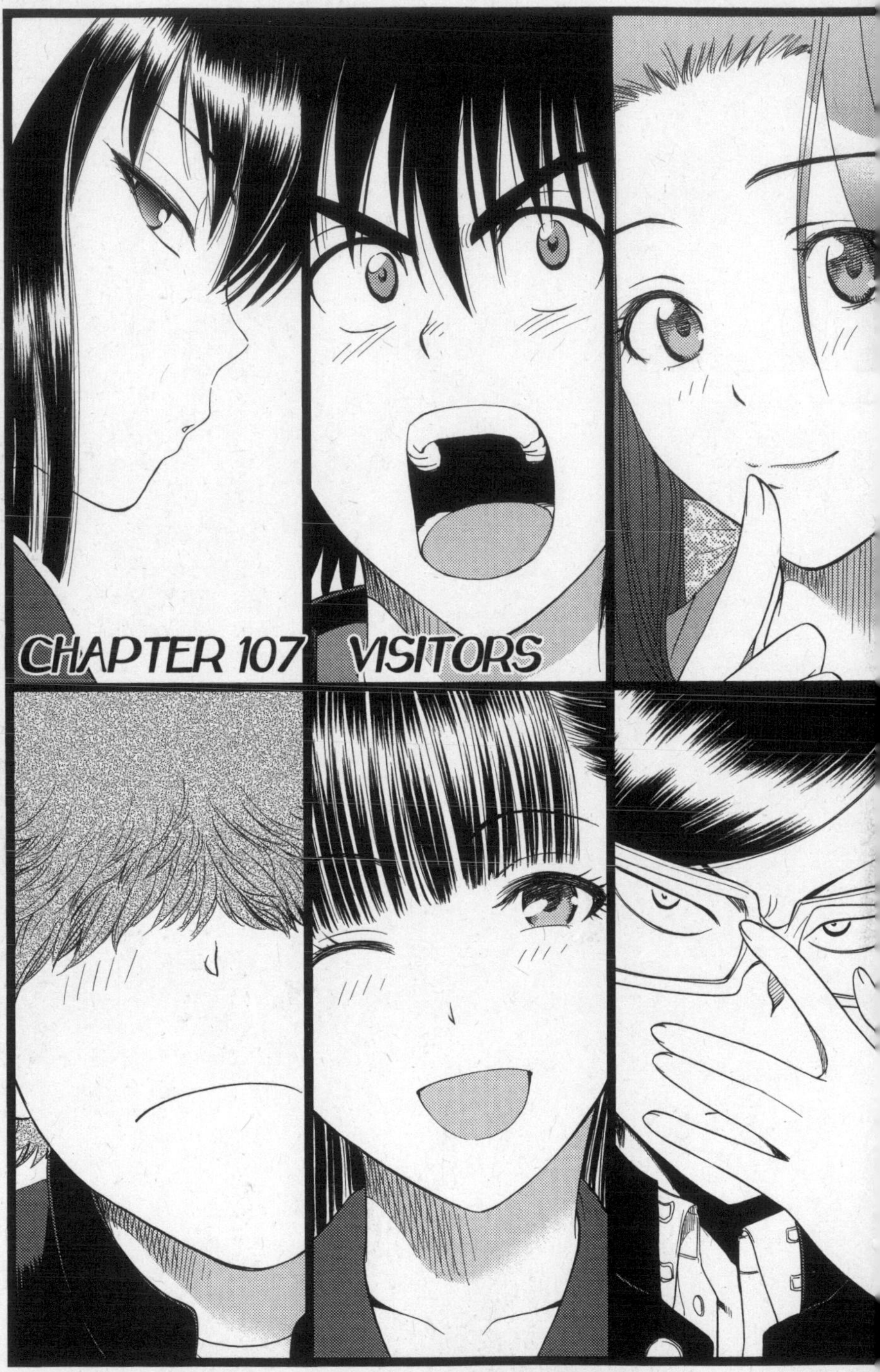
CHAPTER 107 VISITORS

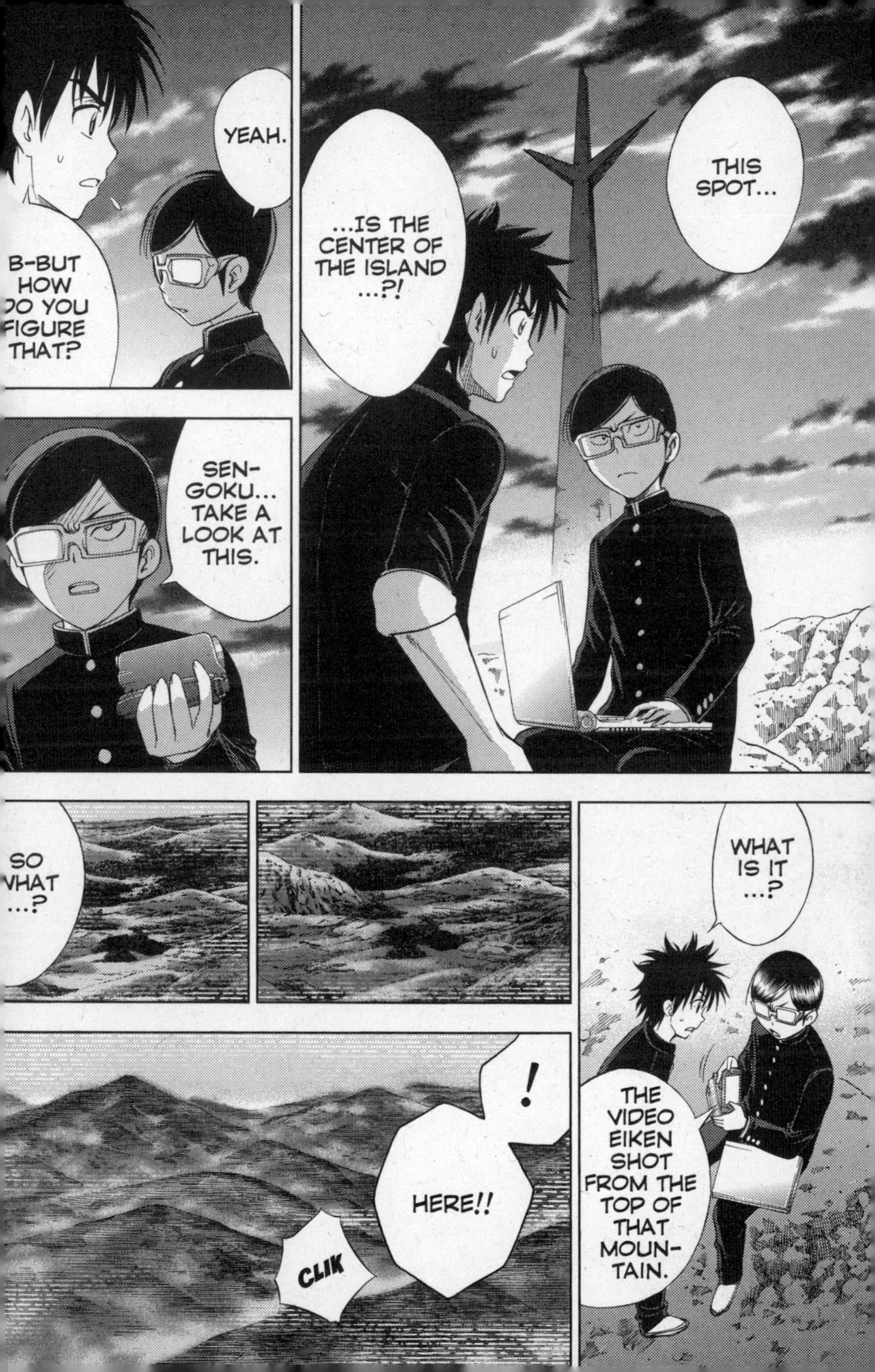
THIS SPOT...
...IS THE CENTER OF THE ISLAND ...?!
YEAH.
B-BUT HOW DO YOU FIGURE THAT?
SEN-GOKU... TAKE A LOOK AT THIS.
WHAT IS IT ...?
THE VIDEO EIKEN SHOT FROM THE TOP OF THAT MOUN-TAIN.
SO WHAT ...?
!
HERE!!
CLIK

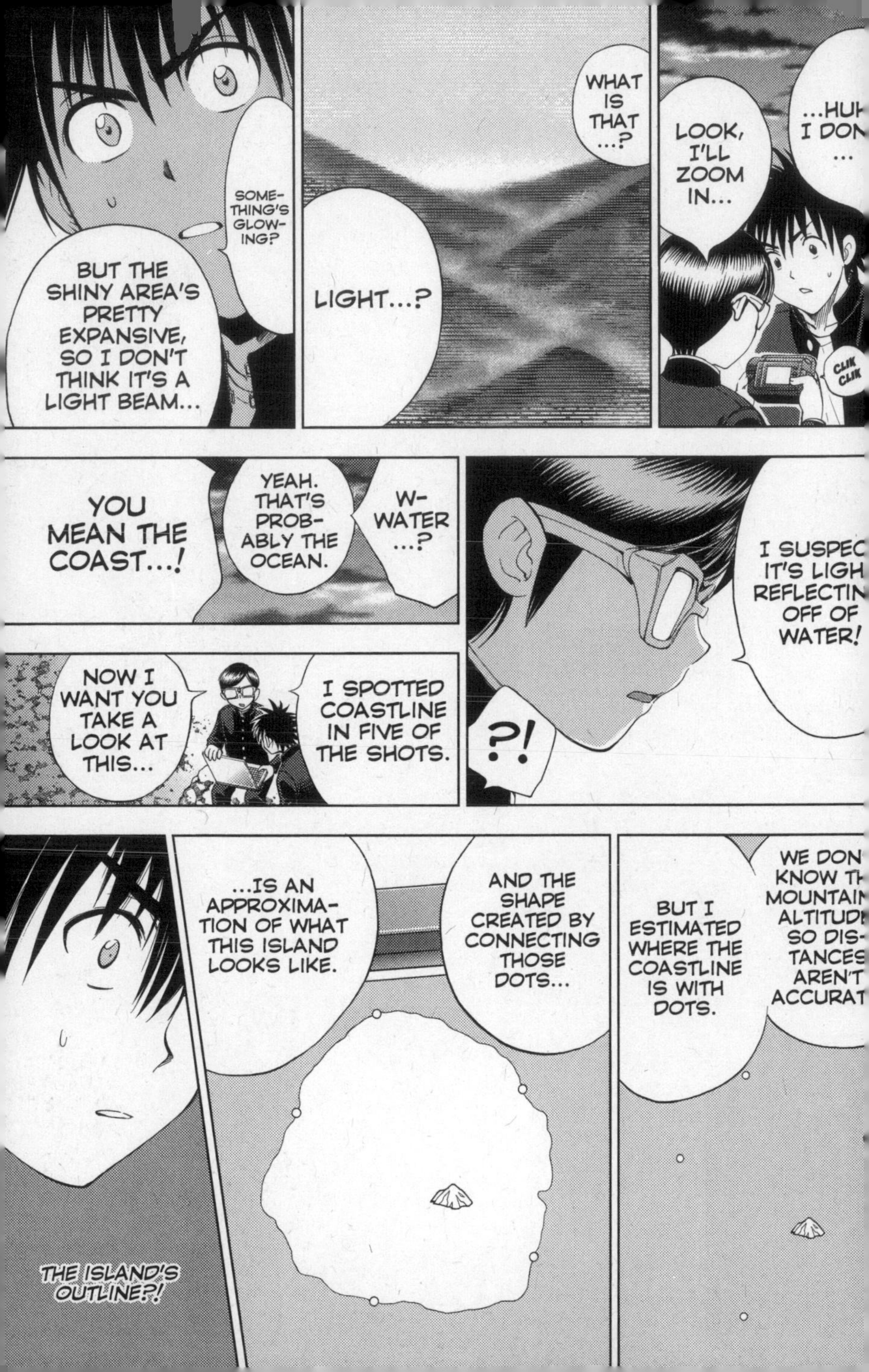
...HUH I DON ...
LOOK, I'LL ZOOM IN...
CLIK CLIK
WHAT IS THAT ...?
LIGHT...?
SOMETHING'S GLOWING?
BUT THE SHINY AREA'S PRETTY EXPANSIVE, SO I DON'T THINK IT'S A LIGHT BEAM...
I SUSPEC IT'S LIGH REFLECTIN OFF OF WATER!
?!
W-WATER ...?
YEAH. THAT'S PROBABLY THE OCEAN.
YOU MEAN THE COAST...!
I SPOTTED COASTLINE IN FIVE OF THE SHOTS.
NOW I WANT YOU TAKE A LOOK AT THIS...
WE DON KNOW TH MOUNTAIN ALTITUDE SO DISTANCES AREN'T ACCURAT
BUT I ESTIMATED WHERE THE COASTLINE IS WITH DOTS.
AND THE SHAPE CREATED BY CONNECTING THOSE DOTS...
...IS AN APPROXIMATION OF WHAT THIS ISLAND LOOKS LIKE.
THE ISLAND'S OUTLINE?!

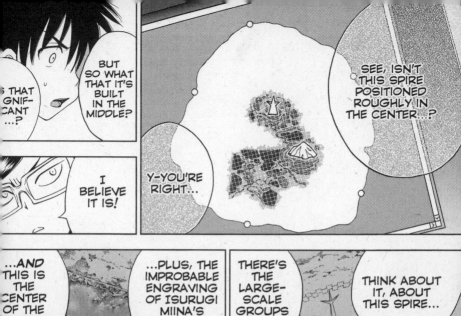

SEE, ISN'T THIS SPIRE POSITIONED ROUGHLY IN THE CENTER...?
Y-YOU'RE RIGHT...
BUT SO WHAT THAT IT'S BUILT IN THE MIDDLE?
S THAT GNIF-CANT ...?
I BELIEVE IT IS!
THINK ABOUT IT, ABOUT THIS SPIRE...
THERE'S THE LARGE-SCALE GROUPS OF TRAPS HERE...
...PLUS, THE IMPROBABLE ENGRAVING OF ISURUGI MIINA'S NAME...
...AND THIS IS THE CENTER OF THE SLAND ...?
YOU REALLY THINK IT'S PURE COINCIDENCE ...?
HUH ...?
YOU KNOW, SENGOKU ...
...WE MAY BE PENETRATING THE HEART OF THIS ISLAND'S MYSTERIES WITHOUT EVEN REALIZING IT...

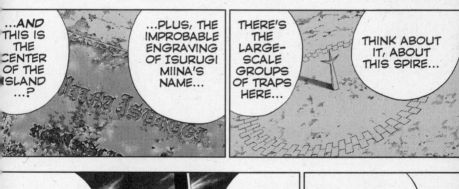

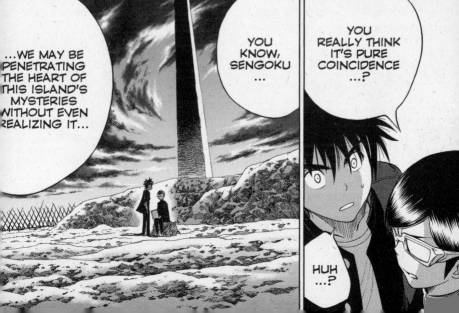

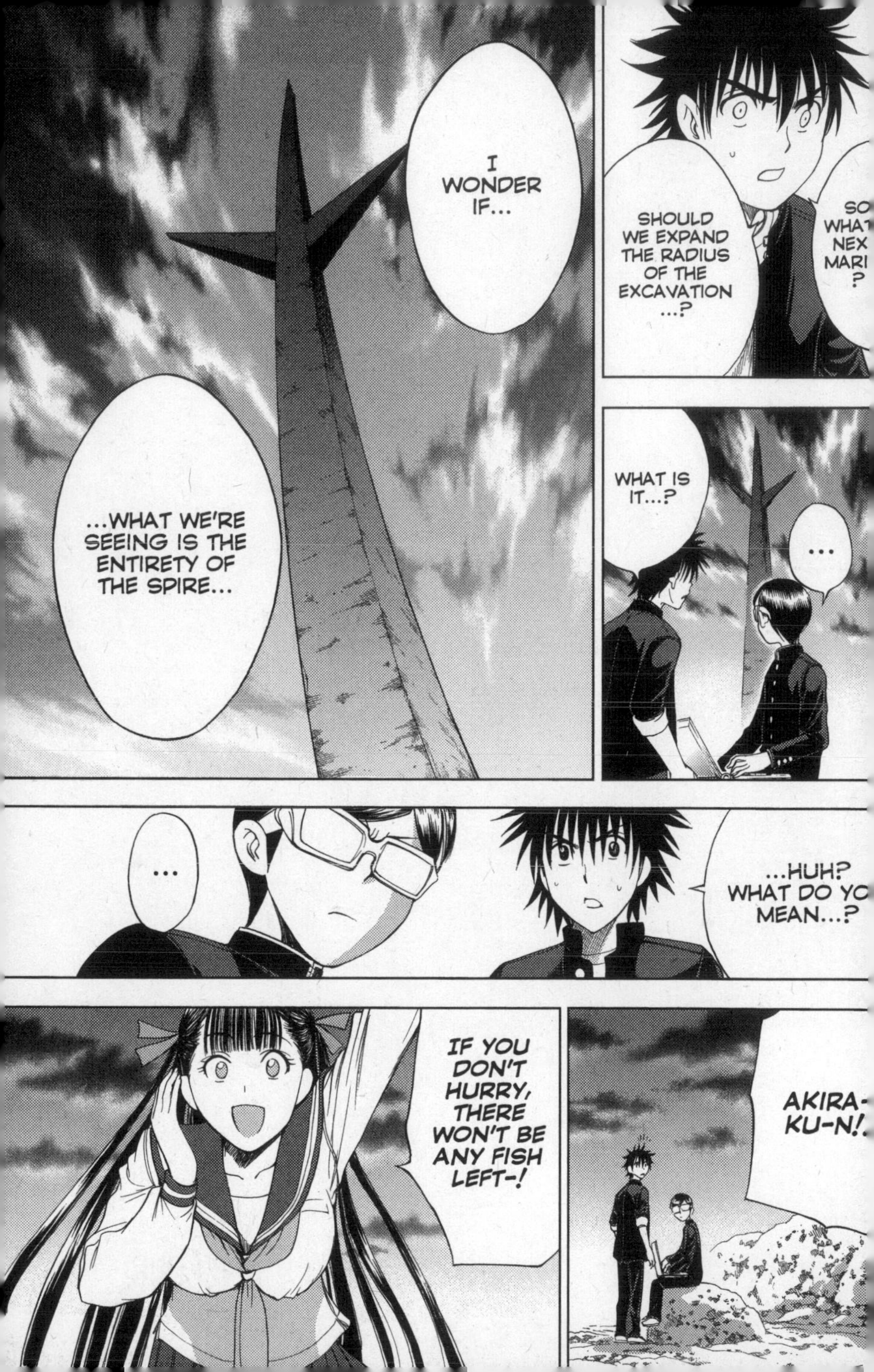
SO WHAT NEX MARI ?
SHOULD WE EXPAND THE RADIUS OF THE EXCAVATION ...?
...
WHAT IS IT...?
I WONDER IF...
...WHAT WE'RE SEEING IS THE ENTIRETY OF THE SPIRE...
...HUH? WHAT DO YO MEAN...?
...
AKIRA-KU-N!
IF YOU DON'T HURRY, THERE WON'T BE ANY FISH LEFT-!

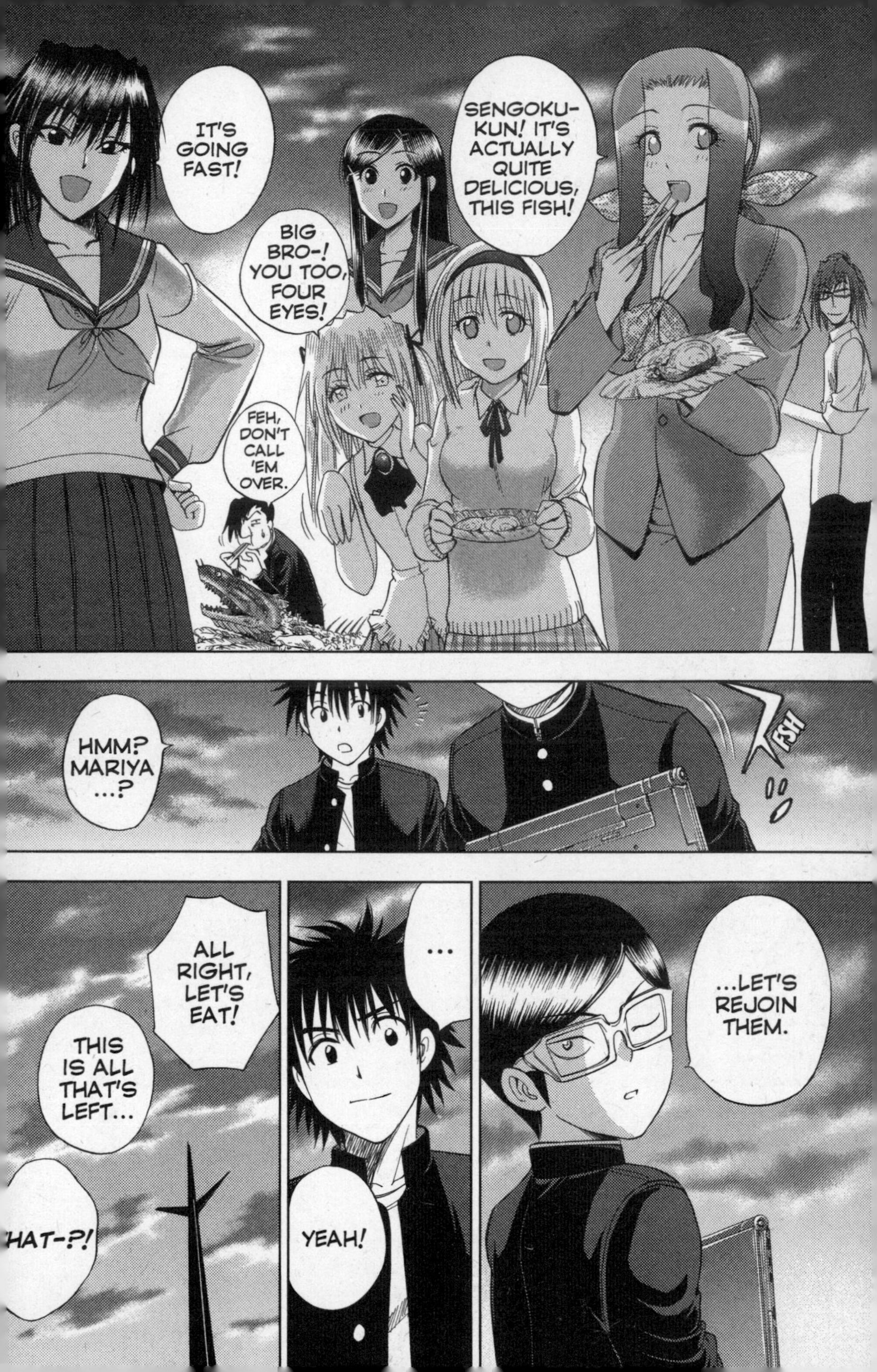
SENGOKU-KUN! IT'S ACTUALLY QUITE DELICIOUS, THIS FISH!
IT'S GOING FAST!
BIG BRO-! YOU TOO, FOUR EYES!
FEH, DON'T CALL 'EM OVER.
FSH
HMM? MARIYA ...?
...LET'S REJOIN THEM.
...
YEAH!
ALL RIGHT, LET'S EAT!
THIS IS ALL THAT'S LEFT...
HAT-?!

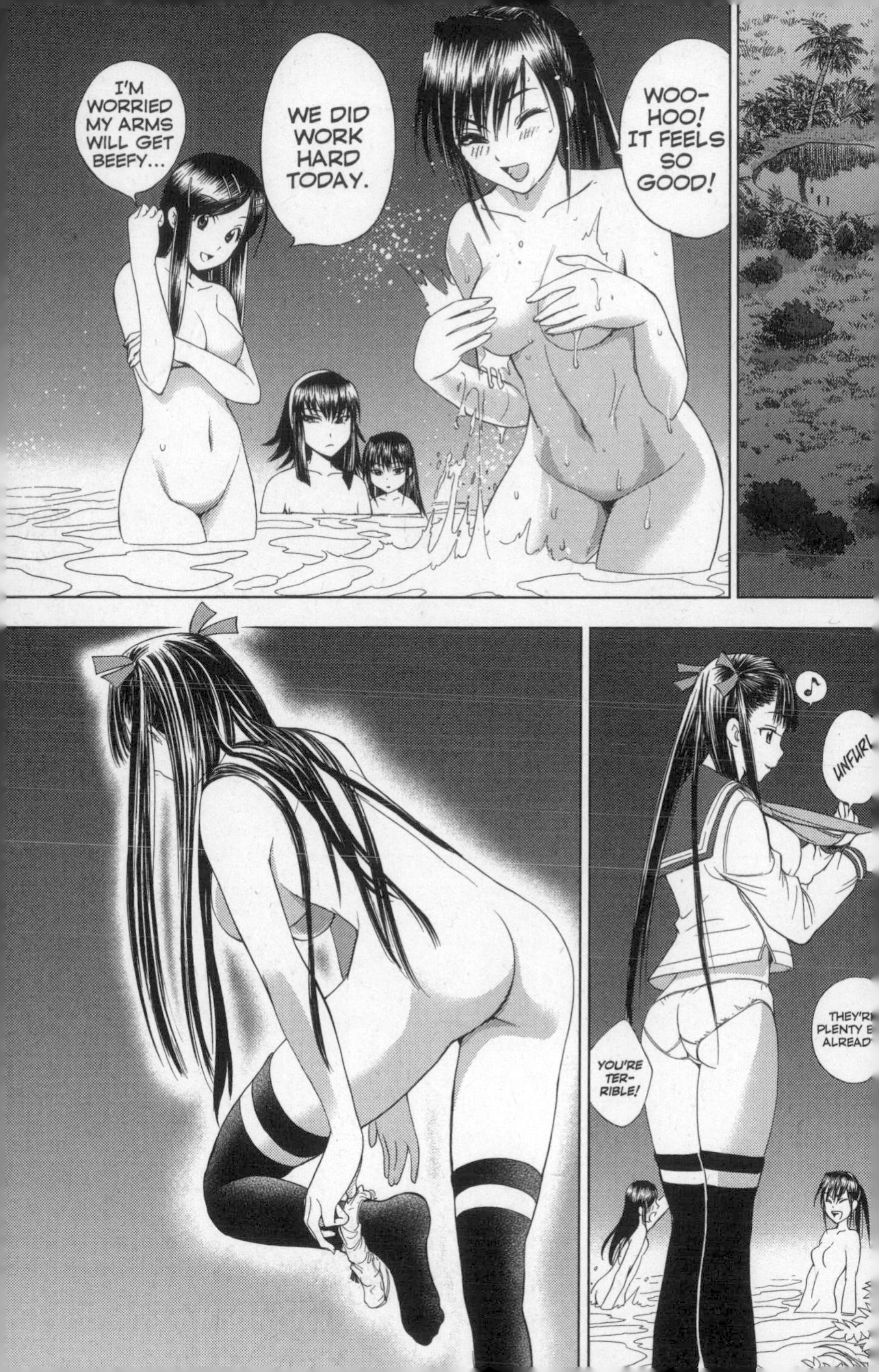
WOO-HOO! IT FEELS SO GOOD!
WE DID WORK HARD TODAY.
I'M WORRIED MY ARMS WILL GET BEEFY...
UNFURL
THEY'R PLENTY B ALREAD
YOU'RE TER-RIBLE!

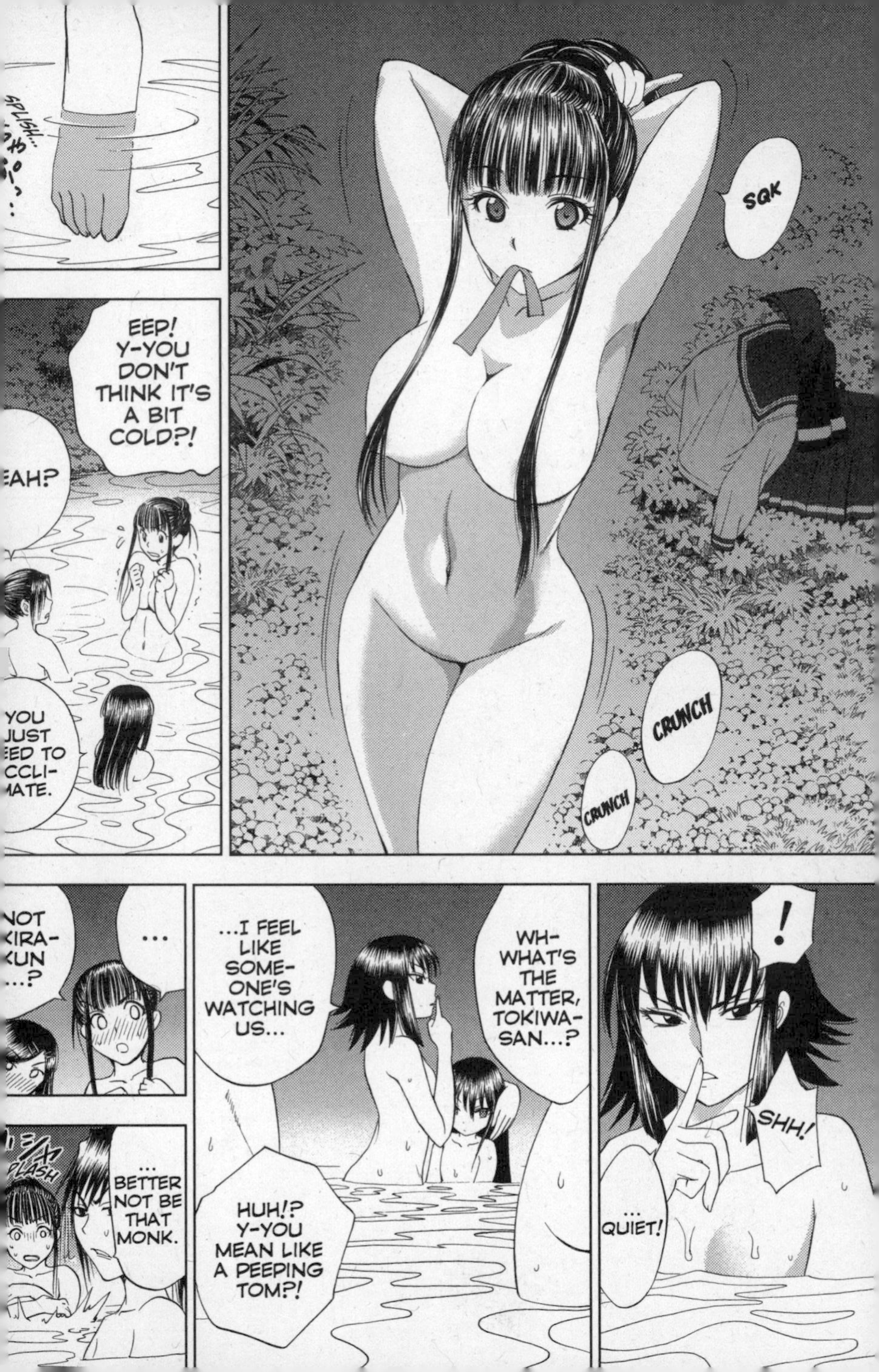
SQK
CRUNCH
CRUNCH
SPLISH...
EEP! Y-YOU DON'T THINK IT'S A BIT COLD?!
EAH?
YOU JUST EED TO CCLI- MATE.
!
SHH!
... QUIET!
WH- WHAT'S THE MATTER, TOKIWA-SAN...?
...I FEEL LIKE SOME- ONE'S WATCHING US...
HUH!? Y-YOU MEAN LIKE A PEEPING TOM?!
...
NOT IRA- UN ...?
... BETTER NOT BE THAT MONK.
PLASH

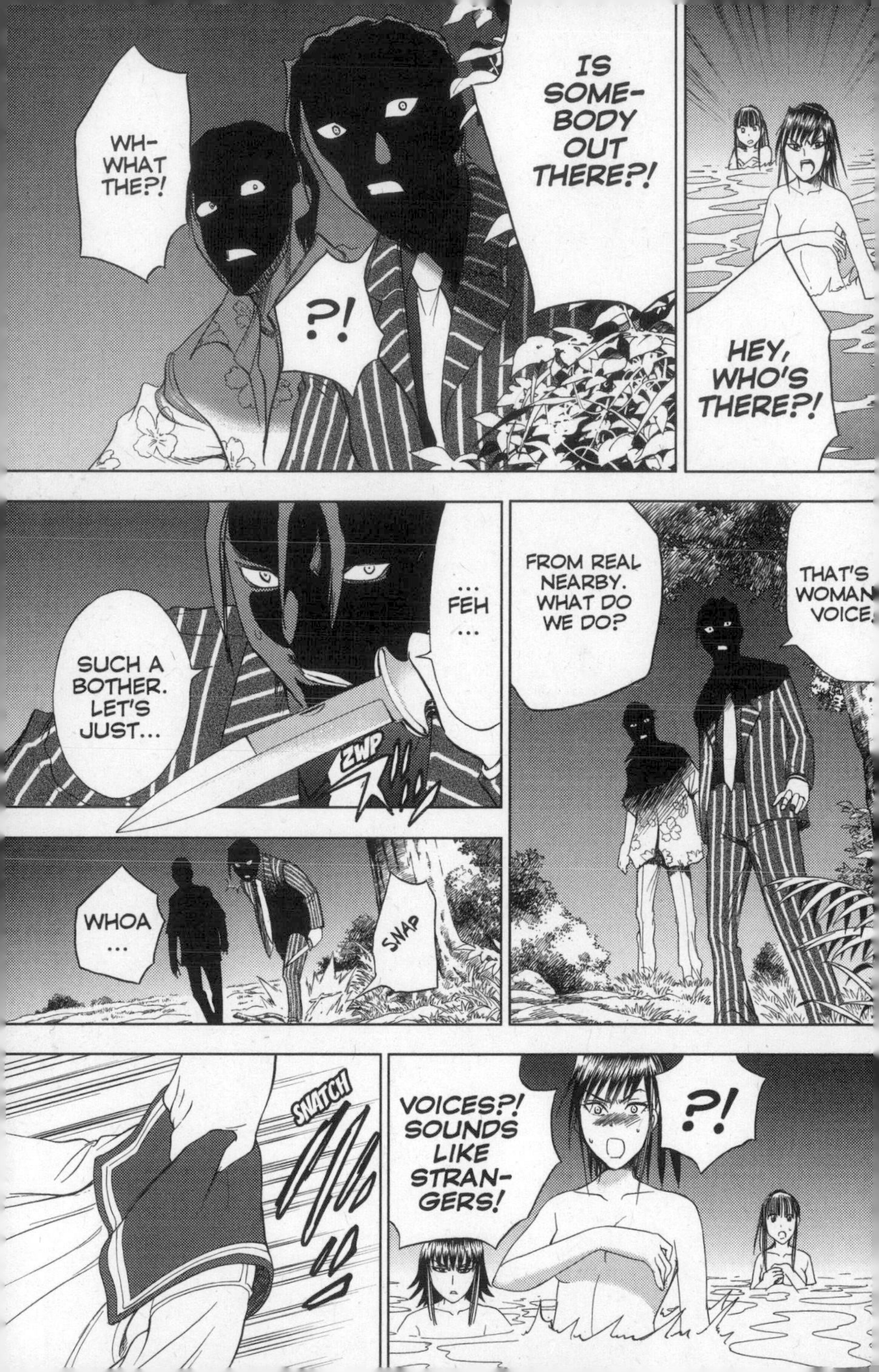
HEY, WHO'S THERE?!
IS SOME-BODY OUT THERE?!
WH-WHAT THE?!
?!
THAT'S WOMAN VOICE.
FROM REAL NEARBY. WHAT DO WE DO?
... FEH ...
SUCH A BOTHER. LET'S JUST...
ZWP
SNAP
WHOA ...
?!
VOICES?! SOUNDS LIKE STRAN-GERS!
SNATCH

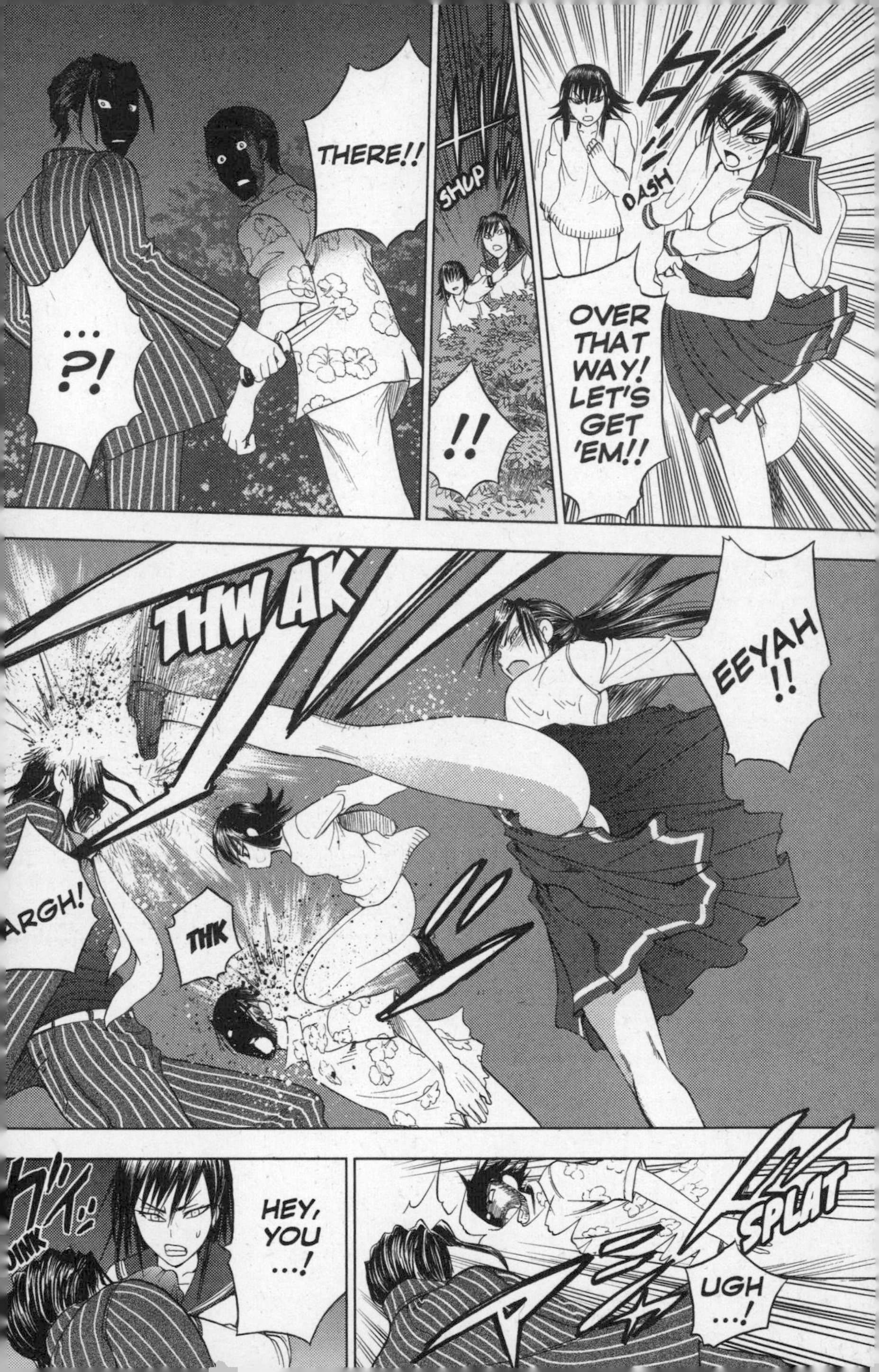
DASH
OVER THAT WAY! LET'S GET 'EM!!
SHUP
!!
THERE!!
...?!
EEYAH!!
THWAK
ARGH!
THK
SPLAT
UGH ...!
HEY, YOU ...!

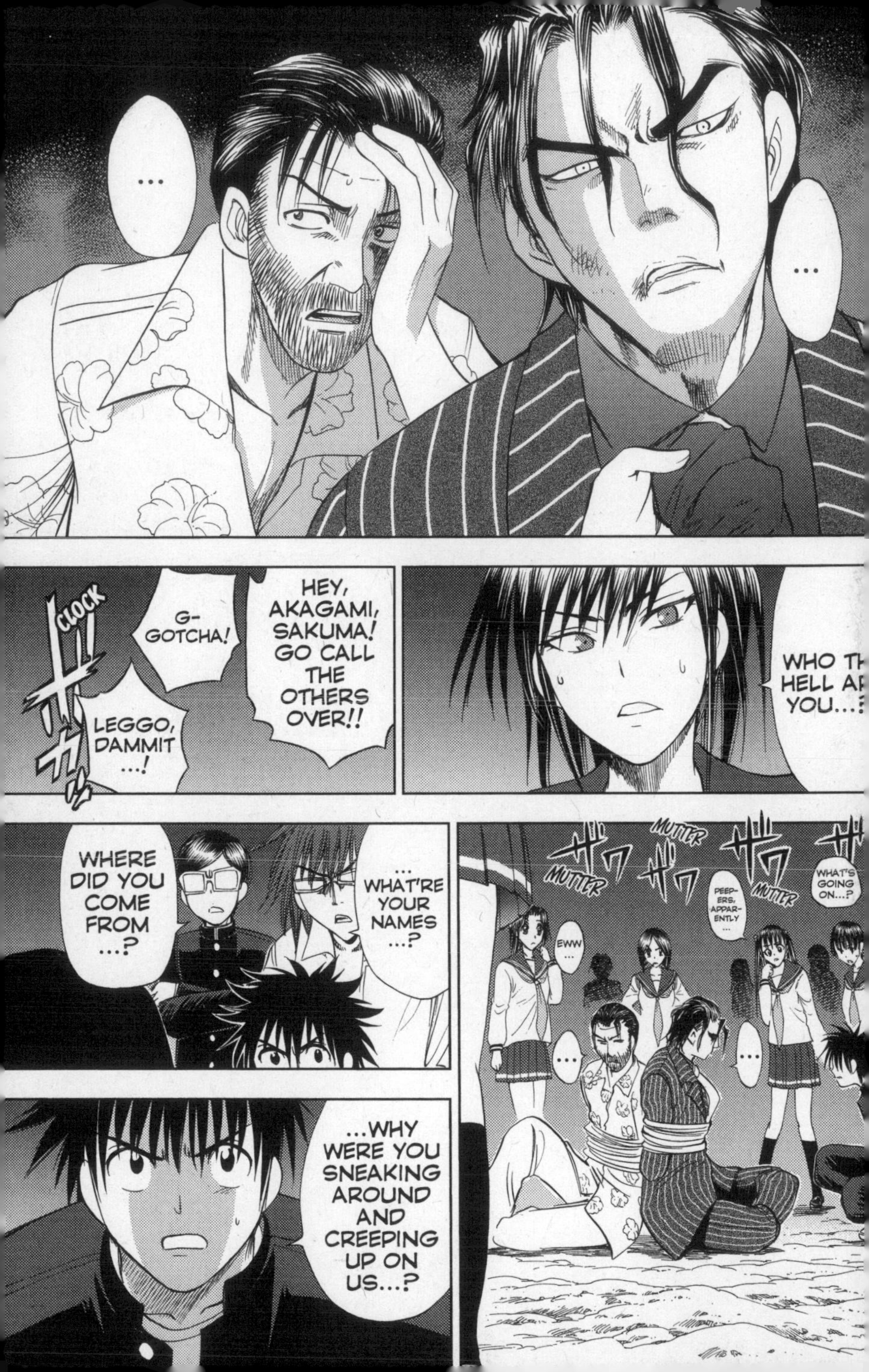
...
...
WHO TH
HELL AR
YOU...?
HEY, AKAGAMI, SAKUMA! GO CALL THE OTHERS OVER!!
G-GOTCHA!
CLOCK
LEGGO, DAMMIT...!
MUTTER
MUTTER
MUTTER
MUTTER
WHAT'S GOING ON...?
PEEPERS, APPARENTLY...
EWW...
...
...
...WHAT'RE YOUR NAMES...?
WHERE DID YOU COME FROM...?
...WHY WERE YOU SNEAKING AROUND AND CREEPING UP ON US...?

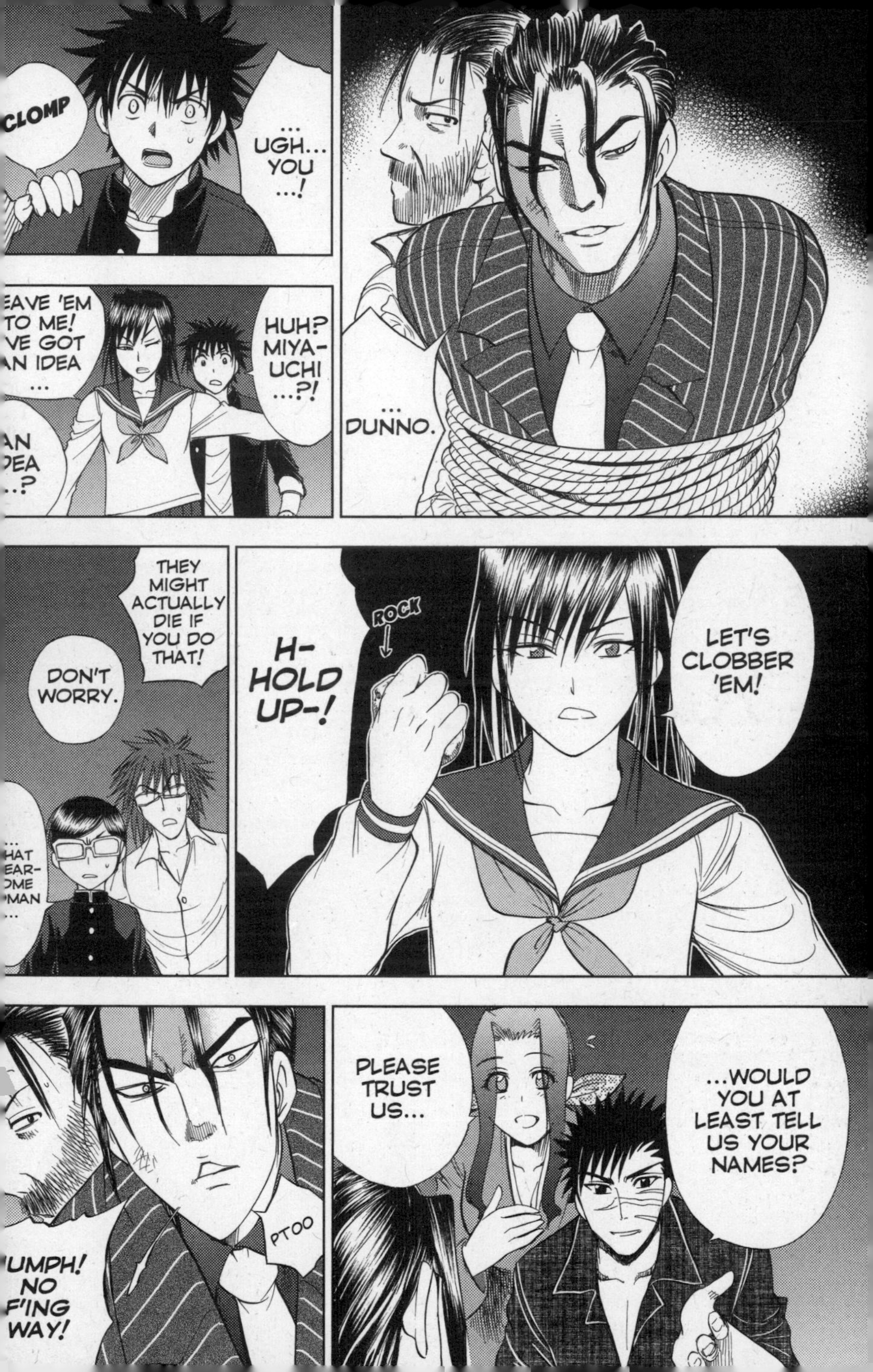
... DUNNO.
... UGH... YOU ...!
CLOMP
HUH? MIYA-UCHI ...?!
EAVE 'EM TO ME! VE GOT AN IDEA ...
AN DEA ...?
LET'S CLOBBER 'EM!
ROCK
H-HOLD UP-!
THEY MIGHT ACTUALLY DIE IF YOU DO THAT!
DON'T WORRY.
... HAT EAR-OME MAN ...
...WOULD YOU AT LEAST TELL US YOUR NAMES?
PLEASE TRUST US...
PTOO
UMPH! NO F'ING WAY!

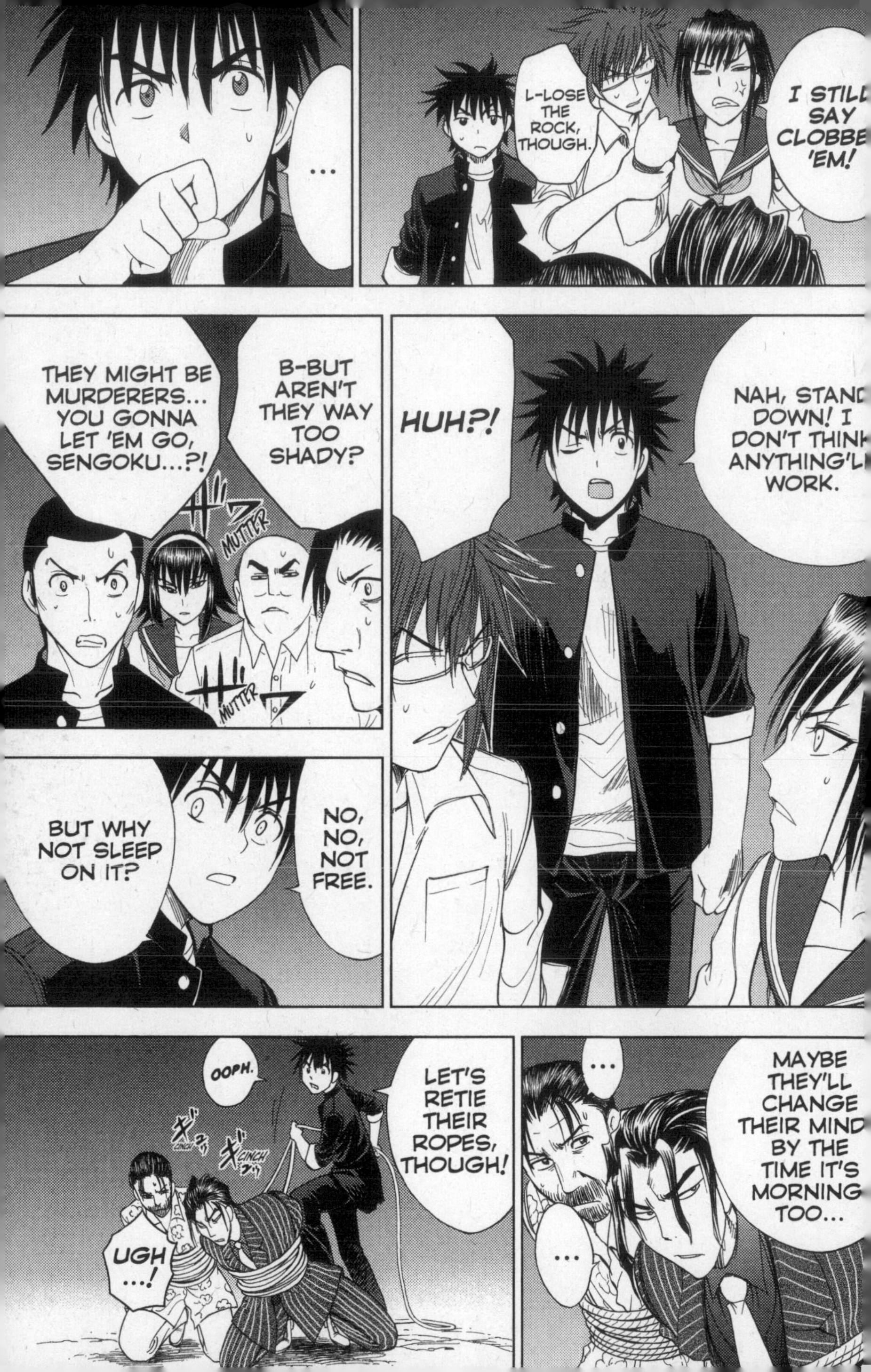
I STILL SAY CLOBBE 'EM!
L-LOSE THE ROCK, THOUGH.
...
NAH, STAND DOWN! I DON'T THINK ANYTHING'L WORK.
HUH?!
B-BUT AREN'T THEY WAY TOO SHADY?
THEY MIGHT BE MURDERERS... YOU GONNA LET 'EM GO, SENGOKU...?!
MUTTER
MUTTER
NO, NO, NOT FREE.
BUT WHY NOT SLEEP ON IT?
MAYBE THEY'LL CHANGE THEIR MIND BY THE TIME IT'S MORNING TOO...
...
...
LET'S RETIE THEIR ROPES, THOUGH!
OOPH.
CINCH
CINCH
UGH ...!

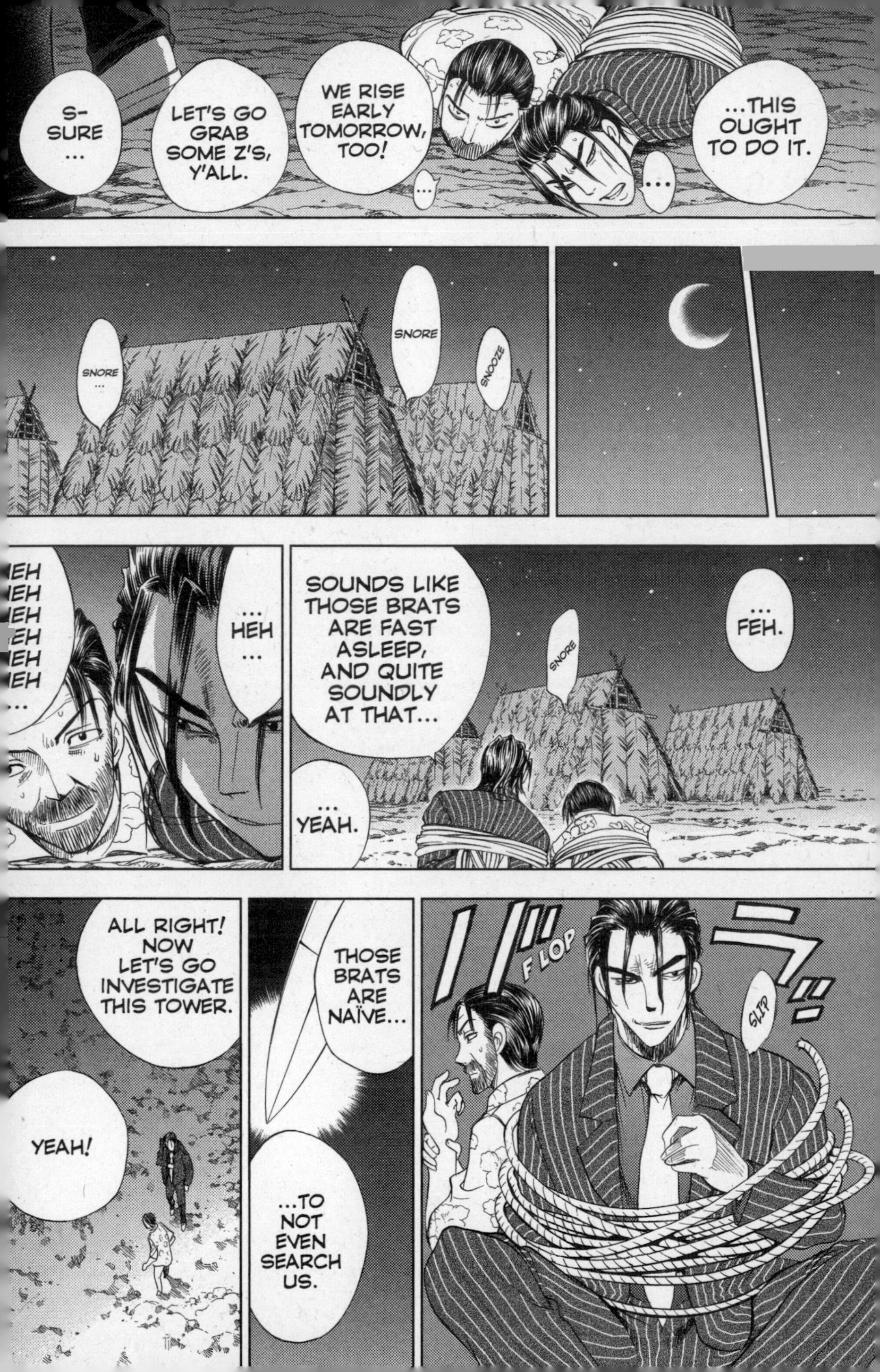
...THIS OUGHT TO DO IT.
...
...
WE RISE EARLY TOMORROW, TOO!
LET'S GO GRAB SOME Z'S, Y'ALL.
S-SURE...
SNOOZE
SNORE
SNORE...
...FEH.
SOUNDS LIKE THOSE BRATS ARE FAST ASLEEP, AND QUITE SOUNDLY AT THAT...
SNORE
...YEAH.
...HEH...
HEH HEH HEH HEH HEH HEH...
SLIP
F LOP
THOSE BRATS ARE NAÏVE...
...TO NOT EVEN SEARCH US.
ALL RIGHT! NOW LET'S GO INVESTIGATE THIS TOWER.
YEAH!

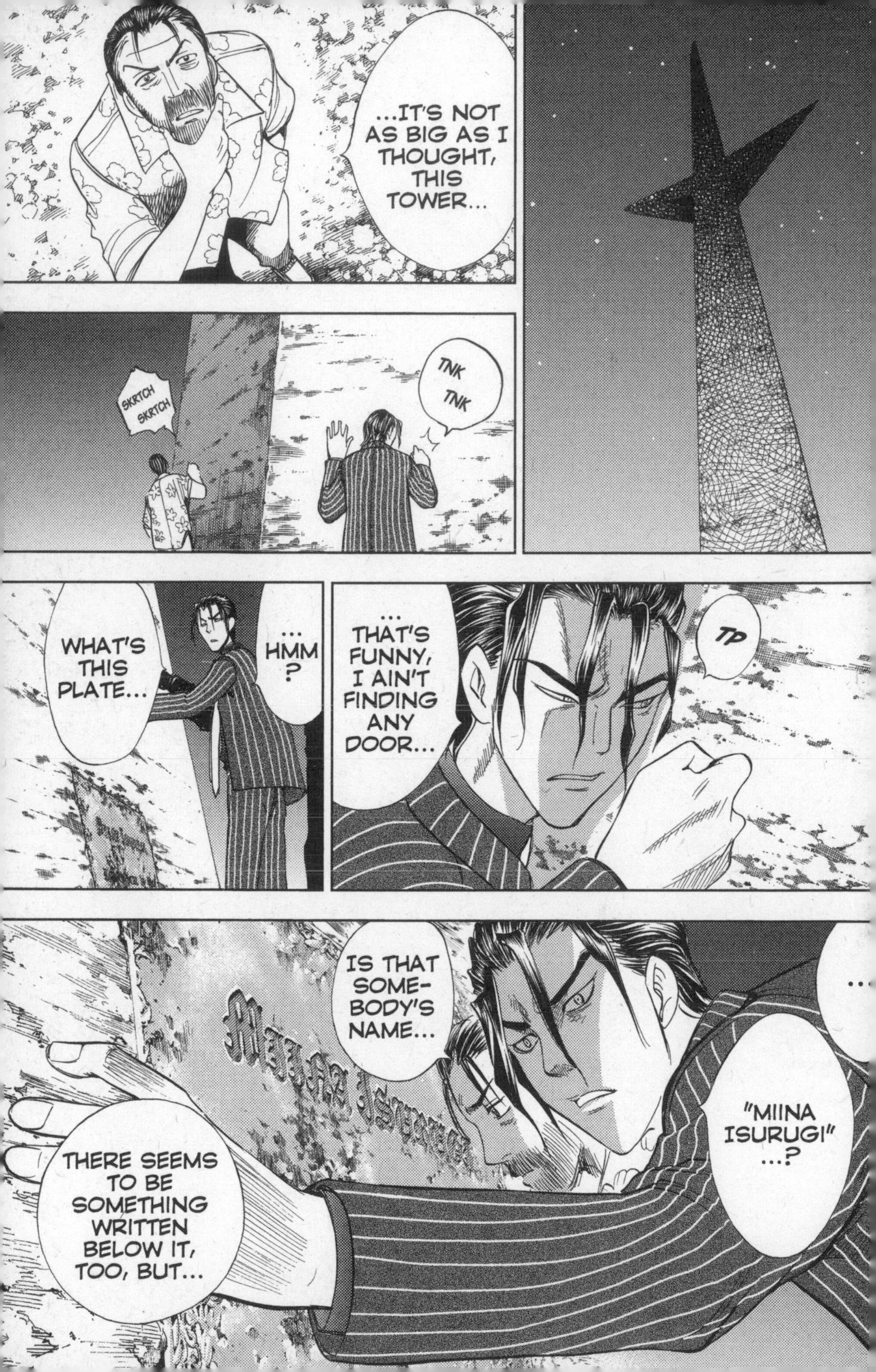
...IT'S NOT AS BIG AS I THOUGHT, THIS TOWER...
TNK TNK
SKRTCH SKRTCH
TP
... THAT'S FUNNY, I AIN'T FINDING ANY DOOR...
... HMM?
WHAT'S THIS PLATE...
...
"MIINA ISURUGI" ...?
IS THAT SOME-BODY'S NAME...
THERE SEEMS TO BE SOMETHING WRITTEN BELOW IT, TOO, BUT...

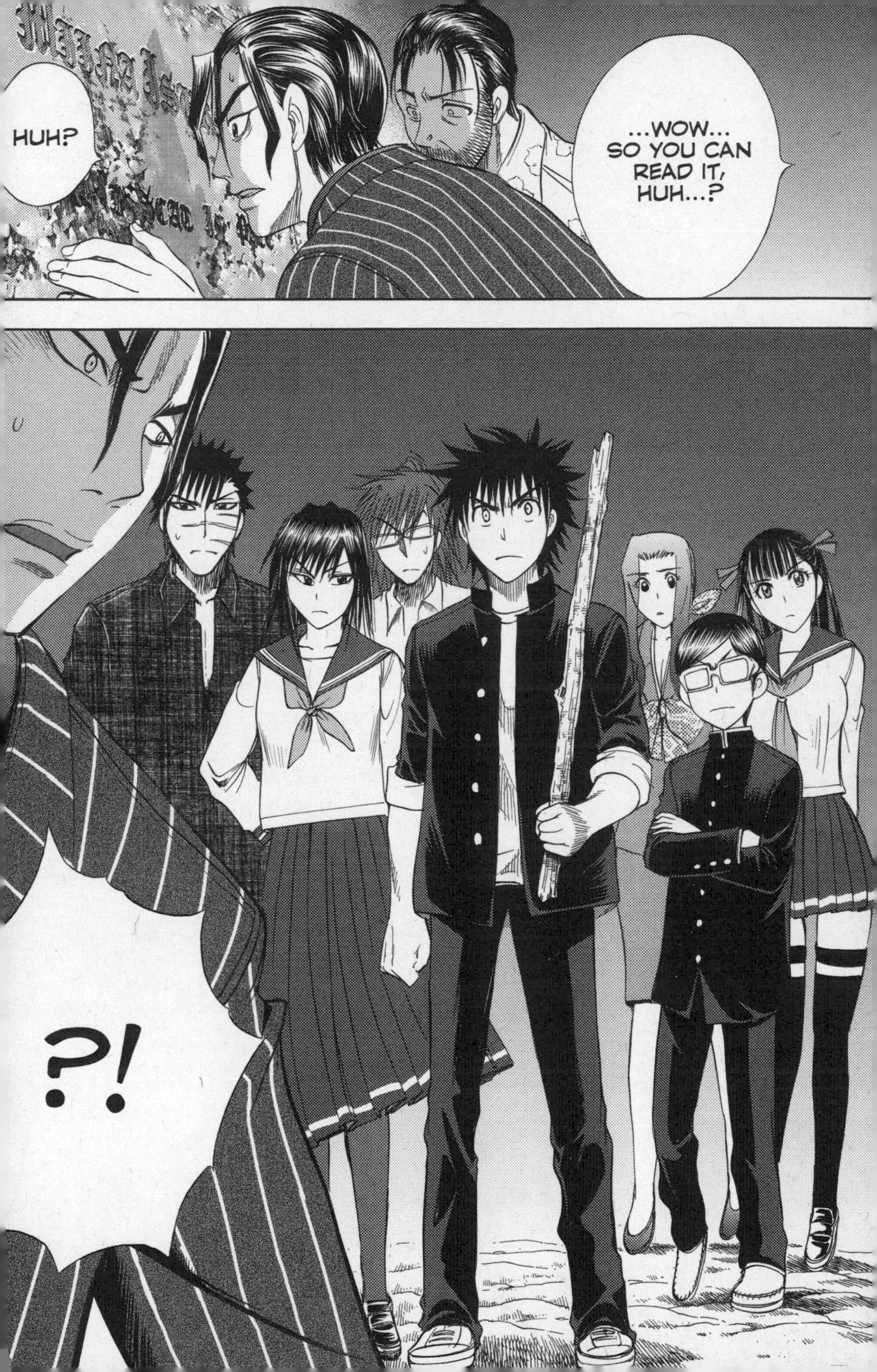
...WOW... SO YOU CAN READ IT, HUH...?
HUH?
?!

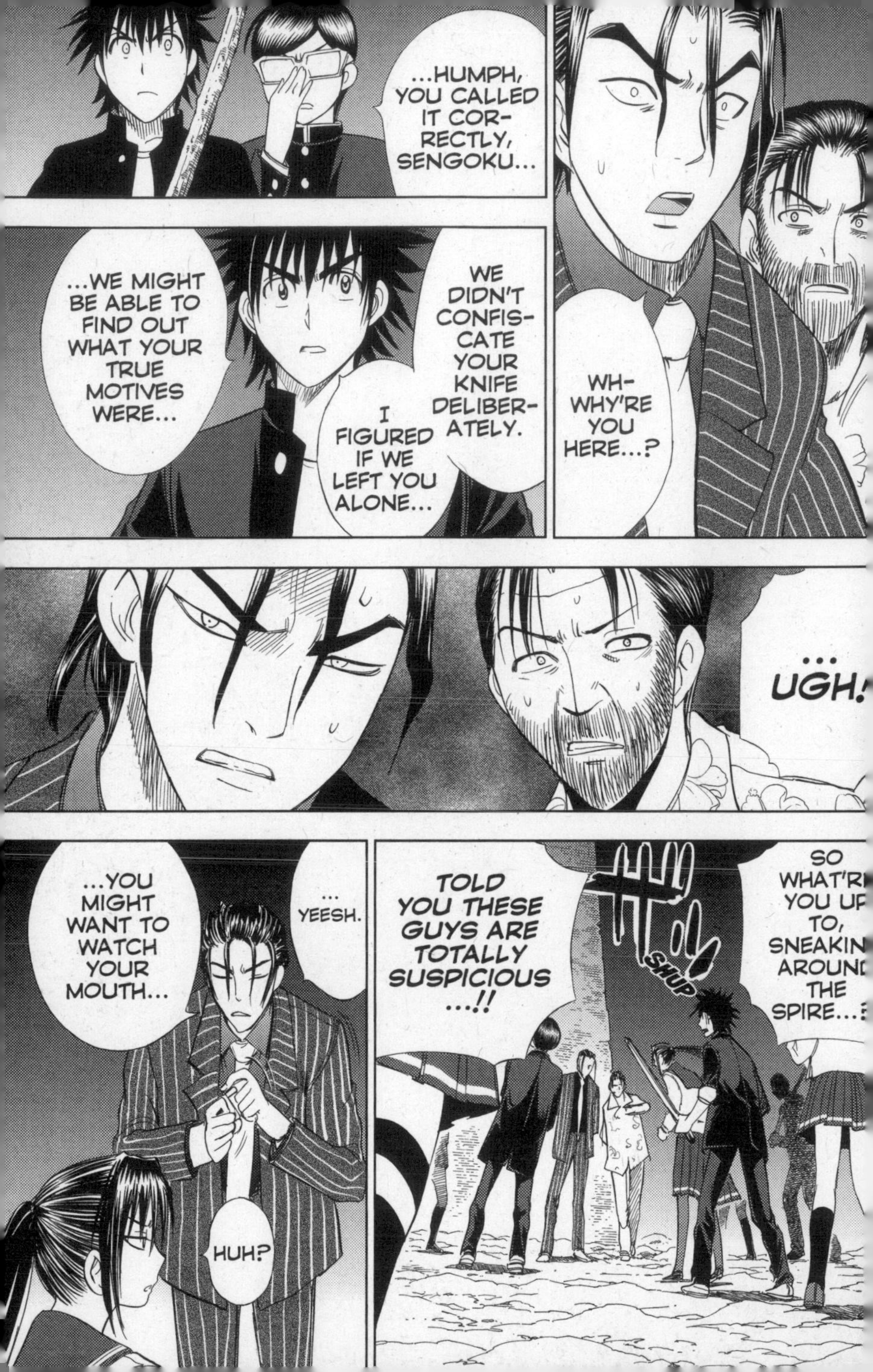
WH- WHY'RE YOU HERE...?
...HUMPH, YOU CALLED IT COR- RECTLY, SENGOKU...
WE DIDN'T CONFIS- CATE YOUR KNIFE DELIBER- ATELY.
I FIGURED IF WE LEFT YOU ALONE...
...WE MIGHT BE ABLE TO FIND OUT WHAT YOUR TRUE MOTIVES WERE...
... UGH!
SO WHAT'R YOU UP TO, SNEAKIN AROUND THE SPIRE...?
SHUP
TOLD YOU THESE GUYS ARE TOTALLY SUSPICIOUS ...!!
... YEESH.
...YOU MIGHT WANT TO WATCH YOUR MOUTH...
HUH?

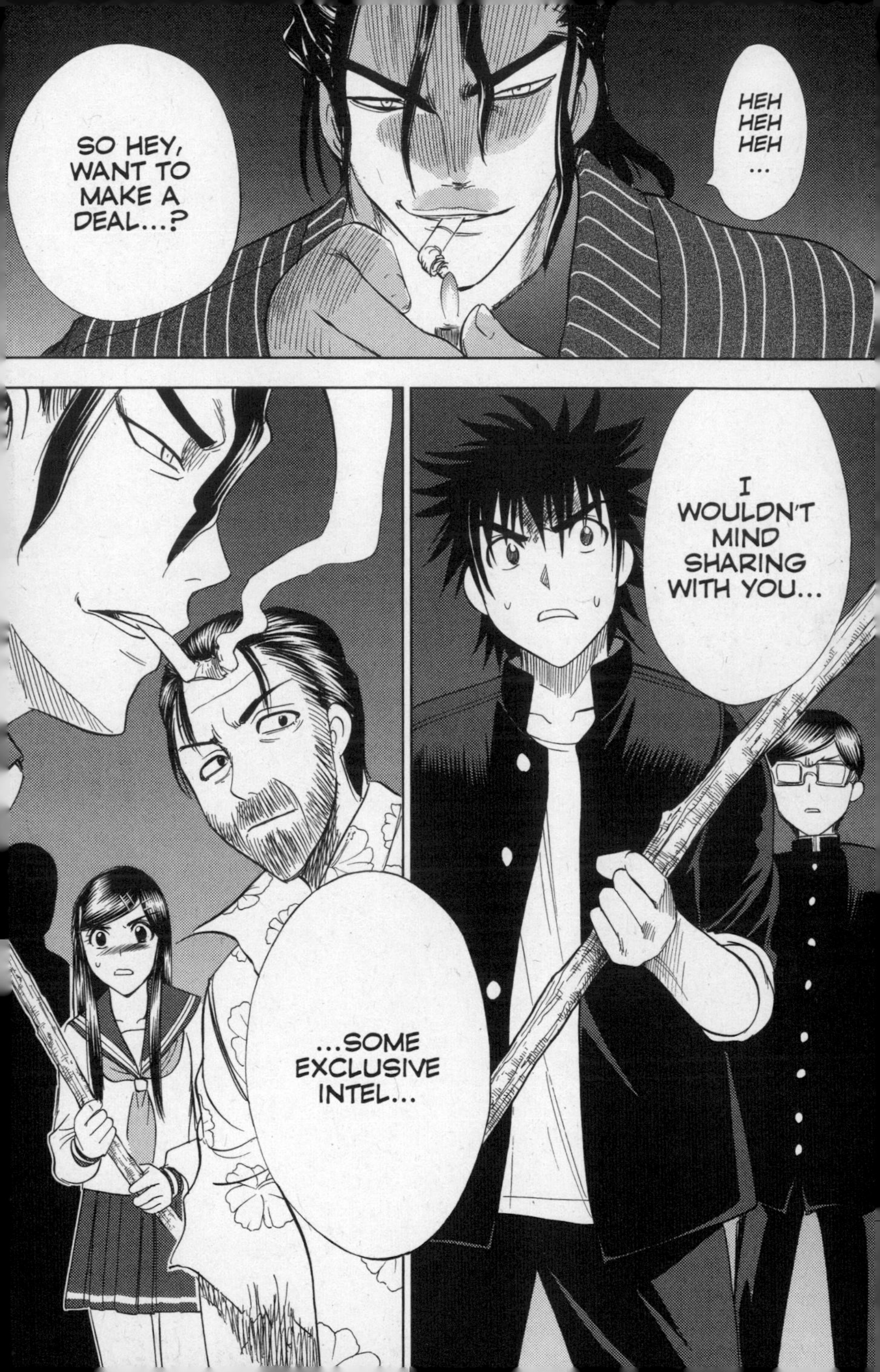
HEH HEH HEH ...
SO HEY, WANT TO MAKE A DEAL...?
I WOULDN'T MIND SHARING WITH YOU...
...SOME EXCLUSIVE INTEL...

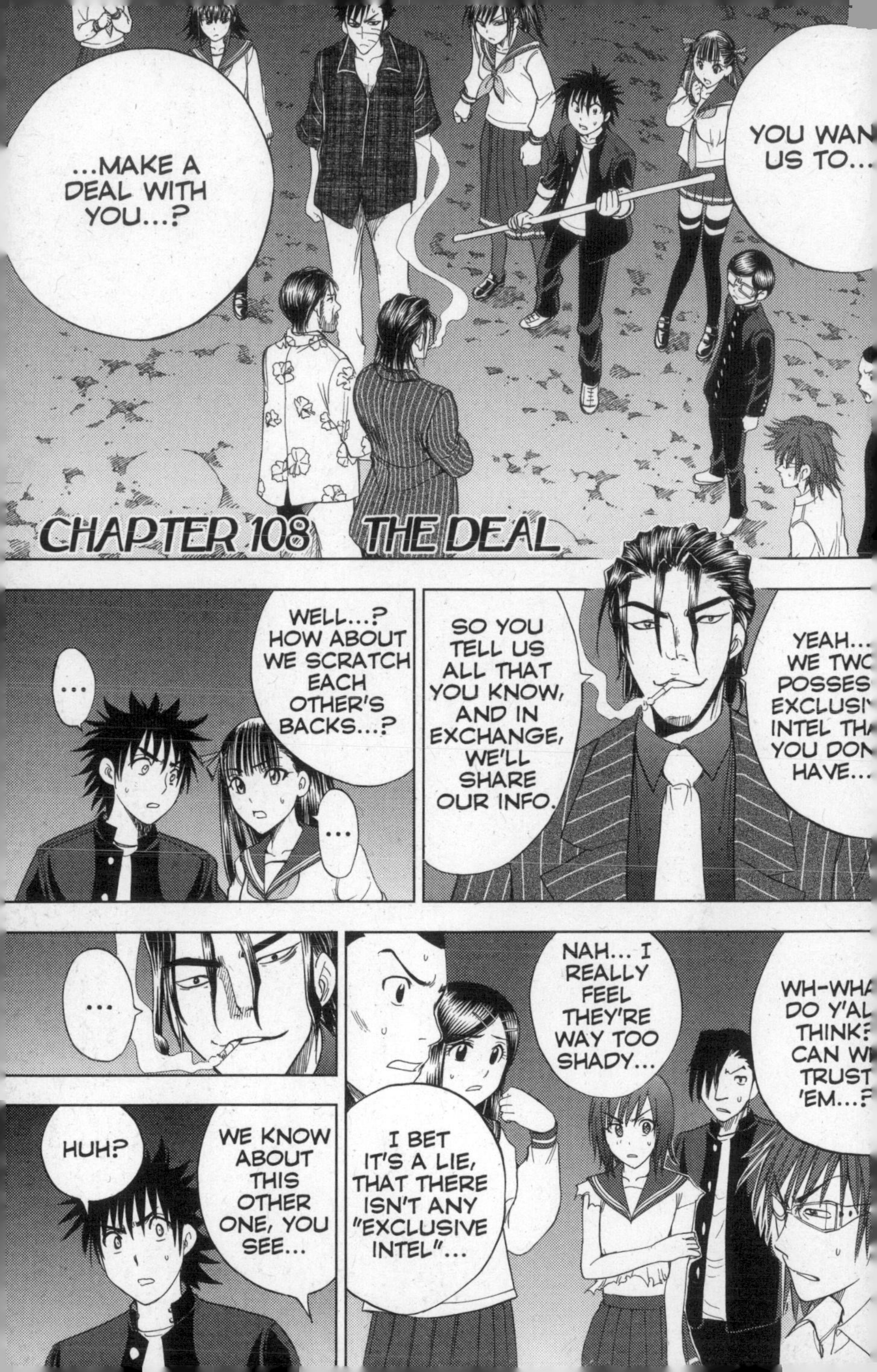
YOU WAN US TO...
...MAKE A DEAL WITH YOU...?
CHAPTER 108 THE DEAL
YEAH... WE TWO POSSES EXCLUSI INTEL THA YOU DON HAVE...
SO YOU TELL US ALL THAT YOU KNOW, AND IN EXCHANGE, WE'LL SHARE OUR INFO.
WELL...? HOW ABOUT WE SCRATCH EACH OTHER'S BACKS...?
...
...
WH-WHA DO Y'AL THINK? CAN W TRUST 'EM...?
NAH... I REALLY FEEL THEY'RE WAY TOO SHADY...
I BET IT'S A LIE, THAT THERE ISN'T ANY "EXCLUSIVE INTEL"...
...
WE KNOW ABOUT THIS OTHER ONE, YOU SEE...
HUH?

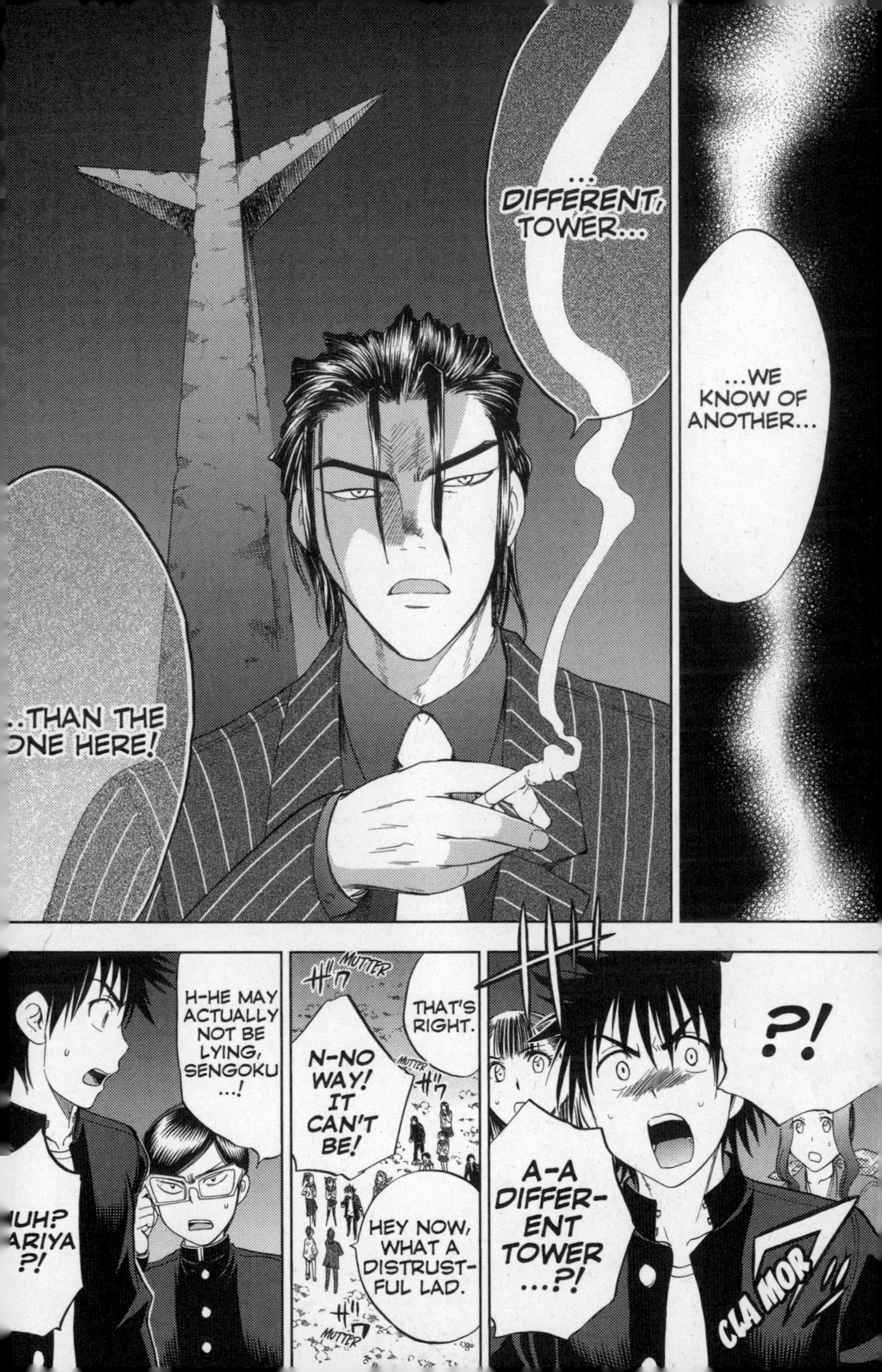
...WE KNOW OF ANOTHER...
...DIFFERENT TOWER...
..THAN THE ONE HERE!
?!
A-A DIFFERENT-ENT TOWER...?!
CLAMOR
THAT'S RIGHT.
MUTTER
N-NO WAY! IT CAN'T BE!
MUTTER
HEY NOW, WHAT A DISTRUST-FUL LAD.
MUTTER
H-HE MAY ACTUALLY NOT BE LYING, SENGOKU...!
UH? ARIYA ?!

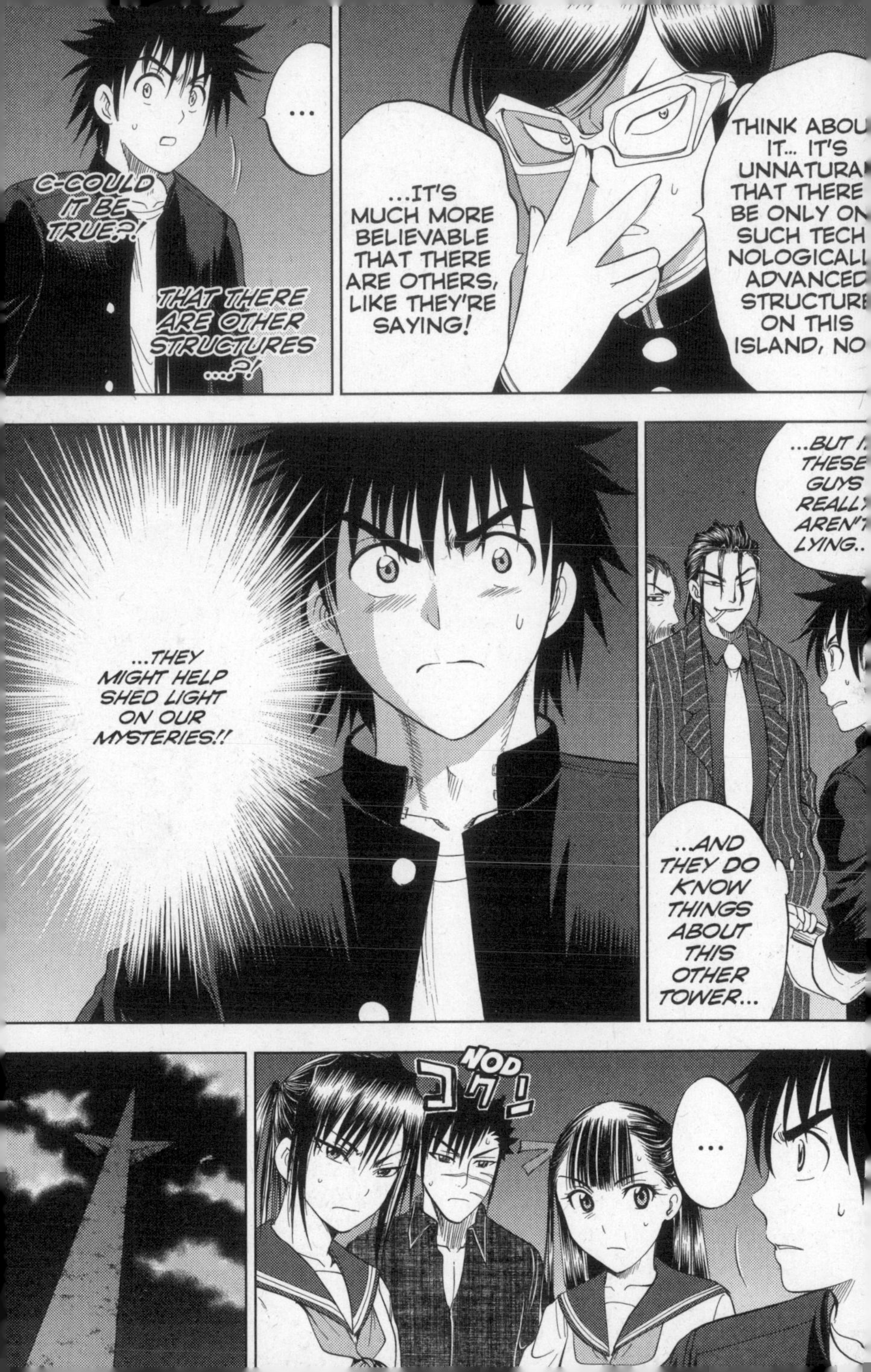
THINK ABOU IT... IT'S UNNATURA THAT THERE BE ONLY ON SUCH TECH NOLOGICALL ADVANCED STRUCTURE ON THIS ISLAND, NO
...IT'S MUCH MORE BELIEVABLE THAT THERE ARE OTHERS, LIKE THEY'RE SAYING!
...
C-COULD IT BE TRUE?!
THAT THERE ARE OTHER STRUCTURES ...?!
...BUT I THESE GUYS REALL AREN'T LYING..
...AND THEY DO KNOW THINGS ABOUT THIS OTHER TOWER...
...THEY MIGHT HELP SHED LIGHT ON OUR MYSTERIES!!
...
NOD
コク!

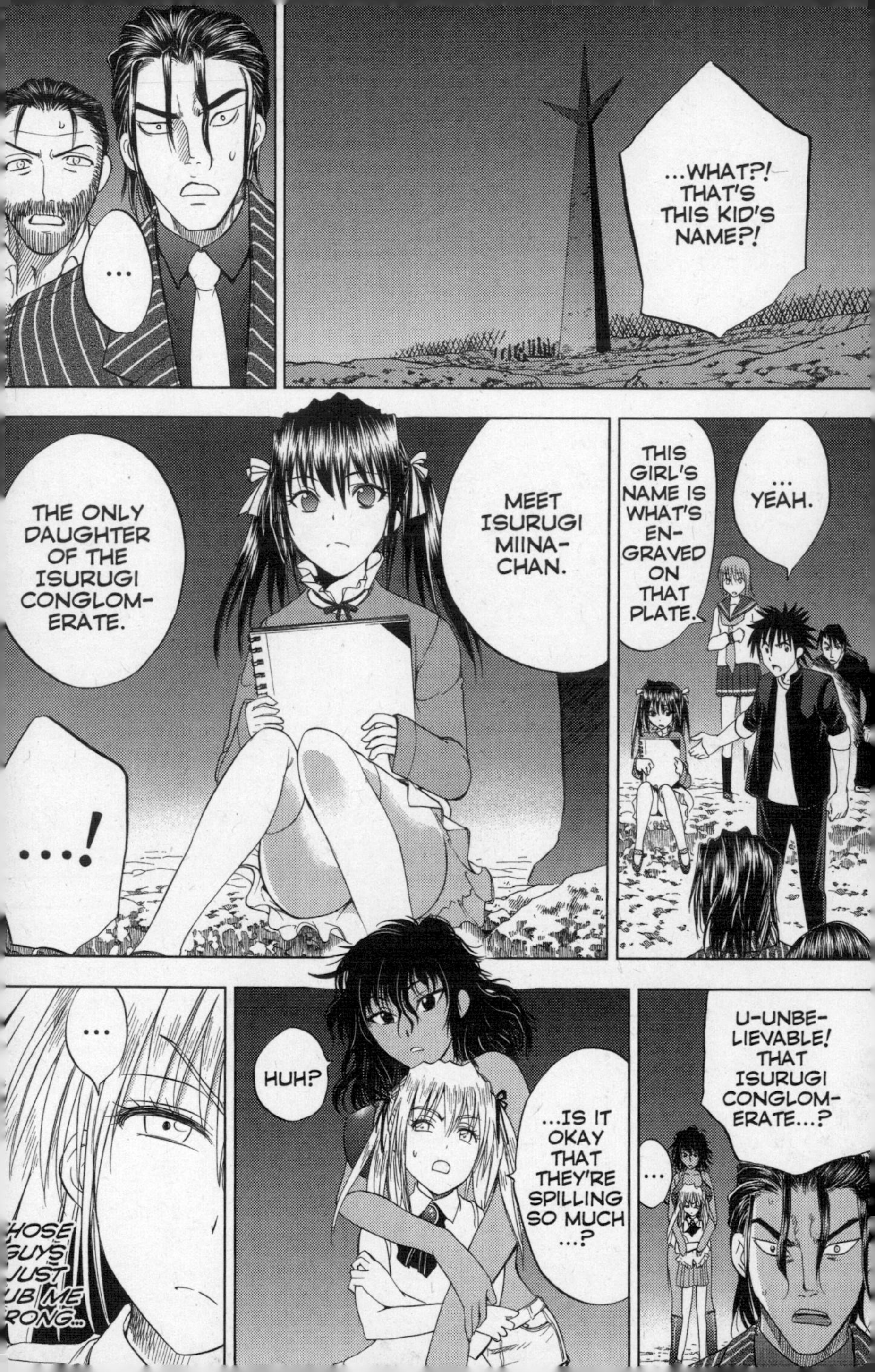
...WHAT?! THAT'S THIS KID'S NAME?!
...
... YEAH.
THIS GIRL'S NAME IS WHAT'S EN-GRAVED ON THAT PLATE.
MEET ISURUGI MIINA-CHAN.
THE ONLY DAUGHTER OF THE ISURUGI CONGLOM-ERATE.
...!
U-UNBE-LIEVABLE! THAT ISURUGI CONGLOM-ERATE...?
...
...IS IT OKAY THAT THEY'RE SPILLING SO MUCH ...?
HUH?
...
HOSE GUYS JUST UB ME RONG...

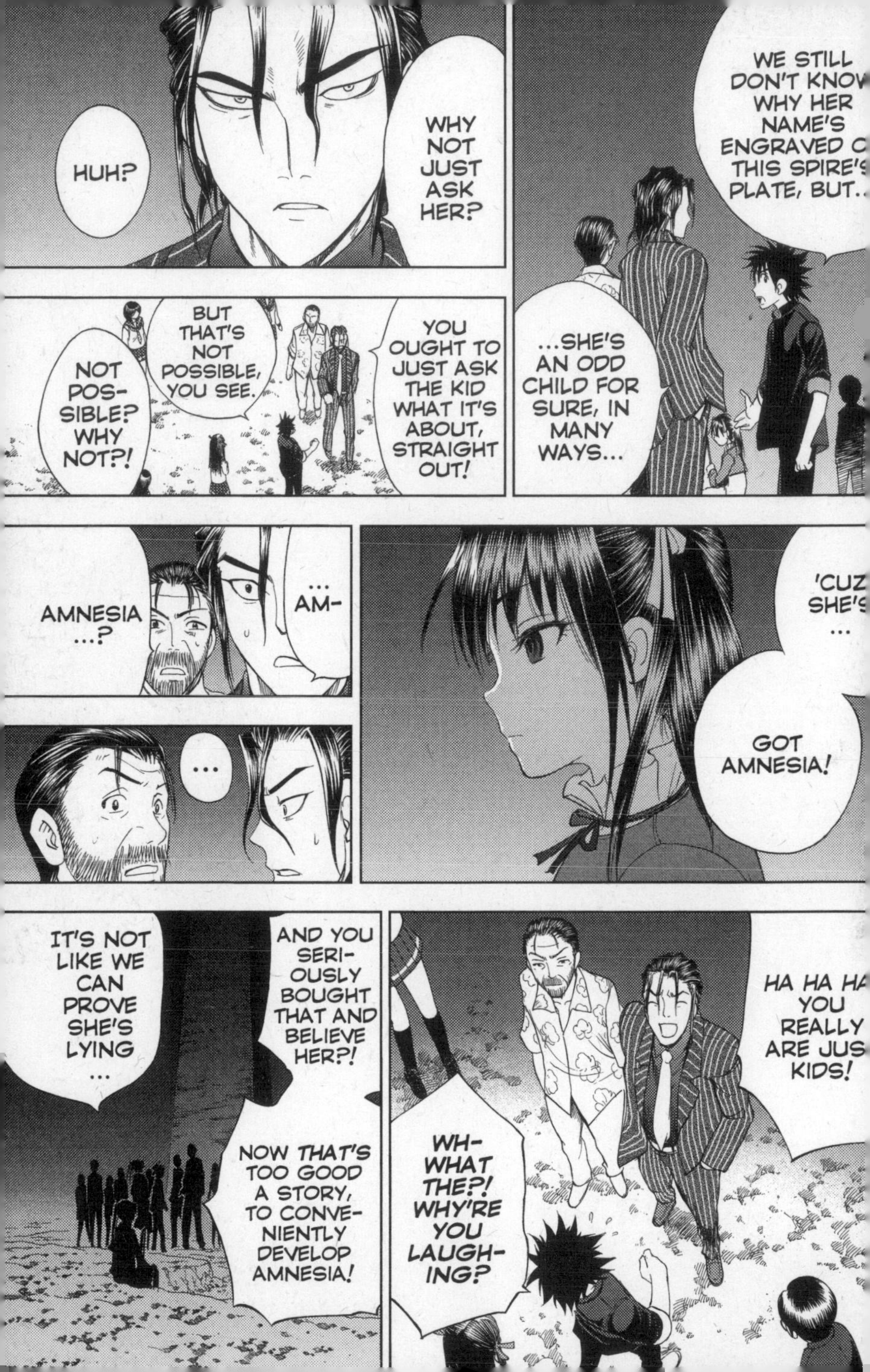
WE STILL DON'T KNOV WHY HER NAME'S ENGRAVED O THIS SPIRE'S PLATE, BUT..
...SHE'S AN ODD CHILD FOR SURE, IN MANY WAYS...
WHY NOT JUST ASK HER?
HUH?
YOU OUGHT TO JUST ASK THE KID WHAT IT'S ABOUT, STRAIGHT OUT!
BUT THAT'S NOT POSSIBLE, YOU SEE.
NOT POS-SIBLE? WHY NOT?!
'CUZ SHE'S ...
GOT AMNESIA!
... AM-
AMNESIA ...?
...
HA HA HA YOU REALLY ARE JUS KIDS!
WH-WHAT THE?! WHY'RE YOU LAUGH-ING?
AND YOU SERI-OUSLY BOUGHT THAT AND BELIEVE HER?!
IT'S NOT LIKE WE CAN PROVE SHE'S LYING ...
NOW THAT'S TOO GOOD A STORY, TO CONVE-NIENTLY DEVELOP AMNESIA!

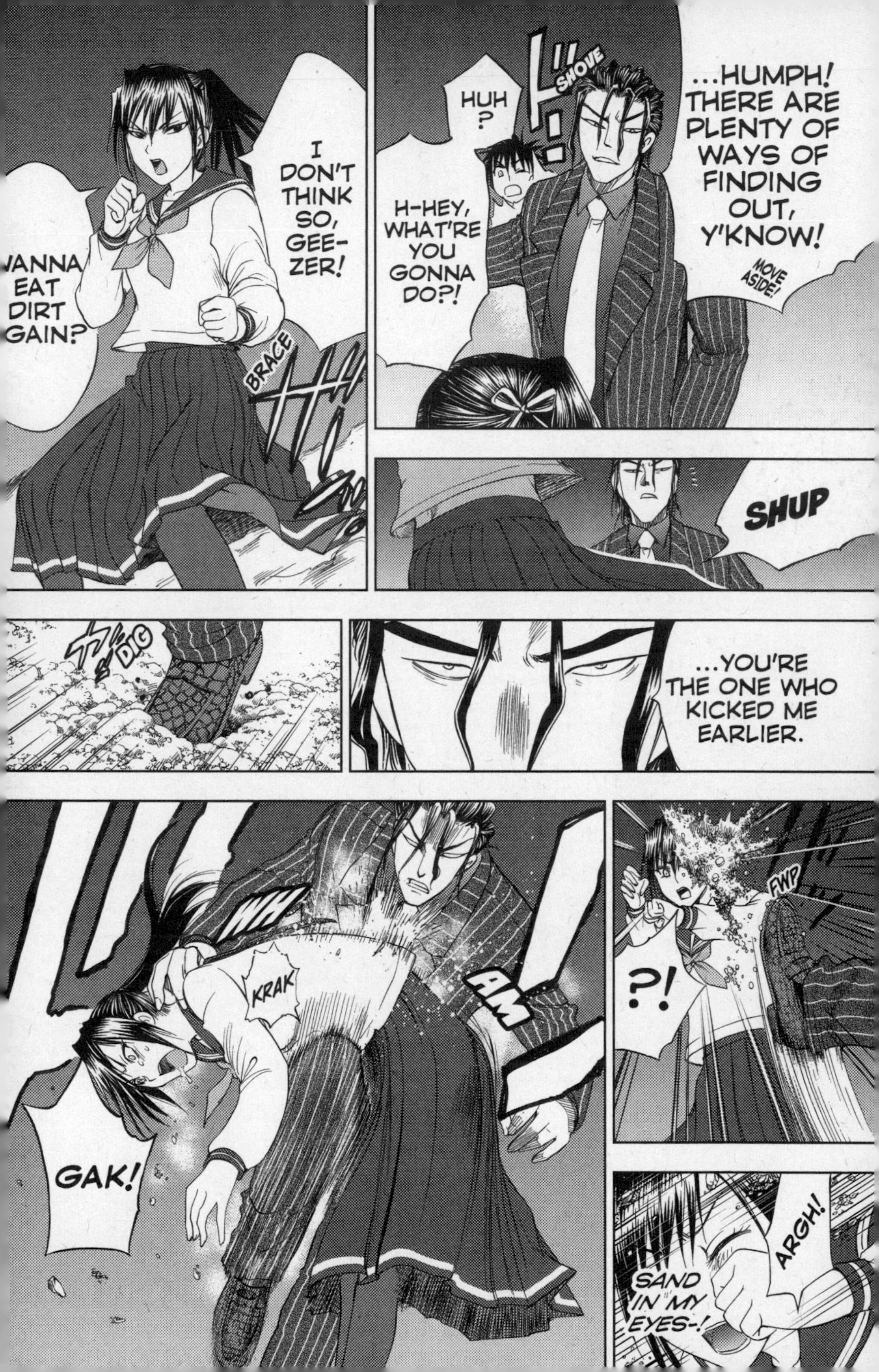
...HUMPH! THERE ARE PLENTY OF WAYS OF FINDING OUT, Y'KNOW!
SHOVE
HUH ?
MOVE ASIDE!
H-HEY, WHAT'RE YOU GONNA DO?!
SHUP
I DON'T THINK SO, GEE-ZER!
ANNA EAT DIRT GAIN?
BRACE
...YOU'RE THE ONE WHO KICKED ME EARLIER.
DIG
FWP
?!
ARGH!
SAND IN MY EYES-!
AM
KRAK
GAK!

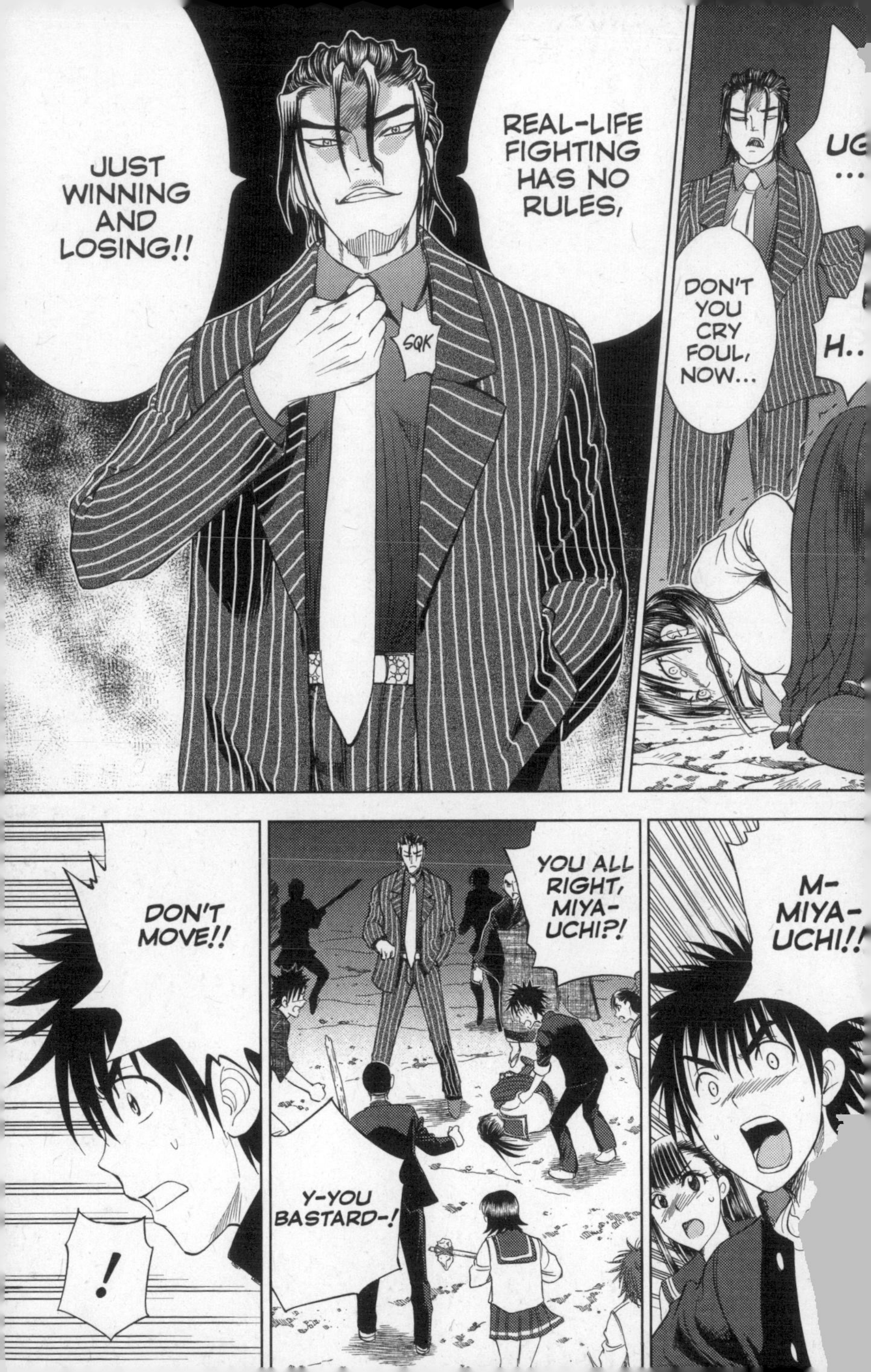
UG...
H..
DON'T YOU CRY FOUL, NOW...
REAL-LIFE FIGHTING HAS NO RULES,
JUST WINNING AND LOSING!!
SQK
M-MIYA-UCHI!!
YOU ALL RIGHT, MIYA-UCHI?!
Y-YOU BASTARD-!
DON'T MOVE!!
!

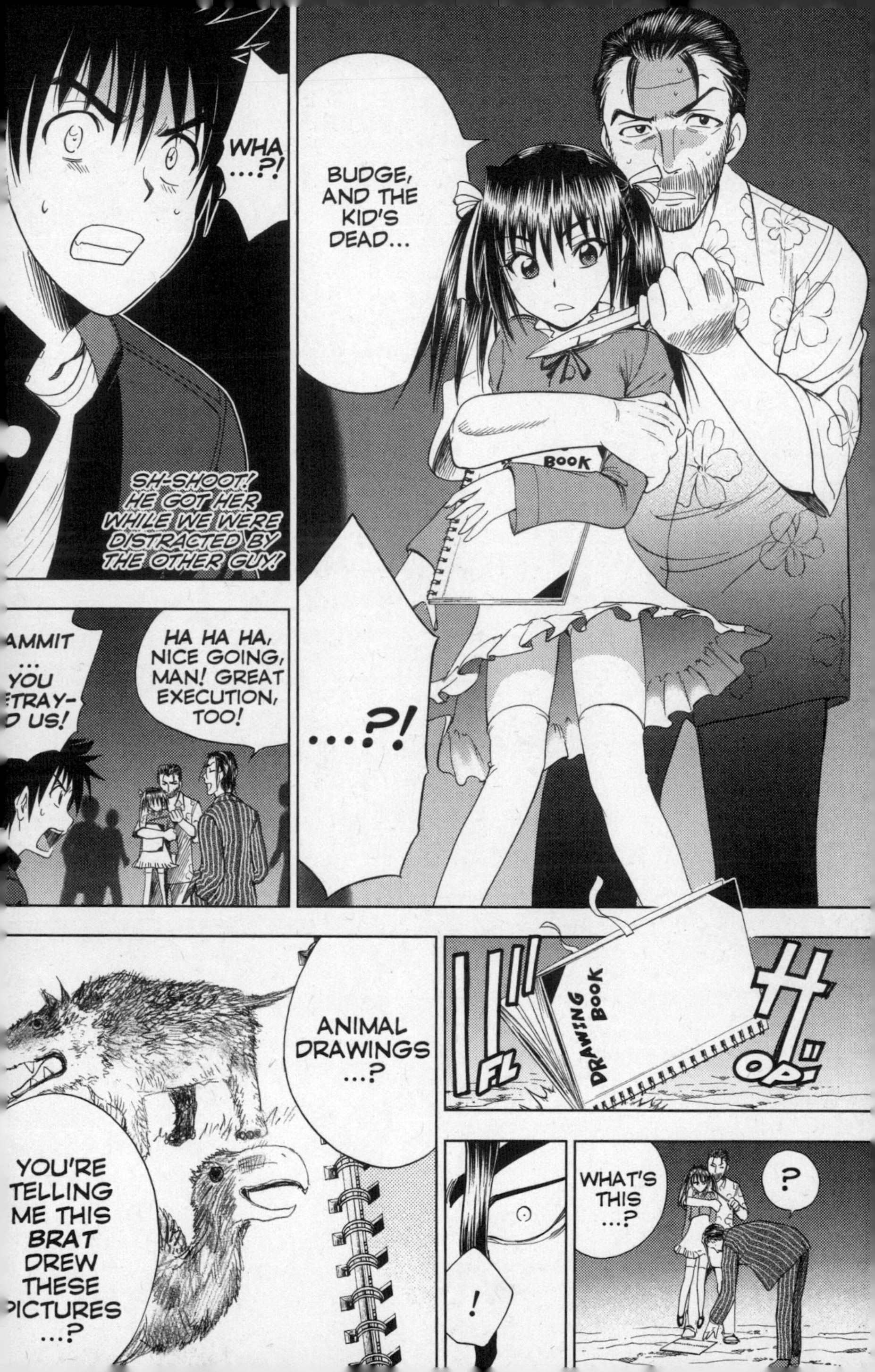
BUDGE, AND THE KID'S DEAD...
BOOK
...?!
WHA ...?!
SH-SHOOT! HE GOT HER WHILE WE WERE DISTRACTED BY THE OTHER GUY!
HA HA HA, NICE GOING, MAN! GREAT EXECUTION, TOO!
AMMIT ... YOU ETRAY- D US!
FL
DRAWING BOOK
OP
?
WHAT'S THIS ...?
!
ANIMAL DRAWINGS ...?
YOU'RE TELLING ME THIS BRAT DREW THESE ICTURES ...?

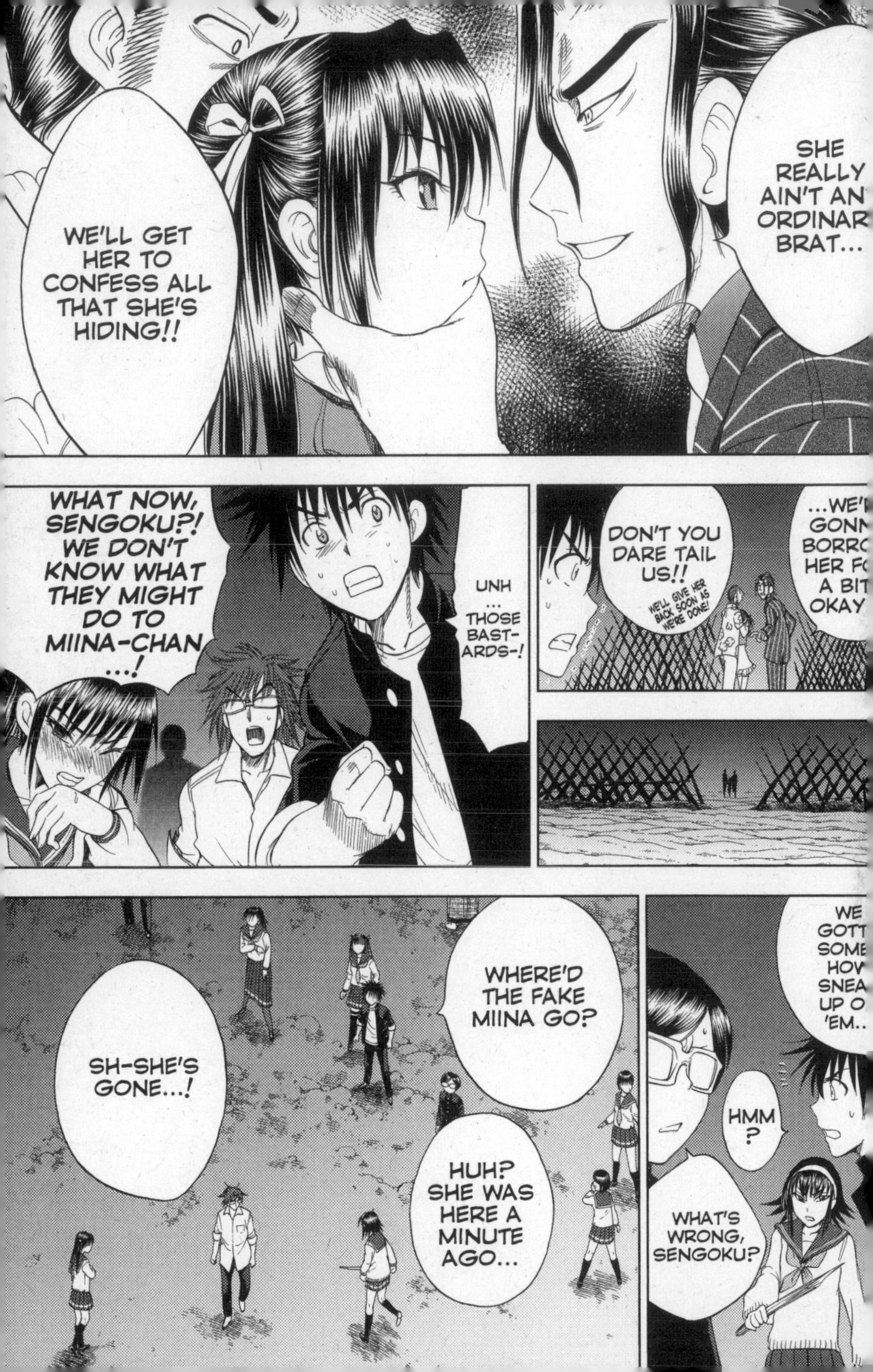
SHE REALLY AIN'T AN ORDINAR BRAT...
WE'LL GET HER TO CONFESS ALL THAT SHE'S HIDING!!
...WE'R GONN BORRO HER FO A BIT OKAY
DON'T YOU DARE TAIL US!!
WE'LL GIVE HER BACK SOON AS WE'RE DONE!
UNH ... THOSE BAST-ARDS-!
WHAT NOW, SENGOKU?! WE DON'T KNOW WHAT THEY MIGHT DO TO MIINA-CHAN ...!
WE GOTT SOME HOW SNEA UP O 'EM..
HMM ?
WHAT'S WRONG, SENGOKU?
WHERE'D THE FAKE MIINA GO?
HUH? SHE WAS HERE A MINUTE AGO...
SH-SHE'S GONE...!

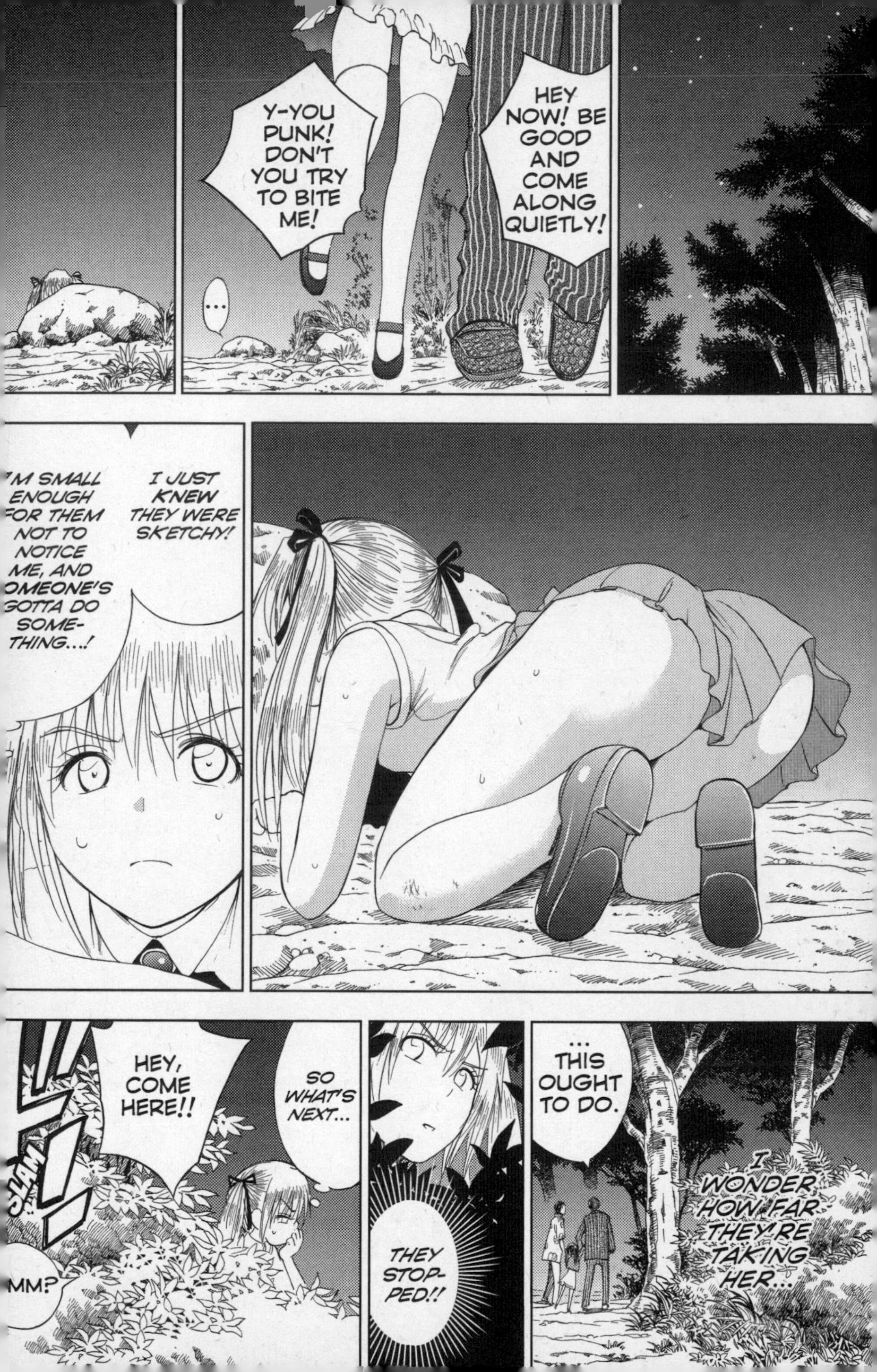
HEY NOW! BE GOOD AND COME ALONG QUIETLY!
Y-YOU PUNK! DON'T YOU TRY TO BITE ME!
...
I JUST KNEW THEY WERE SKETCHY!
I'M SMALL ENOUGH FOR THEM NOT TO NOTICE ME, AND SOMEONE'S GOTTA DO SOME-THING...!
I WONDER HOW FAR THEY'RE TAKING HER...
... THIS OUGHT TO DO.
THEY STOP-PED!!
SO WHAT'S NEXT...
HEY, COME HERE!!
SLAM
MM?

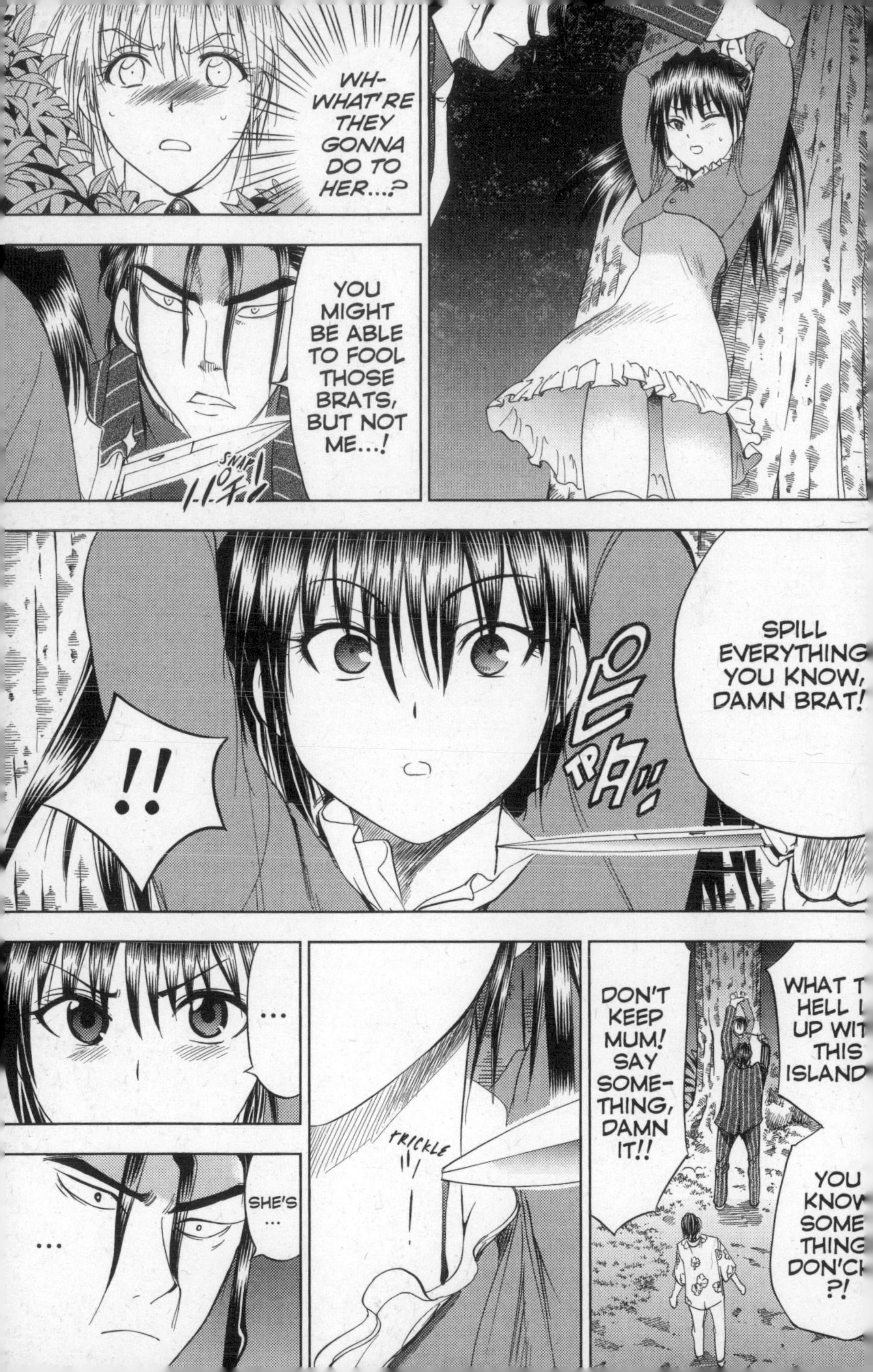
WH-WHAT'RE THEY GONNA DO TO HER...?
YOU MIGHT BE ABLE TO FOOL THOSE BRATS, BUT NOT ME...!
SNAP
SPILL EVERYTHING YOU KNOW, DAMN BRAT!
TP
!!
WHAT T HELL I UP WIT THIS ISLAND
DON'T KEEP MUM! SAY SOME-THING, DAMN IT!!
YOU KNOW SOME THING DON'C ?!
TRICKLE
...
SHE'S ...
...

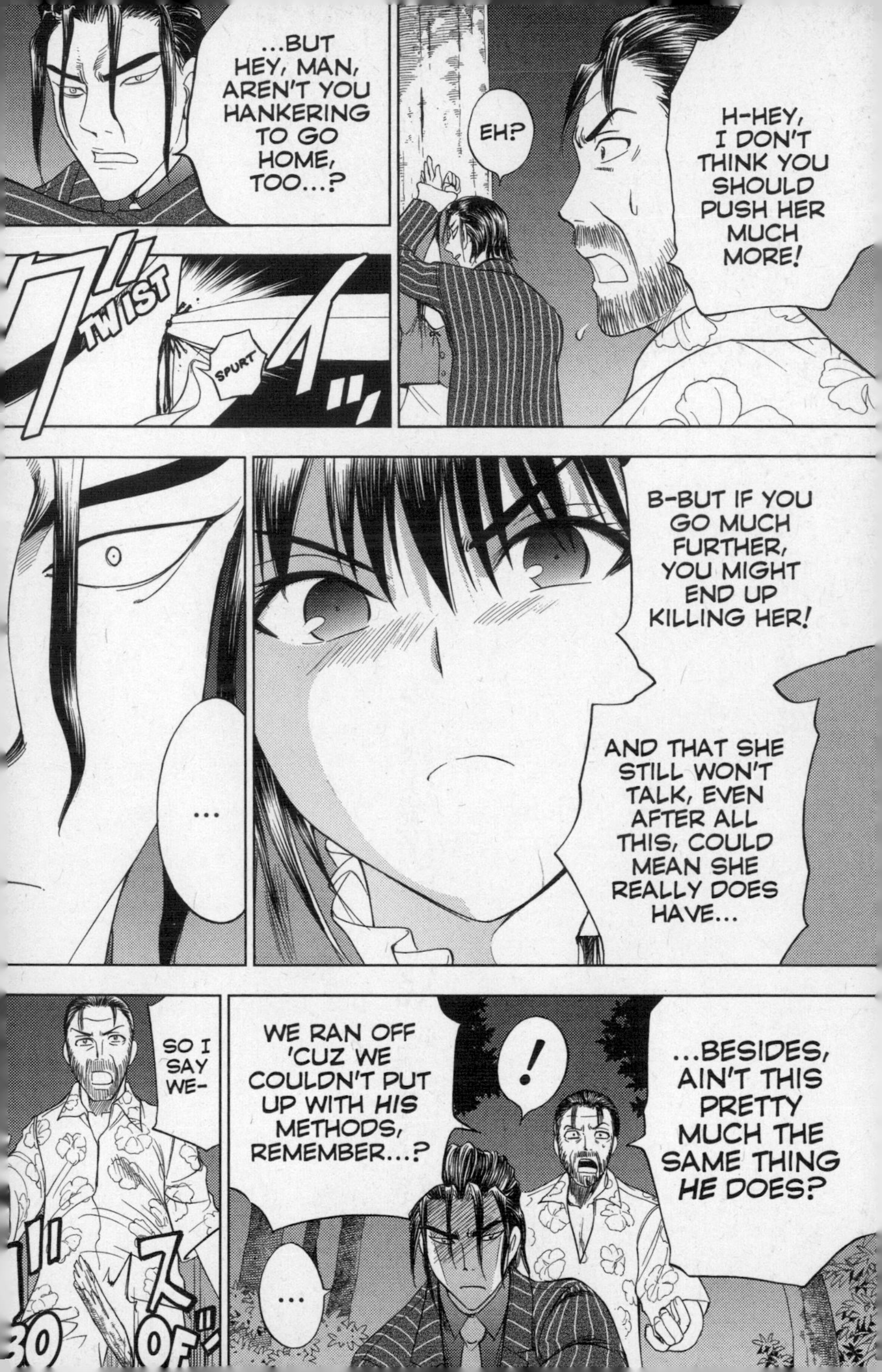
H-HEY, I DON'T THINK YOU SHOULD PUSH HER MUCH MORE!
EH?
...BUT HEY, MAN, AREN'T YOU HANKERING TO GO HOME, TOO...?
TWIST
SPURT
B-BUT IF YOU GO MUCH FURTHER, YOU MIGHT END UP KILLING HER!
AND THAT SHE STILL WON'T TALK, EVEN AFTER ALL THIS, COULD MEAN SHE REALLY DOES HAVE...
...
...BESIDES, AIN'T THIS PRETTY MUCH THE SAME THING *HE* DOES?
!
WE RAN OFF 'CUZ WE COULDN'T PUT UP WITH *HIS* METHODS, REMEMBER...?
...
SO I SAY WE-

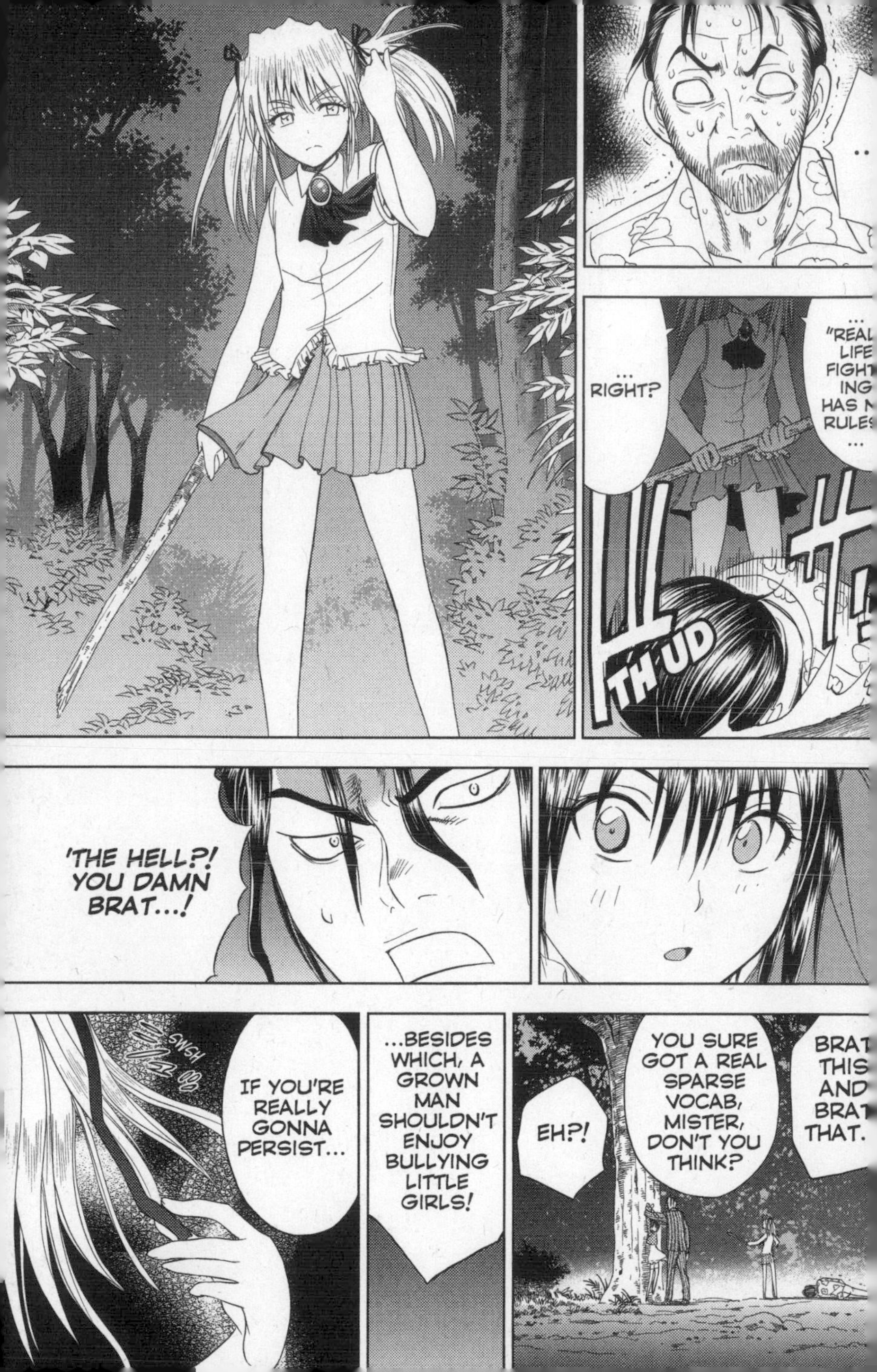
...
..."REAL LIFE FIGHTING HAS N RULES ...
... RIGHT?
THUD
'THE HELL?! YOU DAMN BRAT...!
BRAT THIS AND BRAT THAT.
YOU SURE GOT A REAL SPARSE VOCAB, MISTER, DON'T YOU THINK?
EH?!
...BESIDES WHICH, A GROWN MAN SHOULDN'T ENJOY BULLYING LITTLE GIRLS!
SWSH
IF YOU'RE REALLY GONNA PERSIST...

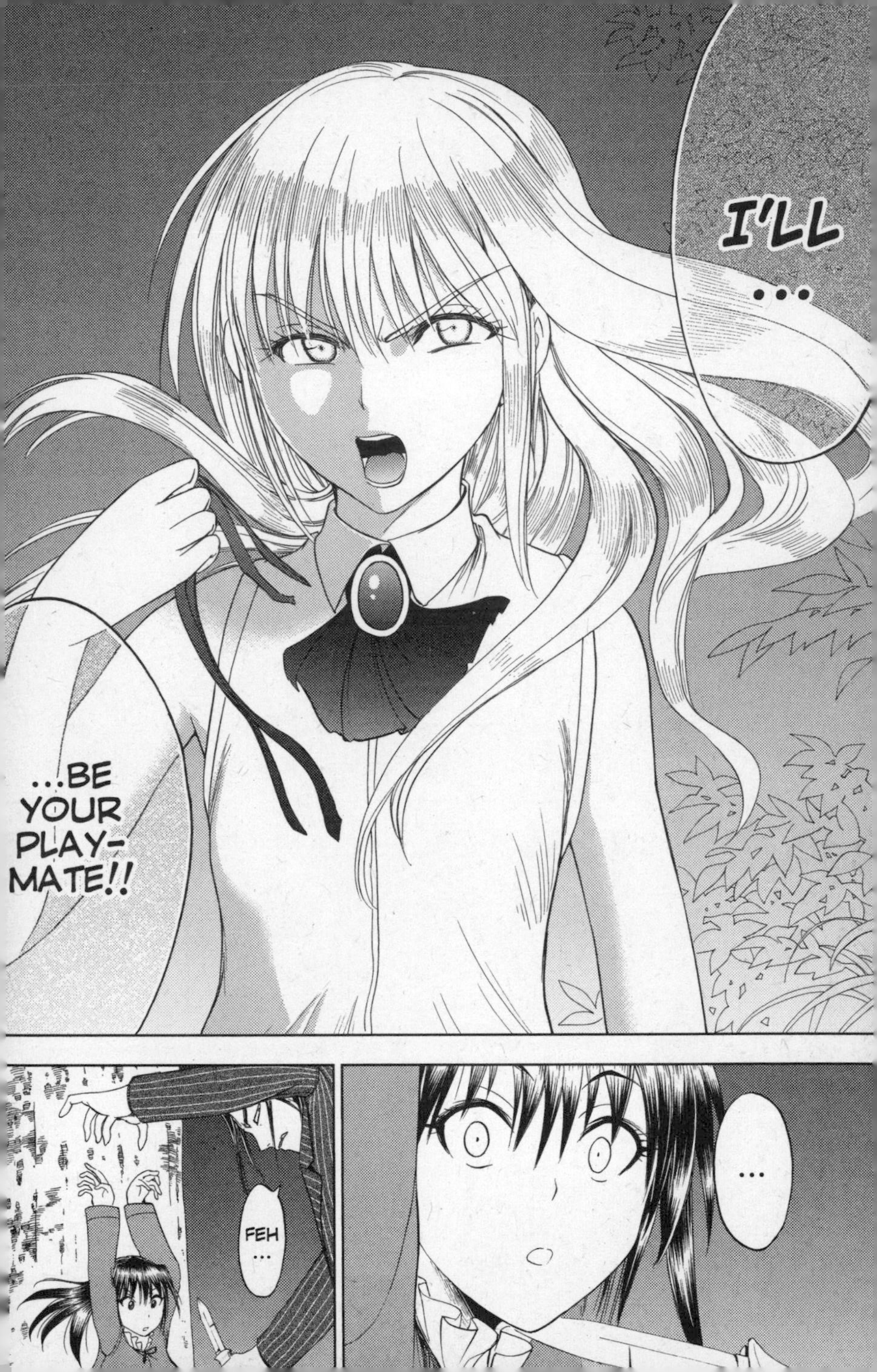
I'LL
...
...BE YOUR PLAY-MATE!!
...
FEH ...

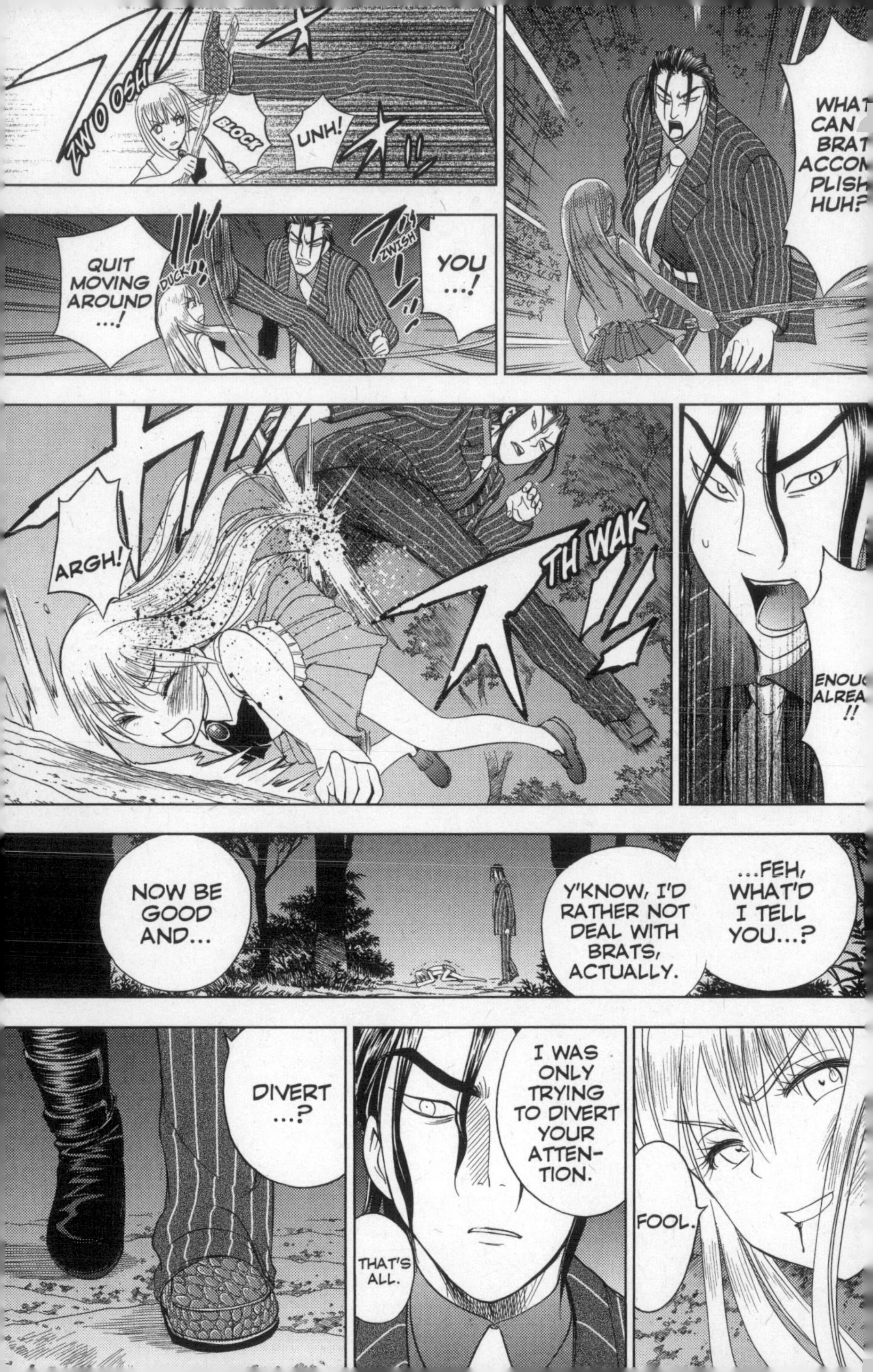

WHAT CAN BRAT ACCOM PLISH HUH?
UNH!
BLOCK
ZWOOSH
YOU ...!
ZWISH
QUIT MOVING AROUND ...!
DUCK
ENOUG ALREA !!
TH WAK
ARGH!
...FEH, WHAT'D I TELL YOU...?
Y'KNOW, I'D RATHER NOT DEAL WITH BRATS, ACTUALLY.
NOW BE GOOD AND...
FOOL.
I WAS ONLY TRYING TO DIVERT YOUR ATTEN- TION.
THAT'S ALL.
DIVERT ...?

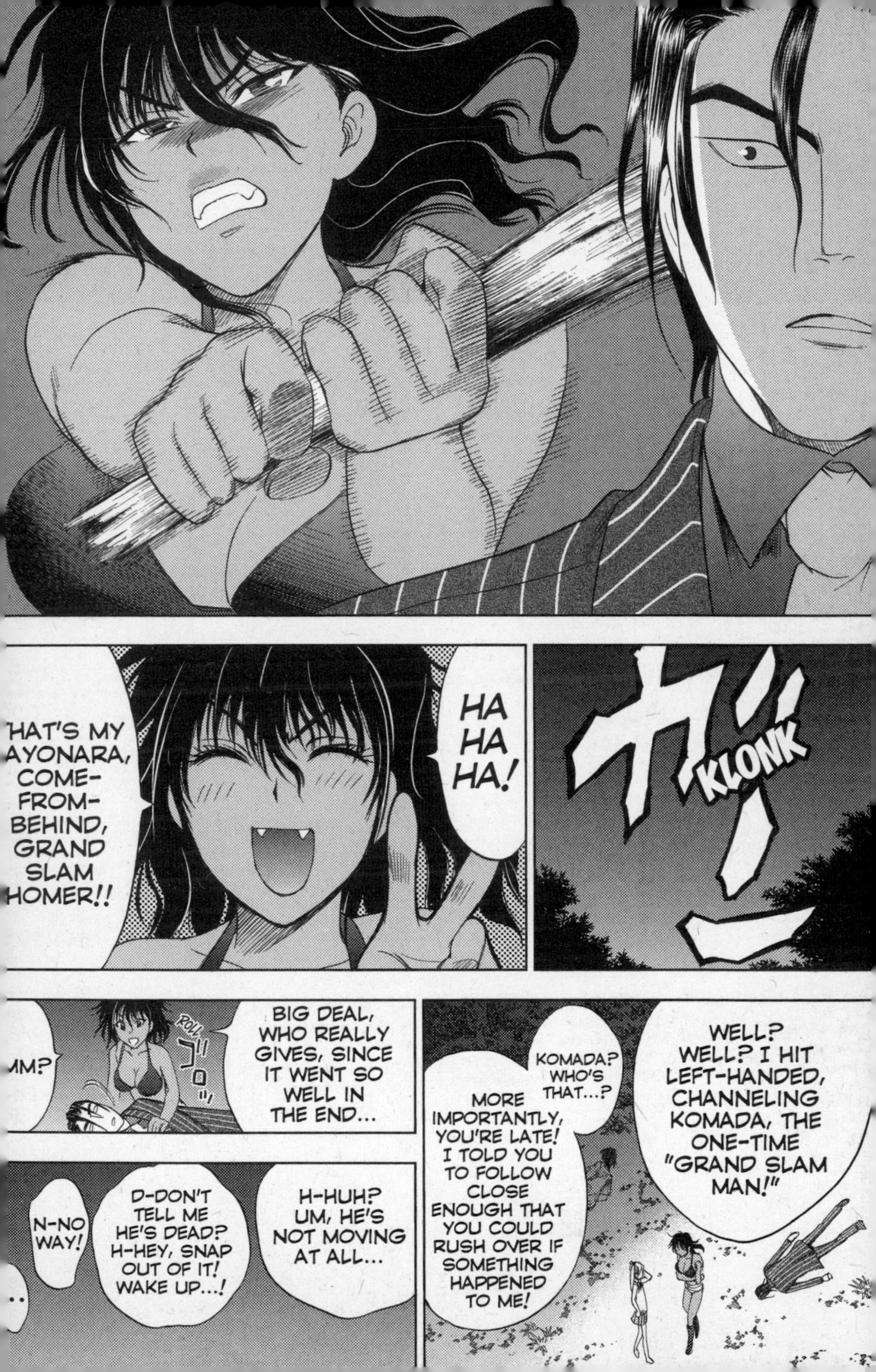
KLONK
HA HA HA!
HAT'S MY AYONARA, COME-FROM-BEHIND, GRAND SLAM HOMER!!
WELL? WELL? I HIT LEFT-HANDED, CHANNELING KOMADA, THE ONE-TIME "GRAND SLAM MAN!"
KOMADA? WHO'S THAT...?
MORE IMPORTANTLY, YOU'RE LATE! I TOLD YOU TO FOLLOW CLOSE ENOUGH THAT YOU COULD RUSH OVER IF SOMETHING HAPPENED TO ME!
BIG DEAL, WHO REALLY GIVES, SINCE IT WENT SO WELL IN THE END...
ROLL
MM?
H-HUH? UM, HE'S NOT MOVING AT ALL...
D-DON'T TELL ME HE'S DEAD? H-HEY, SNAP OUT OF IT! WAKE UP...!
N-NO WAY!
...

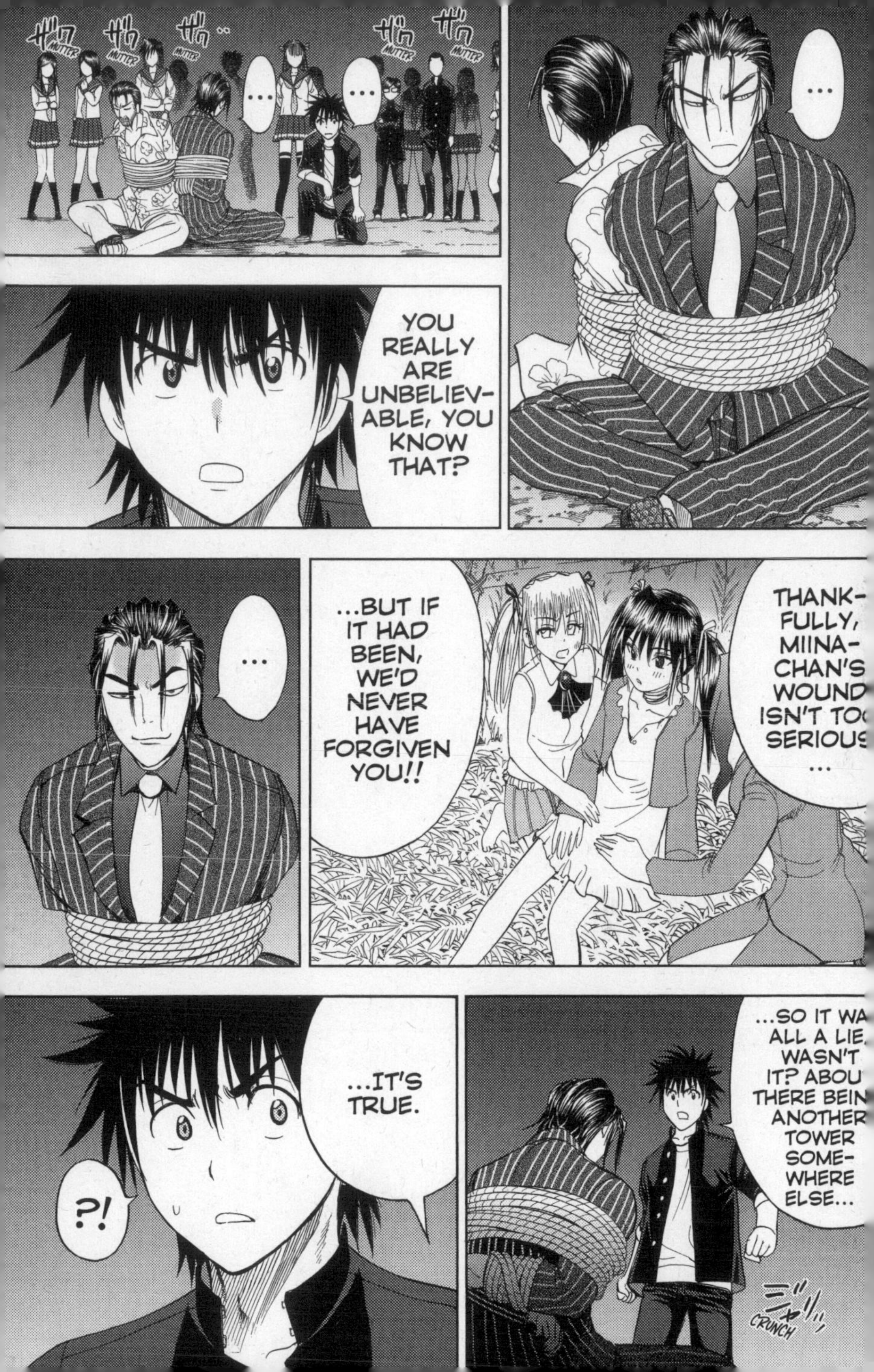
…
MUTTER
MUTTER
…
…
MUTTER
MUTTER
MUTTER
YOU REALLY ARE UNBELIEV-ABLE, YOU KNOW THAT?
THANK-FULLY, MIINA-CHAN'S WOUND ISN'T TOO SERIOUS …
…BUT IF IT HAD BEEN, WE'D NEVER HAVE FORGIVEN YOU!!
…
…SO IT WA ALL A LIE, WASN'T IT? ABOU THERE BEIN ANOTHER TOWER SOME-WHERE ELSE…
CRUNCH
…IT'S TRUE.
?!

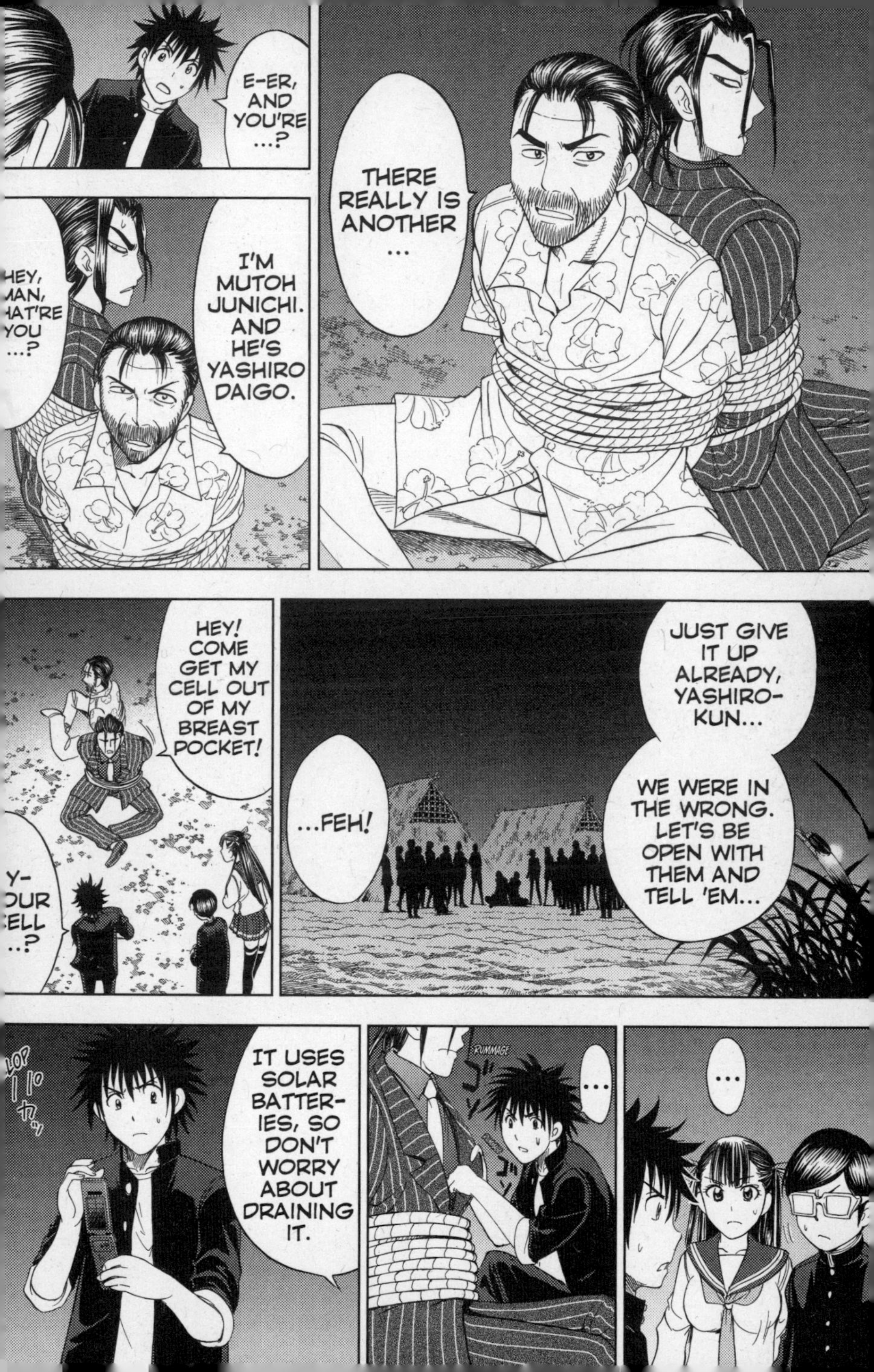
THERE REALLY IS ANOTHER ...
E-ER, AND YOU'RE ...?
I'M MUTOH JUNICHI. AND HE'S YASHIRO DAIGO.
HEY, MAN, HAT'RE YOU ...?
JUST GIVE IT UP ALREADY, YASHIRO-KUN...
WE WERE IN THE WRONG. LET'S BE OPEN WITH THEM AND TELL 'EM...
...FEH!
HEY! COME GET MY CELL OUT OF MY BREAST POCKET!
Y- OUR ELL ...?
...
RUMMAGE
...
IT USES SOLAR BATTER- IES, SO DON'T WORRY ABOUT DRAINING IT.
LOP

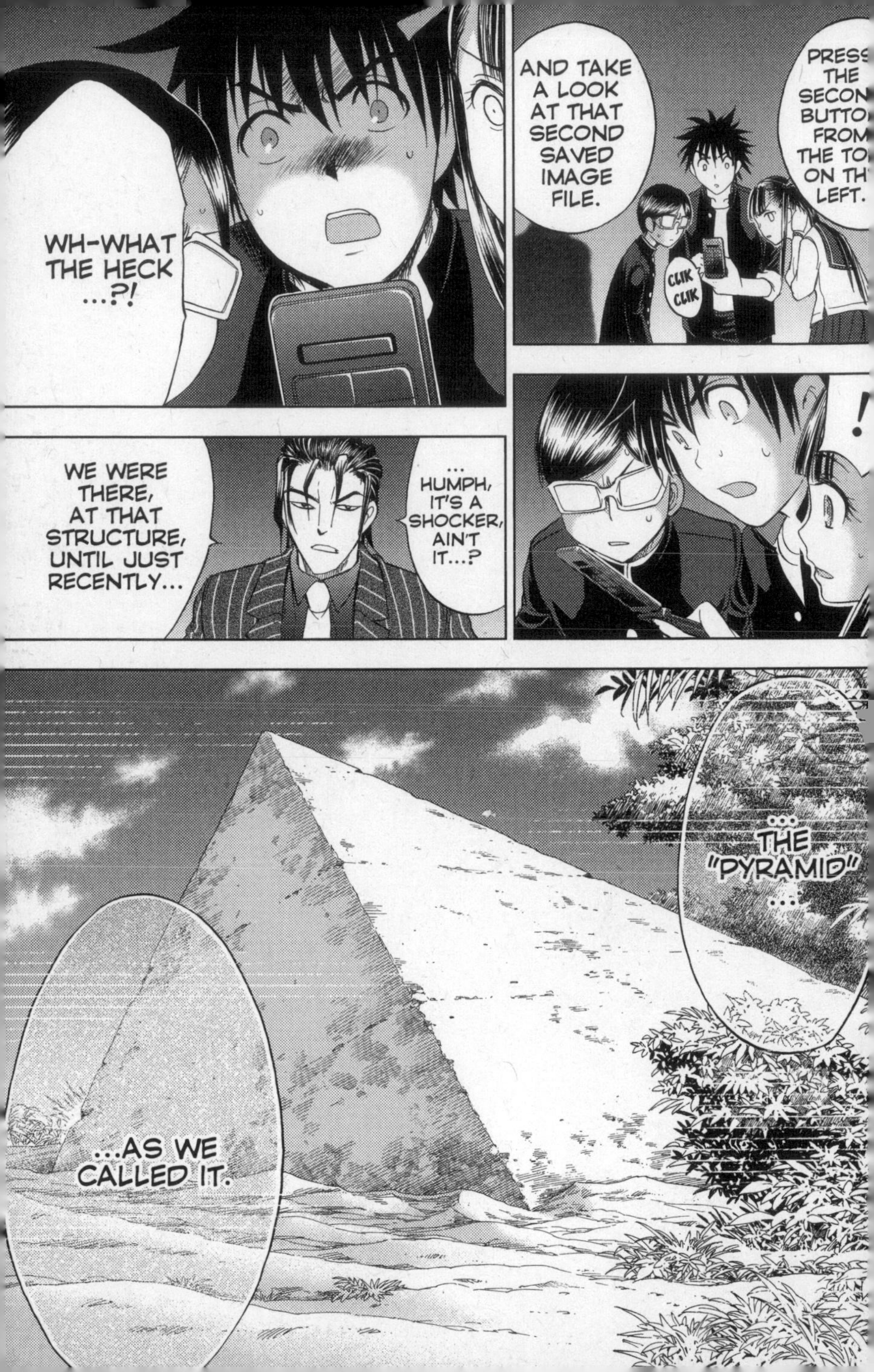
PRESS THE SECON BUTTO FROM THE TO ON TH LEFT.
AND TAKE A LOOK AT THAT SECOND SAVED IMAGE FILE.
CLIK CLIK
WH-WHAT THE HECK ...?!
!
... HUMPH, IT'S A SHOCKER, AIN'T IT...?
WE WERE THERE, AT THAT STRUCTURE, UNTIL JUST RECENTLY...
... THE "PYRAMID" ...
...AS WE CALLED IT.

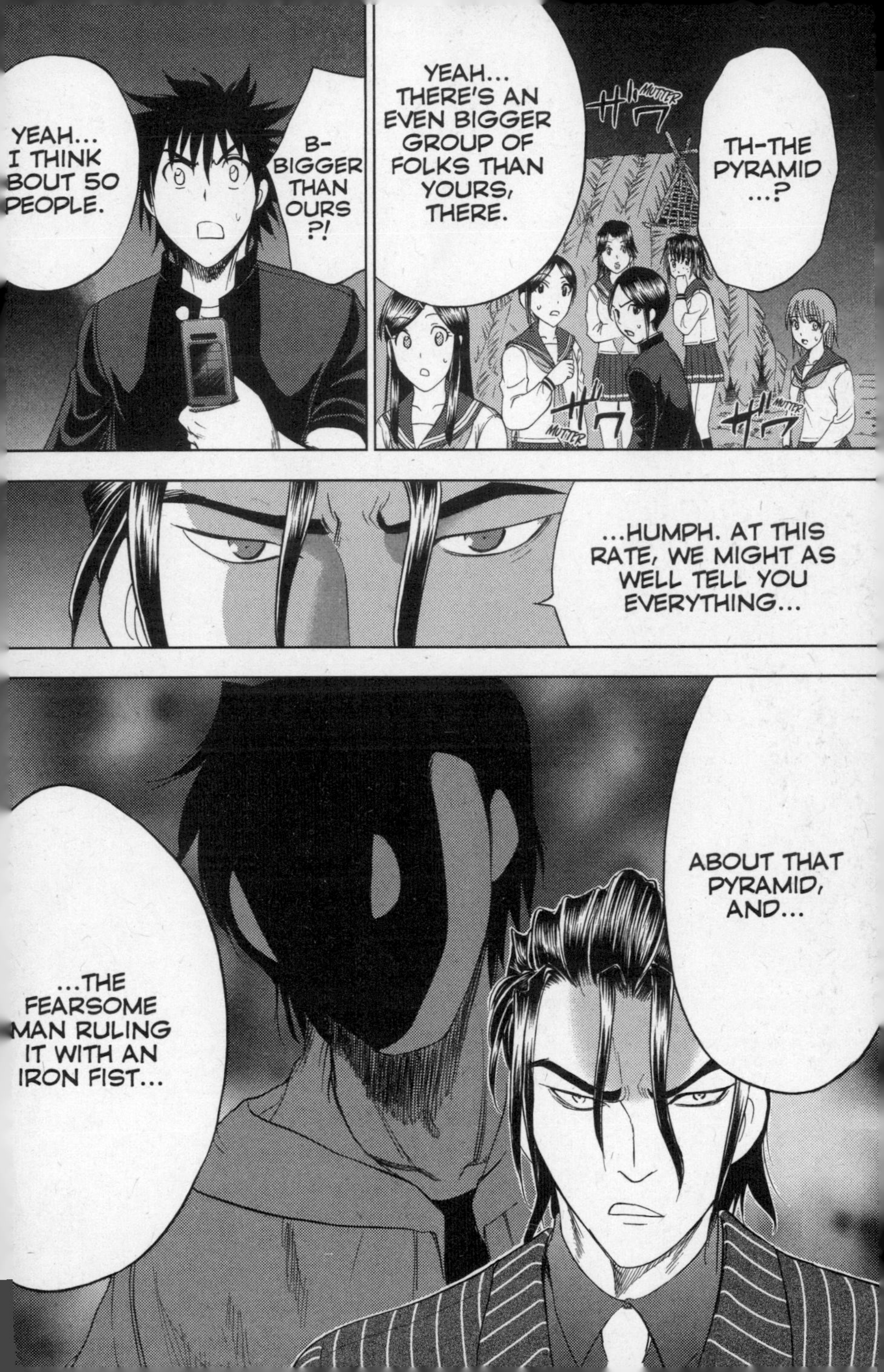
TH-THE PYRAMID ...?
ザワ MUTTER
YEAH... THERE'S AN EVEN BIGGER GROUP OF FOLKS THAN YOURS, THERE.
ザワ MUTTER
ザワ MUTTER
B-BIGGER THAN OURS ?!
YEAH... I THINK BOUT 50 PEOPLE.
...HUMPH. AT THIS RATE, WE MIGHT AS WELL TELL YOU EVERYTHING...
ABOUT THAT PYRAMID, AND...
...THE FEARSOME MAN RULING IT WITH AN IRON FIST...

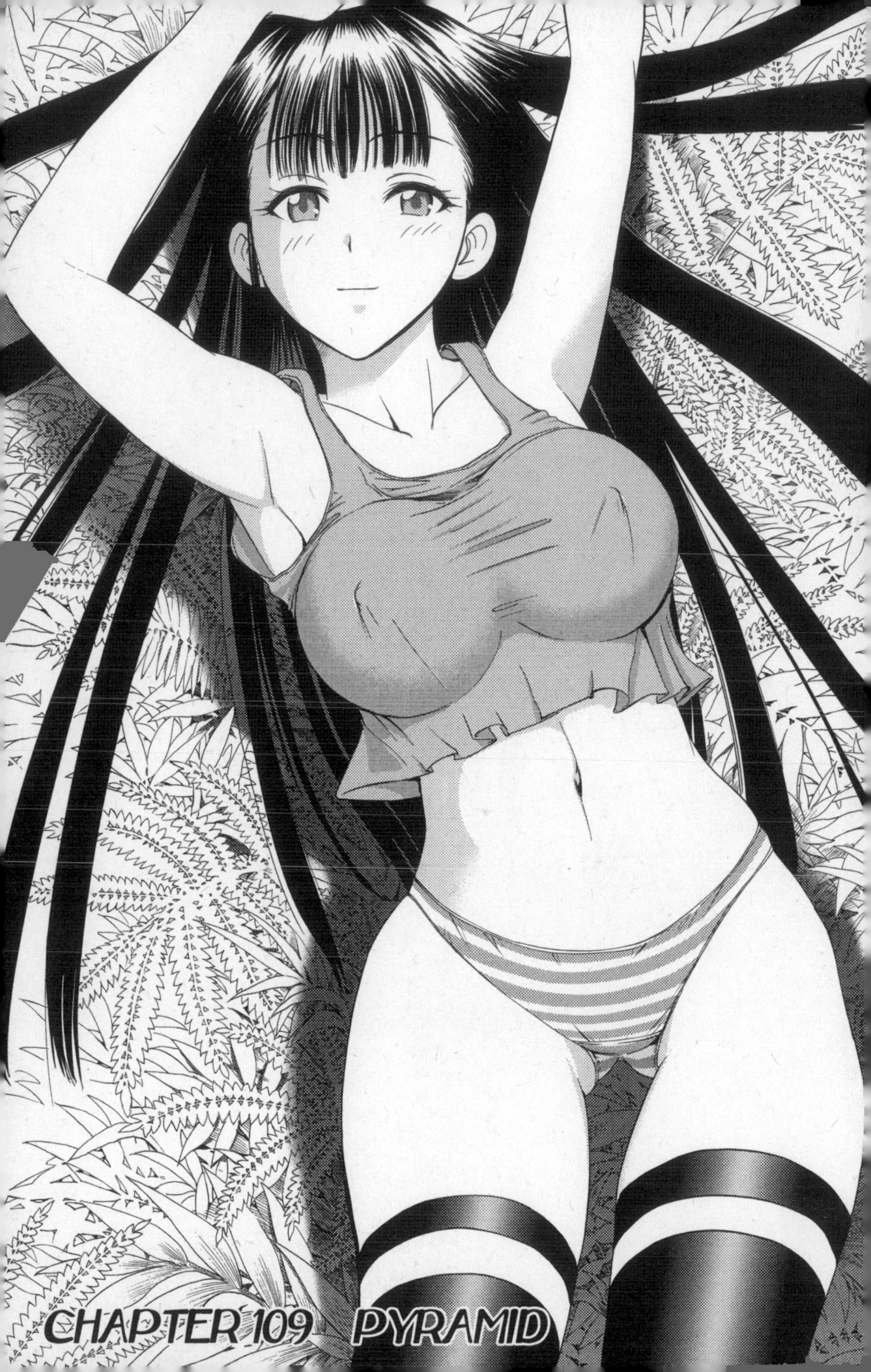
CHAPTER 109 PYRAMID

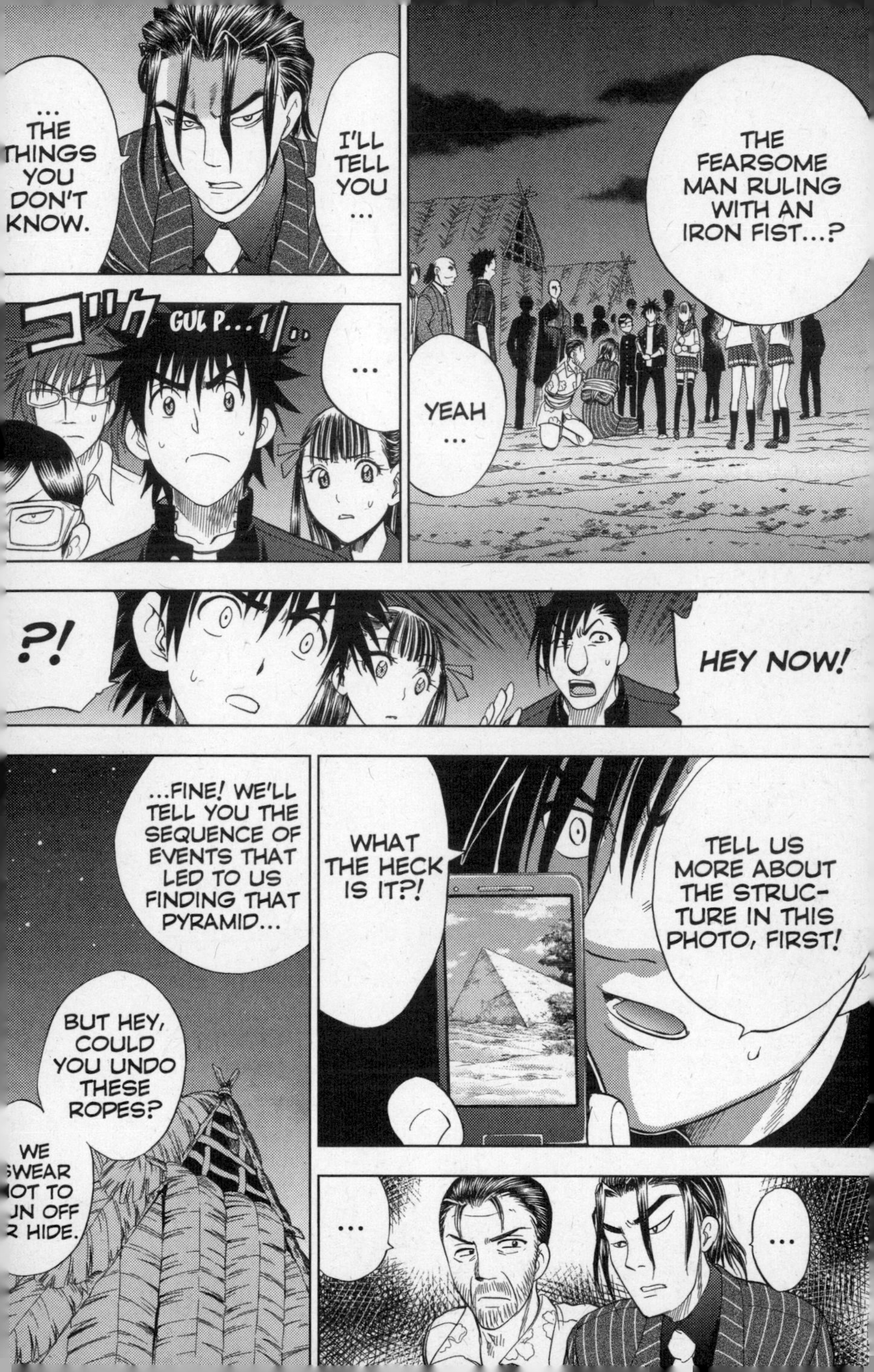

THE FEARSOME MAN RULING WITH AN IRON FIST...?
YEAH ...
I'LL TELL YOU ...
... THE THINGS YOU DON'T KNOW.
...
GULP...!!
HEY NOW!
?!
TELL US MORE ABOUT THE STRUCTURE IN THIS PHOTO, FIRST!
WHAT THE HECK IS IT?!
...
...
...FINE! WE'LL TELL YOU THE SEQUENCE OF EVENTS THAT LED TO US FINDING THAT PYRAMID...
BUT HEY, COULD YOU UNDO THESE ROPES?
WE SWEAR OT TO UN OFF R HIDE.

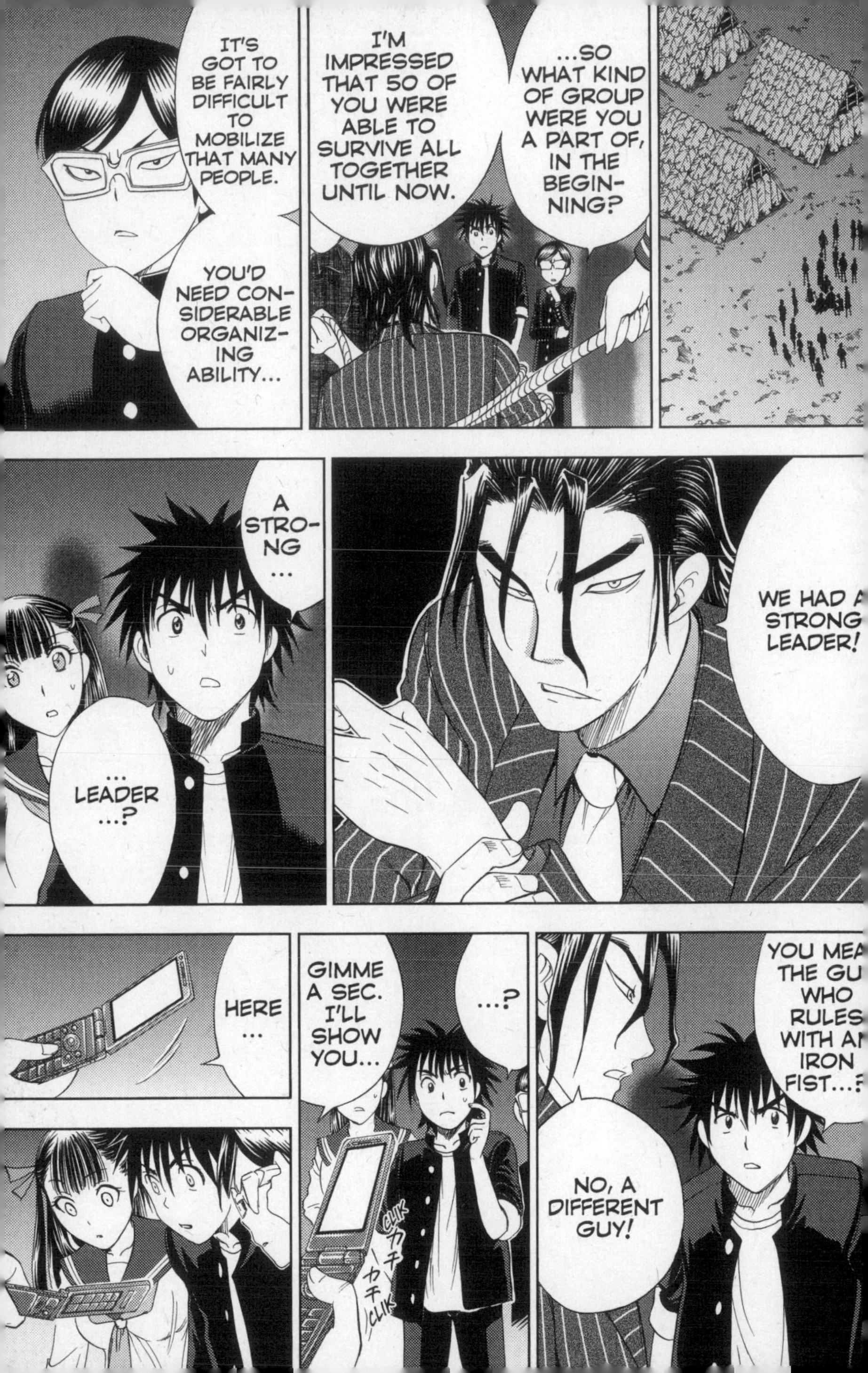
...SO WHAT KIND OF GROUP WERE YOU A PART OF, IN THE BEGINNING?
I'M IMPRESSED THAT 50 OF YOU WERE ABLE TO SURVIVE ALL TOGETHER UNTIL NOW.
IT'S GOT TO BE FAIRLY DIFFICULT TO MOBILIZE THAT MANY PEOPLE.
YOU'D NEED CONSIDERABLE ORGANIZING ABILITY...
WE HAD A STRONG LEADER!
A STRONG...
...LEADER...?
YOU MEA THE GU WHO RULES WITH A IRON FIST...?
NO, A DIFFERENT GUY!
...?
GIMME A SEC. I'LL SHOW YOU...
CLIK
カチ
カチ
CLIK
HERE...

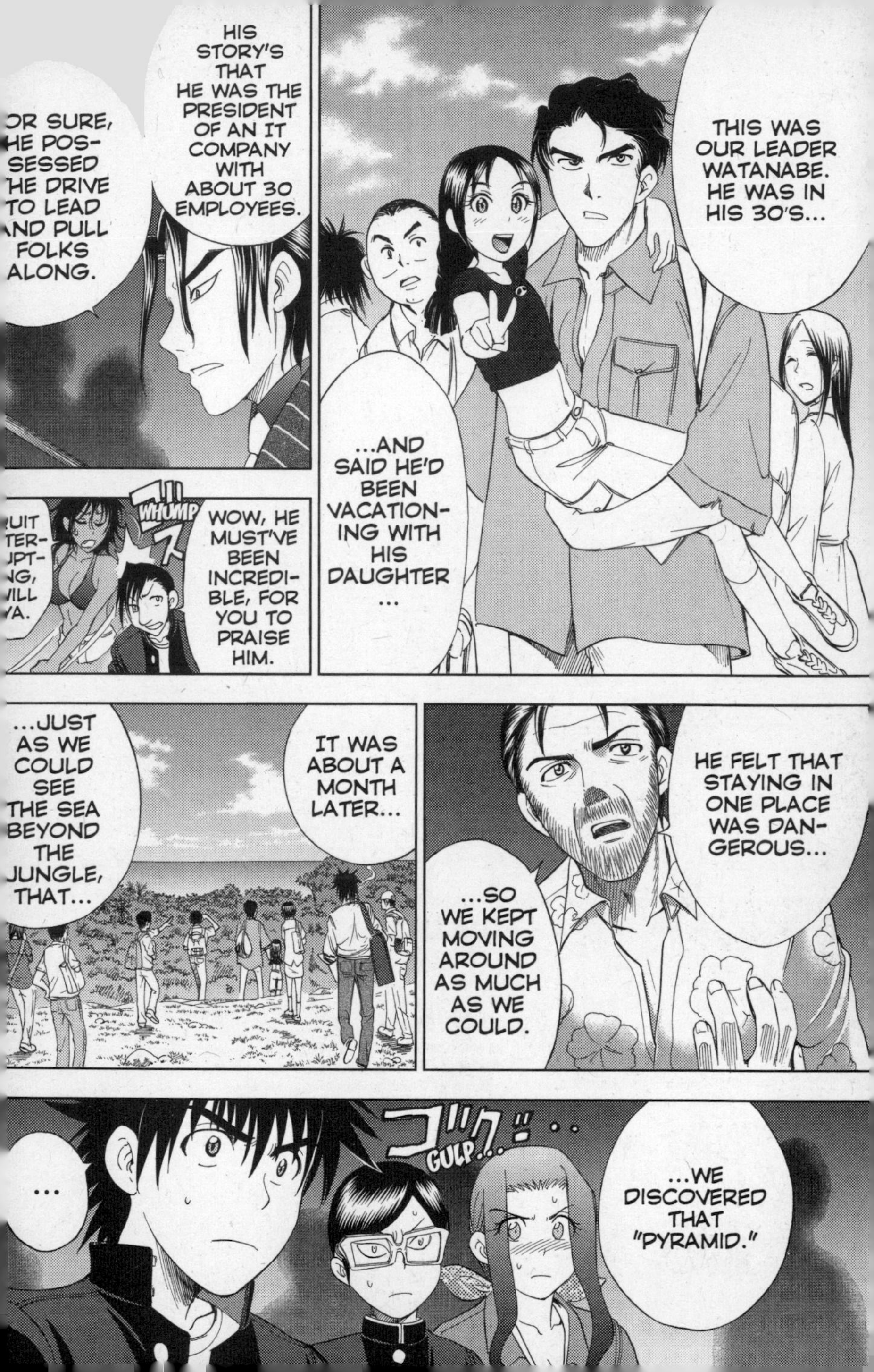
THIS WAS OUR LEADER WATANABE. HE WAS IN HIS 30'S...
...AND SAID HE'D BEEN VACATIONING WITH HIS DAUGHTER...
HIS STORY'S THAT HE WAS THE PRESIDENT OF AN IT COMPANY WITH ABOUT 30 EMPLOYEES.
OR SURE, HE POS-SESSED HE DRIVE TO LEAD ND PULL FOLKS ALONG.
WOW, HE MUST'VE BEEN INCREDI-BLE, FOR YOU TO PRAISE HIM.
WHUMP
UIT TER-UPT-NG, VILL YA.
HE FELT THAT STAYING IN ONE PLACE WAS DAN-GEROUS...
...SO WE KEPT MOVING AROUND AS MUCH AS WE COULD.
IT WAS ABOUT A MONTH LATER...
...JUST AS WE COULD SEE THE SEA BEYOND THE JUNGLE, THAT...
...WE DISCOVERED THAT "PYRAMID."
GULP
...

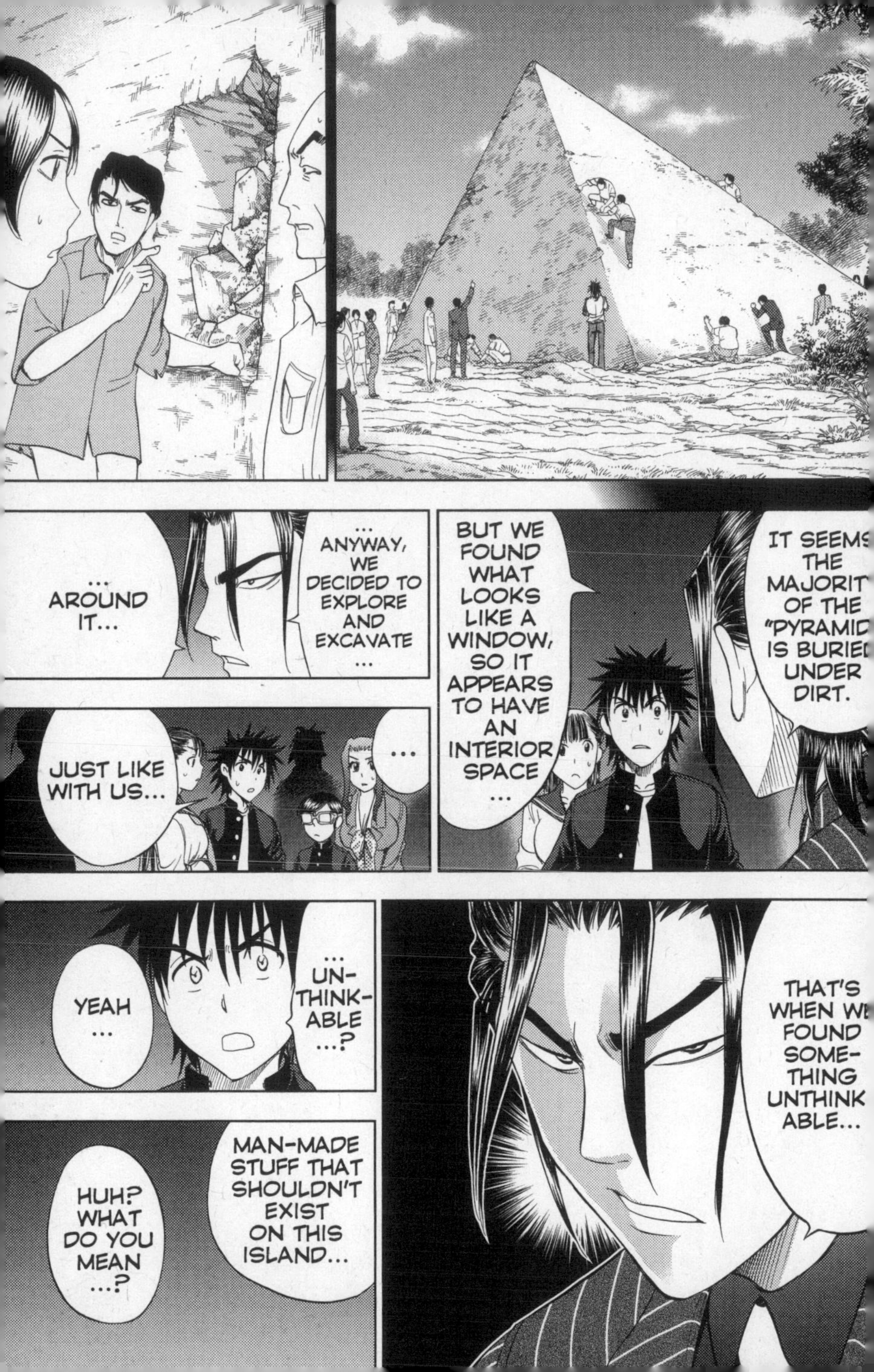

IT SEEMS THE MAJORIT OF THE "PYRAMID IS BURIED UNDER DIRT.
BUT WE FOUND WHAT LOOKS LIKE A WINDOW, SO IT APPEARS TO HAVE AN INTERIOR SPACE ...
... ANYWAY, WE DECIDED TO EXPLORE AND EXCAVATE ...
... AROUND IT...
...
JUST LIKE WITH US...
THAT'S WHEN W FOUND SOME-THING UNTHINK ABLE...
... UN-THINK-ABLE ...?
YEAH ...
MAN-MADE STUFF THAT SHOULDN'T EXIST ON THIS ISLAND...
HUH? WHAT DO YOU MEAN ...?

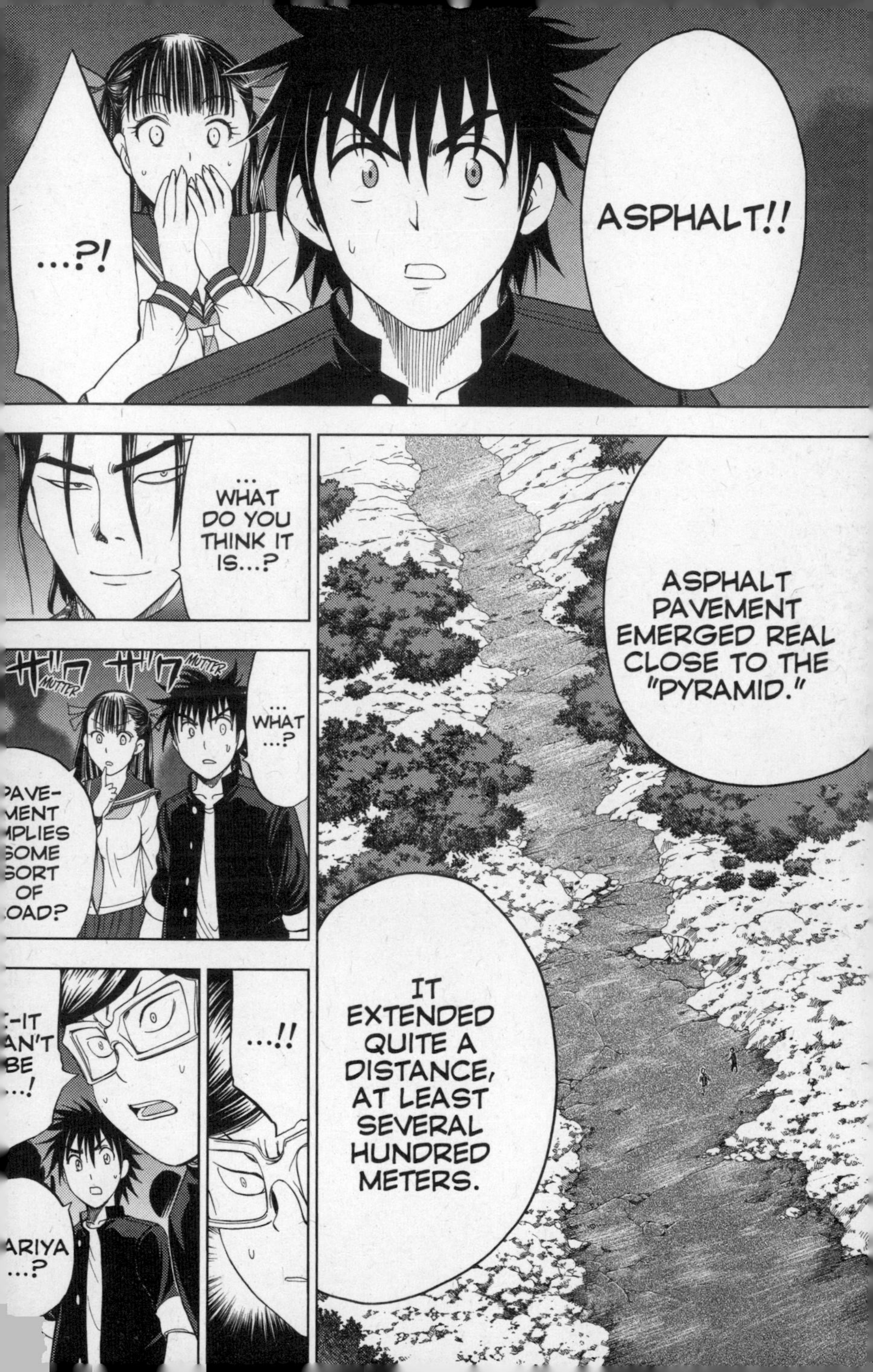
ASPHALT!!
...?!
ASPHALT PAVEMENT EMERGED REAL CLOSE TO THE "PYRAMID."
IT EXTENDED QUITE A DISTANCE, AT LEAST SEVERAL HUNDRED METERS.
... WHAT DO YOU THINK IT IS...?
ザワ ザワ
MUTTER MUTTER
... WHAT ...?
PAVE- MENT MPLIES SOME SORT OF OAD?
...!!
-IT AN'T BE ...!
ARIYA ...?

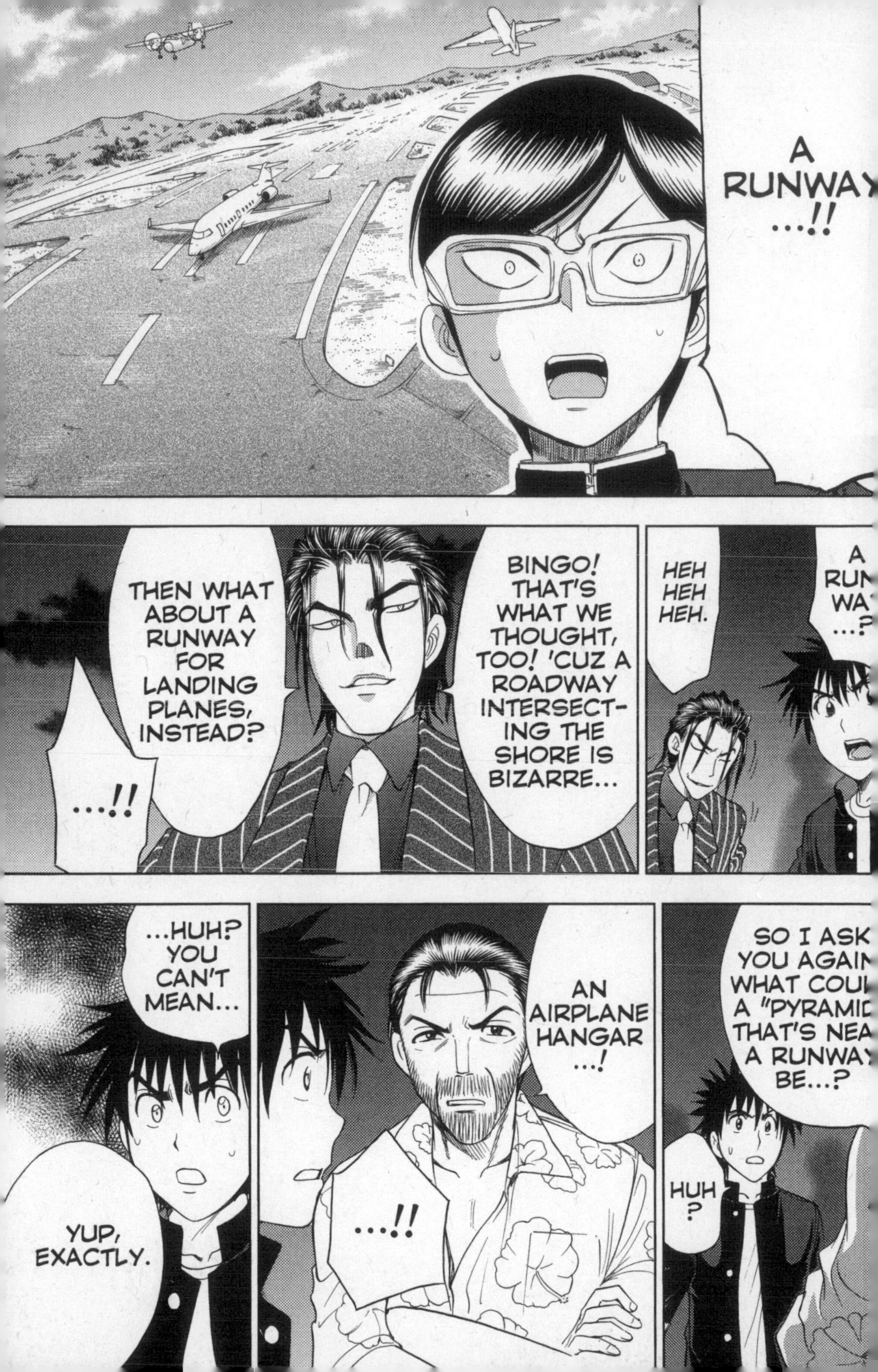
A RUNWAY ...!!
A RUN WA ...?
HEH HEH HEH.
BINGO! THAT'S WHAT WE THOUGHT, TOO! 'CUZ A ROADWAY INTERSECT-ING THE SHORE IS BIZARRE...
THEN WHAT ABOUT A RUNWAY FOR LANDING PLANES, INSTEAD?
...!!
SO I ASK YOU AGAIN WHAT COUL A "PYRAMID THAT'S NEA A RUNWAY BE...?
HUH ?
AN AIRPLANE HANGAR ...!
...!!
...HUH? YOU CAN'T MEAN...
YUP, EXACTLY.

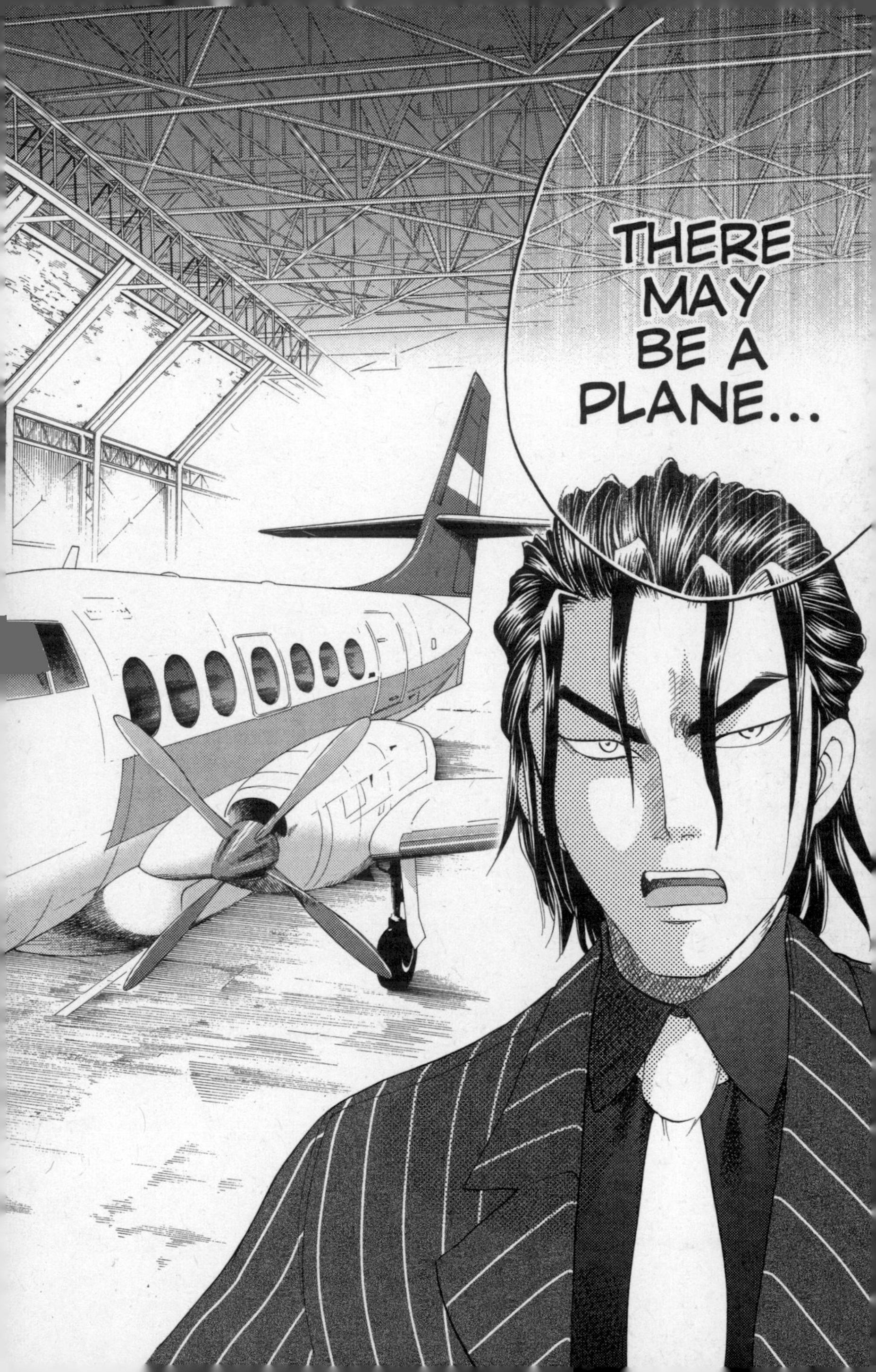
THERE MAY BE A PLANE...

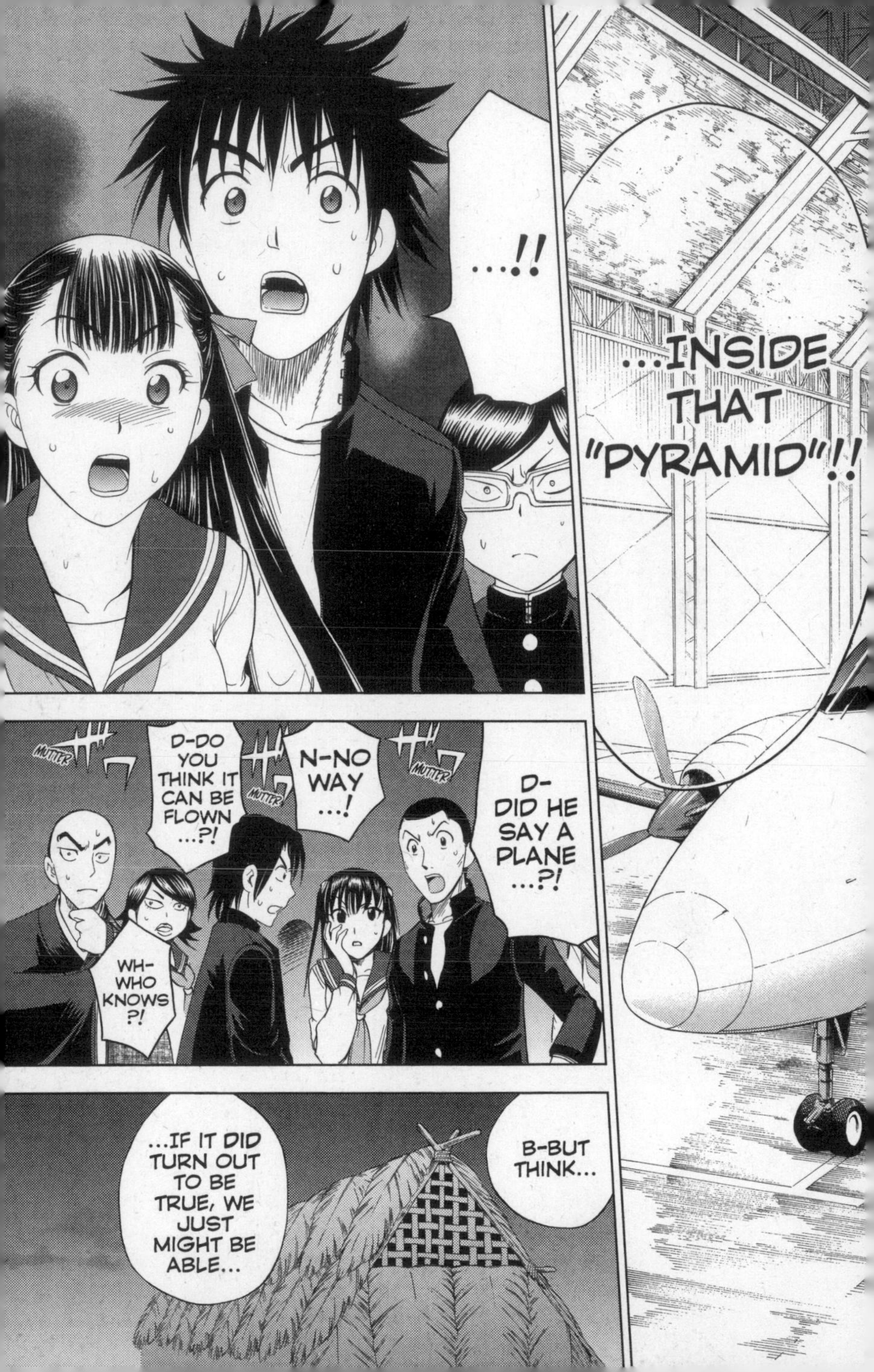
...INSIDE THAT "PYRAMID"!!
...!!
D-DID HE SAY A PLANE ...?!
MUTTER
N-NO WAY ...!
MUTTER
D-DO YOU THINK IT CAN BE FLOWN ...?!
MUTTER
WH-WHO KNOWS ?!
B-BUT THINK...
...IF IT DID TURN OUT TO BE TRUE, WE JUST MIGHT BE ABLE...

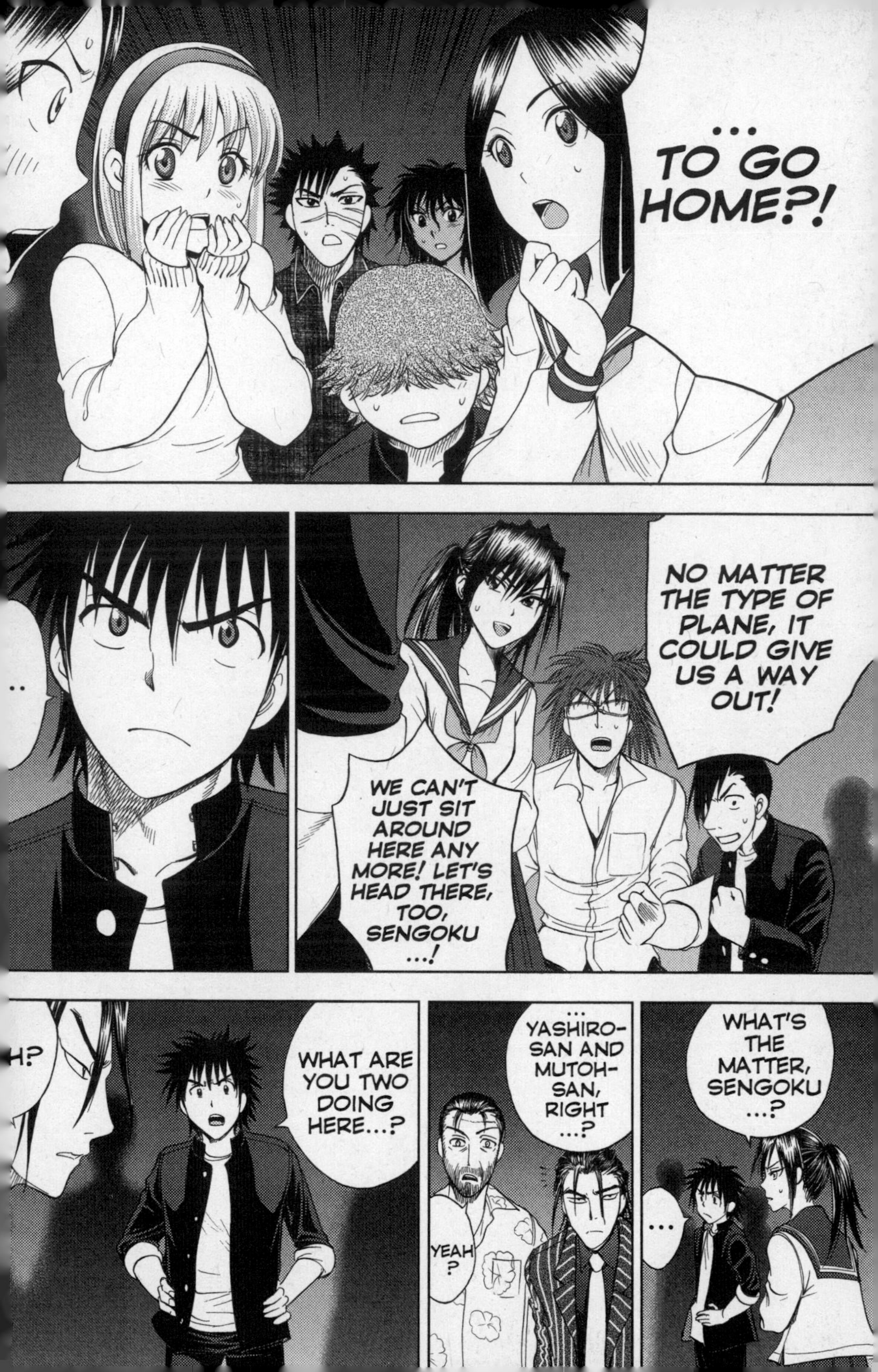
... TO GO HOME?!
NO MATTER THE TYPE OF PLANE, IT COULD GIVE US A WAY OUT!
WE CAN'T JUST SIT AROUND HERE ANY MORE! LET'S HEAD THERE, TOO, SENGOKU ...!
WHAT'S THE MATTER, SENGOKU ...?
...
... YASHIRO-SAN AND MUTOH-SAN, RIGHT ...?
YEAH ?
WHAT ARE YOU TWO DOING HERE...?

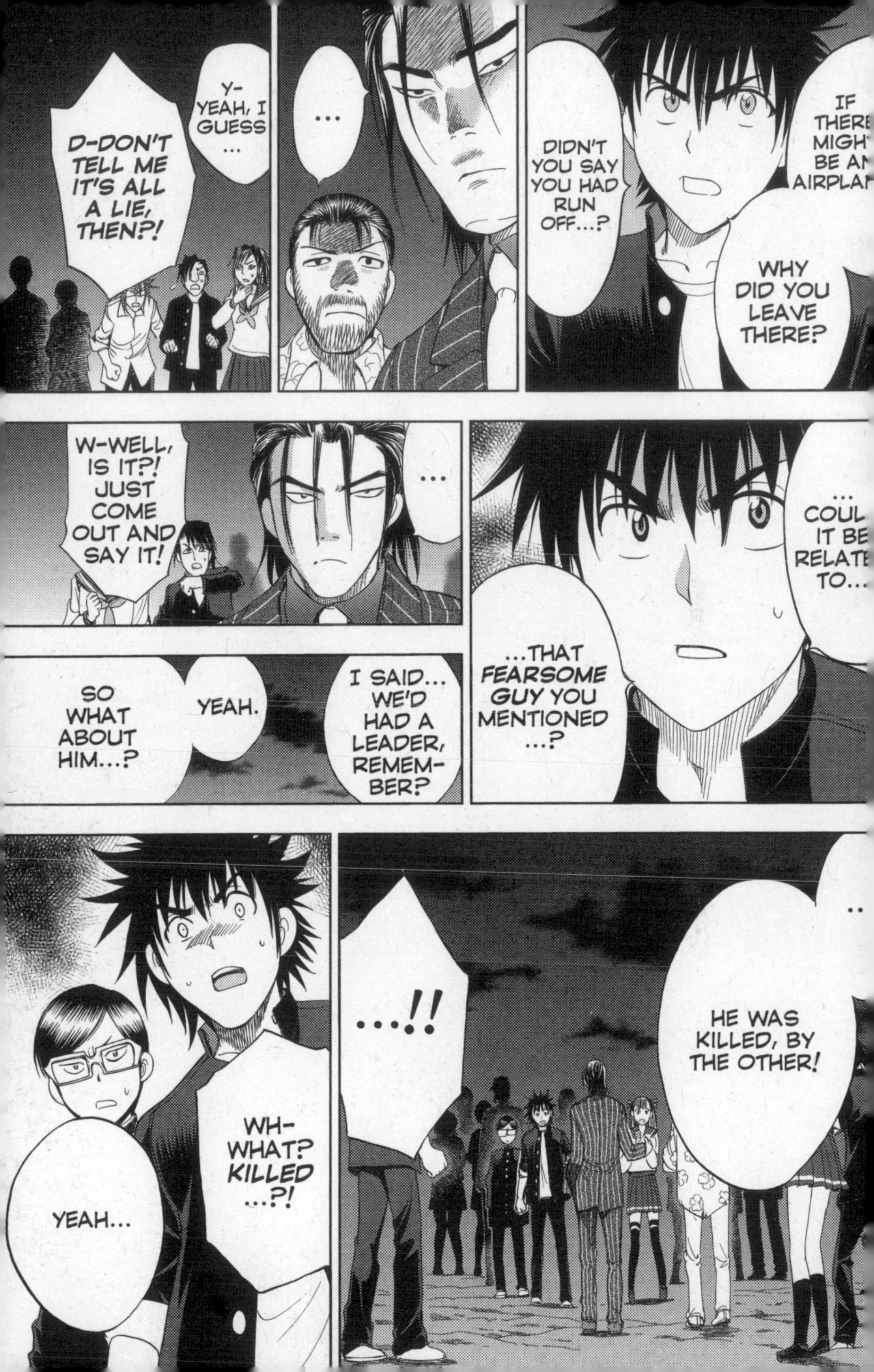
IF THERE MIGHT BE AN AIRPLAN
WHY DID YOU LEAVE THERE?
DIDN'T YOU SAY YOU HAD RUN OFF...?
...
Y-YEAH, I GUESS...
D-DON'T TELL ME IT'S ALL A LIE, THEN?!
... COUL IT BE RELATE TO...
...THAT FEARSOME GUY YOU MENTIONED...?
...
W-WELL, IS IT?! JUST COME OUT AND SAY IT!
I SAID... WE'D HAD A LEADER, REMEMBER?
YEAH.
SO WHAT ABOUT HIM...?
..
HE WAS KILLED, BY THE OTHER!
...!!
WH-WHAT? KILLED...?!
YEAH...

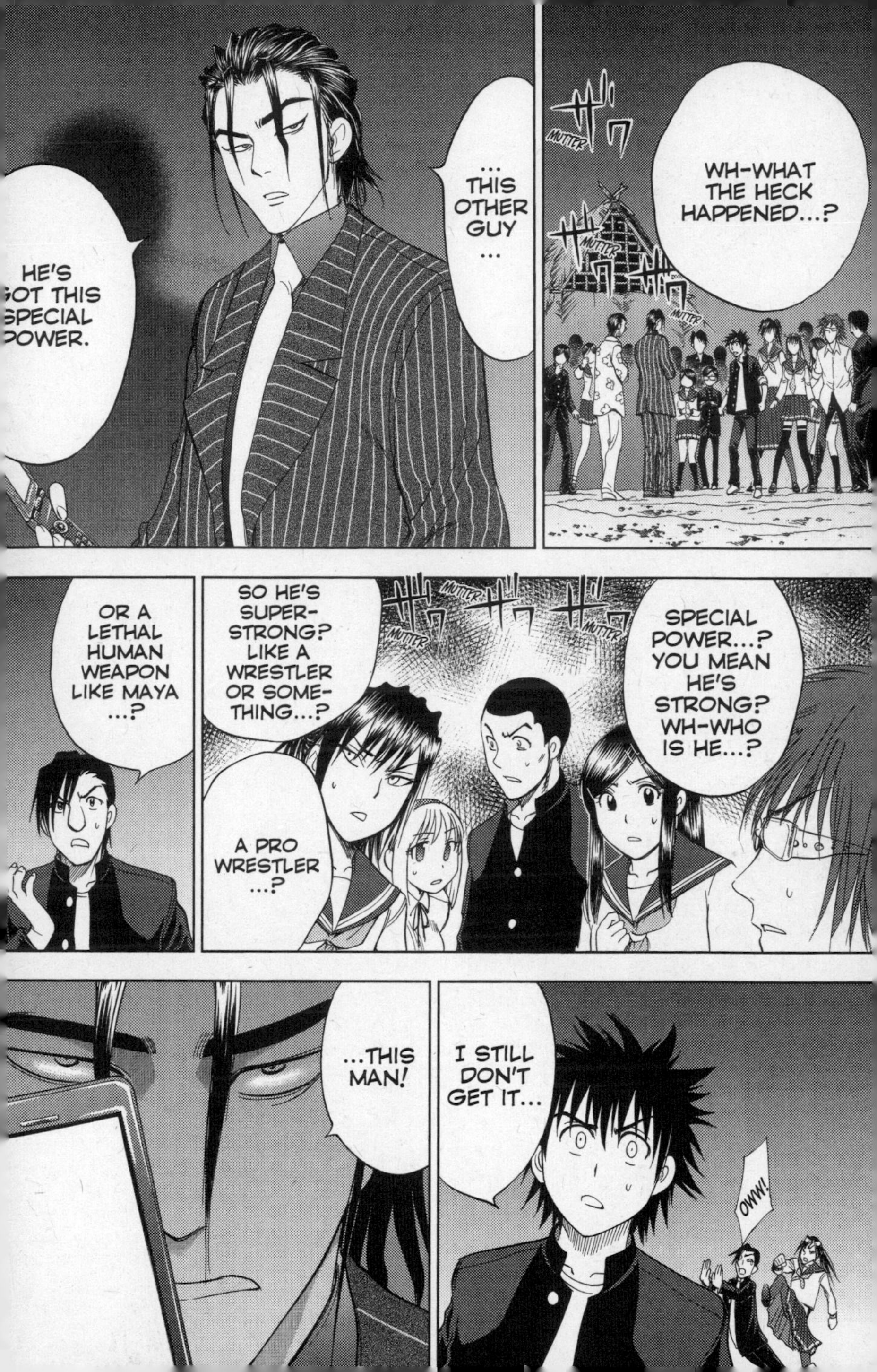
MUTTER
MUTTER
MUTTER
WH-WHAT THE HECK HAPPENED...?
... THIS OTHER GUY ...
HE'S GOT THIS SPECIAL POWER.
SPECIAL POWER...? YOU MEAN HE'S STRONG? WH-WHO IS HE...?
MUTTER
MUTTER
MUTTER
SO HE'S SUPER-STRONG? LIKE A WRESTLER OR SOME-THING...?
A PRO WRESTLER ...?
OR A LETHAL HUMAN WEAPON LIKE MAYA ...?
I STILL DON'T GET IT...
OWW!
...THIS MAN!

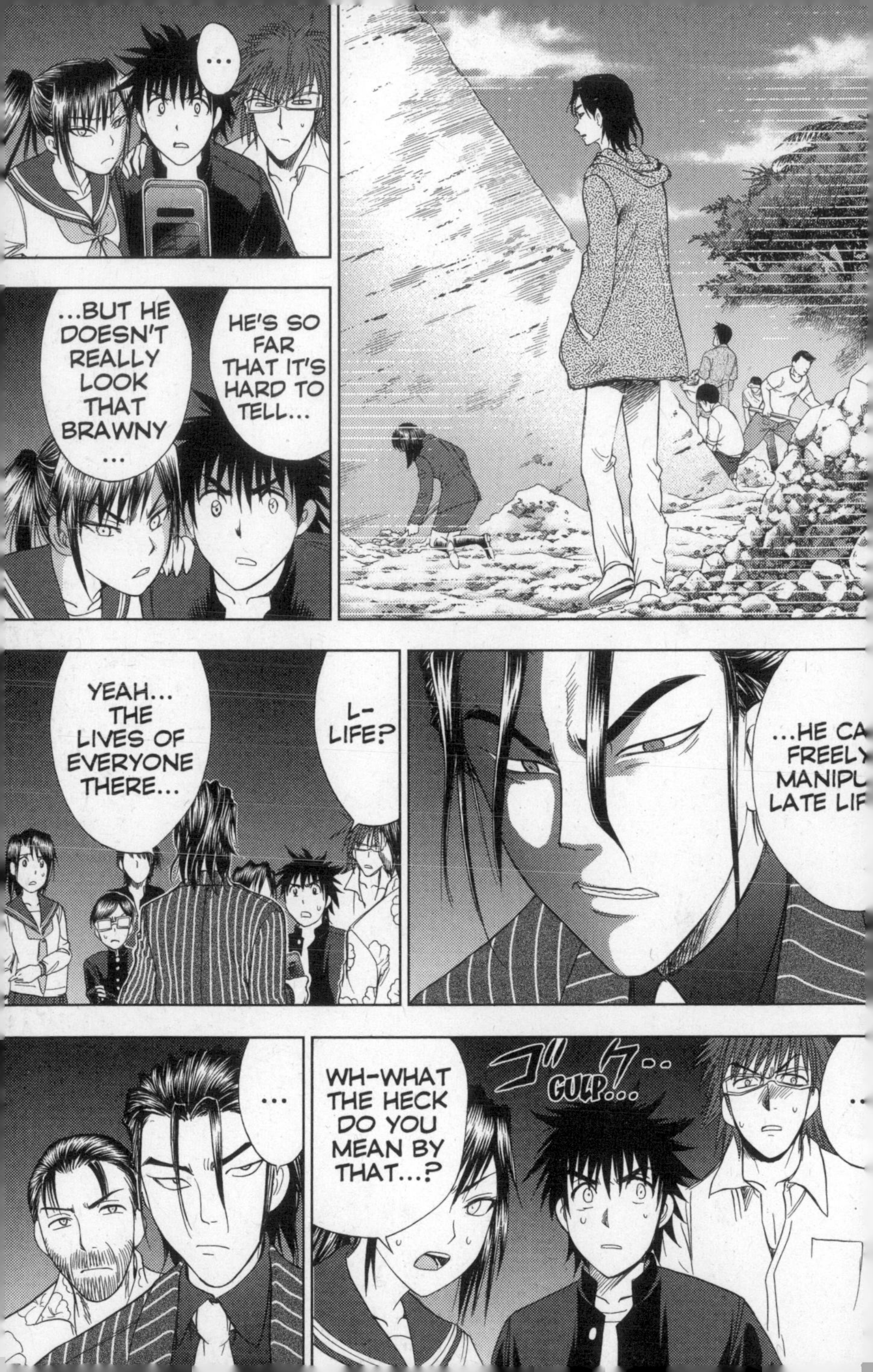
...
HE'S SO FAR THAT IT'S HARD TO TELL...
...BUT HE DOESN'T REALLY LOOK THAT BRAWNY ...
...HE CA FREELY MANIPU LATE LIF
L-LIFE?
YEAH... THE LIVES OF EVERYONE THERE...
GULP...
WH-WHAT THE HECK DO YOU MEAN BY THAT...?
...

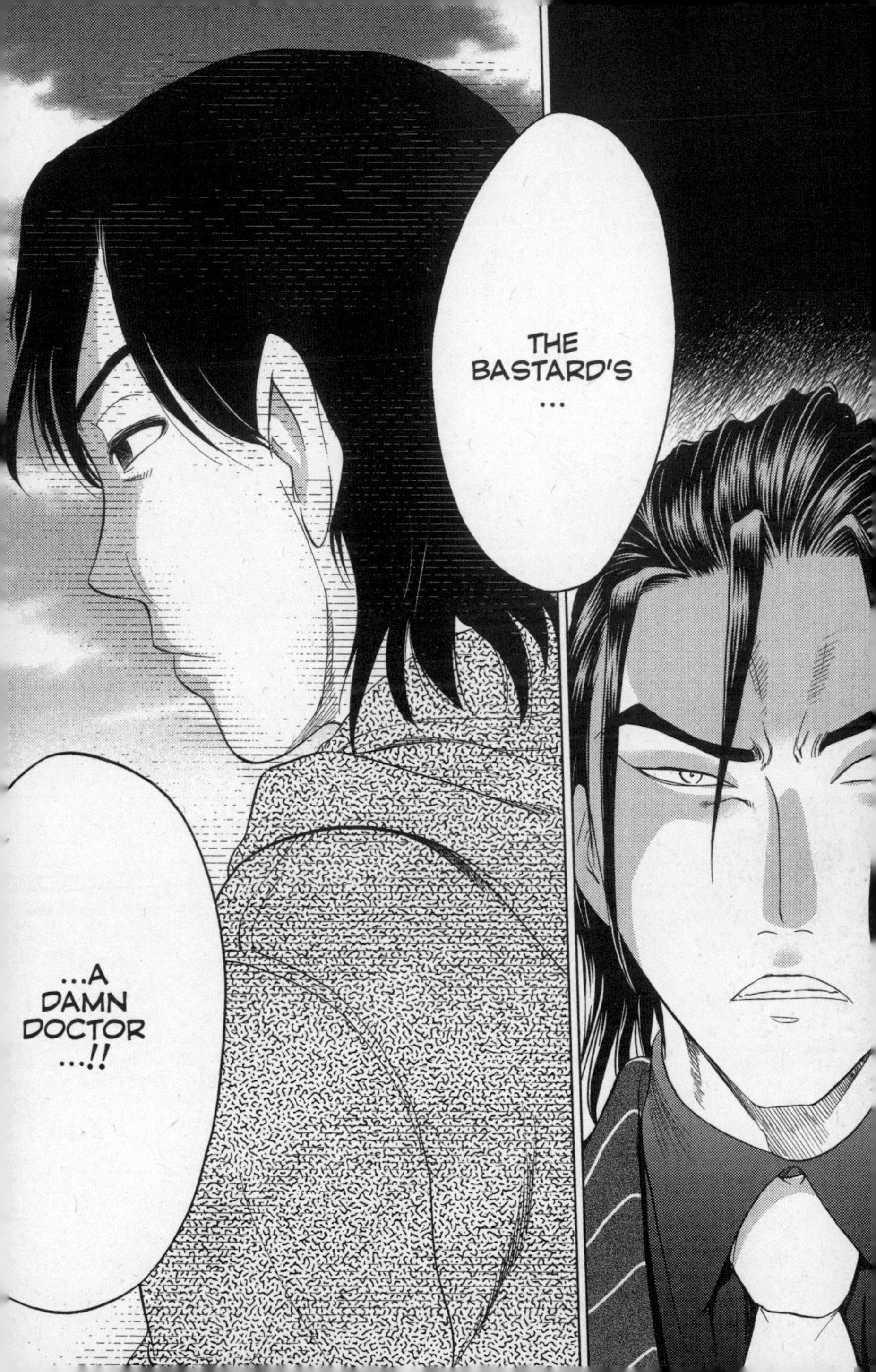
THE BASTARD'S ...
...A DAMN DOCTOR ...!!

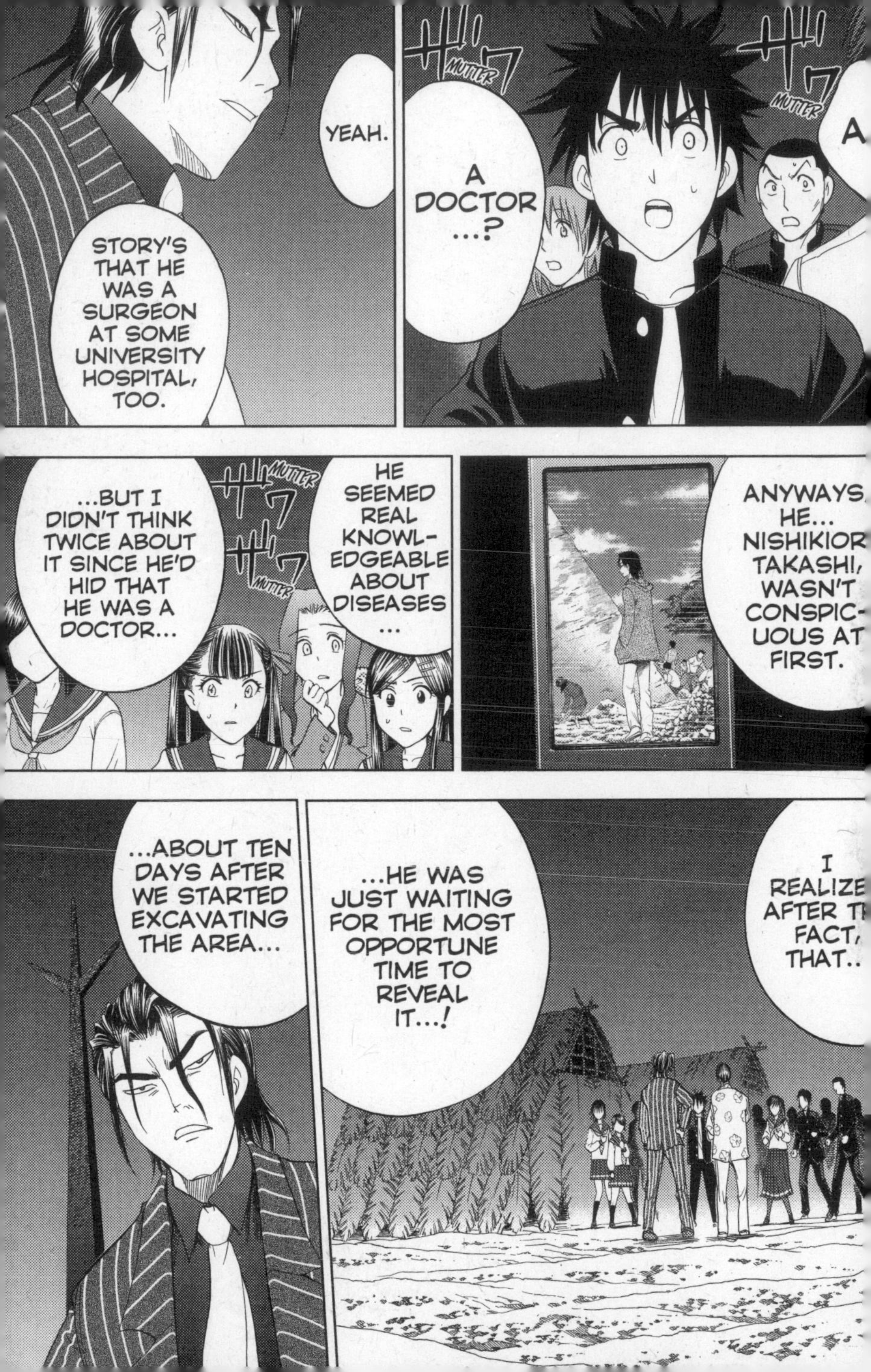
A
MUTTER
A DOCTOR ...?
MUTTER
YEAH.
STORY'S THAT HE WAS A SURGEON AT SOME UNIVERSITY HOSPITAL, TOO.
ANYWAYS, HE... NISHIKIOR TAKASHI, WASN'T CONSPIC-UOUS AT FIRST.
HE SEEMED REAL KNOWL-EDGEABLE ABOUT DISEASES ...
MUTTER
MUTTER
...BUT I DIDN'T THINK TWICE ABOUT IT SINCE HE'D HID THAT HE WAS A DOCTOR...
I REALIZE AFTER T FACT, THAT..
...HE WAS JUST WAITING FOR THE MOST OPPORTUNE TIME TO REVEAL IT...!
...ABOUT TEN DAYS AFTER WE STARTED EXCAVATING THE AREA...

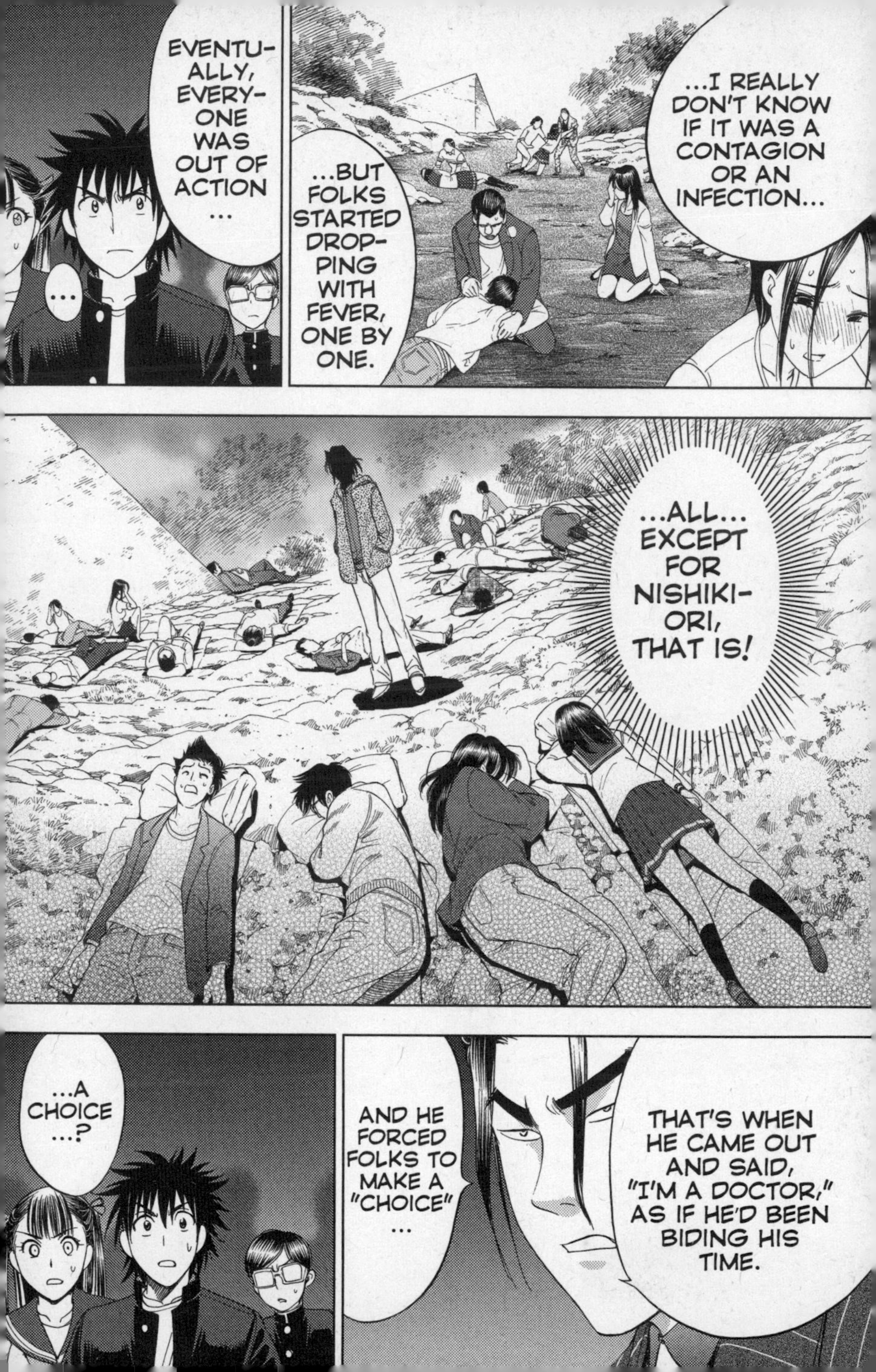
...I REALLY DON'T KNOW IF IT WAS A CONTAGION OR AN INFECTION...
...BUT FOLKS STARTED DROP-PING WITH FEVER, ONE BY ONE.
EVENTU-ALLY, EVERY-ONE WAS OUT OF ACTION ...
....
...ALL... EXCEPT FOR NISHIKI-ORI, THAT IS!
THAT'S WHEN HE CAME OUT AND SAID, "I'M A DOCTOR," AS IF HE'D BEEN BIDING HIS TIME.
AND HE FORCED FOLKS TO MAKE A "CHOICE" ...
...A CHOICE ...?

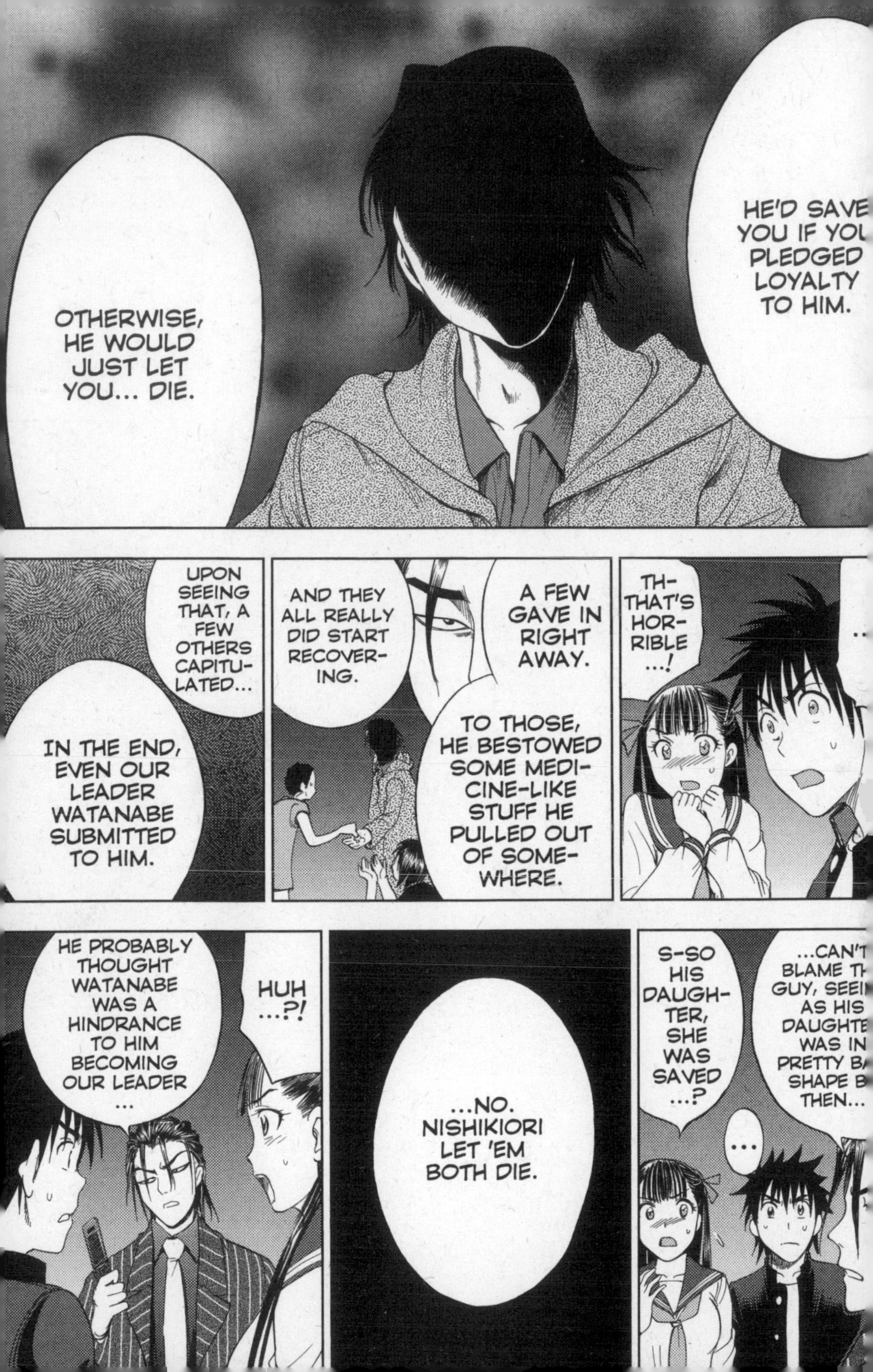
HE'D SAVE YOU IF YOU PLEDGED LOYALTY TO HIM.
OTHERWISE, HE WOULD JUST LET YOU... DIE.
TH-THAT'S HORRIBLE...!
...
A FEW GAVE IN RIGHT AWAY.
TO THOSE, HE BESTOWED SOME MEDICINE-LIKE STUFF HE PULLED OUT OF SOMEWHERE.
AND THEY ALL REALLY DID START RECOVERING.
UPON SEEING THAT, A FEW OTHERS CAPITULATED...
IN THE END, EVEN OUR LEADER WATANABE SUBMITTED TO HIM.
...CAN'T BLAME TH GUY, SEEI AS HIS DAUGHTE WAS IN PRETTY BA SHAPE B THEN...
S-SO HIS DAUGHTER, SHE WAS SAVED...?
...
...NO. NISHIKIORI LET 'EM BOTH DIE.
HUH...?!
HE PROBABLY THOUGHT WATANABE WAS A HINDRANCE TO HIM BECOMING OUR LEADER...

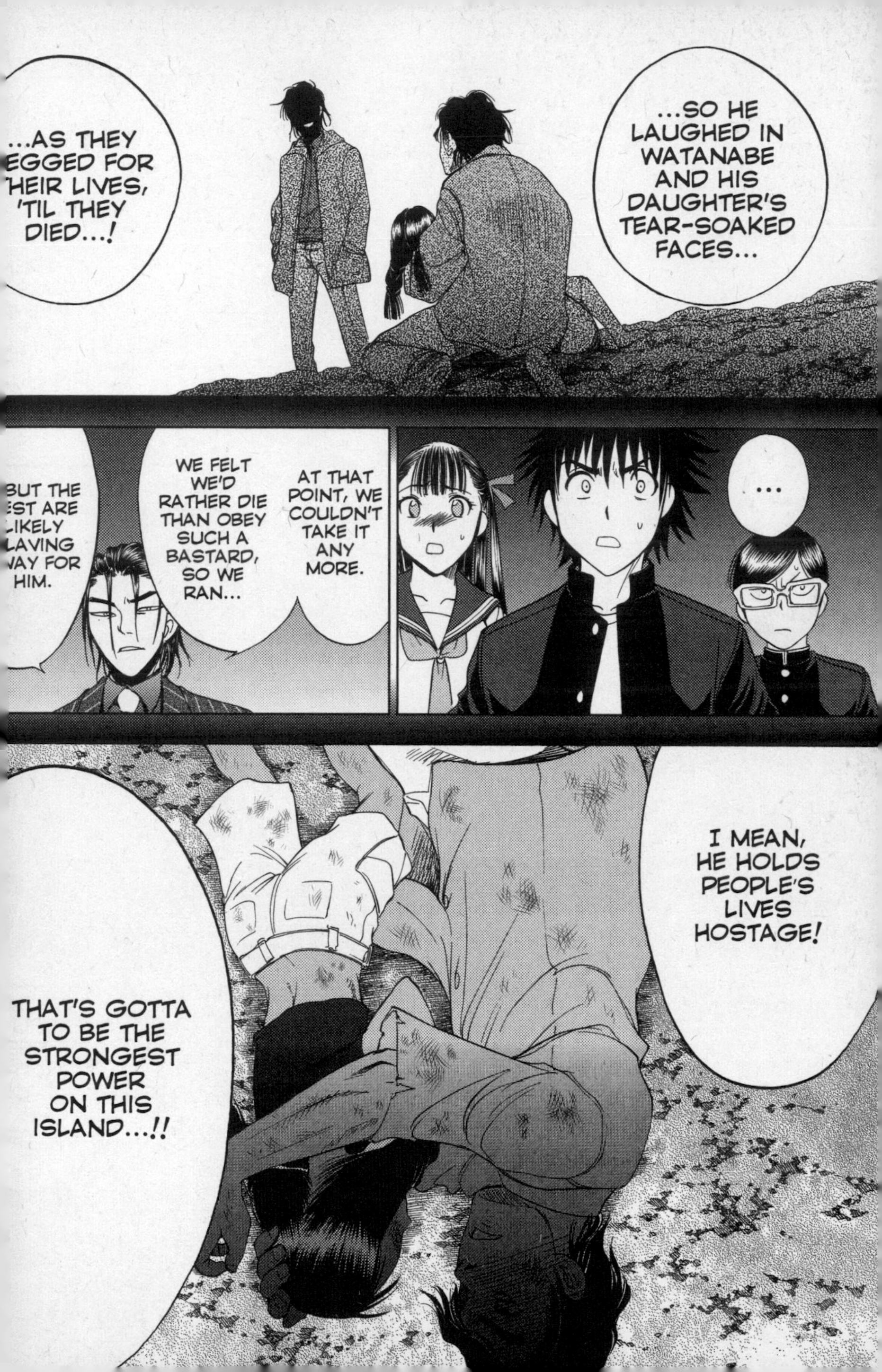
...SO HE LAUGHED IN WATANABE AND HIS DAUGHTER'S TEAR-SOAKED FACES...
...AS THEY EGGED FOR HEIR LIVES, 'TIL THEY DIED...!
...
AT THAT POINT, WE COULDN'T TAKE IT ANY MORE.
WE FELT WE'D RATHER DIE THAN OBEY SUCH A BASTARD, SO WE RAN...
BUT THE EST ARE LIKELY LAVING WAY FOR HIM.
I MEAN, HE HOLDS PEOPLE'S LIVES HOSTAGE!
THAT'S GOTTA TO BE THE STRONGEST POWER ON THIS ISLAND...!!

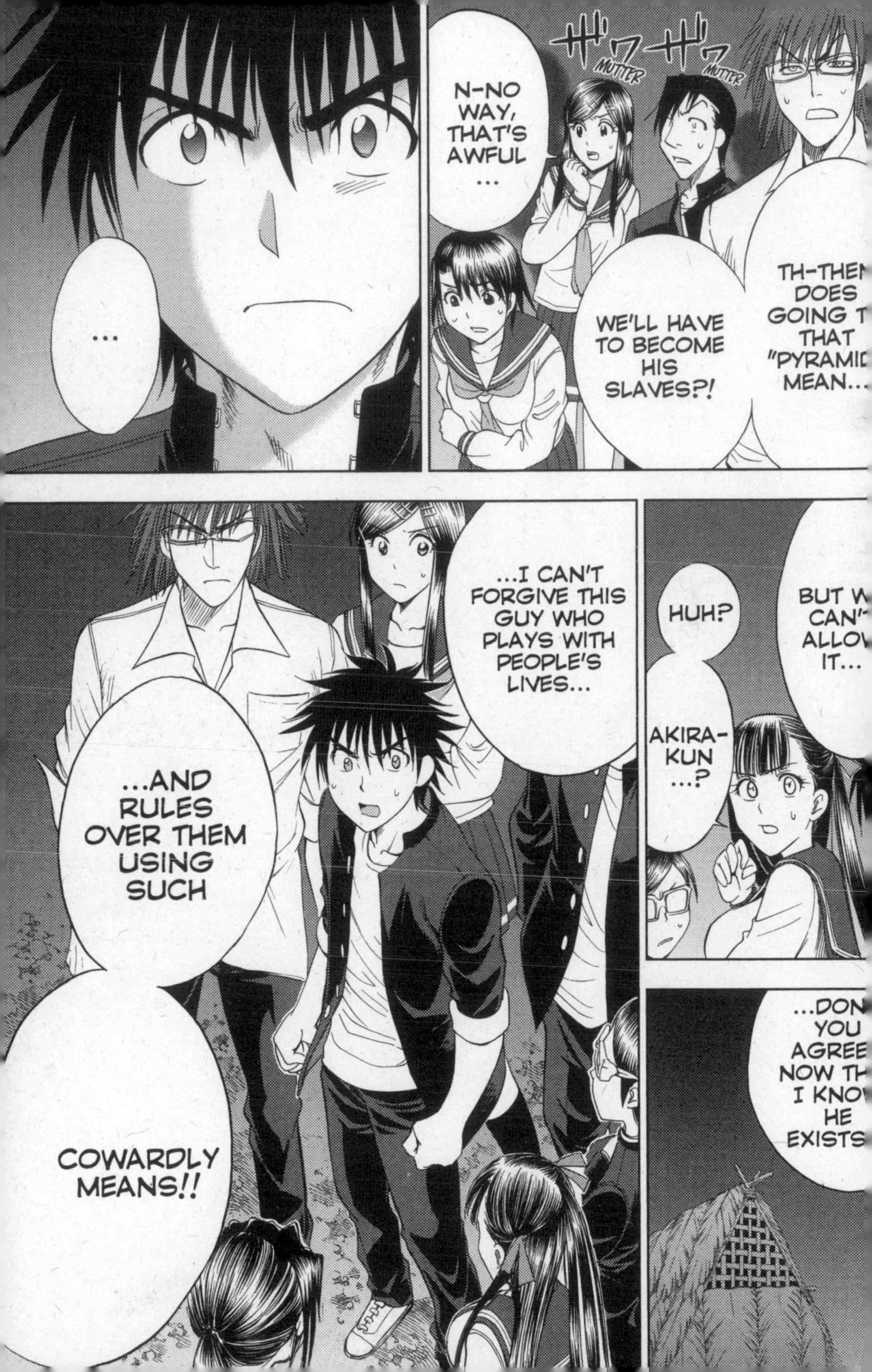
ザワザワ
MUTTER MUTTER
N-NO WAY, THAT'S AWFUL ...
TH-THEN DOES GOING T THAT "PYRAMID MEAN...
WE'LL HAVE TO BECOME HIS SLAVES?!
...
BUT W CAN'T ALLOW IT...
HUH?
AKIRA-KUN ...?
...DON YOU AGREE NOW TH I KNOW HE EXISTS
...I CAN'T FORGIVE THIS GUY WHO PLAYS WITH PEOPLE'S LIVES...
...AND RULES OVER THEM USING SUCH
COWARDLY MEANS!!

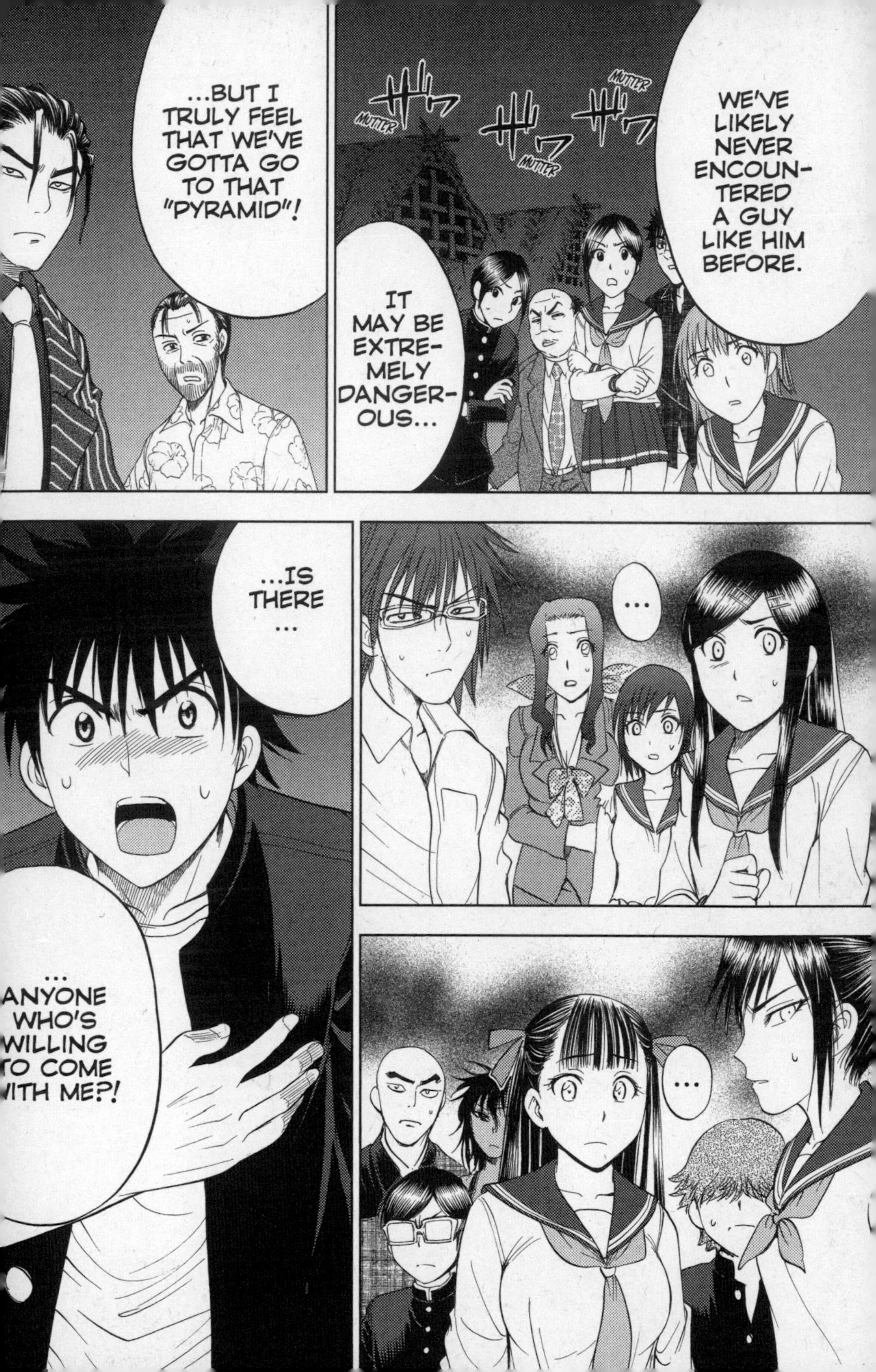
WE'VE LIKELY NEVER ENCOUN-TERED A GUY LIKE HIM BEFORE.
ザワ MUTTER
ザワ MUTTER
ザワ MUTTER
IT MAY BE EXTRE-MELY DANGER-OUS...
...BUT I TRULY FEEL THAT WE'VE GOTTA GO TO THAT "PYRAMID"!
...
...
...IS THERE ...
... ANYONE WHO'S WILLING TO COME WITH ME?!

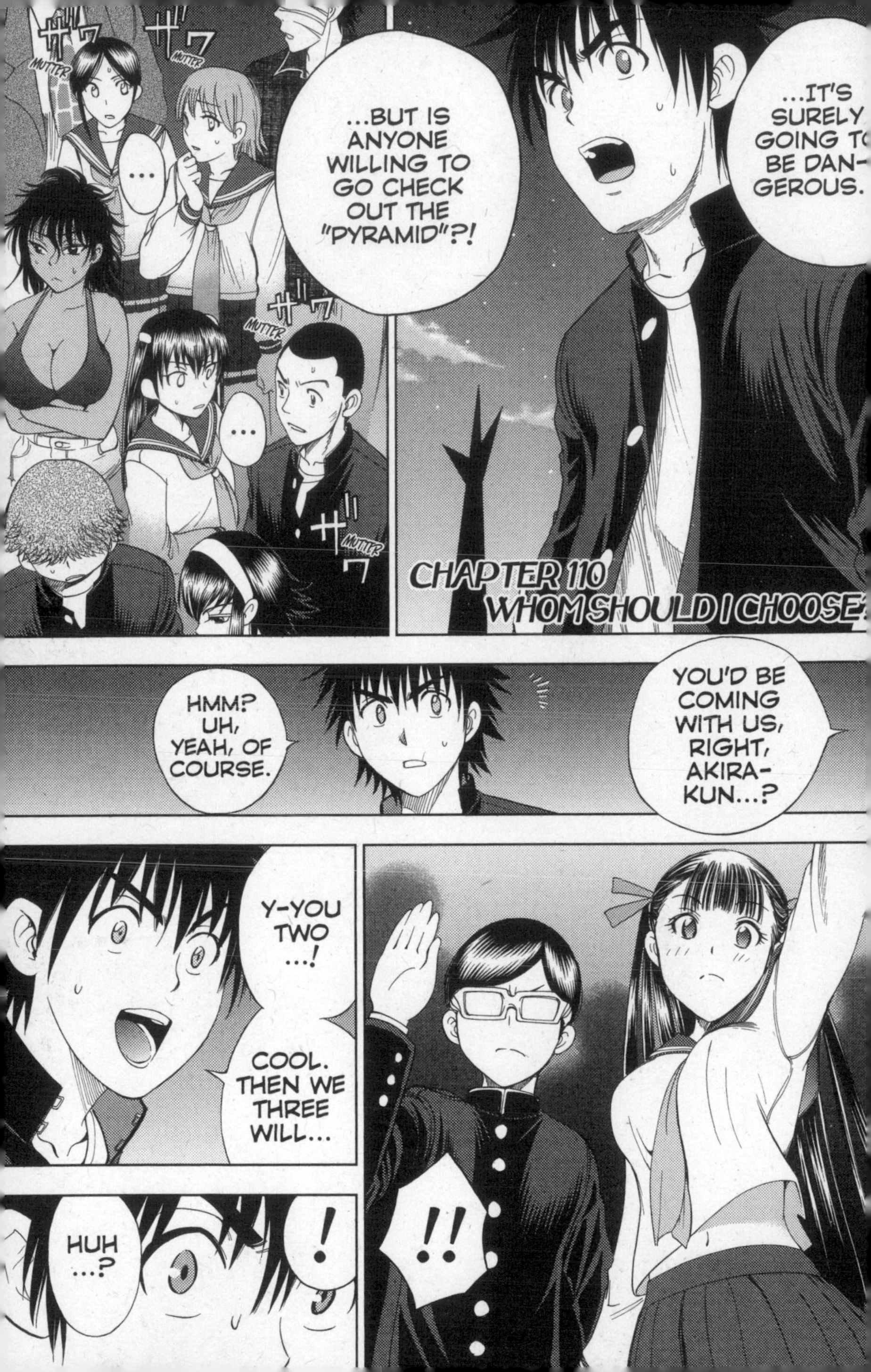
...IT'S SURELY GOING TO BE DANGEROUS.
...BUT IS ANYONE WILLING TO GO CHECK OUT THE "PYRAMID"?!
CHAPTER 110
WHOM SHOULD I CHOOSE?
ザワ MUTTER
ザワ MUTTER
...
ザワ MUTTER
...
ザワ MUTTER
YOU'D BE COMING WITH US, RIGHT, AKIRA-KUN...?
HMM? UH, YEAH, OF COURSE.
!!
!
Y-YOU TWO ...!
COOL. THEN WE THREE WILL...
HUH ...?

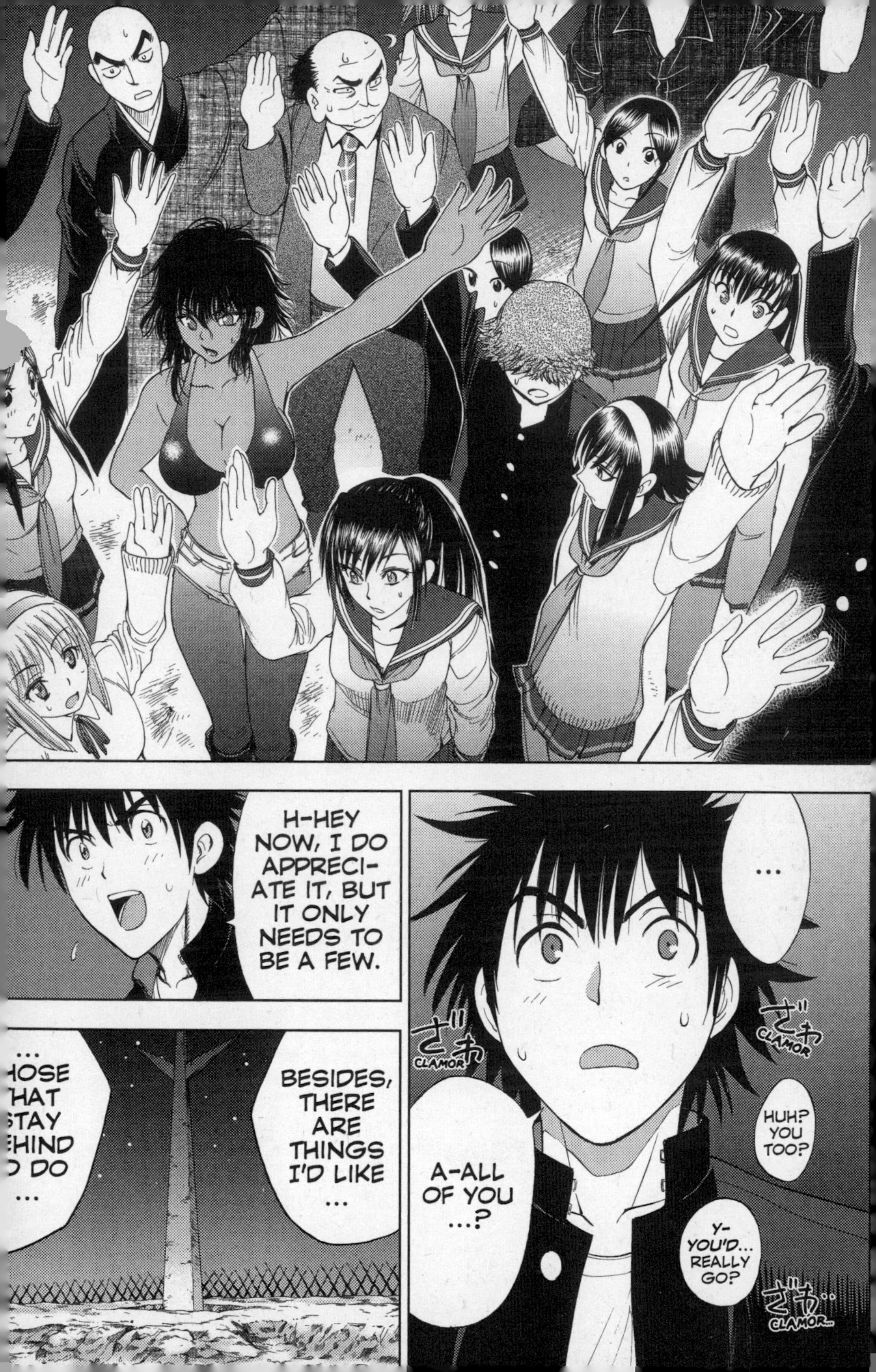
...
ざわ CLAMOR
HUH? YOU TOO?
ざわ CLAMOR
A-ALL OF YOU ...?
Y-YOU'D... REALLY GO?
ざわ.. CLAMOR...
H-HEY NOW, I DO APPRECI-ATE IT, BUT IT ONLY NEEDS TO BE A FEW.
BESIDES, THERE ARE THINGS I'D LIKE ...
... HOSE THAT STAY EHIND O DO ...

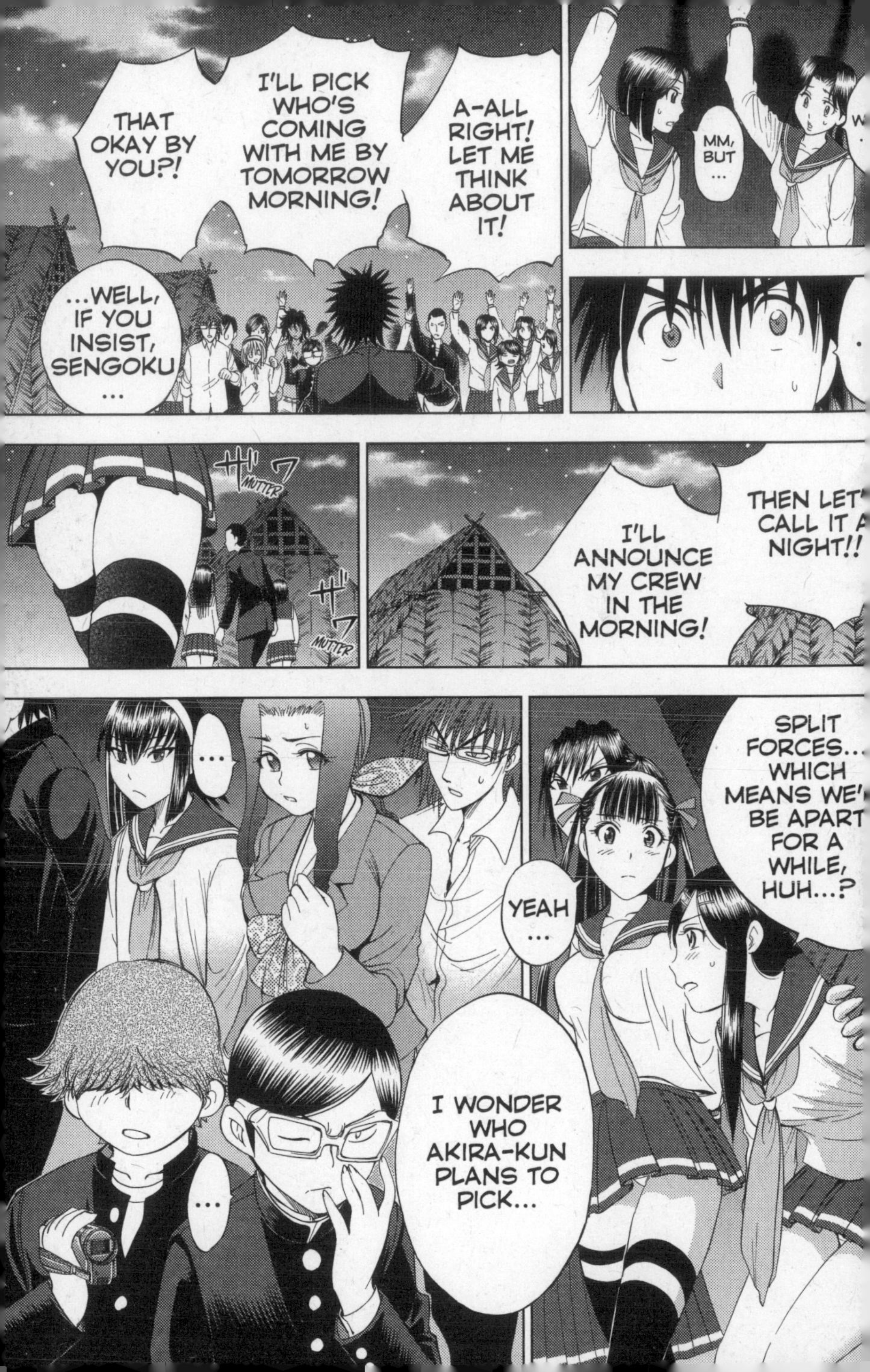
MM, BUT ...
W...
A-ALL RIGHT! LET ME THINK ABOUT IT!
I'LL PICK WHO'S COMING WITH ME BY TOMORROW MORNING!
THAT OKAY BY YOU?!
...WELL, IF YOU INSIST, SENGOKU ...
THEN LET' CALL IT A NIGHT!!
I'LL ANNOUNCE MY CREW IN THE MORNING!
MUTTER
MUTTER
SPLIT FORCES... WHICH MEANS WE' BE APART FOR A WHILE, HUH...?
YEAH ...
...
I WONDER WHO AKIRA-KUN PLANS TO PICK...
...

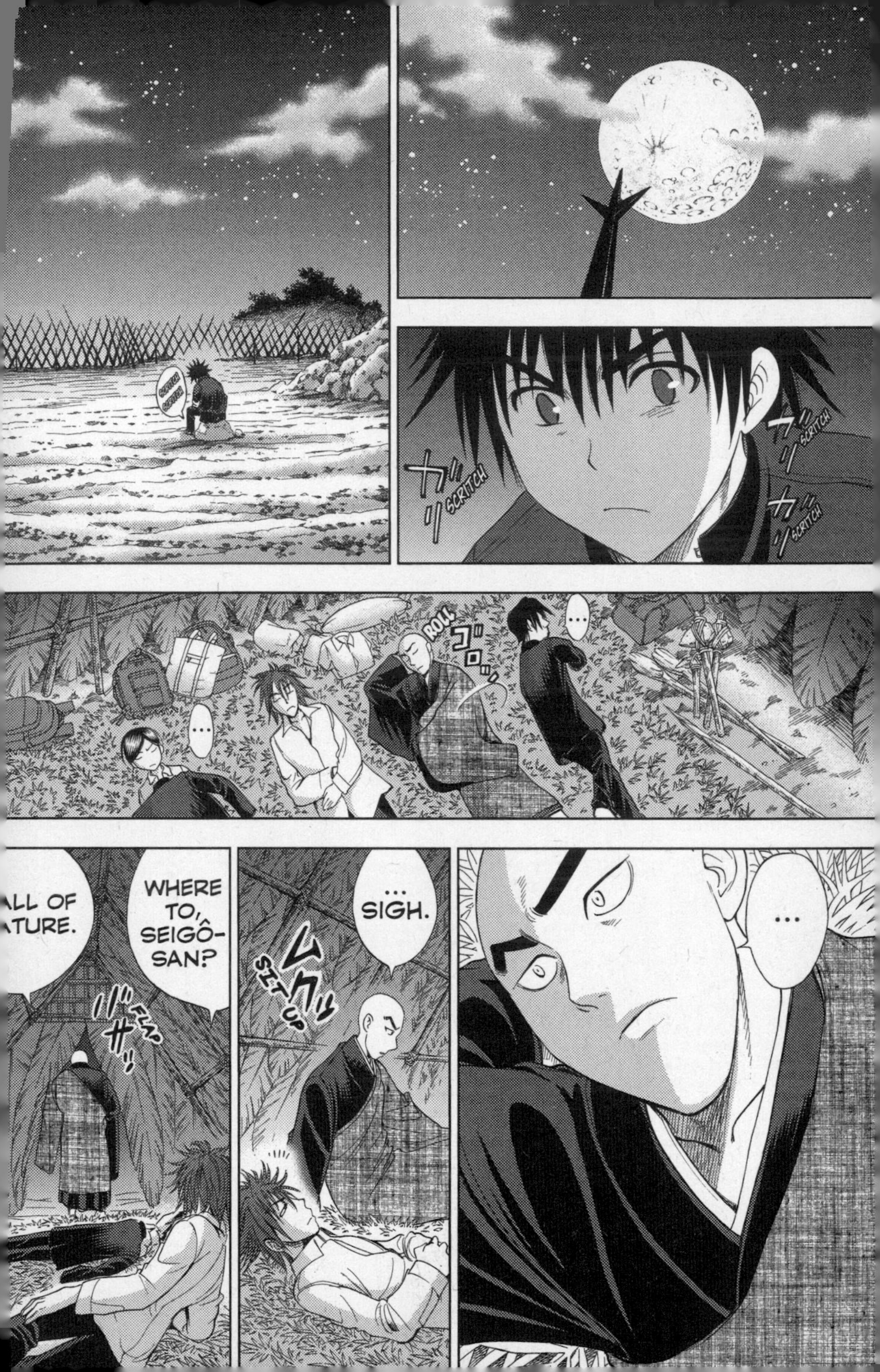
SCRITCH
SCRITCH
SCRITCH
SCRITCH SCRITCH
...
ROLL
...
...
... SIGH.
SIT-UP
WHERE TO, SEIGÔ-SAN?
ALL OF
ATURE.
FLAP

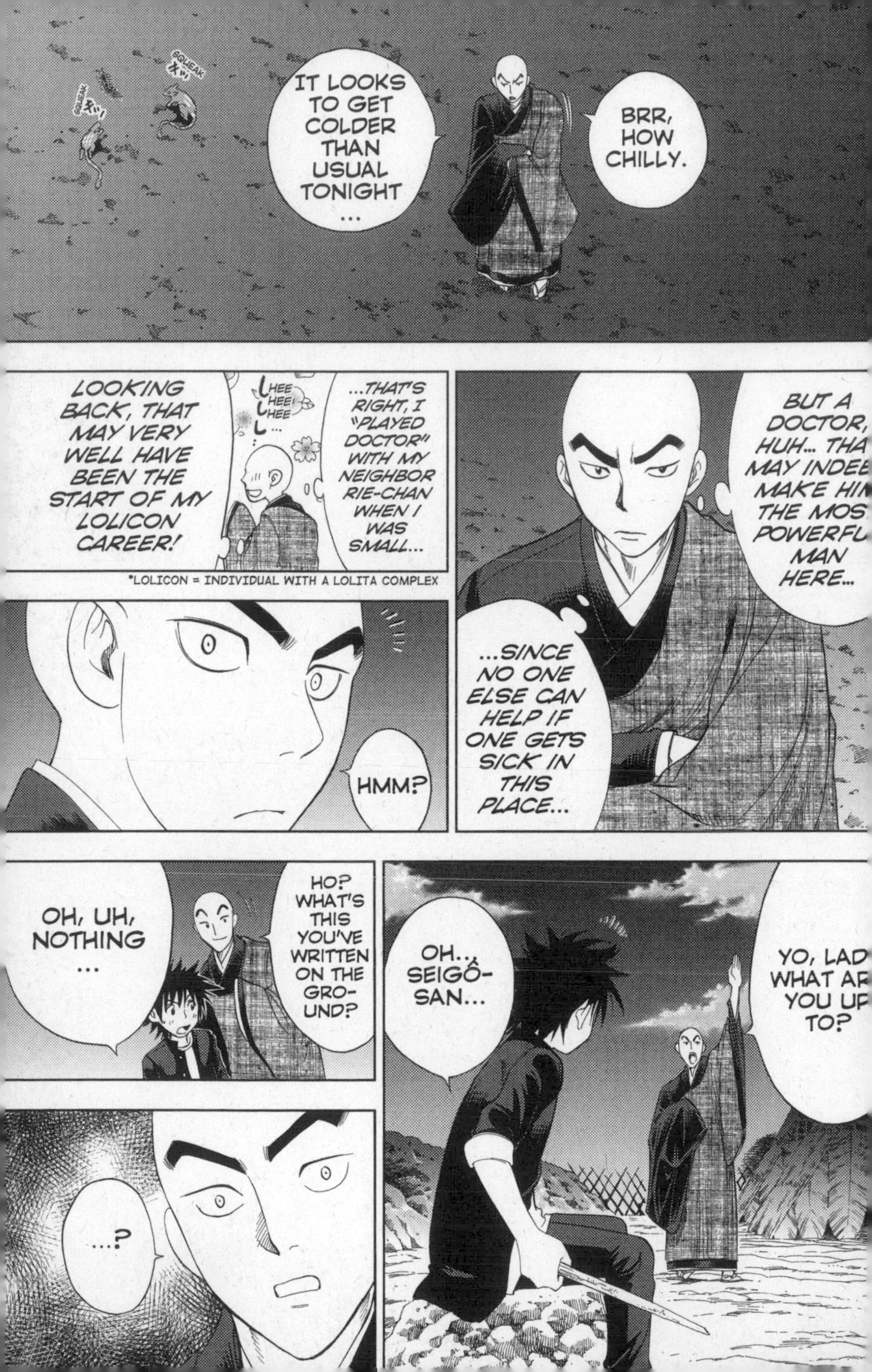
BRR, HOW CHILLY.
IT LOOKS TO GET COLDER THAN USUAL TONIGHT ...
SQUEAK
SQUEAK
BUT A DOCTOR, HUH... THA MAY INDEE MAKE HIM THE MOS POWERFU MAN HERE...
...SINCE NO ONE ELSE CAN HELP IF ONE GETS SICK IN THIS PLACE...
...THAT'S RIGHT, I "PLAYED DOCTOR" WITH MY NEIGHBOR RIE-CHAN WHEN I WAS SMALL...
HEE HEE HEE ...
LOOKING BACK, THAT MAY VERY WELL HAVE BEEN THE START OF MY LOLICON CAREER!
*LOLICON = INDIVIDUAL WITH A LOLITA COMPLEX
HMM?
YO, LAD WHAT AR YOU UP TO?
OH..., SEIGÔ-SAN...
HO? WHAT'S THIS YOU'VE WRITTEN ON THE GRO-UND?
OH, UH, NOTHING ...
...?

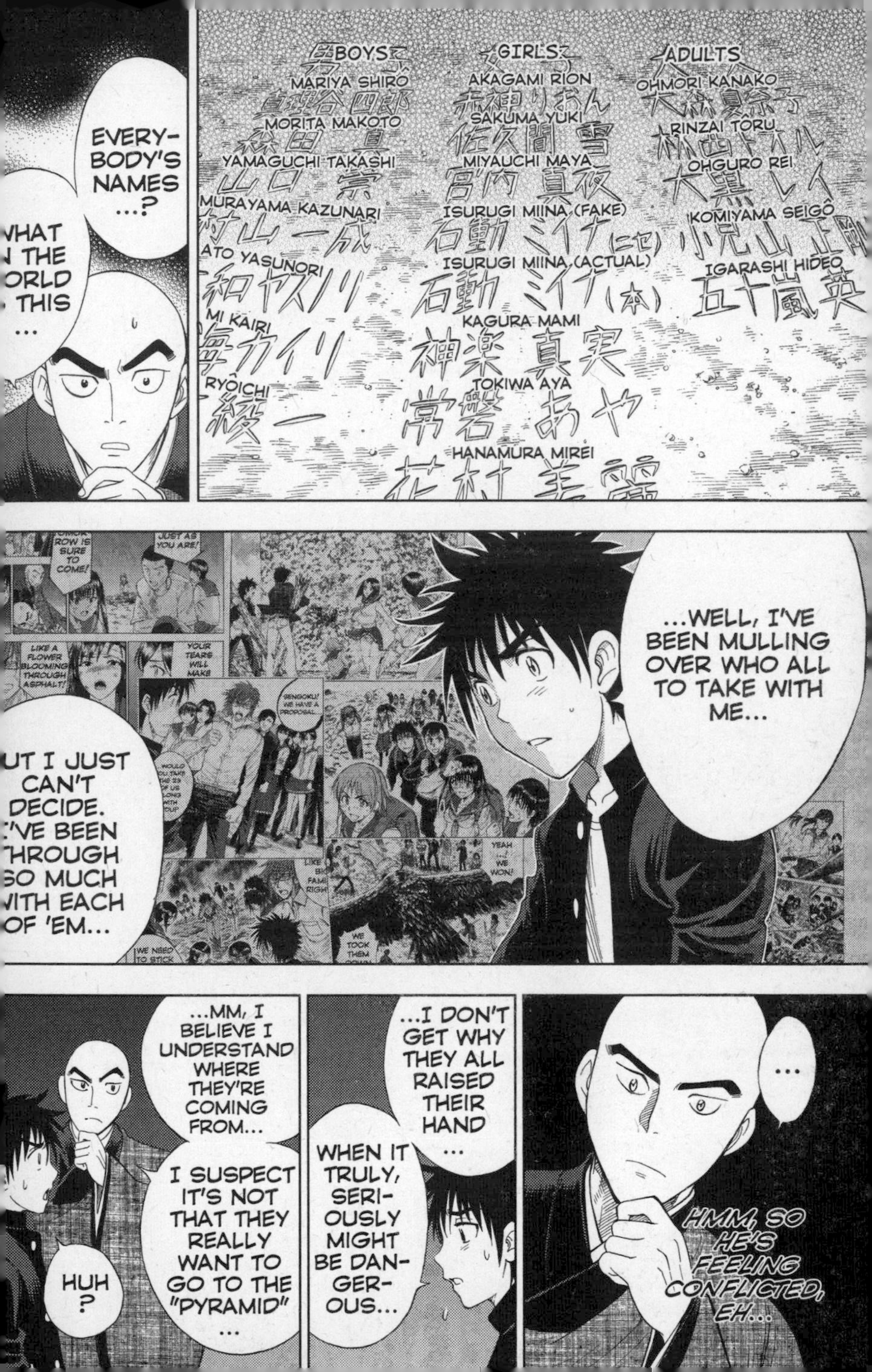
BOYS
MARIYA SHIRO
MORITA MAKOTO
YAMAGUCHI TAKASHI
MURAYAMA KAZUNARI
ATO YASUNORI
MI KAIRI
RYÔICHI
GIRLS
AKAGAMI RION
SAKUMA YUKI
MIYAUCHI MAYA
ISURUGI MIINA (FAKE)
ISURUGI MIINA (ACTUAL)
KAGURA MAMI
TOKIWA AYA
HANAMURA MIREI
ADULTS
OHMORI KANAKO
RINZAI TÔRU
OHGURO REI
KOMIYAMA SEIGÔ
IGARASHI HIDEO
EVERY-BODY'S NAMES ...?
WHAT N THE ORLD THIS ...
...WELL, I'VE BEEN MULLING OVER WHO ALL TO TAKE WITH ME...
JUST AS YOU ARE!
LIKE A FLOWER BLOOMING THROUGH ASPHALT!
YEAH ... WE WON!
UT I JUST CAN'T DECIDE. 'VE BEEN THROUGH SO MUCH WITH EACH OF 'EM...
...
HMM, SO HE'S FEELING CONFLICTED, EH...
...I DON'T GET WHY THEY ALL RAISED THEIR HAND ...
WHEN IT TRULY, SERI-OUSLY MIGHT BE DAN-GER-OUS...
...MM, I BELIEVE I UNDERSTAND WHERE THEY'RE COMING FROM...
I SUSPECT IT'S NOT THAT THEY REALLY WANT TO GO TO THE "PYRAMID" ...
HUH ?

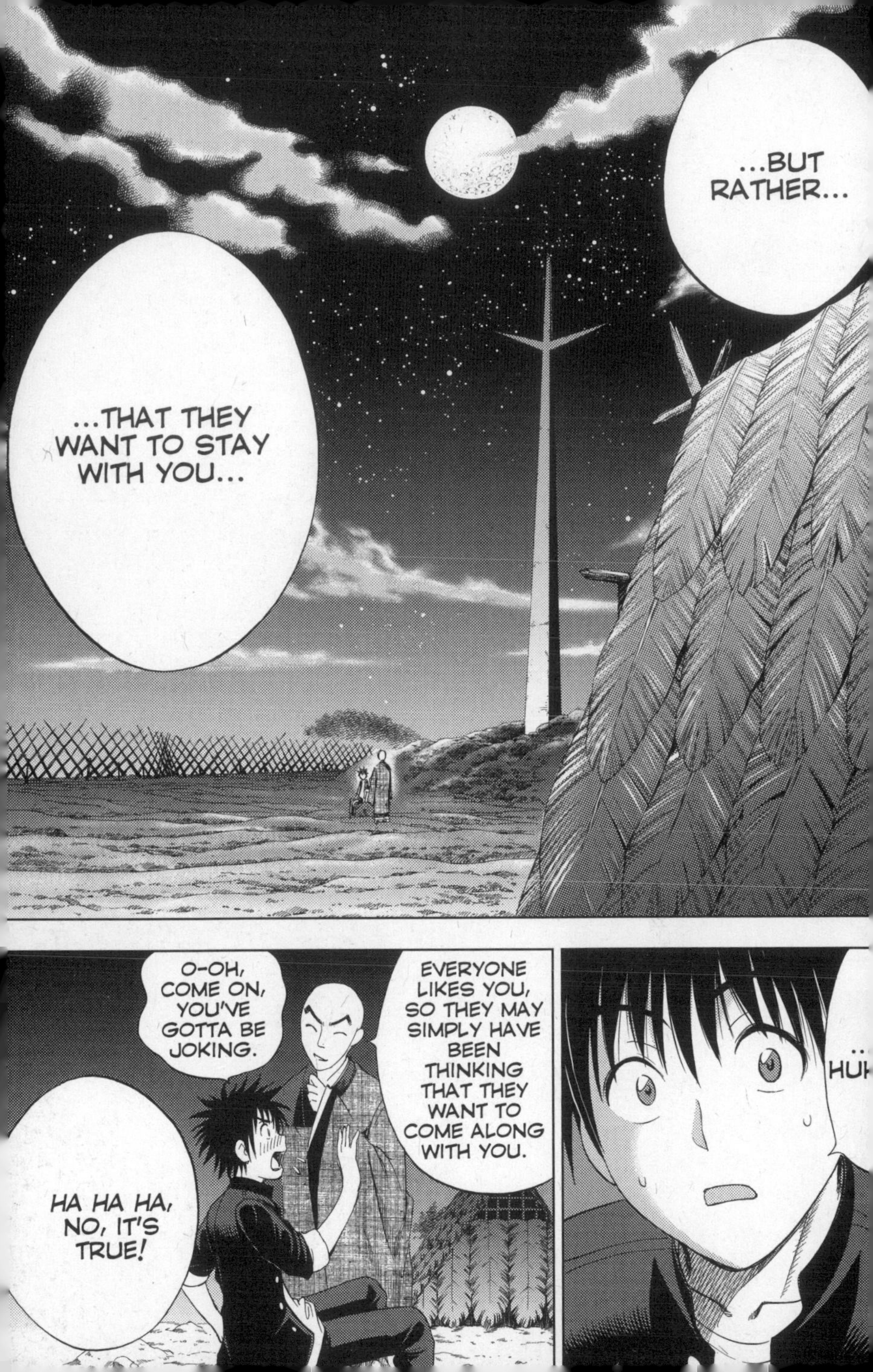
...BUT RATHER...
...THAT THEY WANT TO STAY WITH YOU...
...HUH
EVERYONE LIKES YOU, SO THEY MAY SIMPLY HAVE BEEN THINKING THAT THEY WANT TO COME ALONG WITH YOU.
O-OH, COME ON, YOU'VE GOTTA BE JOKING.
HA HA HA, NO, IT'S TRUE!

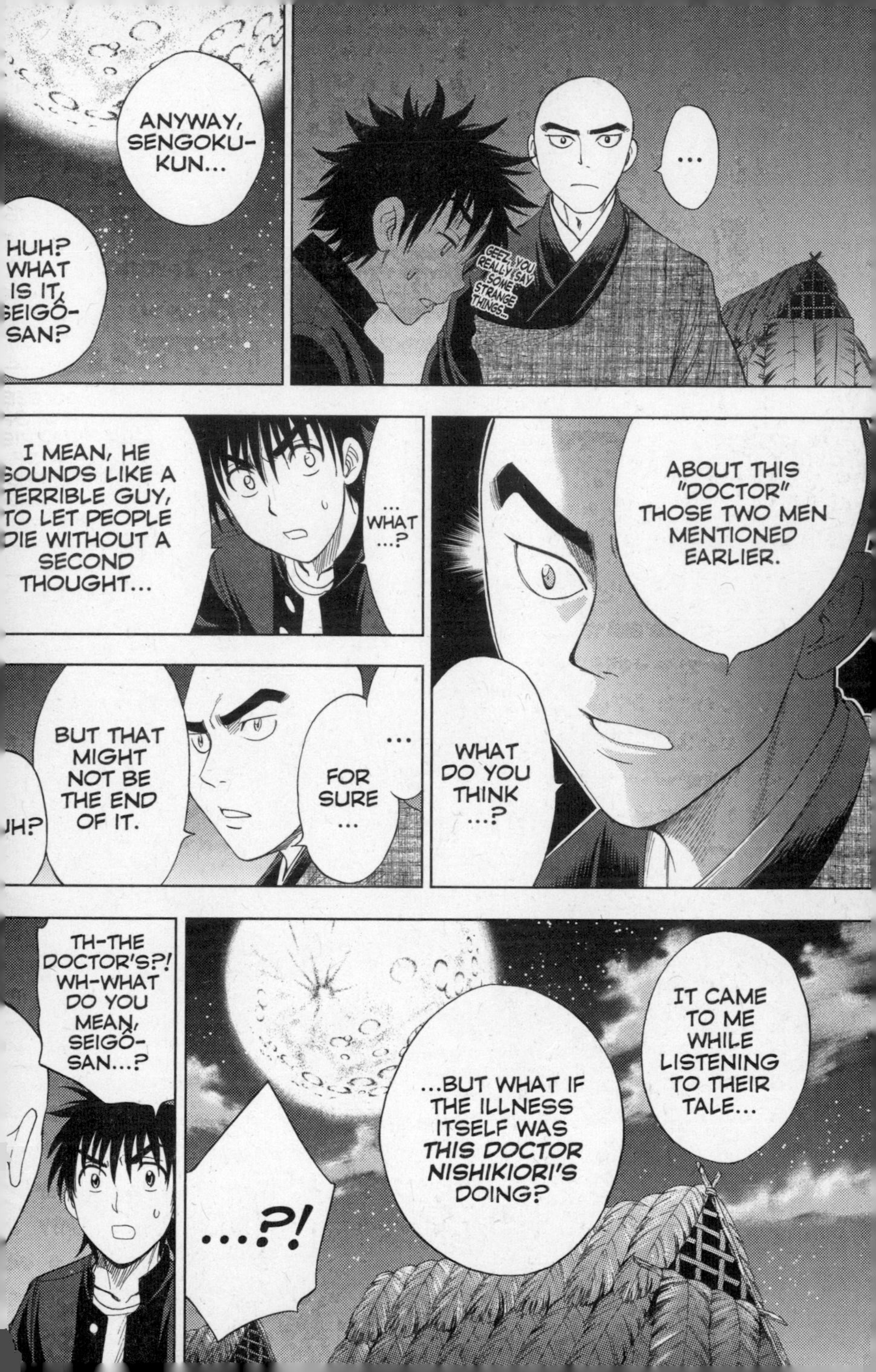
...
GEEZ, YOU REALLY SAY SOME STRANGE THINGS...
ANYWAY, SENGOKU-KUN...
HUH? WHAT IS IT, SEIGŌ-SAN?
ABOUT THIS "DOCTOR" THOSE TWO MEN MENTIONED EARLIER.
WHAT DO YOU THINK ...?
... WHAT ...?
I MEAN, HE SOUNDS LIKE A TERRIBLE GUY, TO LET PEOPLE DIE WITHOUT A SECOND THOUGHT...
... FOR SURE ...
BUT THAT MIGHT NOT BE THE END OF IT.
IT CAME TO ME WHILE LISTENING TO THEIR TALE...
...BUT WHAT IF THE ILLNESS ITSELF WAS *THIS DOCTOR NISHIKIORI'S* DOING?
...?!
TH-THE DOCTOR'S?! WH-WHAT DO YOU MEAN, SEIGŌ-SAN...?

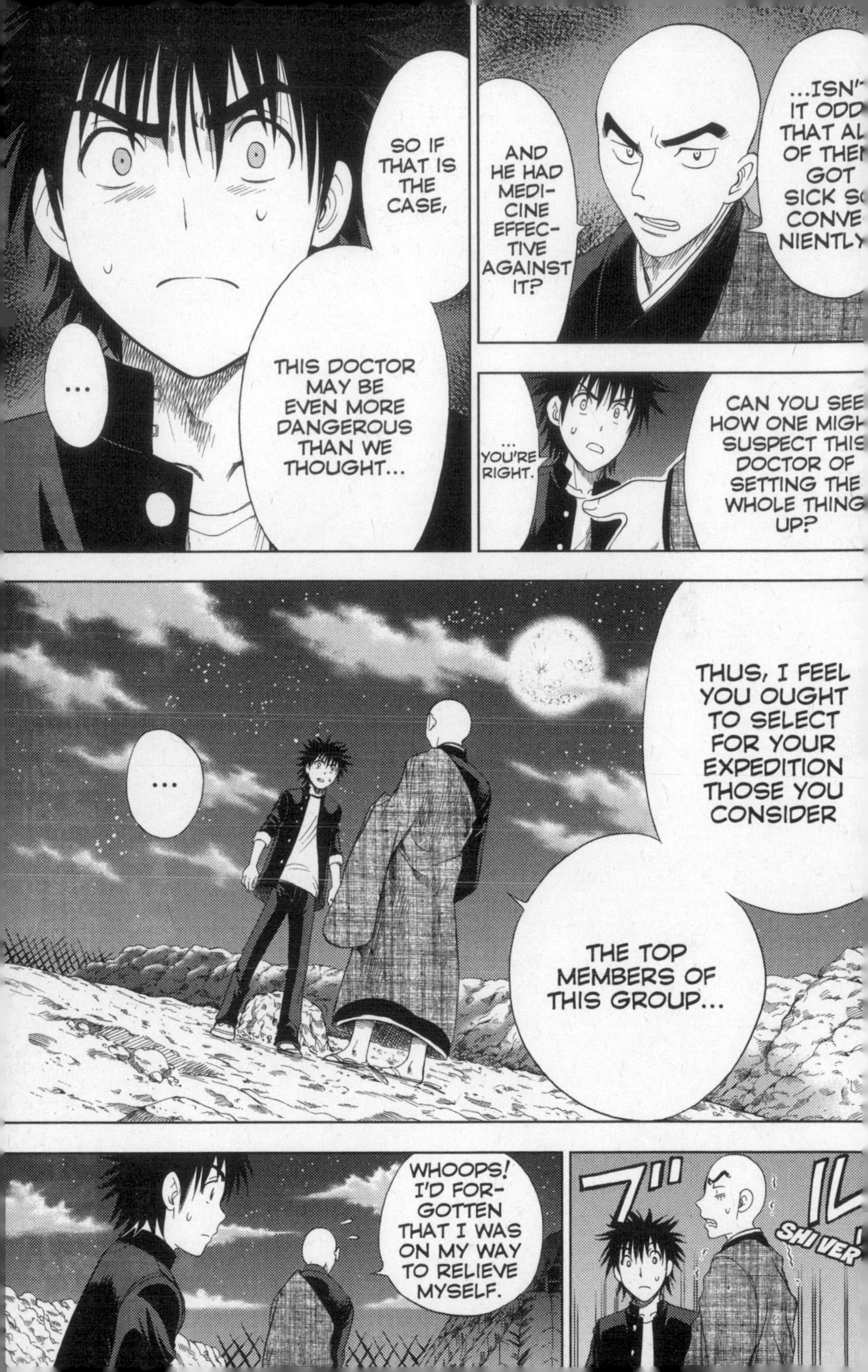
...ISN' IT ODD THAT AL OF THE GOT SICK S CONVE NIENTLY
AND HE HAD MEDICINE EFFECTIVE AGAINST IT?
CAN YOU SEE HOW ONE MIGH SUSPECT THIS DOCTOR OF SETTING THE WHOLE THING UP?
... YOU'RE RIGHT.
SO IF THAT IS THE CASE,
THIS DOCTOR MAY BE EVEN MORE DANGEROUS THAN WE THOUGHT...
...
THUS, I FEEL YOU OUGHT TO SELECT FOR YOUR EXPEDITION THOSE YOU CONSIDER
THE TOP MEMBERS OF THIS GROUP...
...
SHIVER
WHOOPS! I'D FORGOTTEN THAT I WAS ON MY WAY TO RELIEVE MYSELF.

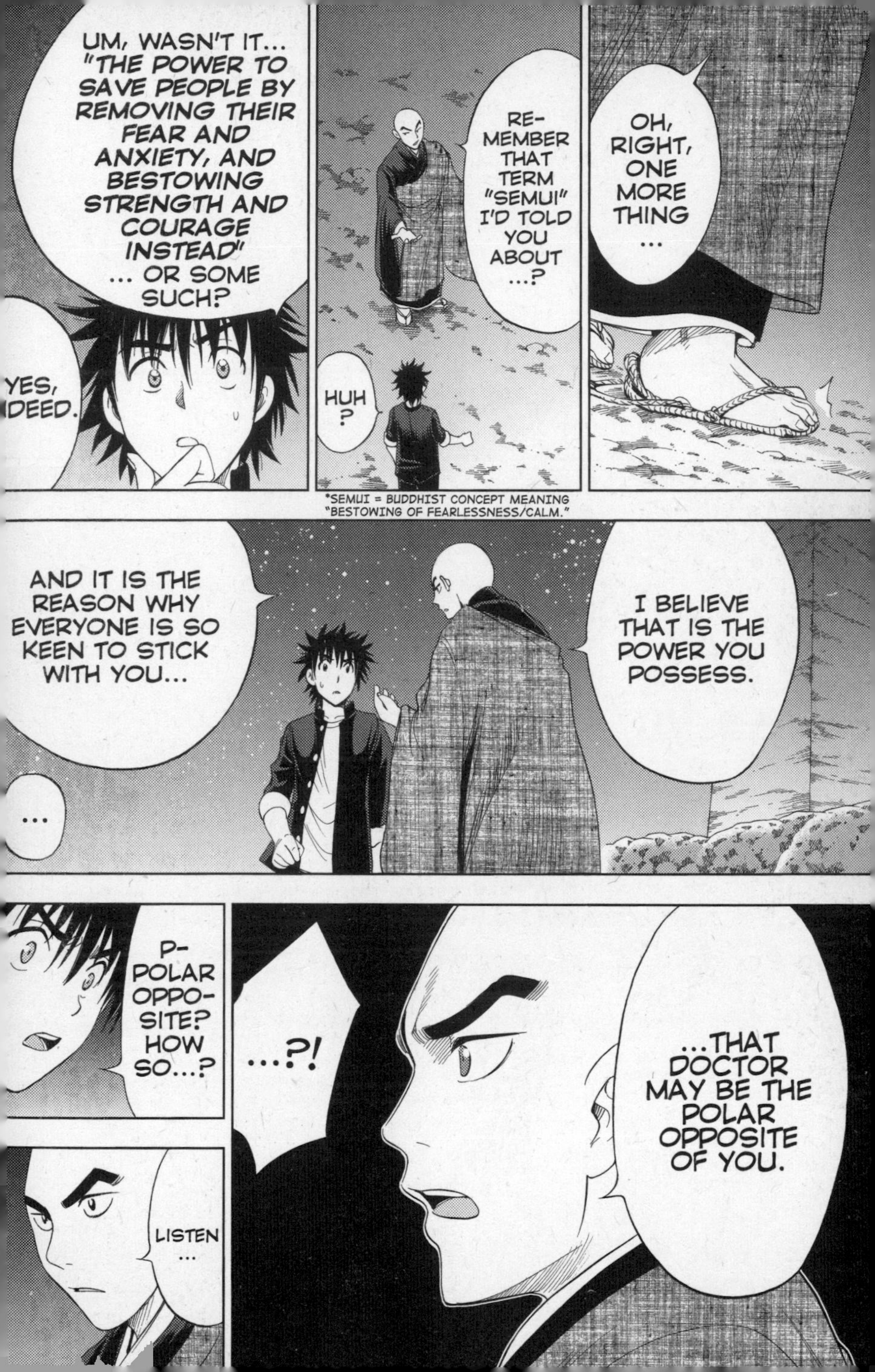
OH, RIGHT, ONE MORE THING ...
RE-MEMBER THAT TERM "SEMUI" I'D TOLD YOU ABOUT ...?
HUH?
UM, WASN'T IT... "THE POWER TO SAVE PEOPLE BY REMOVING THEIR FEAR AND ANXIETY, AND BESTOWING STRENGTH AND COURAGE INSTEAD" ... OR SOME SUCH?
YES, DEED.
*SEMUI = BUDDHIST CONCEPT MEANING "BESTOWING OF FEARLESSNESS/CALM."
I BELIEVE THAT IS THE POWER YOU POSSESS.
AND IT IS THE REASON WHY EVERYONE IS SO KEEN TO STICK WITH YOU...
...
...THAT DOCTOR MAY BE THE POLAR OPPOSITE OF YOU.
...?!
P-POLAR OPPO-SITE? HOW SO...?
LISTEN ...

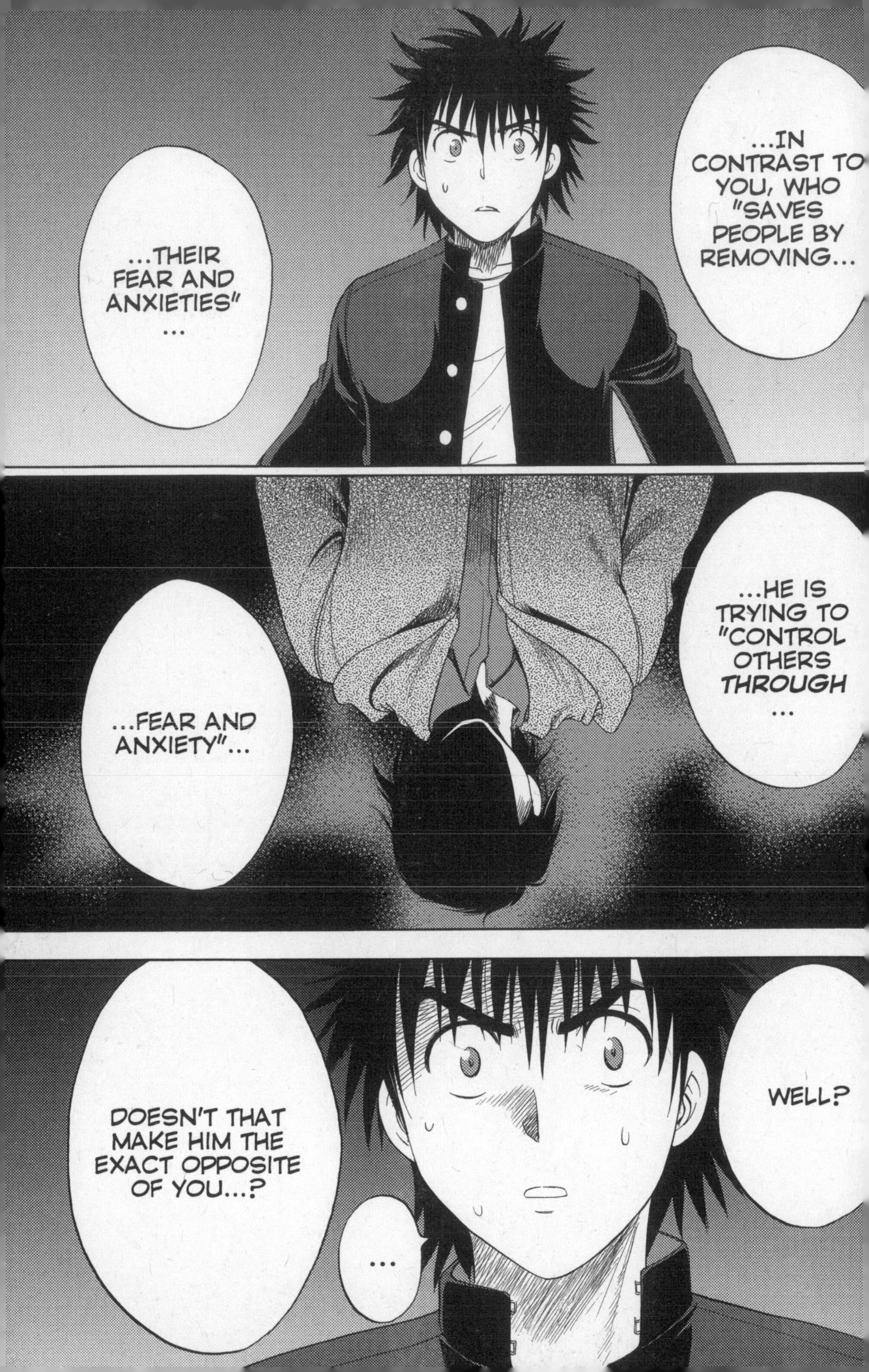
...IN CONTRAST TO YOU, WHO "SAVES PEOPLE BY REMOVING...
...THEIR FEAR AND ANXIETIES" ...
...HE IS TRYING TO "CONTROL OTHERS *THROUGH* ...
...FEAR AND ANXIETY"...
WELL?
DOESN'T THAT MAKE HIM THE EXACT OPPOSITE OF YOU...?
...

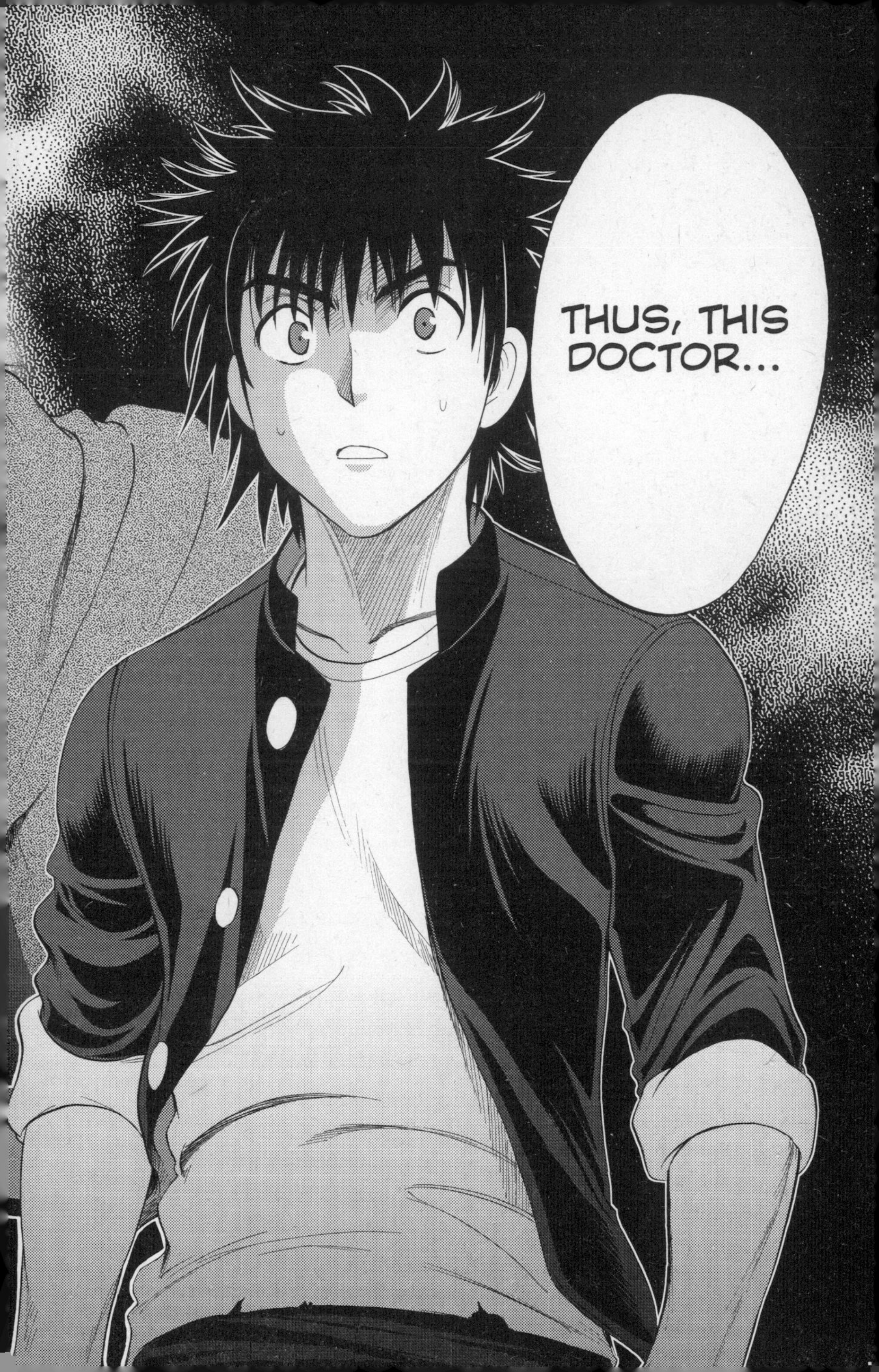
THUS, THIS DOCTOR...

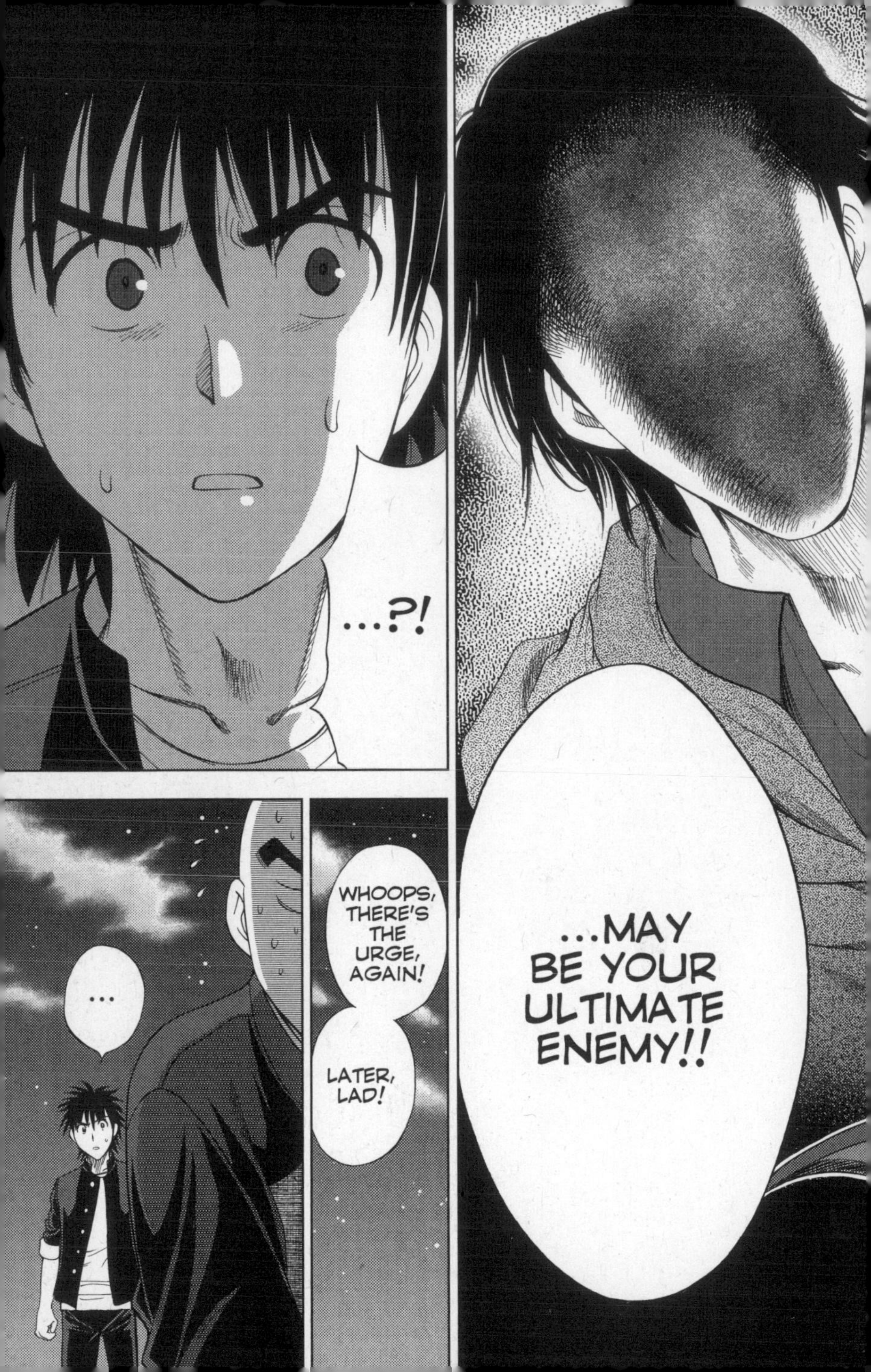
...MAY BE YOUR ULTIMATE ENEMY!!
...?!
WHOOPS, THERE'S THE URGE, AGAIN!
LATER, LAD!
...

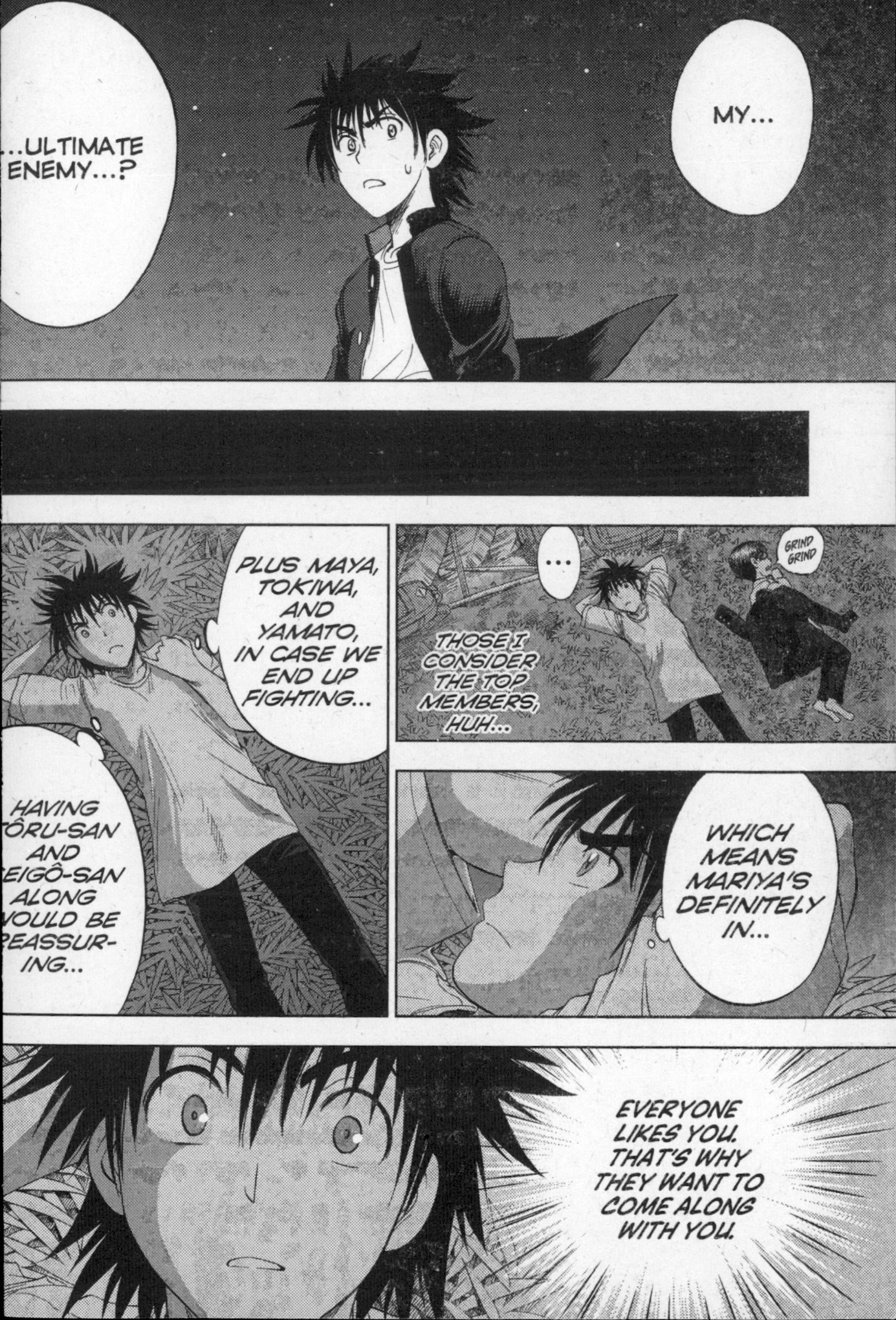
MY...
...ULTIMATE ENEMY...?
...
THOSE I CONSIDER THE TOP MEMBERS, HUH...
GRIND GRIND
WHICH MEANS MARIYA'S DEFINITELY IN...
PLUS MAYA, TOKIWA, AND YAMATO, IN CASE WE END UP FIGHTING...
HAVING TÔRU-SAN AND SEIGÔ-SAN ALONG WOULD BE REASSURING...
EVERYONE LIKES YOU. THAT'S WHY THEY WANT TO COME ALONG WITH YOU.

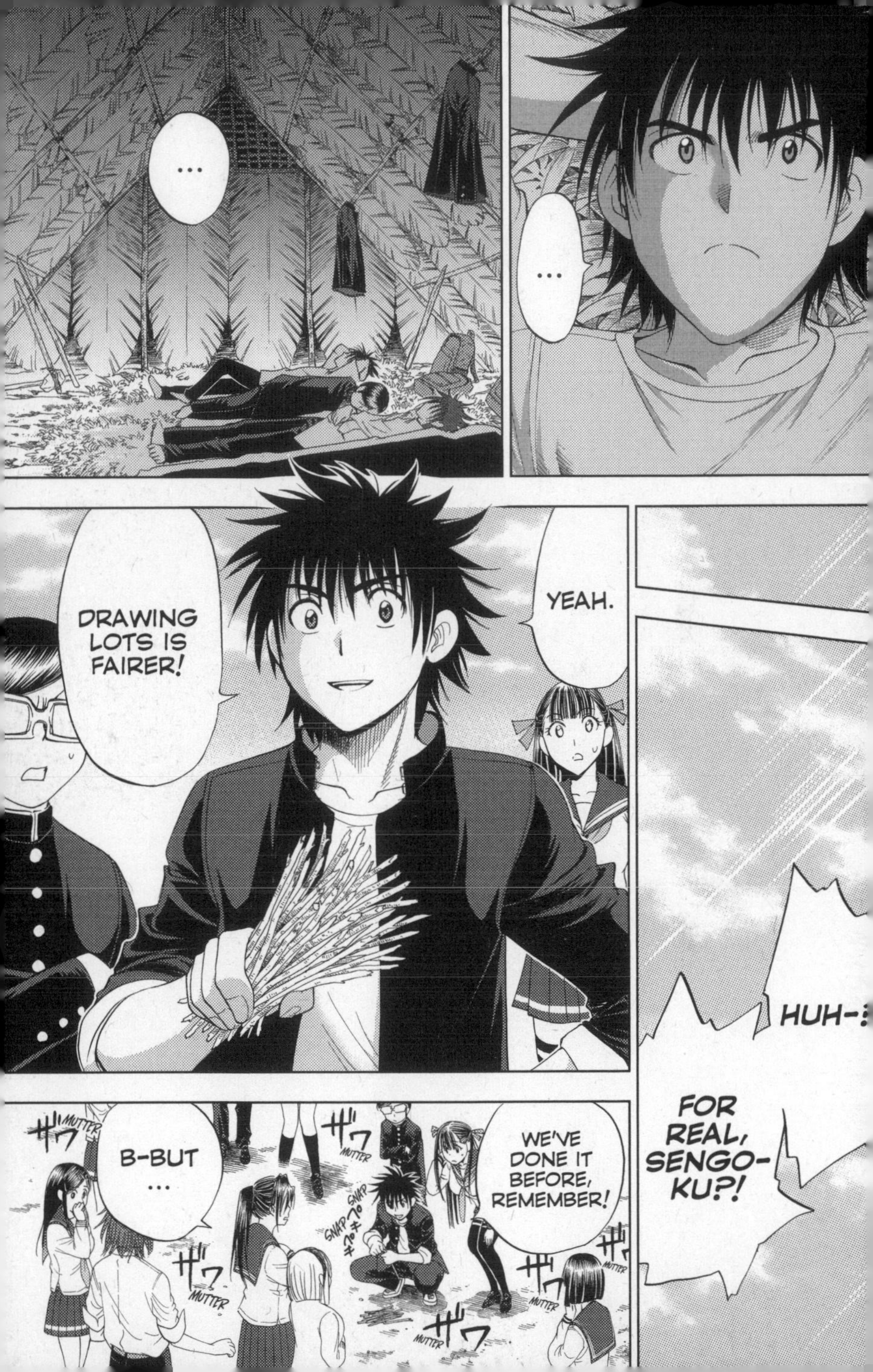
...
...
HUH-!?
FOR REAL, SENGOKU?!
YEAH.
DRAWING LOTS IS FAIRER!
WE'VE DONE IT BEFORE, REMEMBER!
ザワ MUTTER
SNAP ペキ SNAP ペキ
B-BUT ...
ザワ MUTTER
ザワ MUTTER
ザワ MUTTER
ザワ MUTTER
ザワ MUTTER

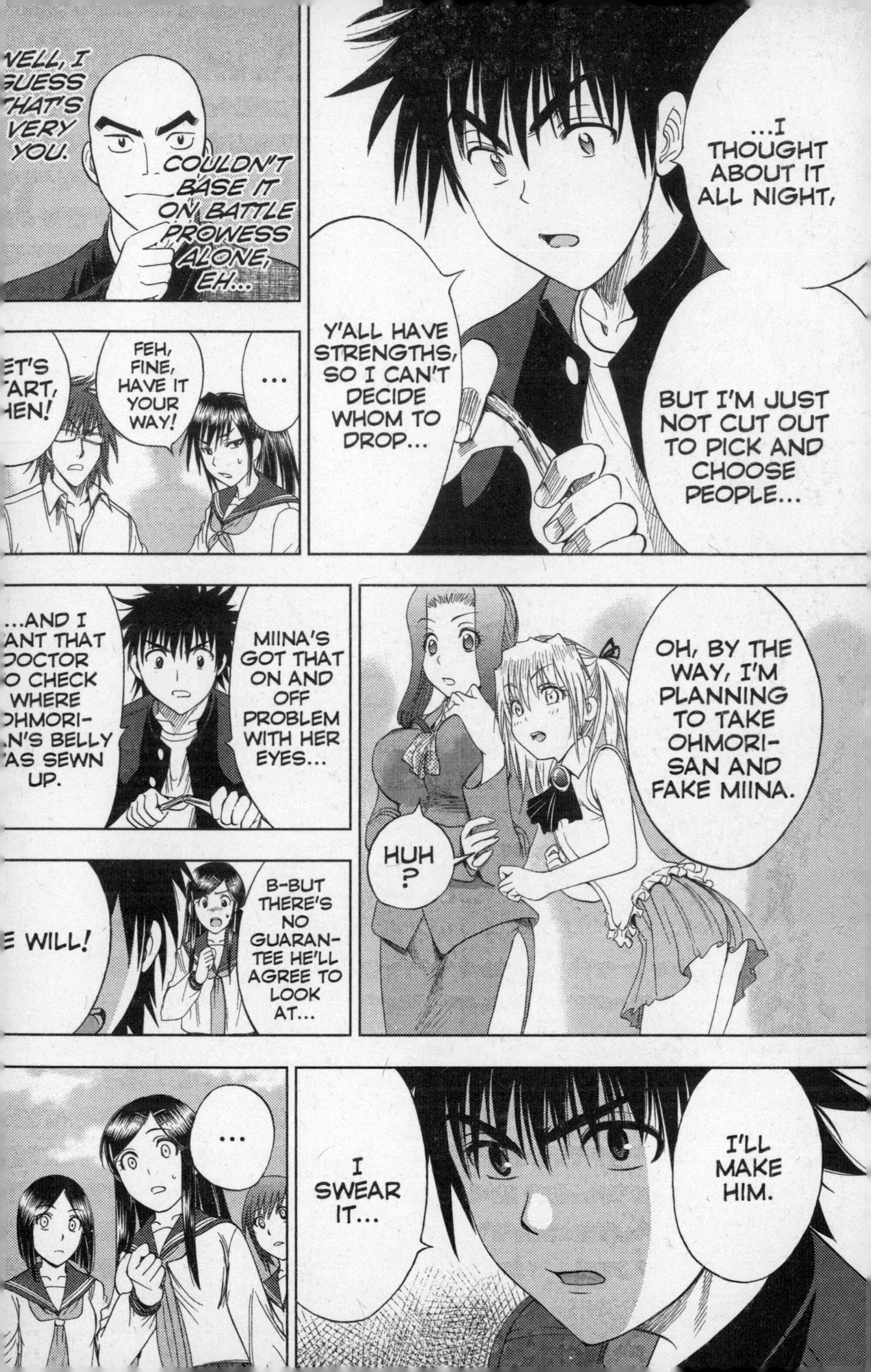
...I THOUGHT ABOUT IT ALL NIGHT,
BUT I'M JUST NOT CUT OUT TO PICK AND CHOOSE PEOPLE...
Y'ALL HAVE STRENGTHS, SO I CAN'T DECIDE WHOM TO DROP...
WELL, I GUESS THAT'S VERY YOU.
COULDN'T BASE IT ON BATTLE PROWESS ALONE, EH...
...
FEH, FINE, HAVE IT YOUR WAY!
ET'S TART, HEN!
OH, BY THE WAY, I'M PLANNING TO TAKE OHMORI-SAN AND FAKE MIINA.
HUH?
MIINA'S GOT THAT ON AND OFF PROBLEM WITH HER EYES...
...AND I ANT THAT OCTOR O CHECK WHERE OHMORI- N'S BELLY AS SEWN UP.
B-BUT THERE'S NO GUARANTEE HE'LL AGREE TO LOOK AT...
E WILL!
I'LL MAKE HIM.
I SWEAR IT...
...

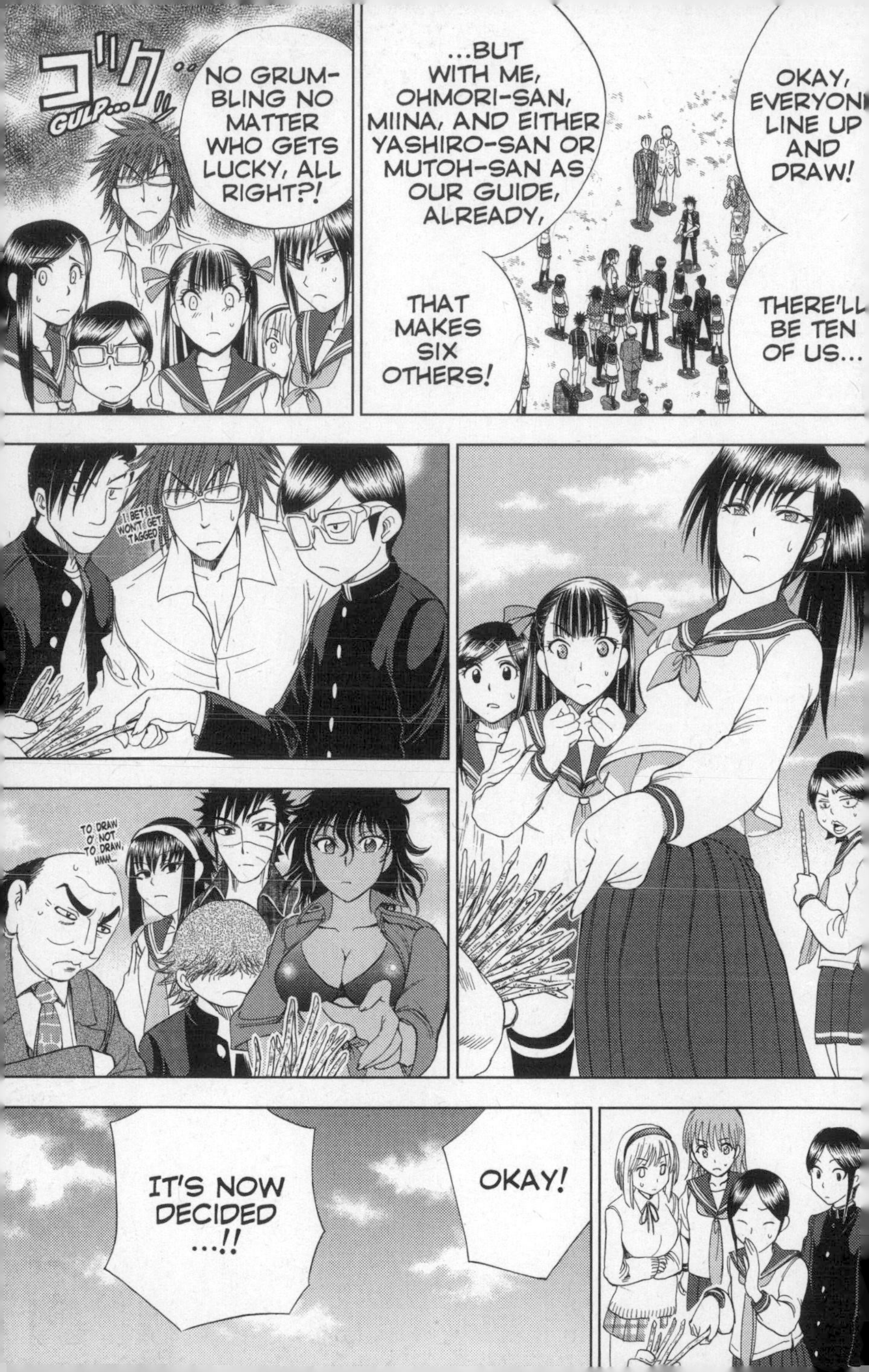
OKAY, EVERYON LINE UP AND DRAW!
THERE'LL BE TEN OF US...
...BUT WITH ME, OHMORI-SAN, MIINA, AND EITHER YASHIRO-SAN OR MUTOH-SAN AS OUR GUIDE, ALREADY,
THAT MAKES SIX OTHERS!
NO GRUM-BLING NO MATTER WHO GETS LUCKY, ALL RIGHT?!
ゴク
GULP...
I BET I WON'T GET TAGGED
TO DRAW O' NOT TO DRAW, HMM...
OKAY!
IT'S NOW DECIDED ...!!

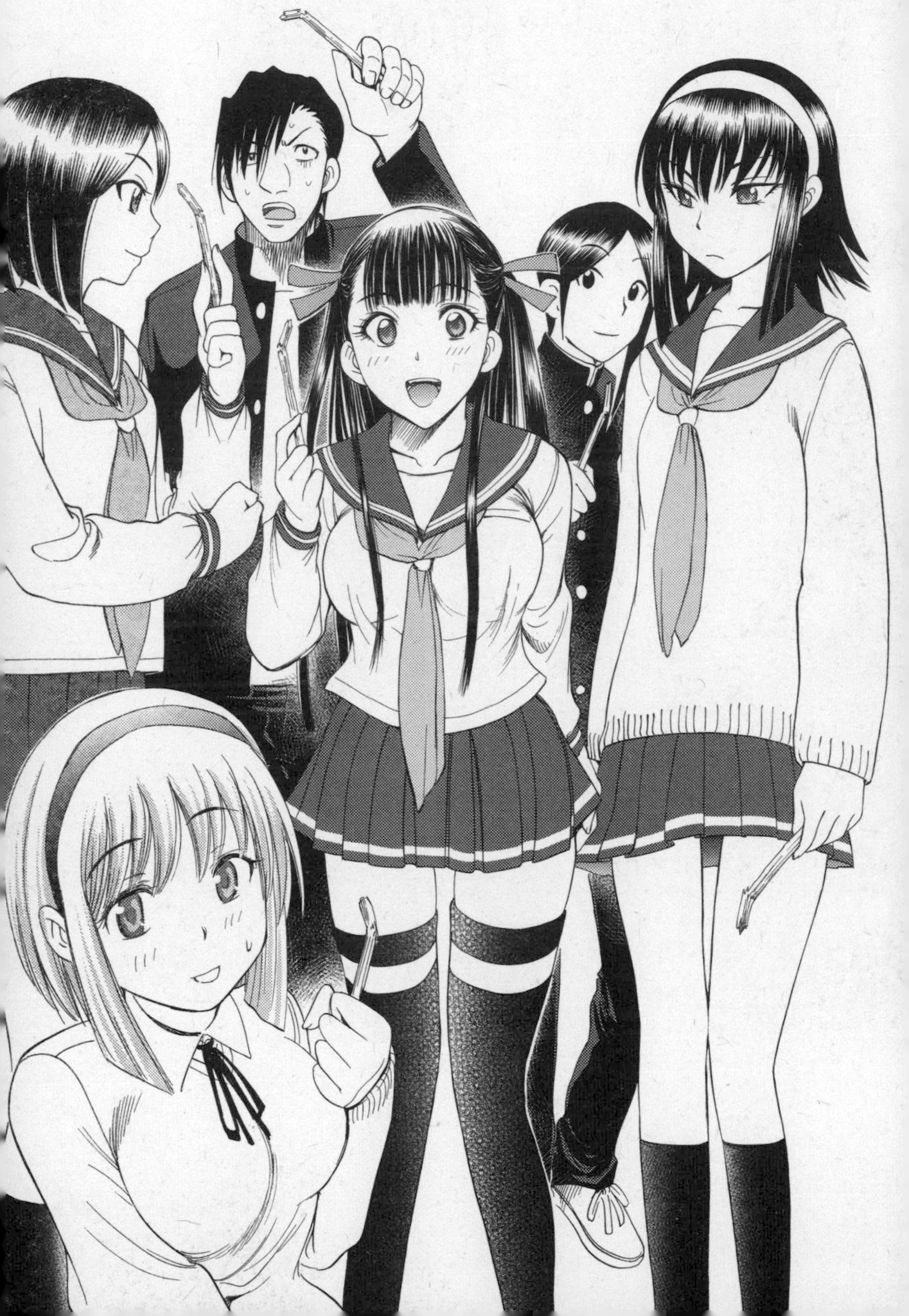

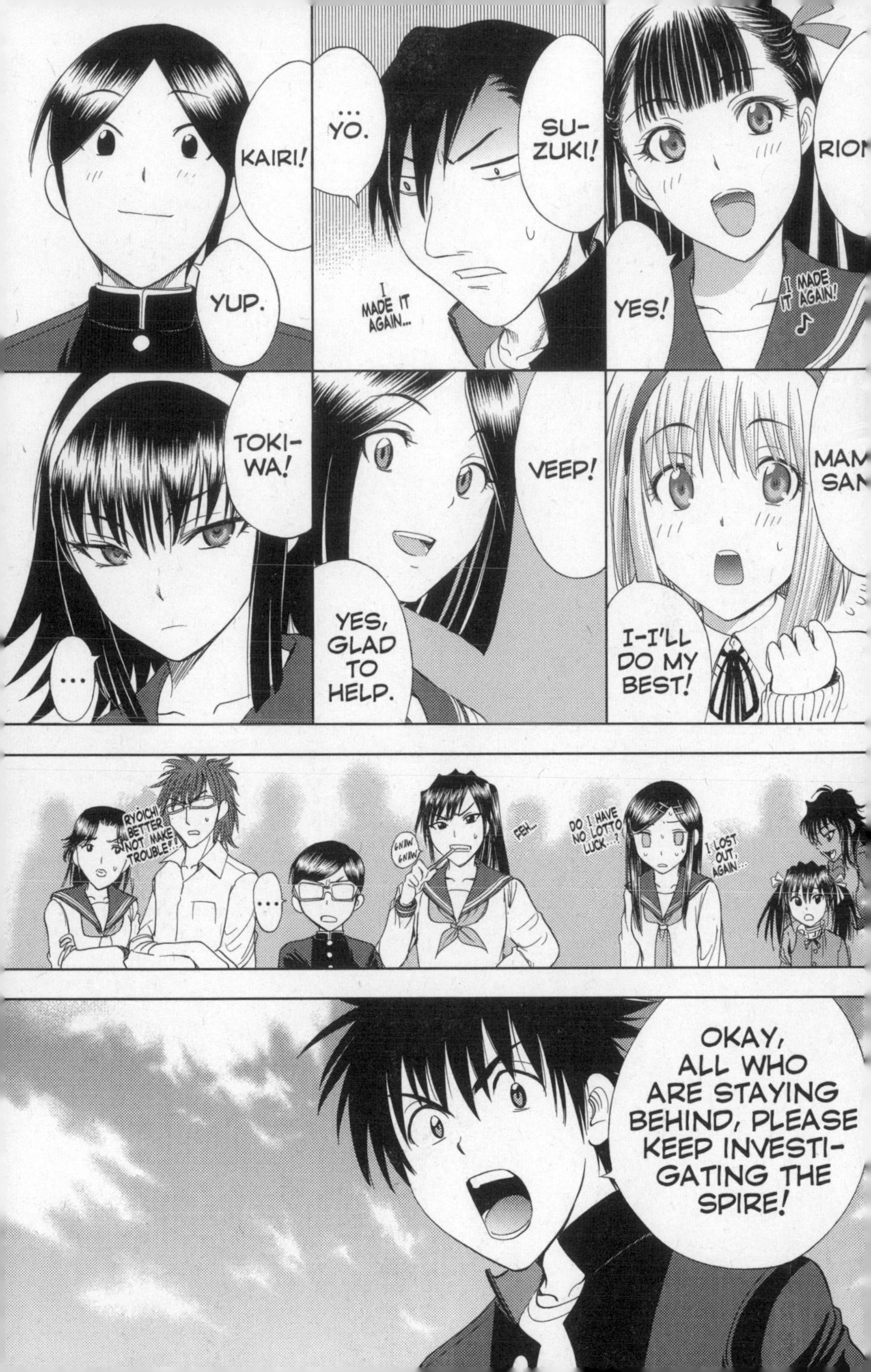
RION
YES!
I MADE IT AGAIN! ♪
SU-ZUKI!
...YO.
I MADE IT AGAIN...
KAIRI!
YUP.
MAM SAN
I-I'LL DO MY BEST!
VEEP!
YES, GLAD TO HELP.
TOKI-WA!
...
I LOST OUT, AGAIN...
DO I HAVE NO LOTTO LUCK...?
FEH...
GNAW GNAW
...
RYOICHI BETTER NOT MAKE TROUBLE!!
OKAY, ALL WHO ARE STAYING BEHIND, PLEASE KEEP INVESTI-GATING THE SPIRE!

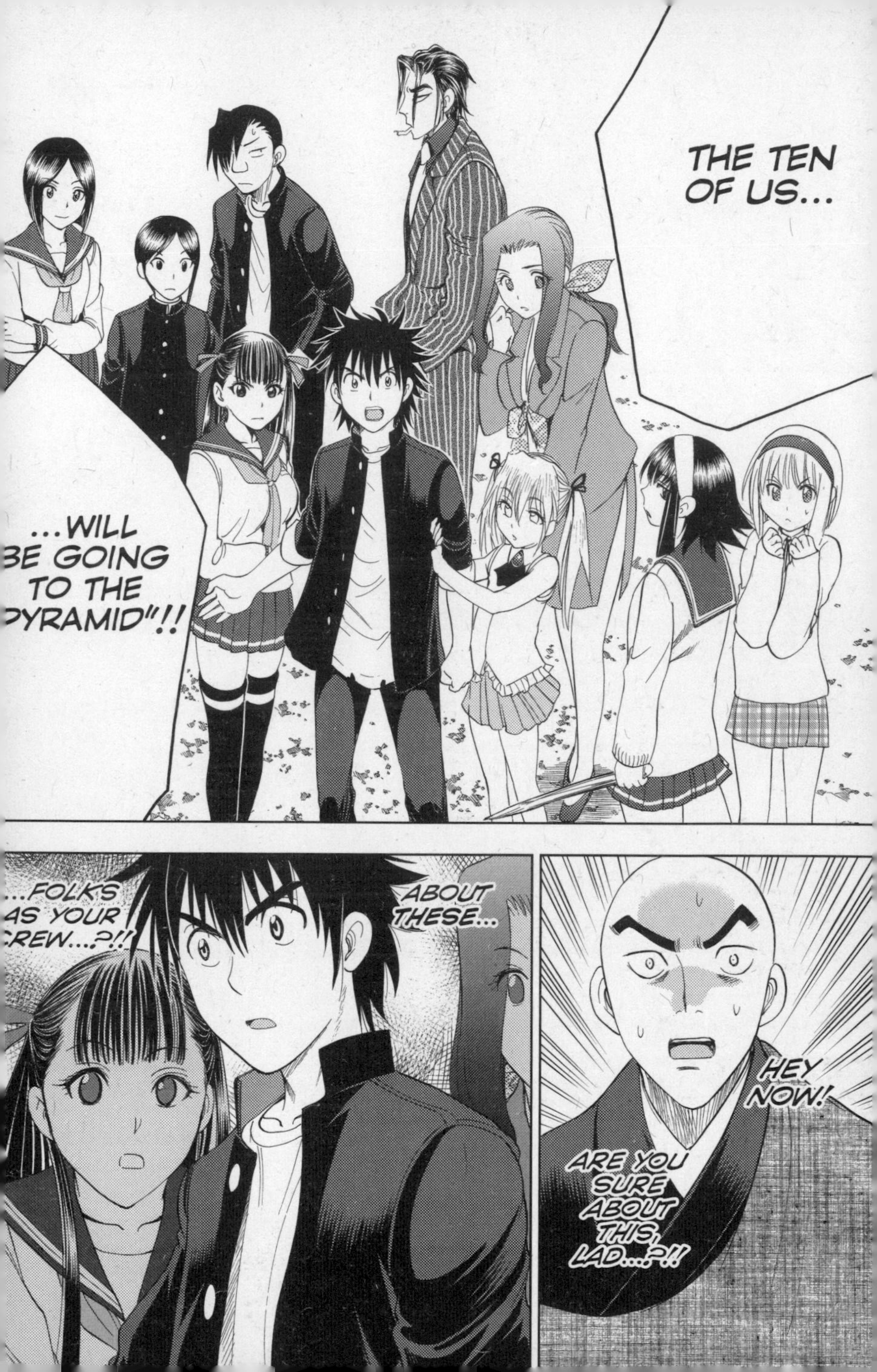
THE TEN OF US...
...WILL BE GOING TO THE PYRAMID"!!
HEY NOW!
ARE YOU SURE ABOUT THIS, LAD...?!!
ABOUT THESE...
...FOLKS AS YOUR CREW...?!!

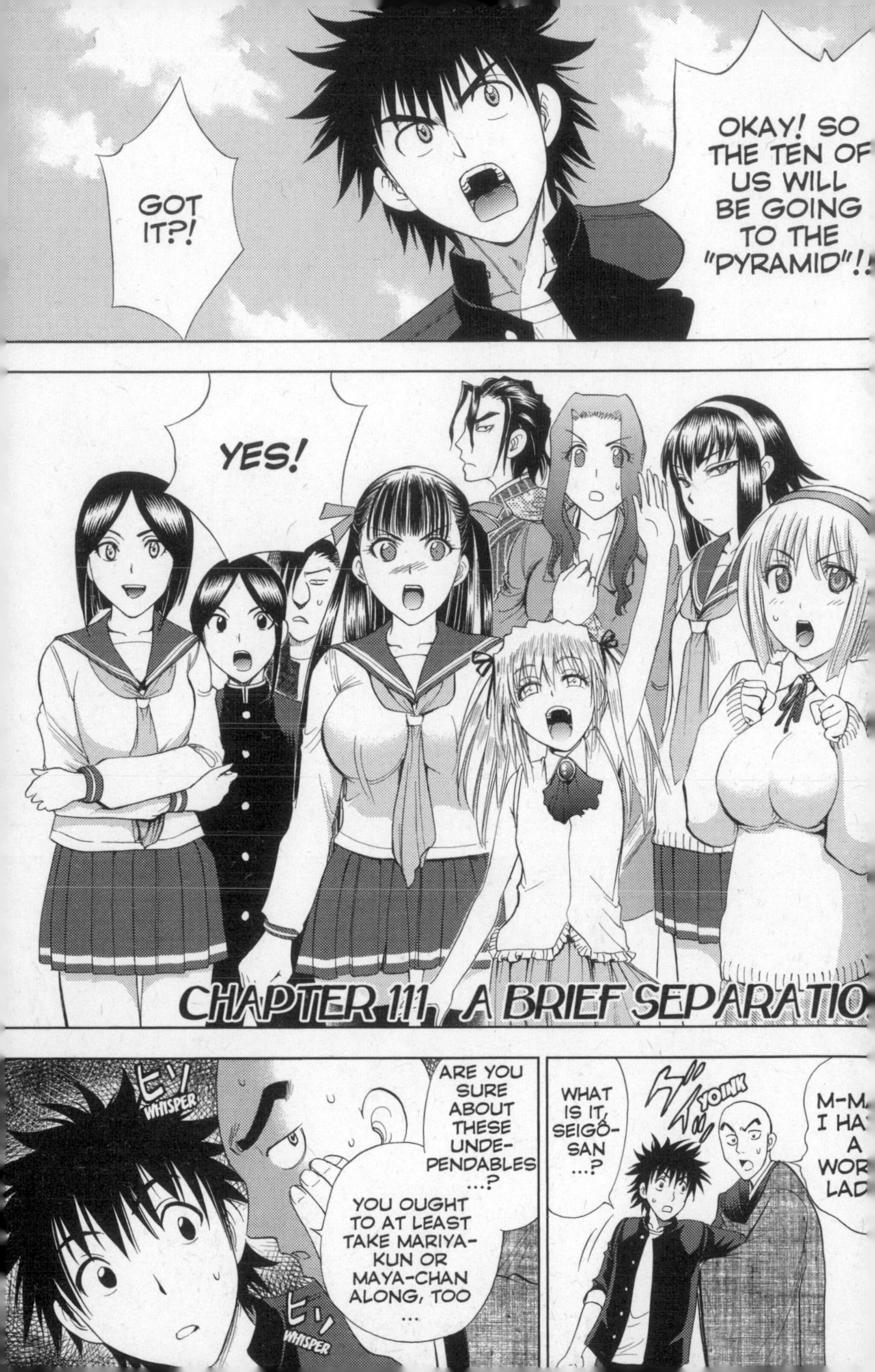
OKAY! SO THE TEN OF US WILL BE GOING TO THE "PYRAMID"!!
GOT IT?!
YES!
CHAPTER 111 A BRIEF SEPARATIO
M-MA I HA A WOR LAD
YOINK
WHAT IS IT, SEIGÔ-SAN ...?
ARE YOU SURE ABOUT THESE UNDE-PENDABLES ...?
YOU OUGHT TO AT LEAST TAKE MARIYA-KUN OR MAYA-CHAN ALONG, TOO ...
WHISPER
WHISPER

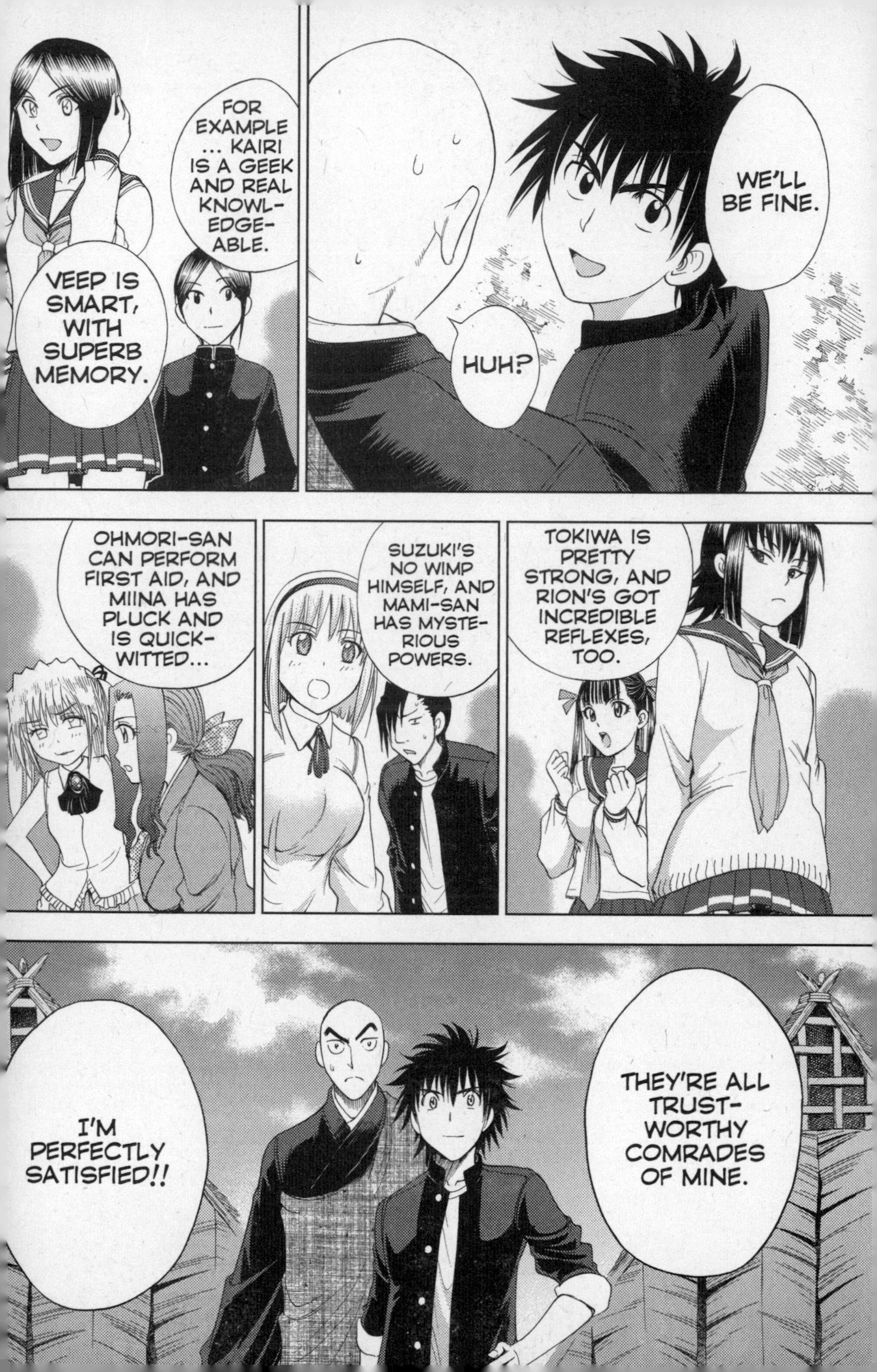
WE'LL BE FINE.
HUH?
FOR EXAMPLE ... KAIRI IS A GEEK AND REAL KNOWL-EDGE-ABLE.
VEEP IS SMART, WITH SUPERB MEMORY.
TOKIWA IS PRETTY STRONG, AND RION'S GOT INCREDIBLE REFLEXES, TOO.
SUZUKI'S NO WIMP HIMSELF, AND MAMI-SAN HAS MYSTE-RIOUS POWERS.
OHMORI-SAN CAN PERFORM FIRST AID, AND MIINA HAS PLUCK AND IS QUICK-WITTED...
THEY'RE ALL TRUST-WORTHY COMRADES OF MINE.
I'M PERFECTLY SATISFIED!!

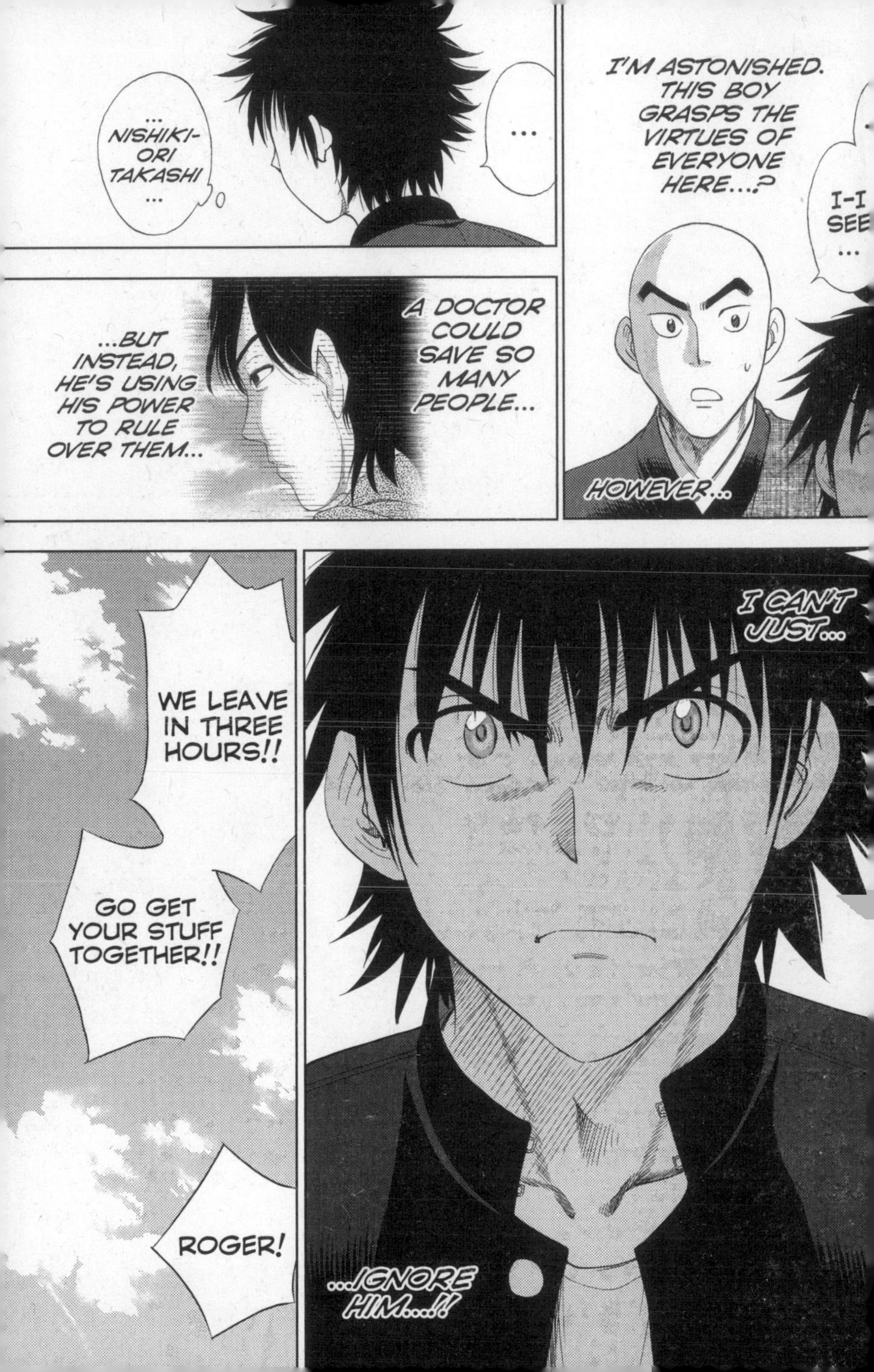

I-I SEE...
I'M ASTONISHED. THIS BOY GRASPS THE VIRTUES OF EVERYONE HERE...?
HOWEVER...
...
... NISHIKI-ORI TAKASHI ...
A DOCTOR COULD SAVE SO MANY PEOPLE...
...BUT INSTEAD, HE'S USING HIS POWER TO RULE OVER THEM...
I CAN'T JUST...
...IGNORE HIM...!!
WE LEAVE IN THREE HOURS!!
GO GET YOUR STUFF TOGETHER!!
ROGER!

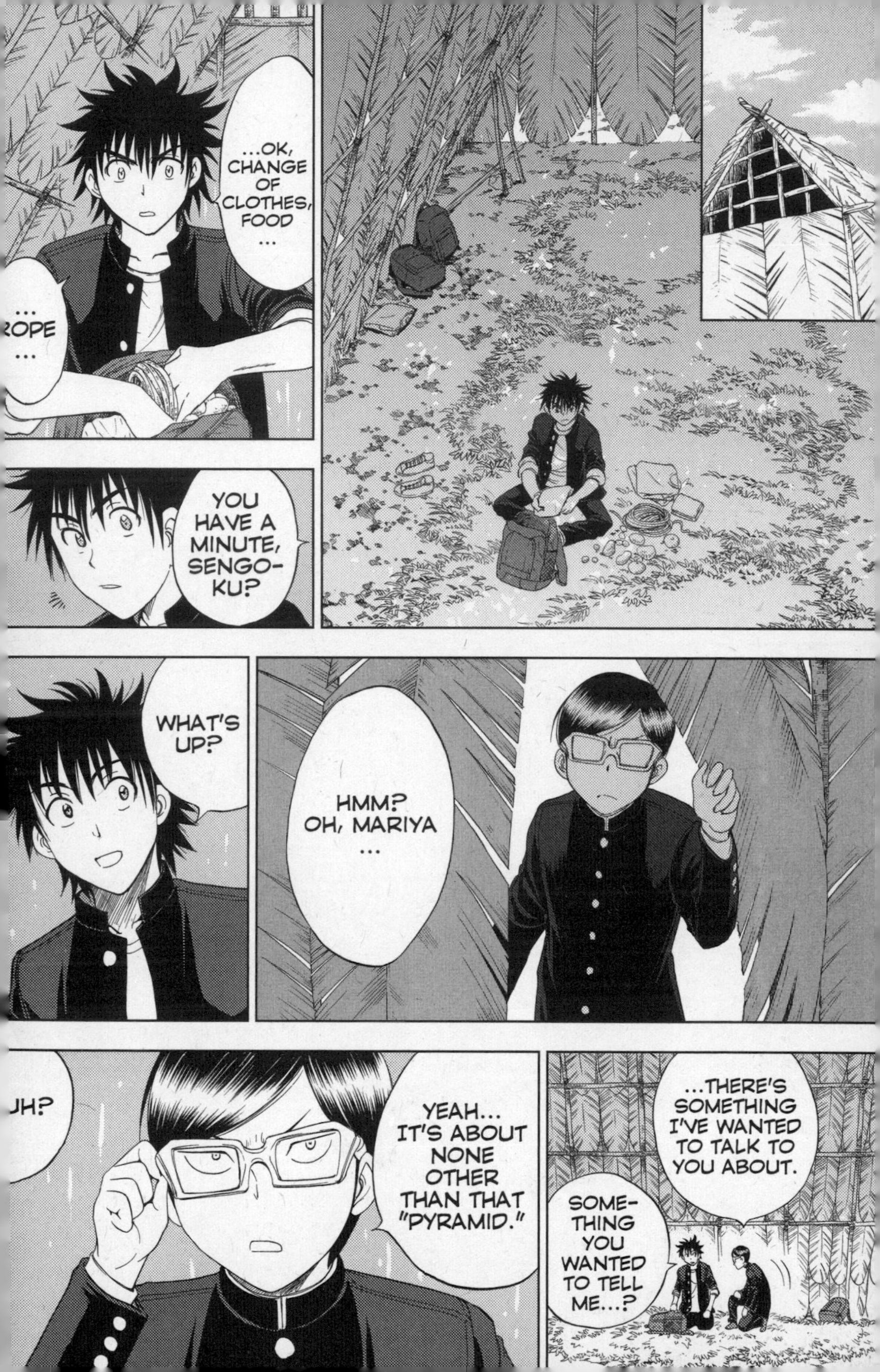
...OK, CHANGE OF CLOTHES, FOOD ...
... ROPE ...
YOU HAVE A MINUTE, SENGO-KU?
HMM? OH, MARIYA ...
WHAT'S UP?
...THERE'S SOMETHING I'VE WANTED TO TALK TO YOU ABOUT.
SOME-THING YOU WANTED TO TELL ME...?
YEAH... IT'S ABOUT NONE OTHER THAN THAT "PYRAMID."
UH?

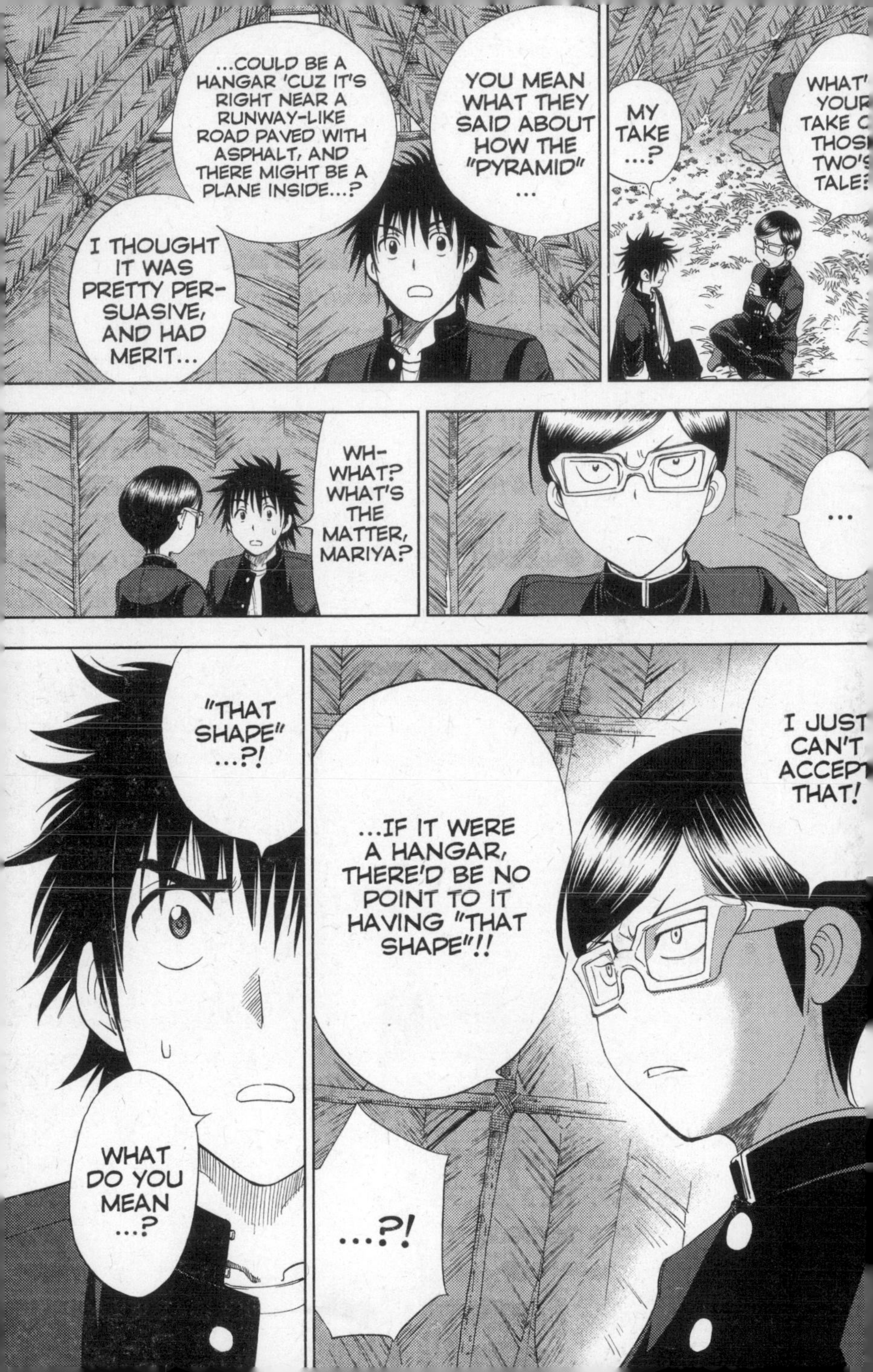
WHAT' YOUR TAKE O THOS TWO'S TALE?
MY TAKE ...?
YOU MEAN WHAT THEY SAID ABOUT HOW THE "PYRAMID" ...
...COULD BE A HANGAR 'CUZ IT'S RIGHT NEAR A RUNWAY-LIKE ROAD PAVED WITH ASPHALT, AND THERE MIGHT BE A PLANE INSIDE...?
I THOUGHT IT WAS PRETTY PER-SUASIVE, AND HAD MERIT...
...
WH-WHAT? WHAT'S THE MATTER, MARIYA?
I JUST CAN'T ACCEPT THAT!
...IF IT WERE A HANGAR, THERE'D BE NO POINT TO IT HAVING "THAT SHAPE"!!
...?!
"THAT SHAPE" ...?!
WHAT DO YOU MEAN ...?

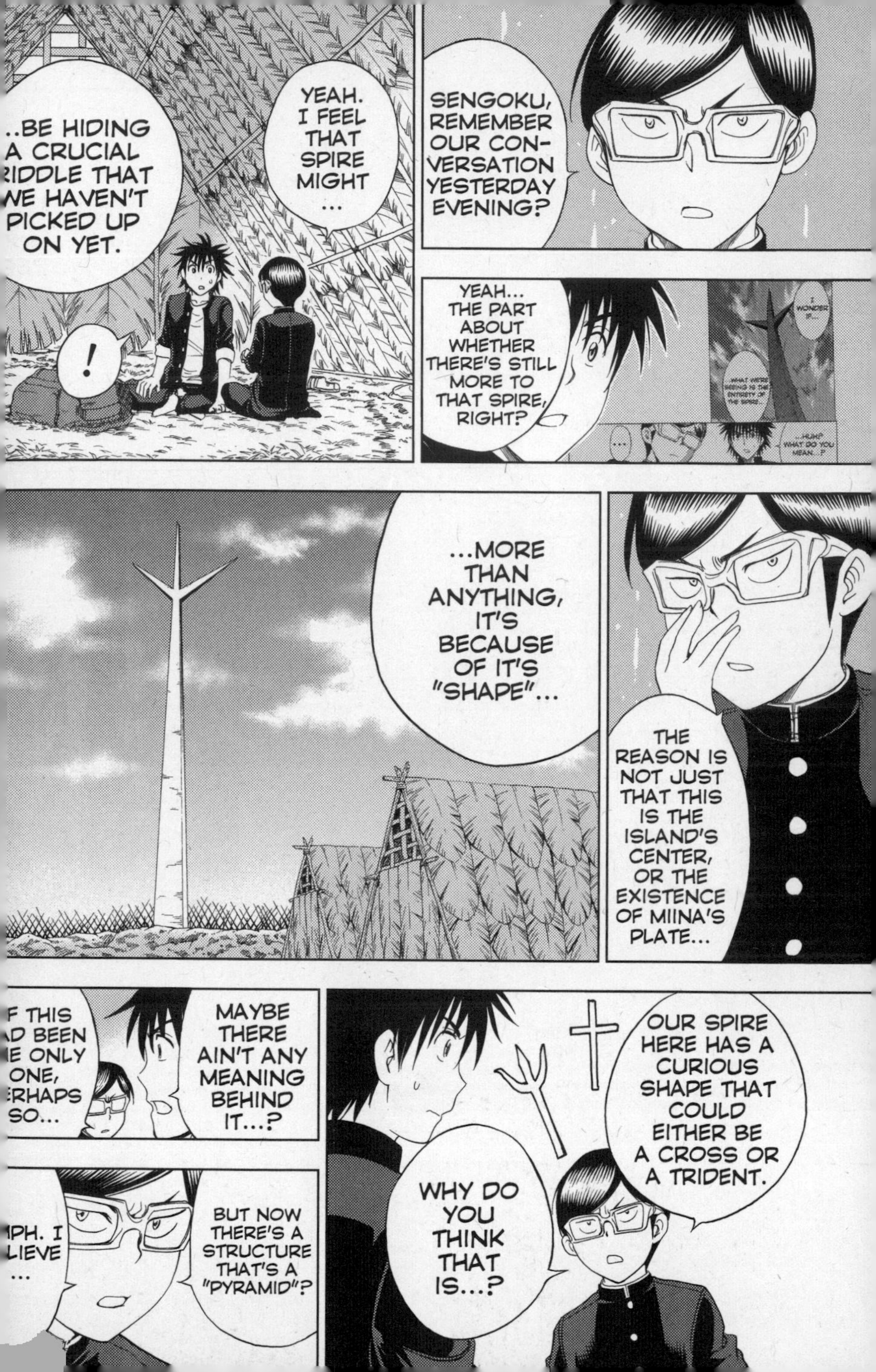
SENGOKU, REMEMBER OUR CON-VERSATION YESTERDAY EVENING?
YEAH... THE PART ABOUT WHETHER THERE'S STILL MORE TO THAT SPIRE, RIGHT?
I WONDER IF...
...WHAT WE'RE SEEING IS THE ENTIRETY OF THE SPIRE...
...HUH? WHAT DO YOU MEAN...?
...
YEAH. I FEEL THAT SPIRE MIGHT ...
..BE HIDING A CRUCIAL RIDDLE THAT WE HAVEN'T PICKED UP ON YET.
!
THE REASON IS NOT JUST THAT THIS IS THE ISLAND'S CENTER, OR THE EXISTENCE OF MIINA'S PLATE...
...MORE THAN ANYTHING, IT'S BECAUSE OF IT'S "SHAPE"...
OUR SPIRE HERE HAS A CURIOUS SHAPE THAT COULD EITHER BE A CROSS OR A TRIDENT.
WHY DO YOU THINK THAT IS...?
MAYBE THERE AIN'T ANY MEANING BEHIND IT...?
F THIS D BEEN E ONLY ONE, ERHAPS SO...
BUT NOW THERE'S A STRUCTURE THAT'S A "PYRAMID"?
PH. I LIEVE ...

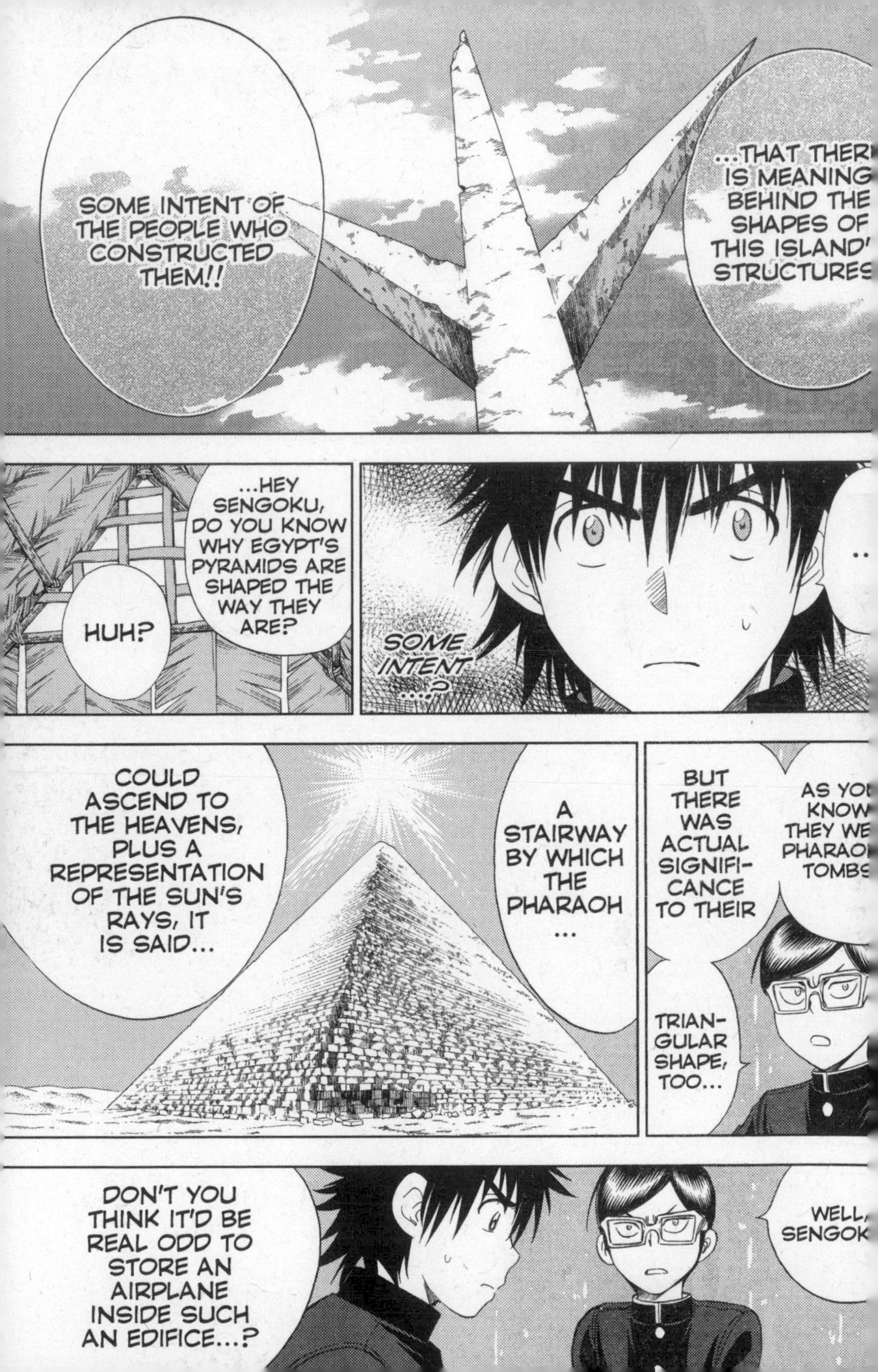
...THAT THER IS MEANING BEHIND THE SHAPES OF THIS ISLAND' STRUCTURES
SOME INTENT OF THE PEOPLE WHO CONSTRUCTED THEM!!
..
SOME INTENT ...?
...HEY SENGOKU, DO YOU KNOW WHY EGYPT'S PYRAMIDS ARE SHAPED THE WAY THEY ARE?
HUH?
AS YO KNOW THEY WE PHARAO TOMBS
BUT THERE WAS ACTUAL SIGNIFI-CANCE TO THEIR
TRIAN-GULAR SHAPE, TOO...
A STAIRWAY BY WHICH THE PHARAOH ...
COULD ASCEND TO THE HEAVENS, PLUS A REPRESENTATION OF THE SUN'S RAYS, IT IS SAID...
WELL, SENGOK
DON'T YOU THINK IT'D BE REAL ODD TO STORE AN AIRPLANE INSIDE SUCH AN EDIFICE...?

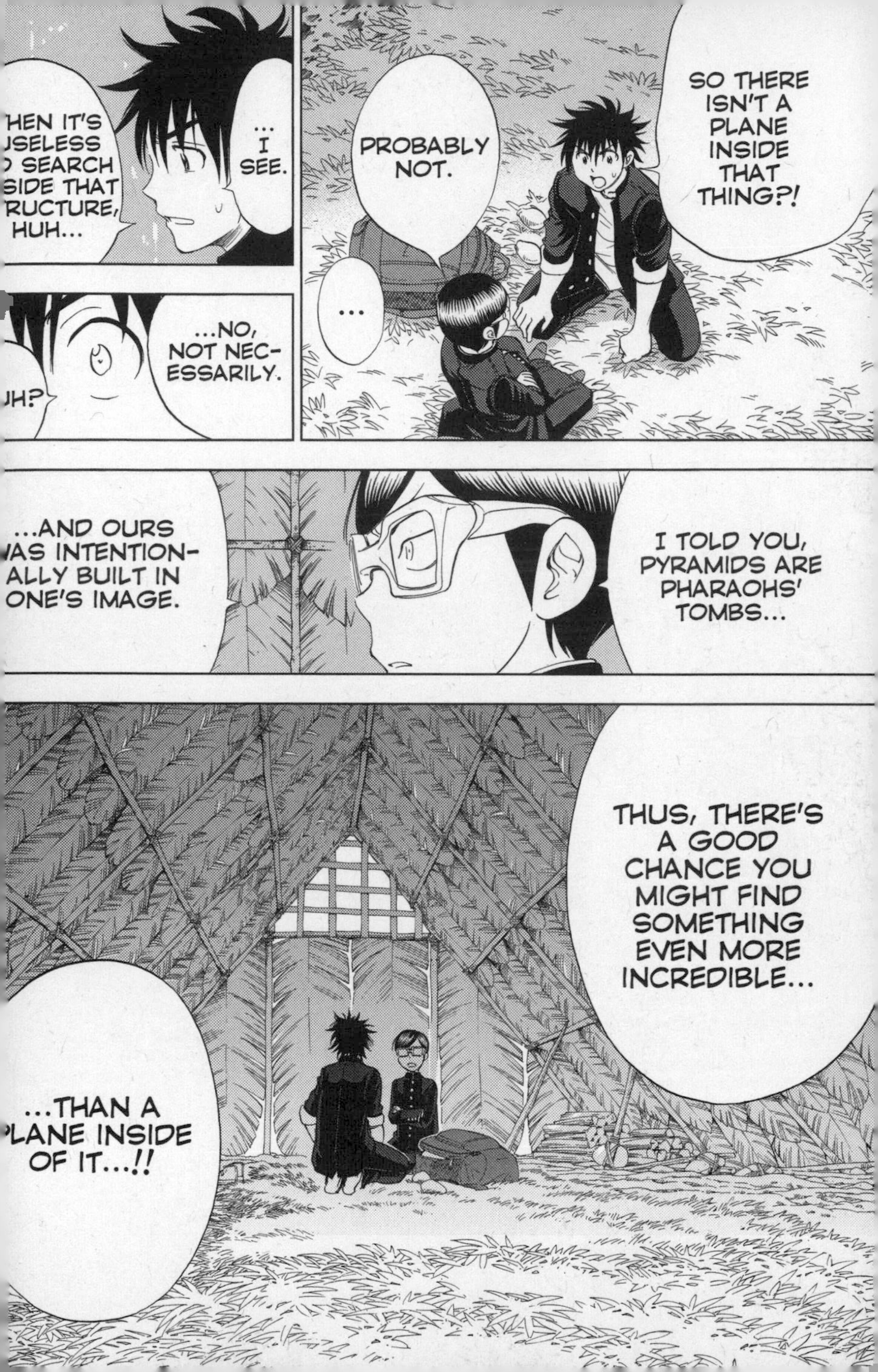
SO THERE ISN'T A PLANE INSIDE THAT THING?!
PROBABLY NOT.
...
... I SEE.
HEN IT'S USELESS) SEARCH SIDE THAT RUCTURE, HUH...
...NO, NOT NEC-ESSARILY.
JH?
I TOLD YOU, PYRAMIDS ARE PHARAOHS' TOMBS...
...AND OURS VAS INTENTION-ALLY BUILT IN ONE'S IMAGE.
THUS, THERE'S A GOOD CHANCE YOU MIGHT FIND SOMETHING EVEN MORE INCREDIBLE...
...THAN A LANE INSIDE OF IT...!!

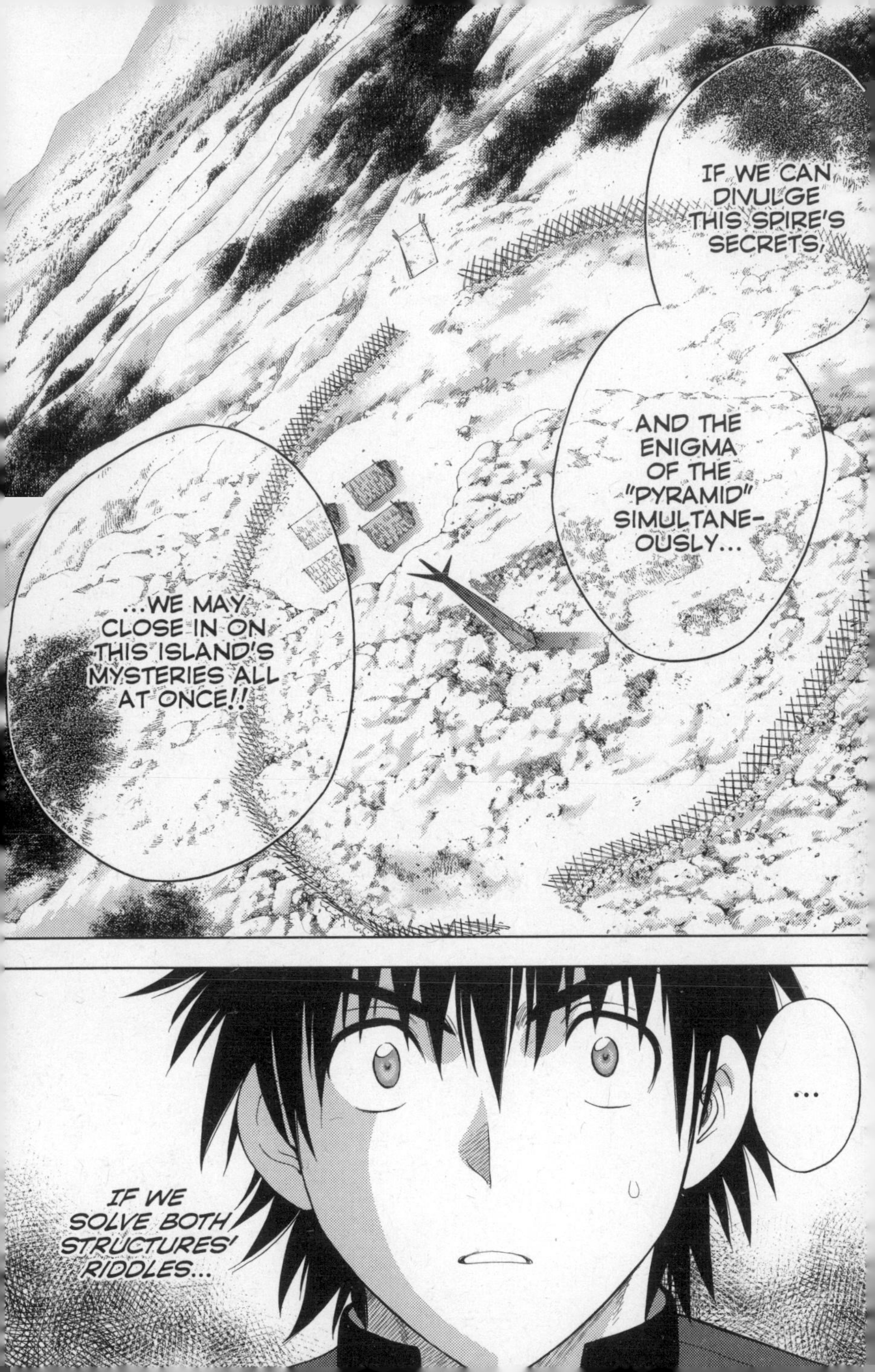
IF WE CAN DIVULGE THIS SPIRE'S SECRETS,
AND THE ENIGMA OF THE "PYRAMID" SIMULTANE-OUSLY...
...WE MAY CLOSE IN ON THIS ISLAND'S MYSTERIES ALL AT ONCE!!
...
IF WE SOLVE BOTH STRUCTURES' RIDDLES...

... ANYWAY, THAT'S ALL I HAD TO SAY.

YOU BE CAREFUL OUT THERE, ALL RIGHT?!

...

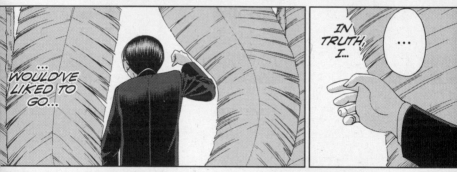

...WOULD'VE LIKED TO GO...

IN TRUTH, I...

...

COURSE... !KE DUH!!

MARIYA, YOU...

...

...CAME 'CUZ YOU'RE WORRIED...

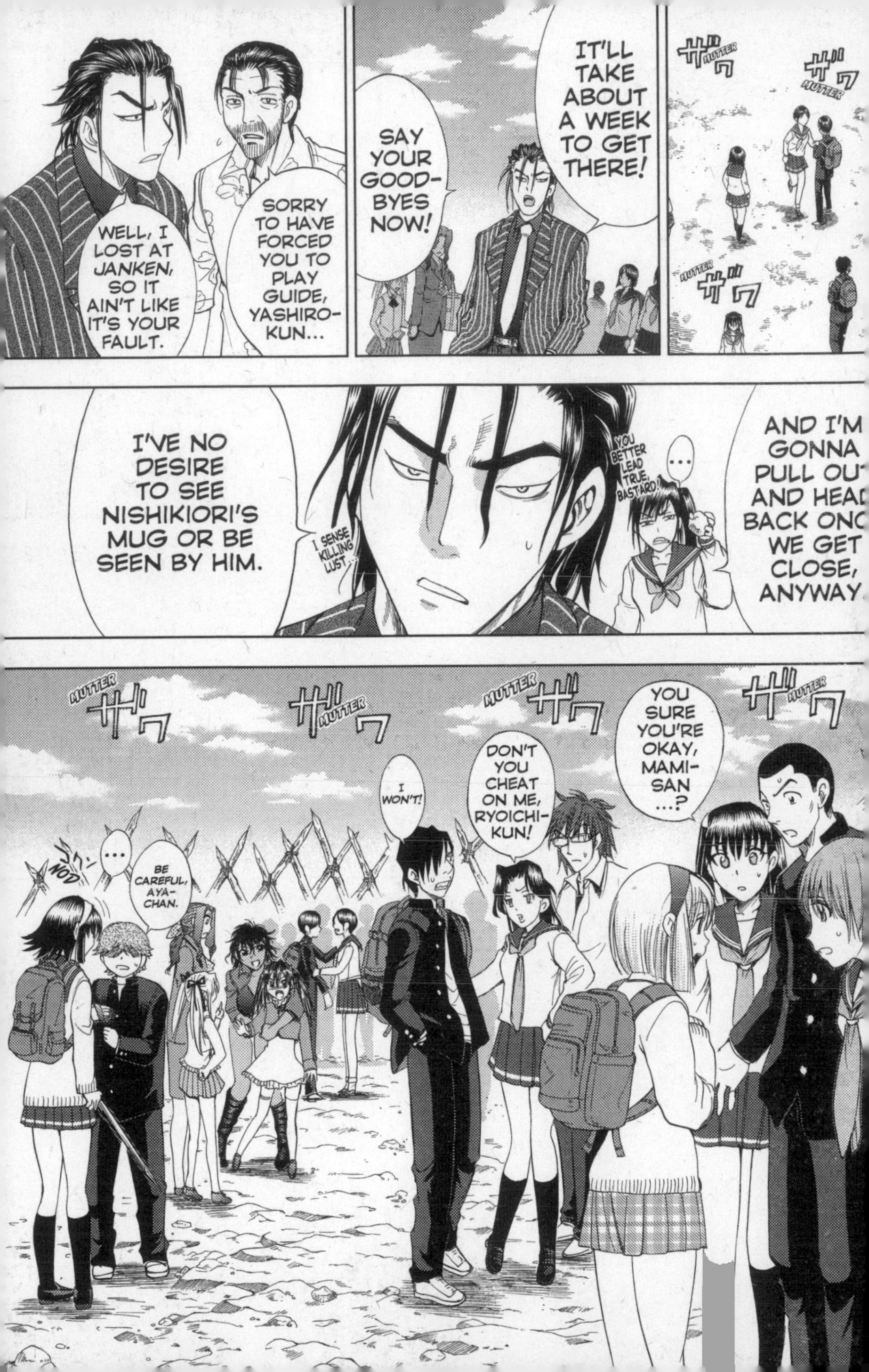

ザワ MUTTER
ザワ MUTTER
ザワ MUTTER
IT'LL TAKE ABOUT A WEEK TO GET THERE!
SAY YOUR GOOD-BYES NOW!
SORRY TO HAVE FORCED YOU TO PLAY GUIDE, YASHIRO-KUN...
WELL, I LOST AT JANKEN, SO IT AIN'T LIKE IT'S YOUR FAULT.
AND I'M GONNA PULL OUT AND HEAD BACK ONCE WE GET CLOSE, ANYWAY.
...
YOU BETTER LEAD TRUE, BASTARD!
I'VE NO DESIRE TO SEE NISHIKIORI'S MUG OR BE SEEN BY HIM.
I SENSE KILLING LUST...
ザワ MUTTER
ザワ MUTTER
YOU SURE YOU'RE OKAY, MAMI-SAN ...?
ザワ MUTTER
ザワ MUTTER
DON'T YOU CHEAT ON ME, RYOICHI-KUN!
I WON'T!
BE CAREFUL, AYA-CHAN.
...
コクン NOD

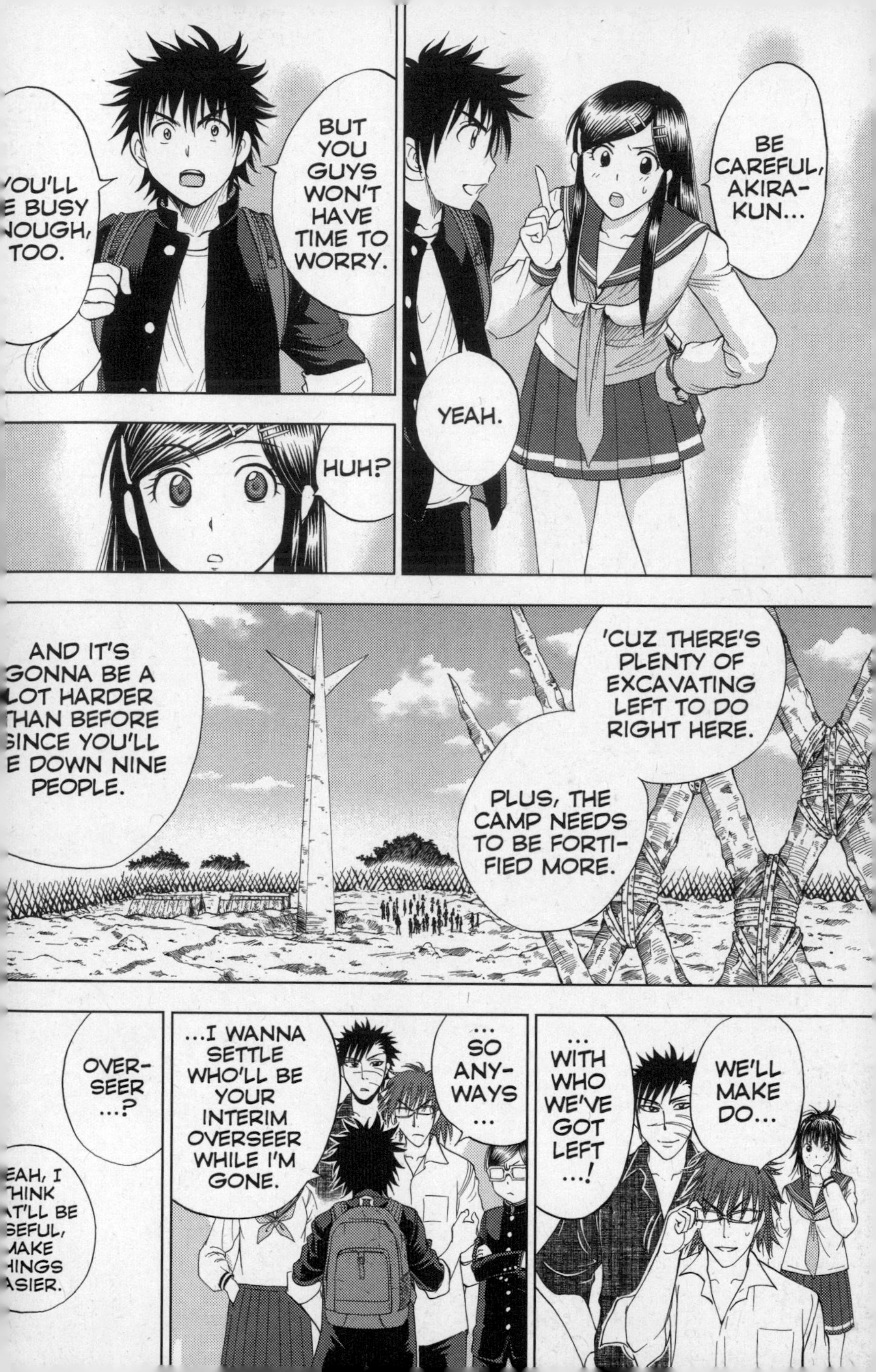
BE CAREFUL, AKIRA-KUN...
YEAH.
BUT YOU GUYS WON'T HAVE TIME TO WORRY.
OU'LL E BUSY NOUGH, TOO.
HUH?
'CUZ THERE'S PLENTY OF EXCAVATING LEFT TO DO RIGHT HERE.
PLUS, THE CAMP NEEDS TO BE FORTI-FIED MORE.
AND IT'S GONNA BE A LOT HARDER THAN BEFORE SINCE YOU'LL E DOWN NINE PEOPLE.
WE'LL MAKE DO...
...WITH WHO WE'VE GOT LEFT...!
...SO ANY-WAYS...
...I WANNA SETTLE WHO'LL BE YOUR INTERIM OVERSEER WHILE I'M GONE.
OVER-SEER...?
EAH, I THINK AT'LL BE SEFUL, MAKE HINGS ASIER.

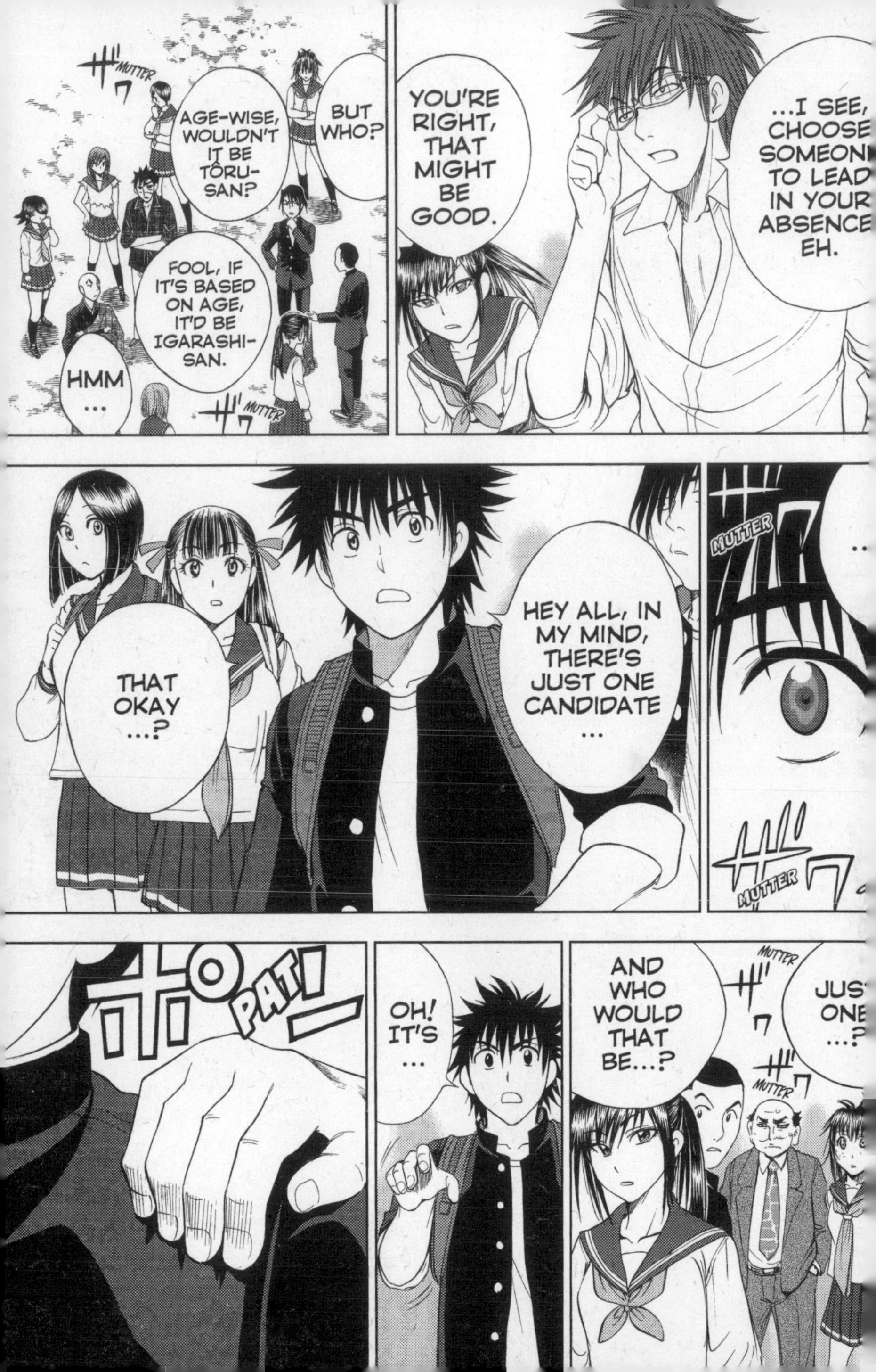
...I SEE, CHOOSE SOMEON TO LEAD IN YOUR ABSENCE EH.
YOU'RE RIGHT, THAT MIGHT BE GOOD.
BUT WHO?
MUTTER
AGE-WISE, WOULDN'T IT BE TÔRU-SAN?
FOOL, IF IT'S BASED ON AGE, IT'D BE IGARASHI-SAN.
HMM ...
MUTTER
MUTTER
MUTTER
HEY ALL, IN MY MIND, THERE'S JUST ONE CANDIDATE ...
THAT OKAY ...?
JUS ONE ...?
MUTTER
MUTTER
AND WHO WOULD THAT BE...?
OH! IT'S ...
PAT!

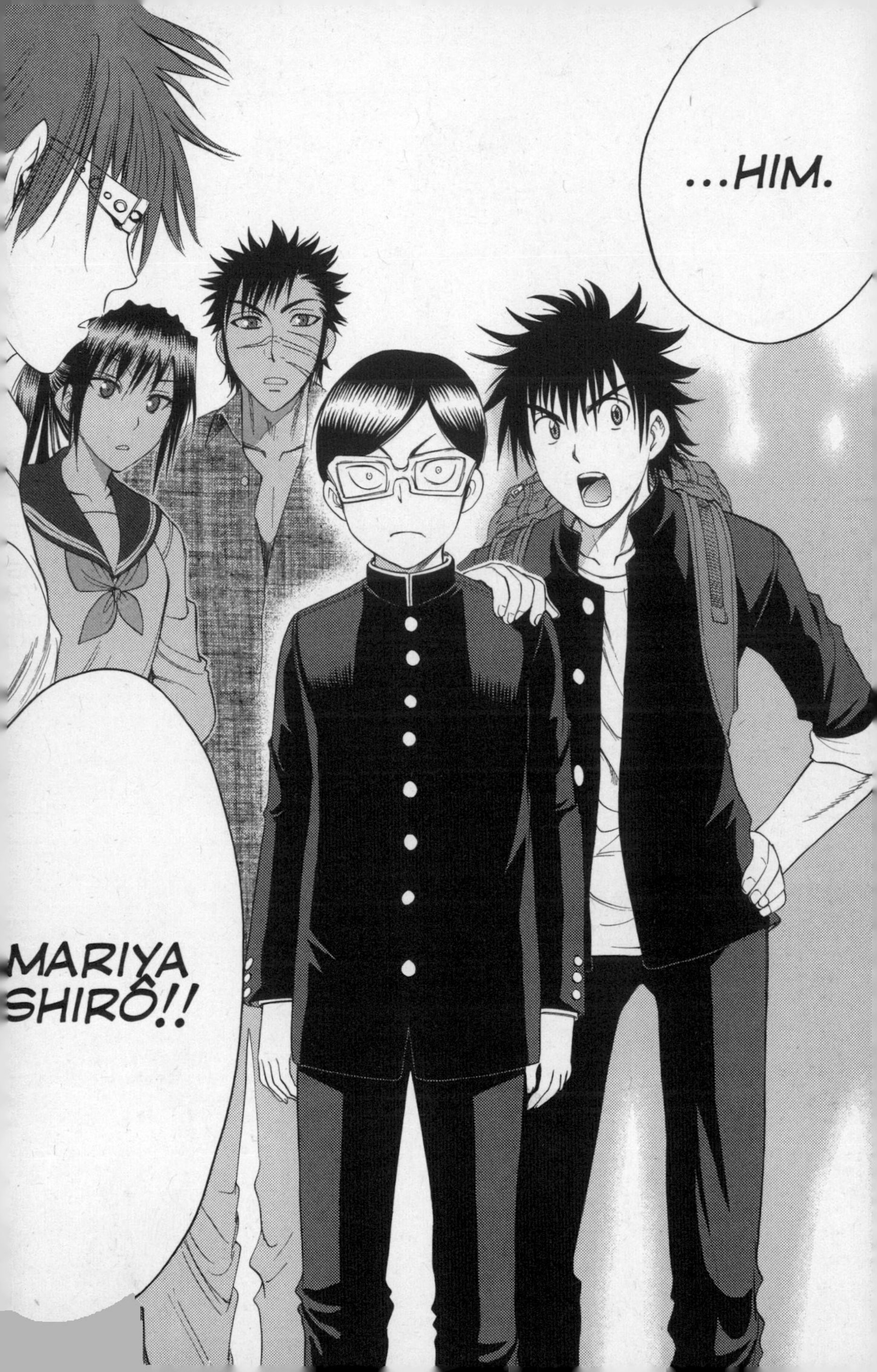
...HIM.
MARIYA SHIRÔ!!

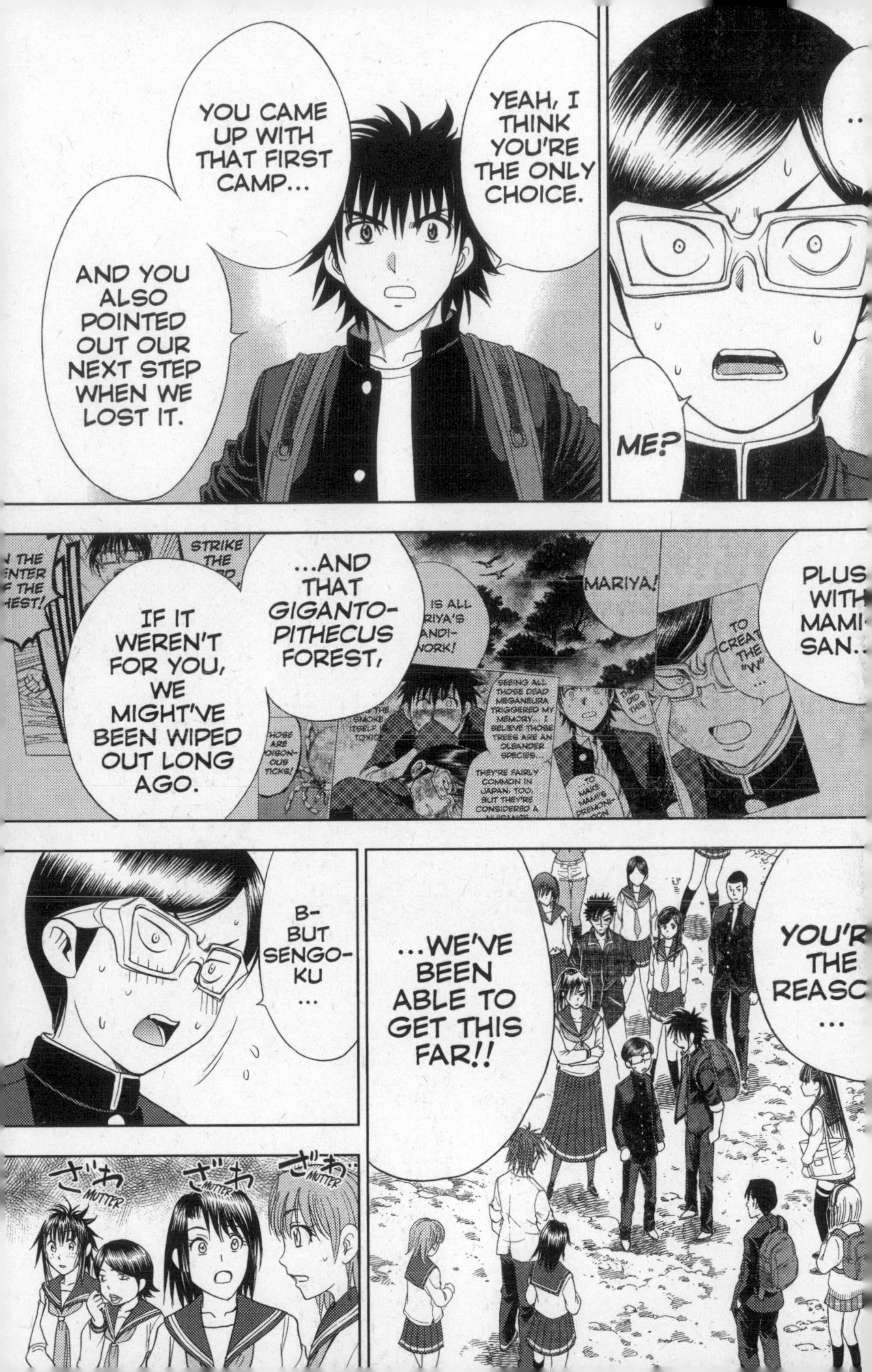
...
ME?
YEAH, I THINK YOU'RE THE ONLY CHOICE.
YOU CAME UP WITH THAT FIRST CAMP...
AND YOU ALSO POINTED OUT OUR NEXT STEP WHEN WE LOST IT.
PLUS WITH MAMI-SAN...
MARIYA!
SEEING ALL THOSE DEAD MEGANEURA TRIGGERED MY MEMORY... I BELIEVE THOSE TREES ARE AN OLEANDER SPECIES...
...AND THAT GIGANTO-PITHECUS FOREST,
IF IT WEREN'T FOR YOU, WE MIGHT'VE BEEN WIPED OUT LONG AGO.
YOU'R THE REASC ...
...WE'VE BEEN ABLE TO GET THIS FAR!!
B-BUT SENGOKU...
MUTTER
MUTTER
MUTTER

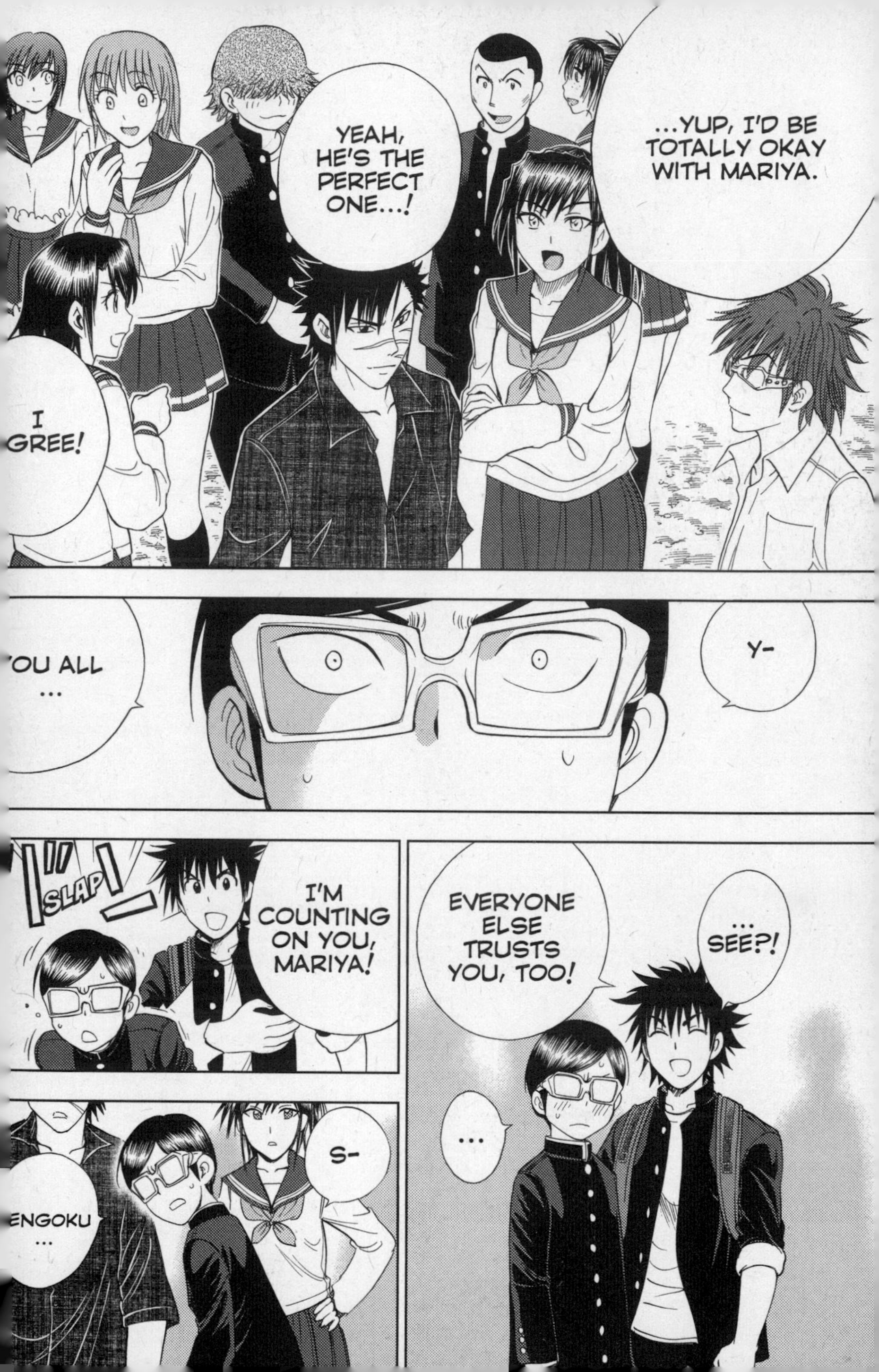
...YUP, I'D BE TOTALLY OKAY WITH MARIYA.
YEAH, HE'S THE PERFECT ONE...!
I GREE!
Y-
YOU ALL ...
... SEE?!
EVERYONE ELSE TRUSTS YOU, TOO!
...
SLAP
I'M COUNTING ON YOU, MARIYA!
S-
ENGOKU ...

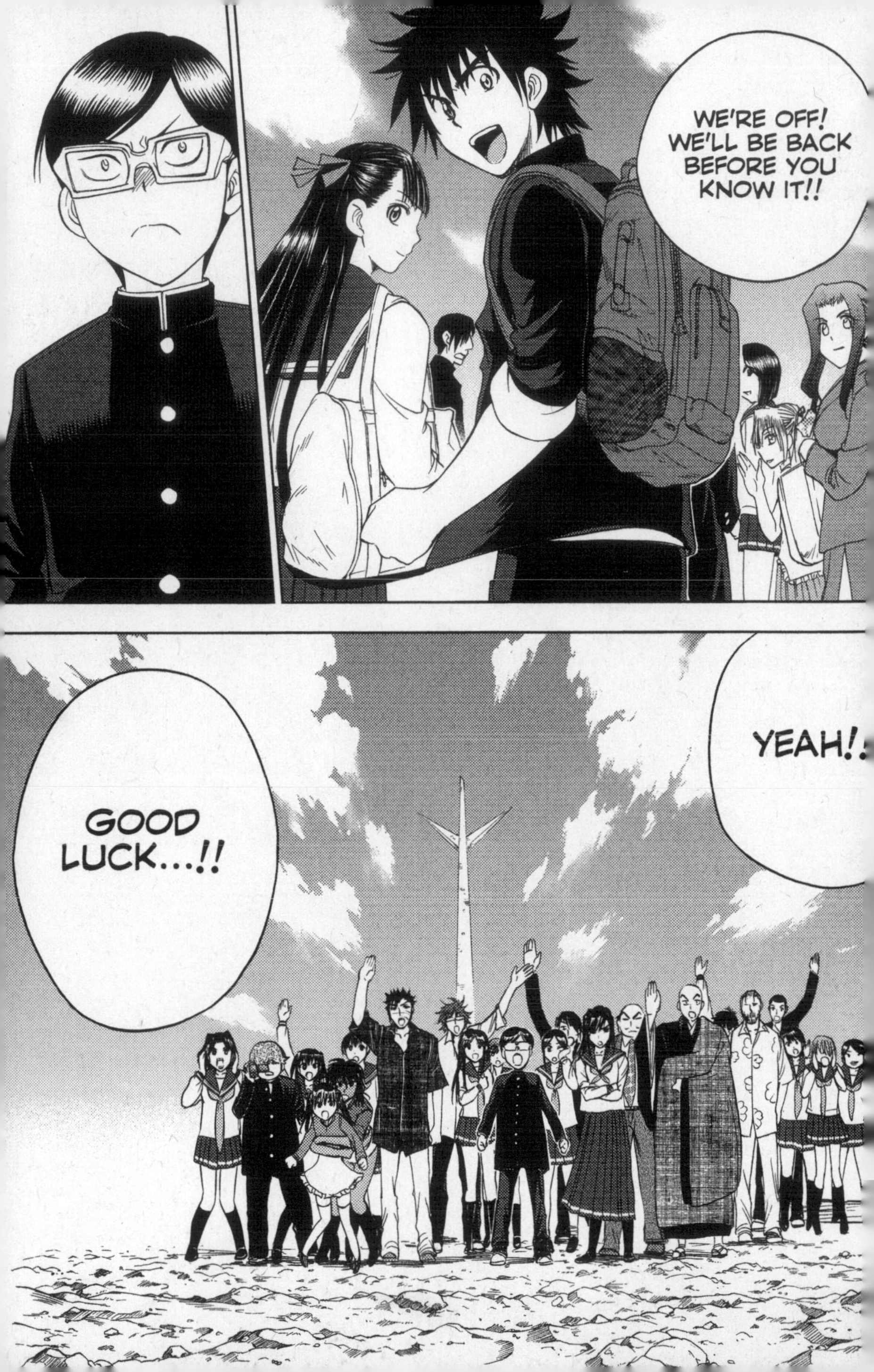
WE'RE OFF! WE'LL BE BACK BEFORE YOU KNOW IT!!
YEAH!!
GOOD LUCK...!!

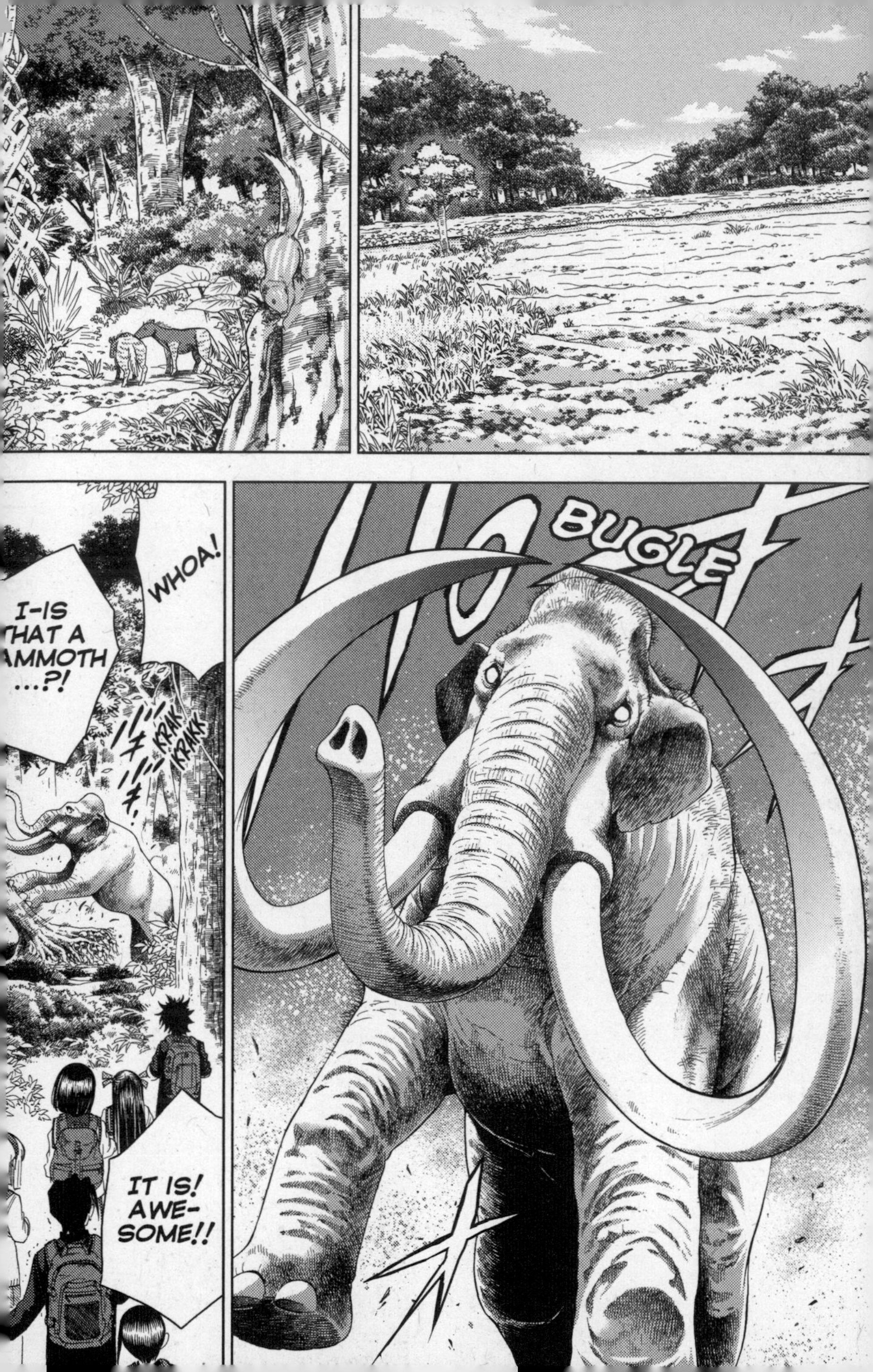
BUGLE
WHOA!
I-IS THAT A AMMOTH ...?!
KRAK KRAKK
IT IS! AWE- SOME!!

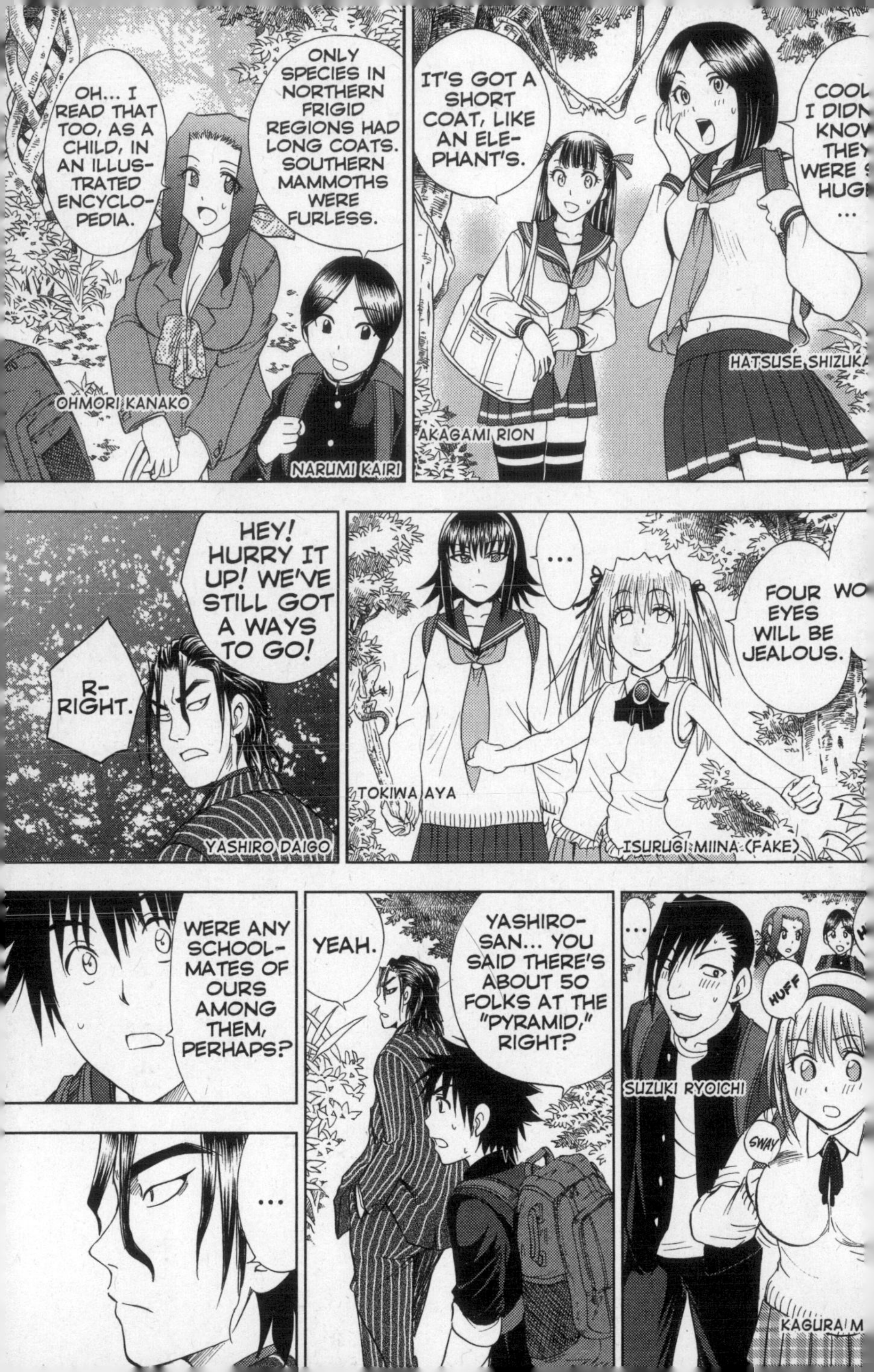
COOL I DIDN KNOW THEY WERE S HUG ...
IT'S GOT A SHORT COAT, LIKE AN ELE-PHANT'S.
HATSUSE SHIZUKA
AKAGAMI RION
ONLY SPECIES IN NORTHERN FRIGID REGIONS HAD LONG COATS. SOUTHERN MAMMOTHS WERE FURLESS.
OH... I READ THAT TOO, AS A CHILD, IN AN ILLUS-TRATED ENCYCLO-PEDIA.
OHMORI KANAKO
NARUMI KAIRI
FOUR WO EYES WILL BE JEALOUS.
...
TOKIWA AYA
ISURUGI MIINA (FAKE)
HEY! HURRY IT UP! WE'VE STILL GOT A WAYS TO GO!
R-RIGHT.
YASHIRO DAIGO
...
HUFF
SUZUKI RYOICHI
SWAY
KAGURA M
YASHIRO-SAN... YOU SAID THERE'S ABOUT 50 FOLKS AT THE "PYRAMID," RIGHT?
YEAH.
WERE ANY SCHOOL-MATES OF OURS AMONG THEM, PERHAPS?
...

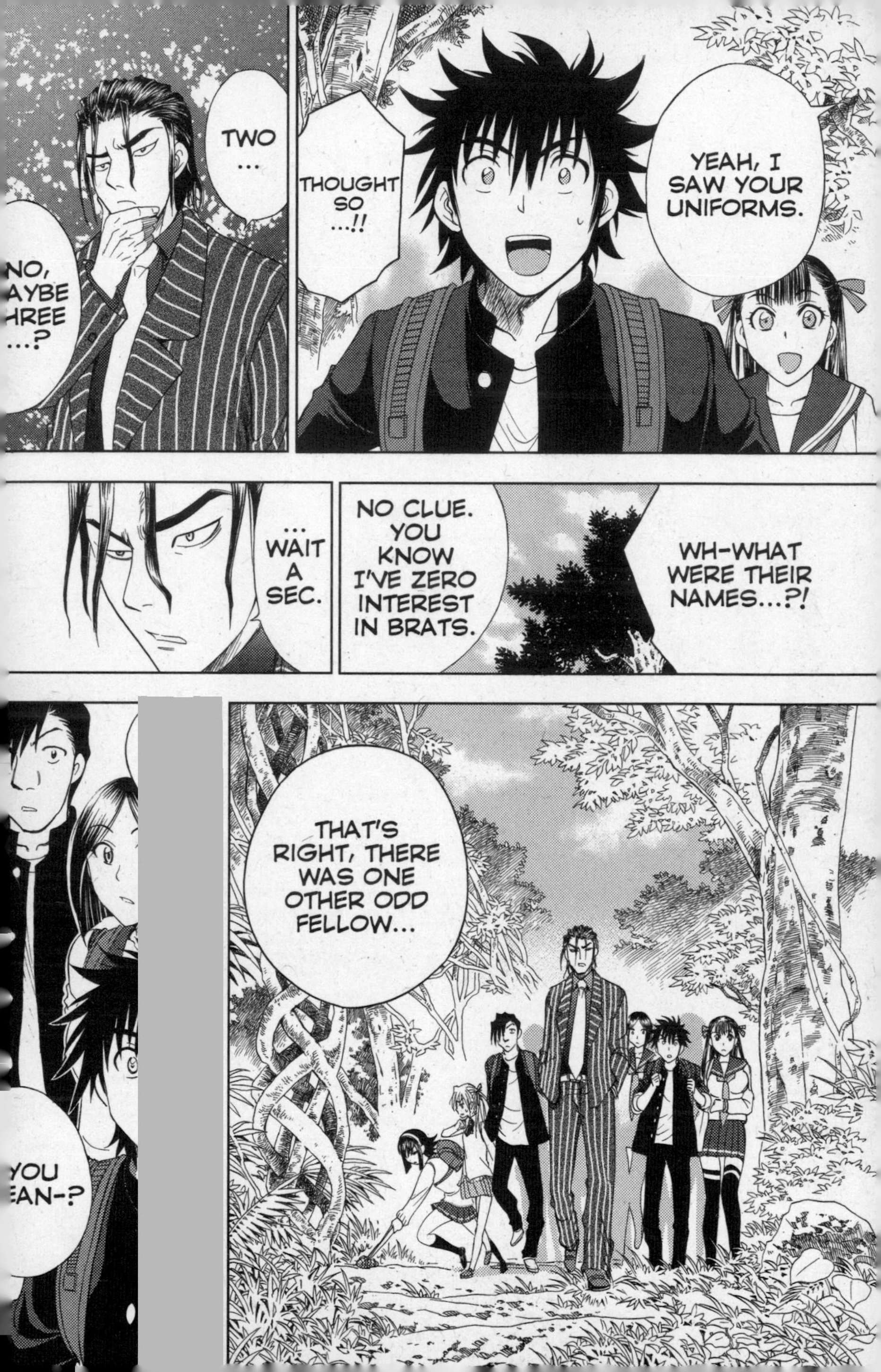
YEAH, I SAW YOUR UNIFORMS.
THOUGHT SO ...!!
TWO ...
NO, AYBE HREE ...?
WH-WHAT WERE THEIR NAMES...?!
NO CLUE. YOU KNOW I'VE ZERO INTEREST IN BRATS.
... WAIT A SEC.
THAT'S RIGHT, THERE WAS ONE OTHER ODD FELLOW...
YOU EAN-?

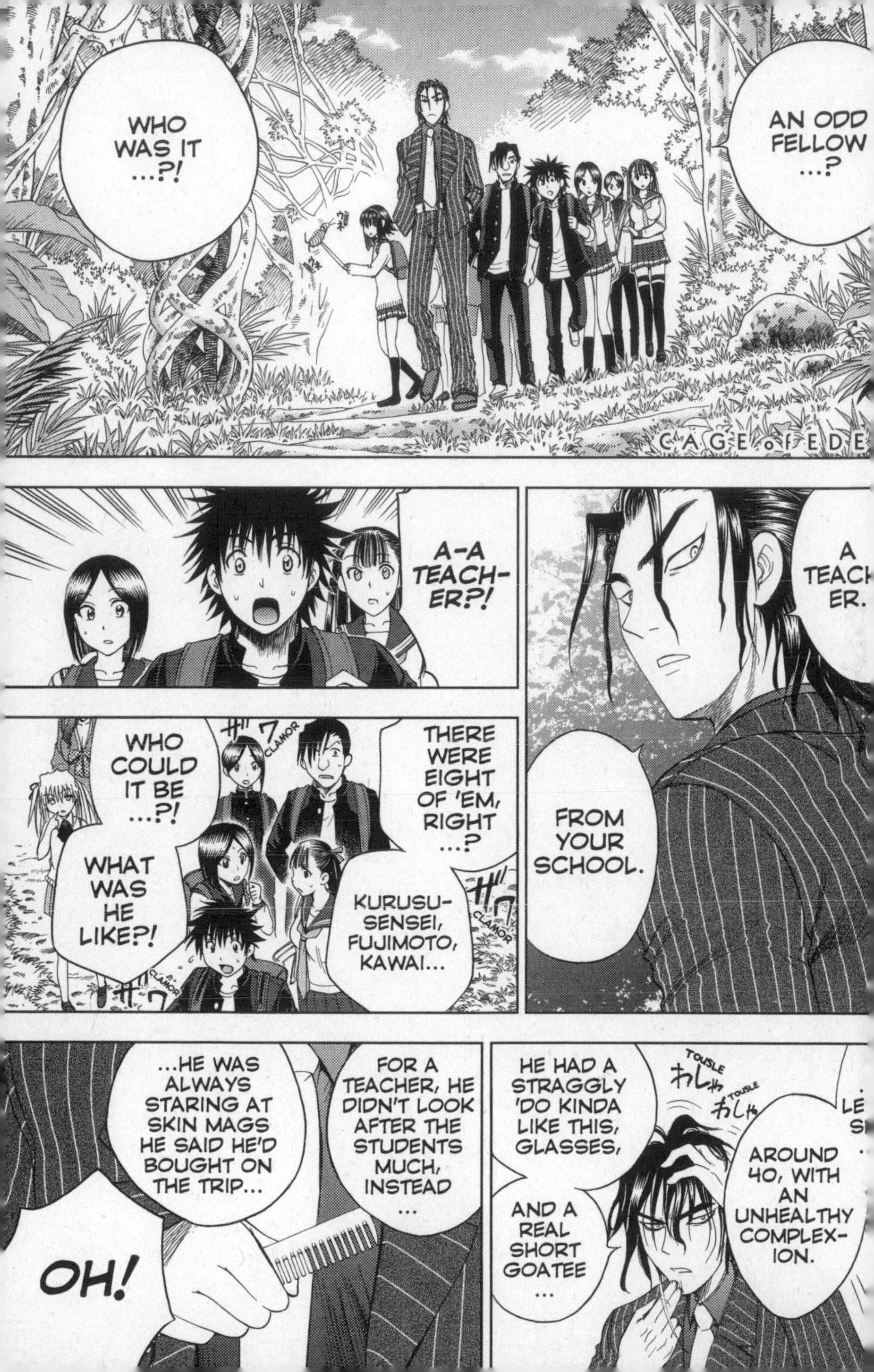
AN ODD FELLOW ...?
WHO WAS IT ...?!
CAGE of EDE
A TEACH ER.
FROM YOUR SCHOOL.
A-A TEACH-ER?!
THERE WERE EIGHT OF 'EM, RIGHT ...?
KURUSU-SENSEI, FUJIMOTO, KAWAI...
CLAMOR
WHO COULD IT BE ...?!
WHAT WAS HE LIKE?!
CLAMOR
CLAMOR
AROUND 40, WITH AN UNHEALTHY COMPLEX-ION.
TOUSLE
TOUSLE
HE HAD A STRAGGLY 'DO KINDA LIKE THIS, GLASSES,
AND A REAL SHORT GOATEE ...
FOR A TEACHER, HE DIDN'T LOOK AFTER THE STUDENTS MUCH, INSTEAD ...
...HE WAS ALWAYS STARING AT SKIN MAGS HE SAID HE'D BOUGHT ON THE TRIP...
OH!

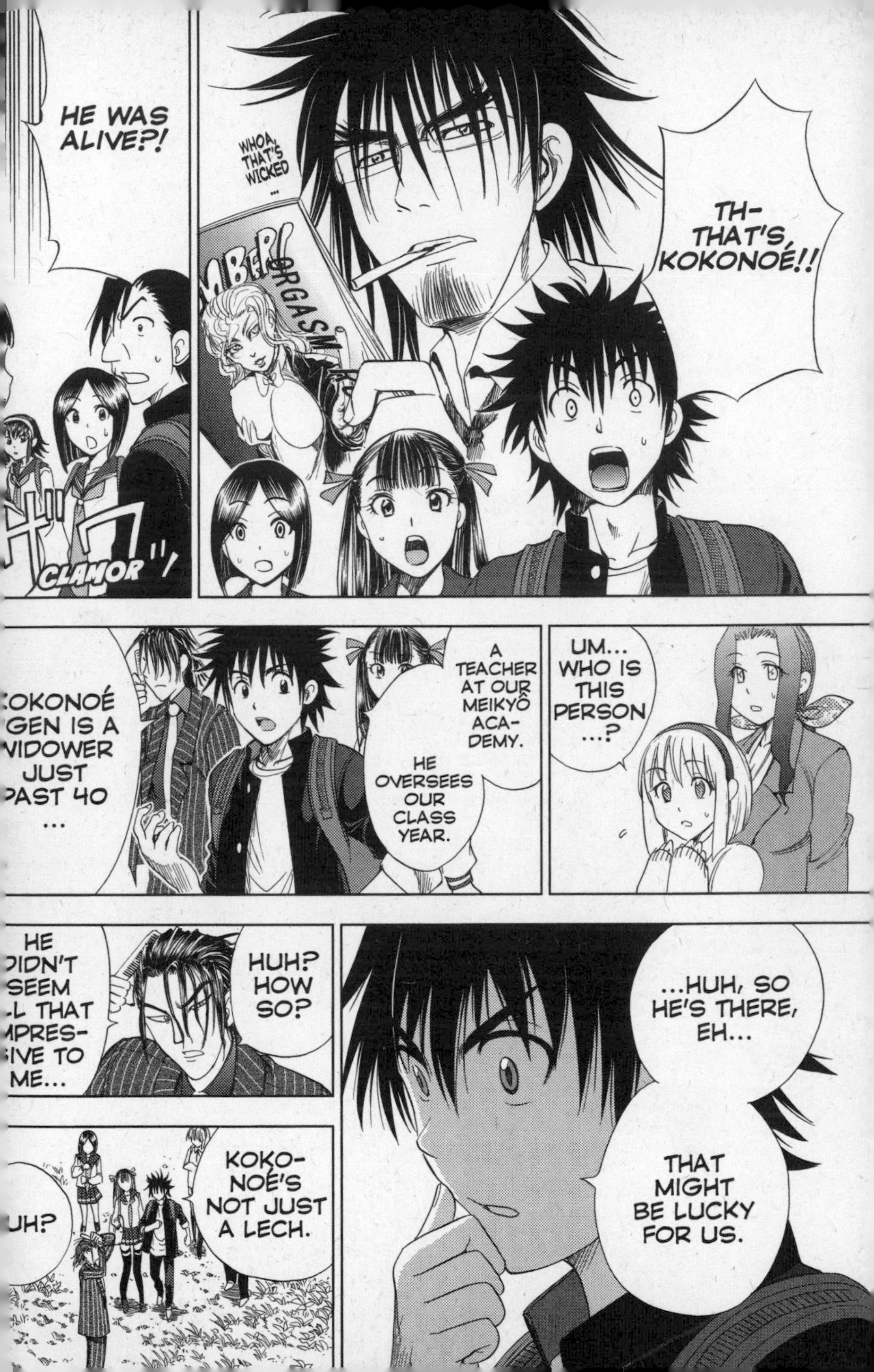
WHOA, THAT'S WICKED ...
TH- THAT'S, KOKONOÉ!!
HE WAS ALIVE?!
CLAMOR
UM... WHO IS THIS PERSON ...?
A TEACHER AT OUR MEIKYÔ ACA- DEMY.
HE OVERSEES OUR CLASS YEAR.
OKONOÉ GEN IS A IDOWER JUST PAST 40 ...
...HUH, SO HE'S THERE, EH...
THAT MIGHT BE LUCKY FOR US.
HUH? HOW SO?
HE IDN'T SEEM L THAT MPRES- IVE TO ME...
KOKO- NOÉ'S NOT JUST A LECH.
UH?

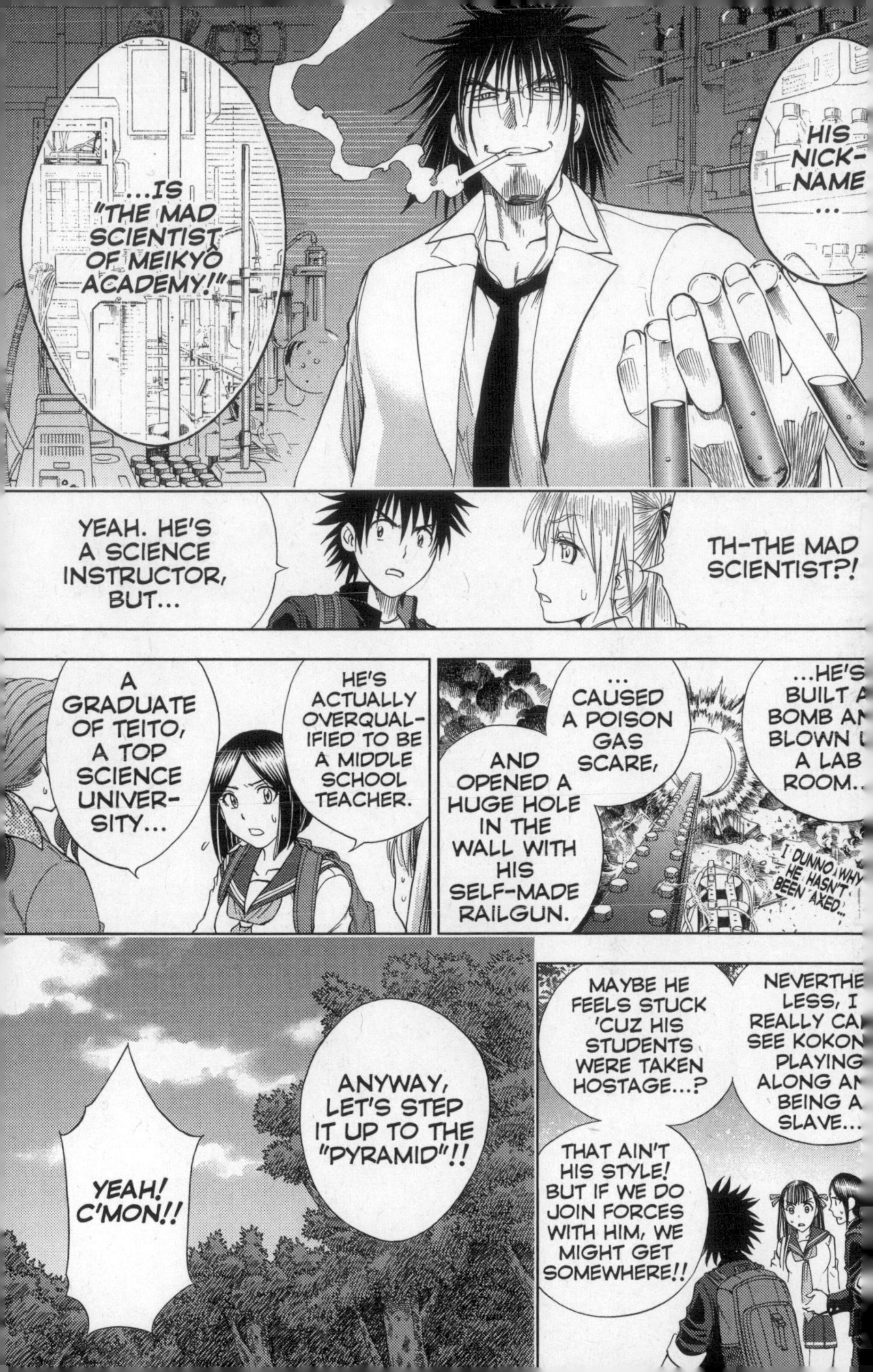
HIS NICK-NAME ...
...IS "THE MAD SCIENTIST OF MEIKYŌ ACADEMY!"
TH-THE MAD SCIENTIST?!
YEAH. HE'S A SCIENCE INSTRUCTOR, BUT...
...HE'S BUILT A BOMB AN BLOWN U A LAB ROOM..
... CAUSED A POISON GAS SCARE,
AND OPENED A HUGE HOLE IN THE WALL WITH HIS SELF-MADE RAILGUN.
I DUNNO WHY HE HASN'T BEEN AXED...
HE'S ACTUALLY OVERQUALIFIED TO BE A MIDDLE SCHOOL TEACHER.
A GRADUATE OF TEITO, A TOP SCIENCE UNIVERSITY...
NEVERTHE LESS, I REALLY CA SEE KOKON PLAYING ALONG AN BEING A SLAVE...
MAYBE HE FEELS STUCK 'CUZ HIS STUDENTS WERE TAKEN HOSTAGE...?
THAT AIN'T HIS STYLE! BUT IF WE DO JOIN FORCES WITH HIM, WE MIGHT GET SOMEWHERE!!
ANYWAY, LET'S STEP IT UP TO THE "PYRAMID"!!
YEAH! C'MON!!

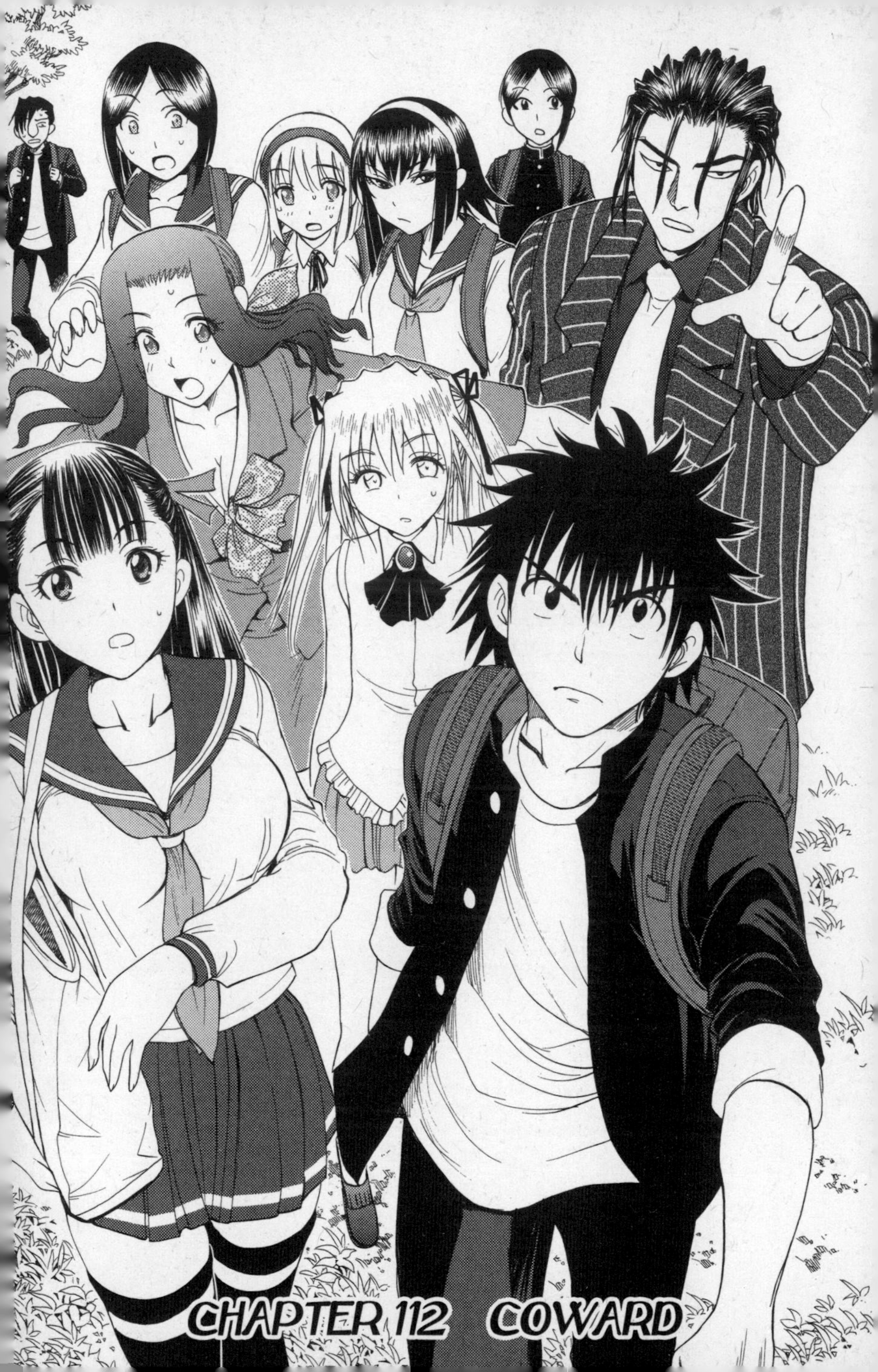
CHAPTER 112 COWARD

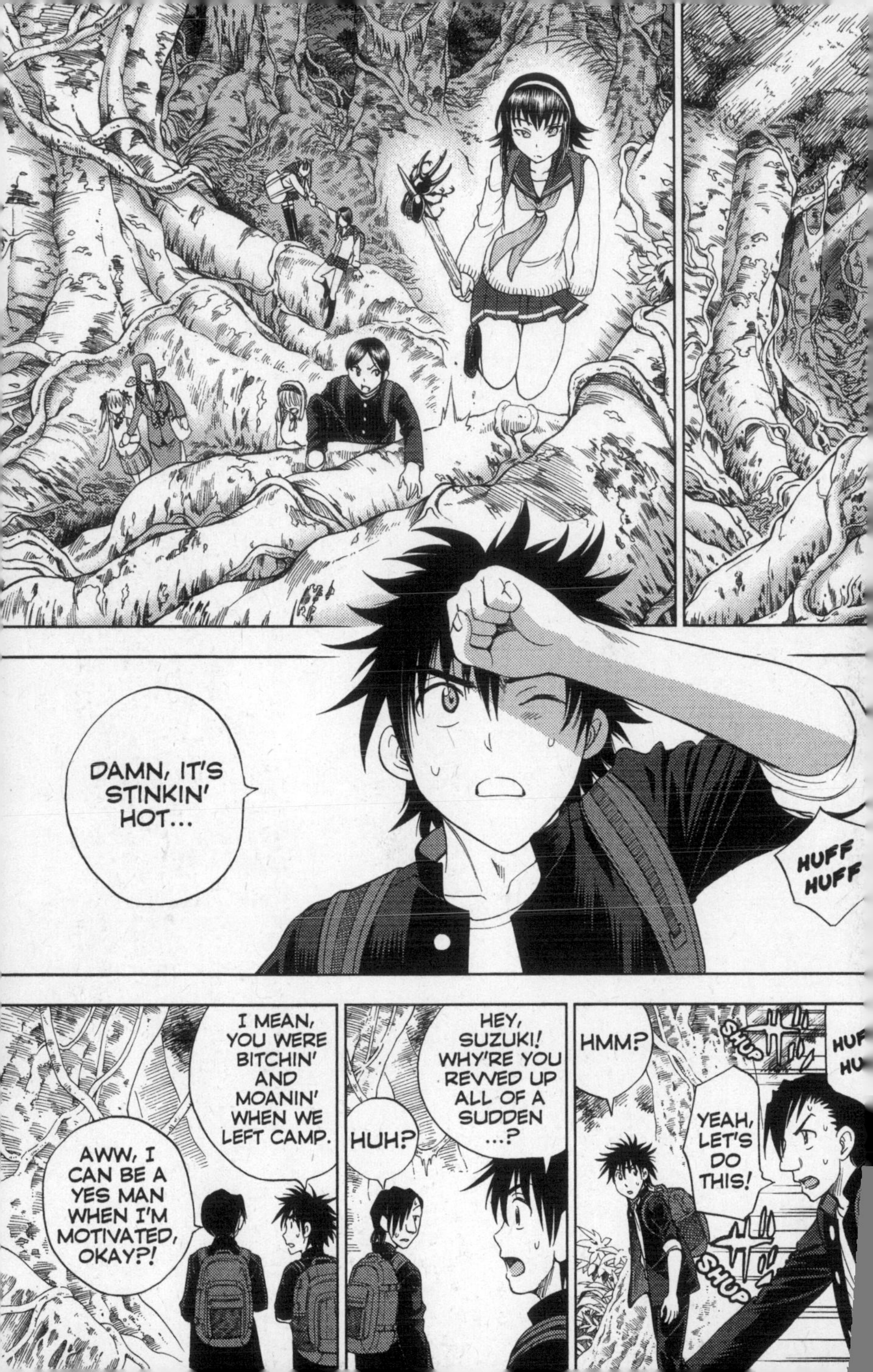
DAMN, IT'S STINKIN' HOT...
HUFF HUFF
HUF HU
SHUP
HMM?
YEAH, LET'S DO THIS!
SHUP
HEY, SUZUKI! WHY'RE YOU REVVED UP ALL OF A SUDDEN ...?
HUH?
I MEAN, YOU WERE BITCHIN' AND MOANIN' WHEN WE LEFT CAMP.
AWW, I CAN BE A YES MAN WHEN I'M MOTIVATED, OKAY?!

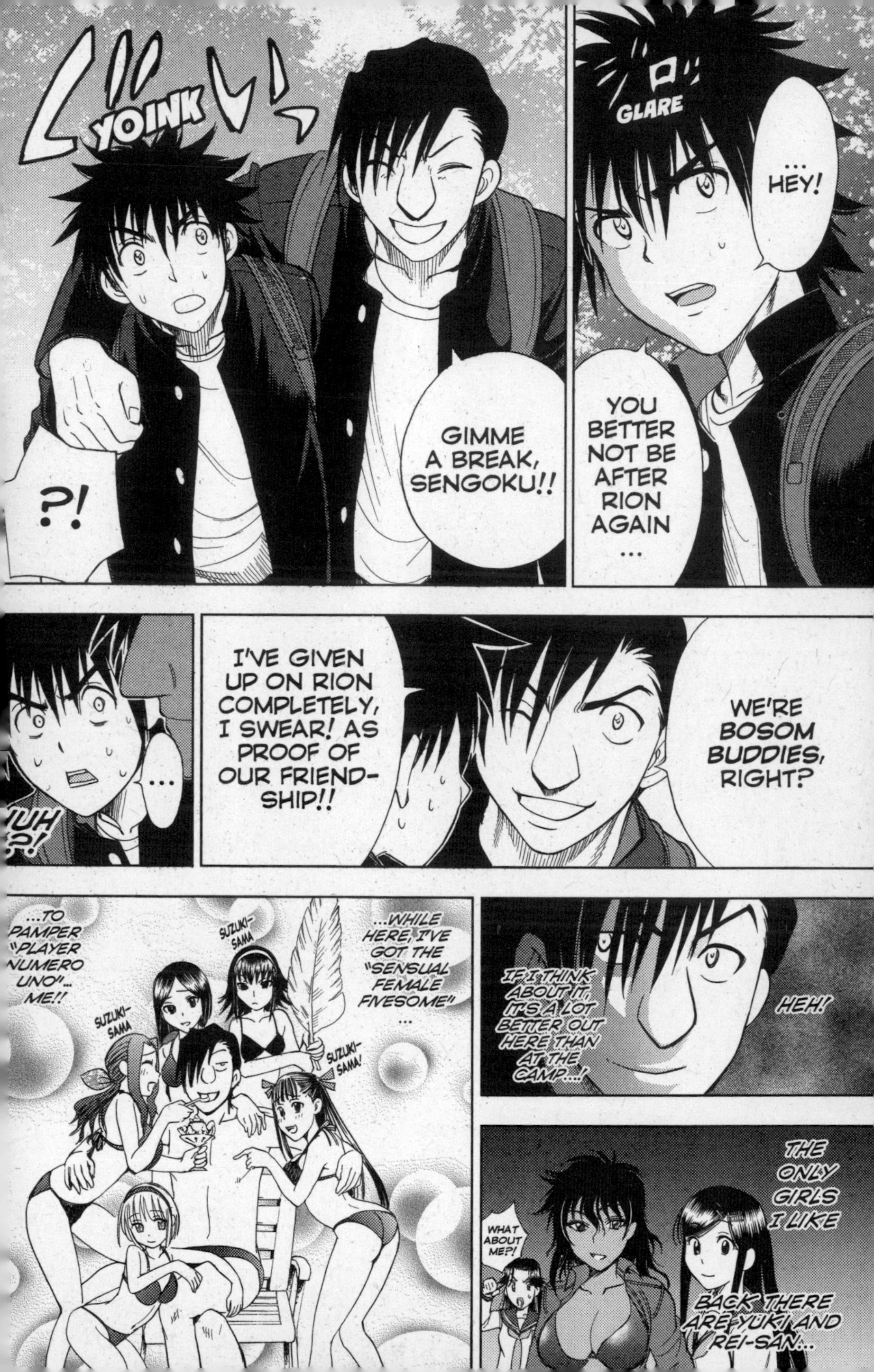
GLARE
...HEY!
YOU BETTER NOT BE AFTER RION AGAIN...
YOINK
GIMME A BREAK, SENGOKU!!
?!
WE'RE BOSOM BUDDIES, RIGHT?
I'VE GIVEN UP ON RION COMPLETELY, I SWEAR! AS PROOF OF OUR FRIENDSHIP!!
...
HEH!
IF I THINK ABOUT IT, IT'S A LOT BETTER OUT HERE THAN AT THE CAMP...!
THE ONLY GIRLS I LIKE
BACK THERE ARE YUKI AND REI-SAN...
WHAT ABOUT ME?!
...WHILE HERE, I'VE GOT THE "SENSUAL FEMALE FIVESOME"...
SUZUKI-SAMA
SUZUKI-SAMA!
...TO PAMPER "PLAYER NUMERO UNO"... ME!!
SUZUKI-SAMA

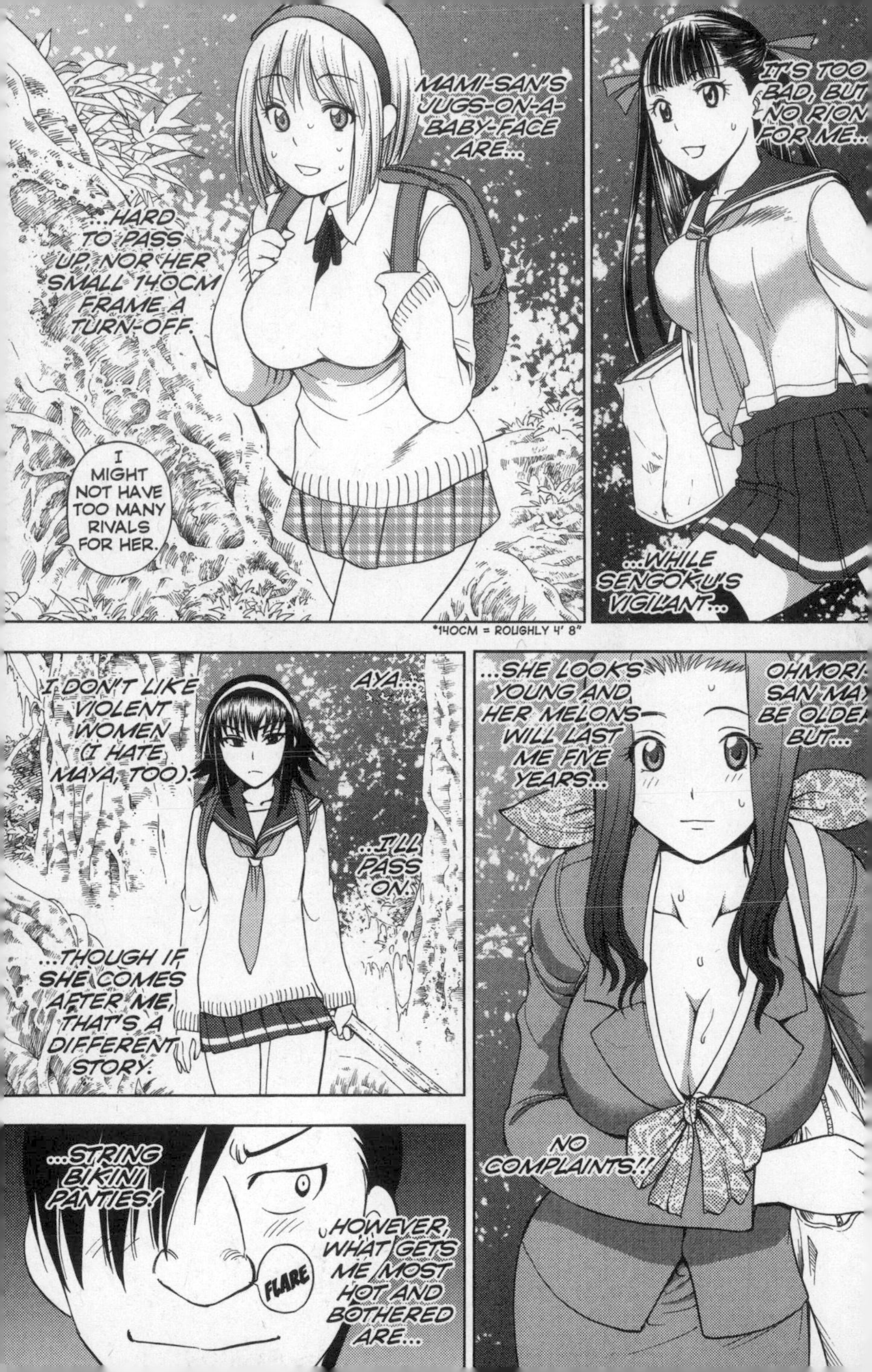
IT'S TOO BAD, BUT NO RION FOR ME...
...WHILE SENGOKU'S VIGILANT...
MAMI-SAN'S JUGS-ON-A-BABY-FACE ARE...
...HARD TO PASS UP, NOR HER SMALL 140CM FRAME A TURN-OFF.
I MIGHT NOT HAVE TOO MANY RIVALS FOR HER.
*140CM = ROUGHLY 4' 8"
OHMORI-SAN MAY BE OLDER BUT...
...SHE LOOKS YOUNG AND HER MELONS WILL LAST ME FIVE YEARS...
NO COMPLAINTS!!
AYA...
...I'LL PASS ON.
I DON'T LIKE VIOLENT WOMEN (I HATE MAYA, TOO).
...THOUGH IF SHE COMES AFTER ME, THAT'S A DIFFERENT STORY.
HOWEVER, WHAT GETS ME MOST HOT AND BOTHERED ARE...
FLARE
...STRING BIKINI PANTIES!

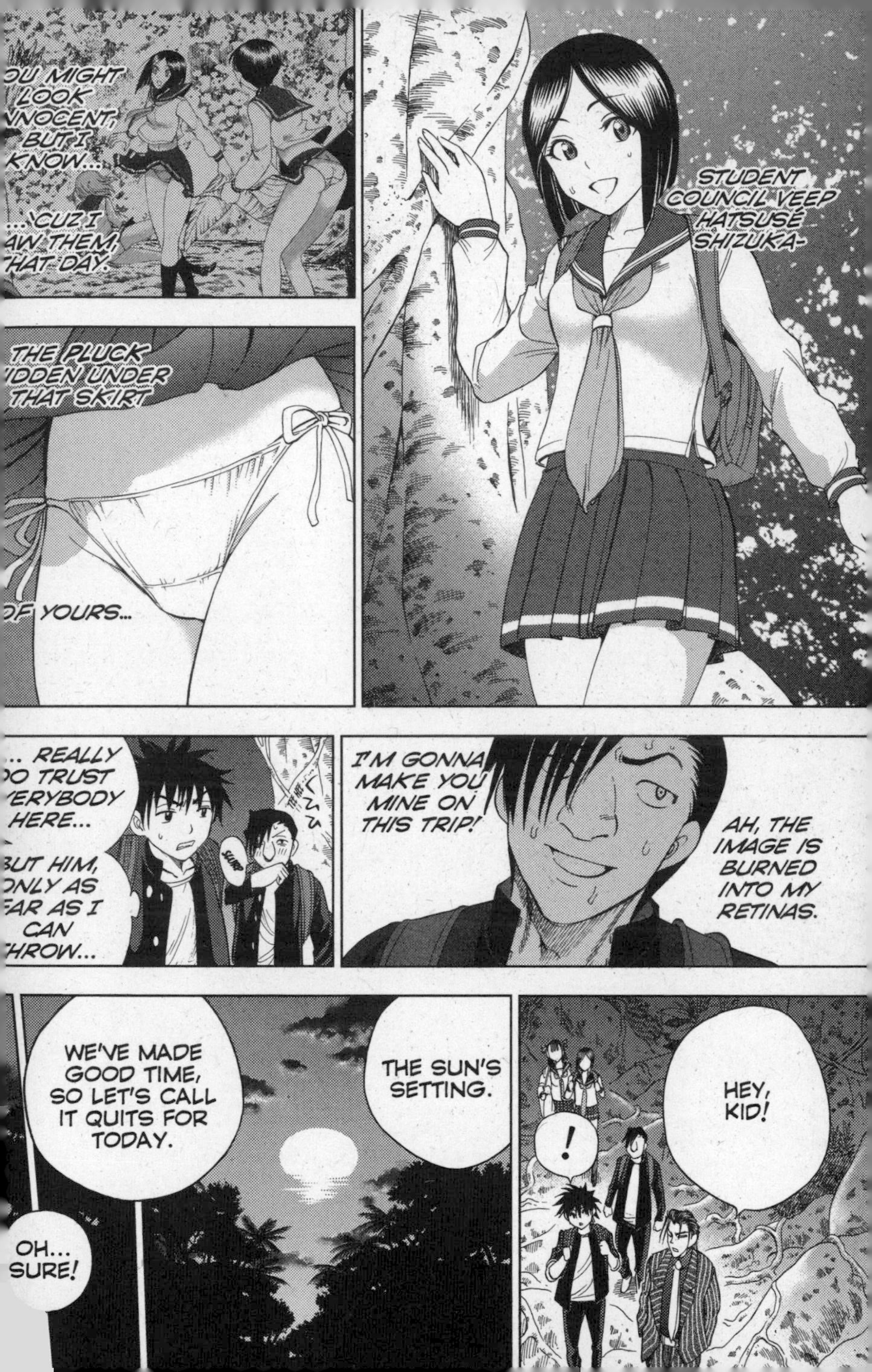
STUDENT COUNCIL VEEP HATSUSÉ SHIZUKA-
OU MIGHT LOOK NNOCENT, BUT I KNOW...
... CUZ I AW THEM, HAT DAY.
THE PLUCK IDDEN UNDER THAT SKIRT
OF YOURS...
I'M GONNA MAKE YOU MINE ON THIS TRIP!
AH, THE IMAGE IS BURNED INTO MY RETINAS.
... REALLY DO TRUST ERYBODY HERE...
UT HIM, NLY AS AR AS I CAN HROW...
HEY, KID!
!
THE SUN'S SETTING.
WE'VE MADE GOOD TIME, SO LET'S CALL IT QUITS FOR TODAY.
OH... SURE!

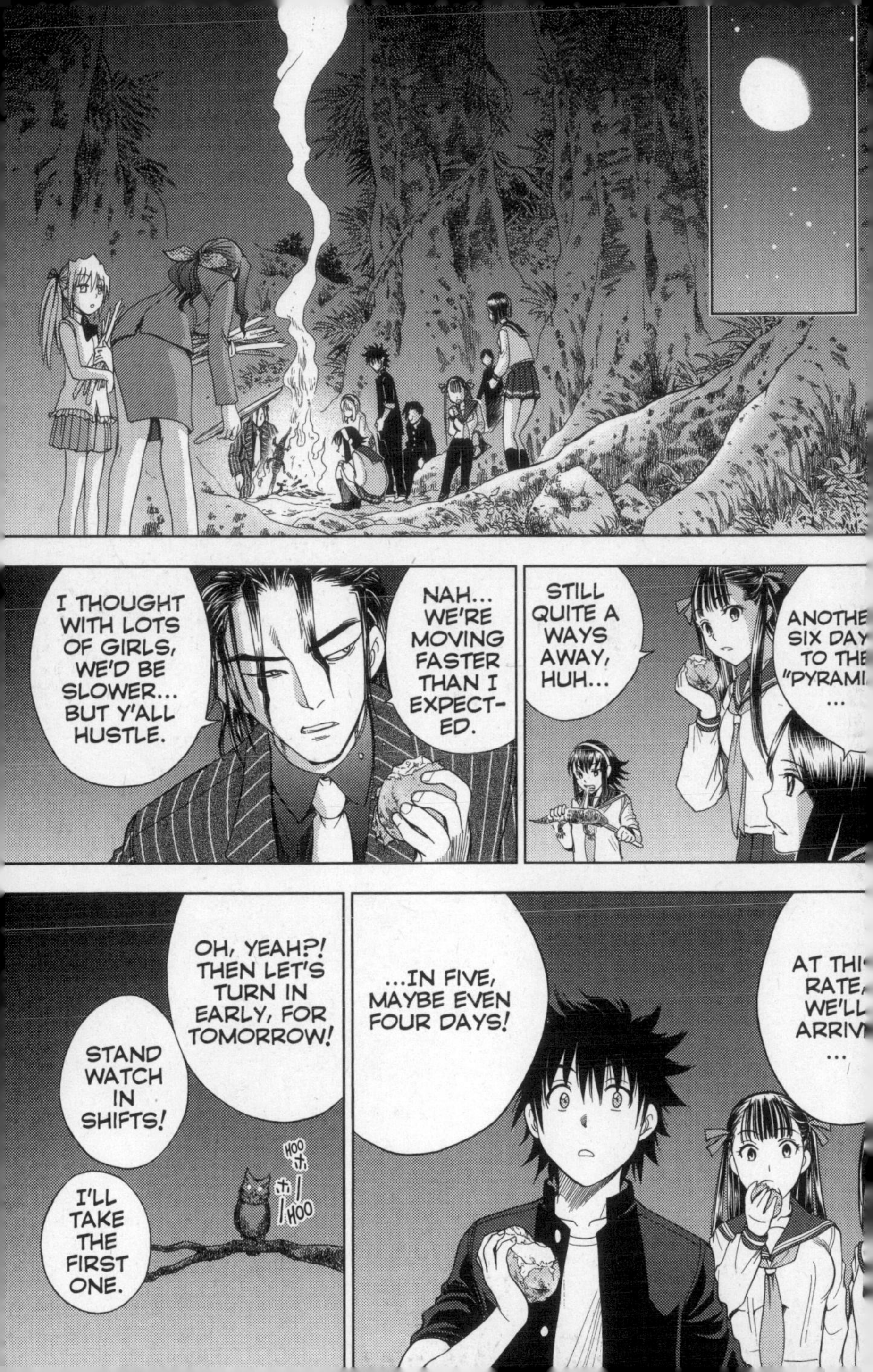
ANOTHE SIX DAY TO THE "PYRAMI ...
STILL QUITE A WAYS AWAY, HUH...
NAH... WE'RE MOVING FASTER THAN I EXPECT-ED.
I THOUGHT WITH LOTS OF GIRLS, WE'D BE SLOWER... BUT Y'ALL HUSTLE.
AT THI RATE, WE'LL ARRIV ...
...IN FIVE, MAYBE EVEN FOUR DAYS!
OH, YEAH?! THEN LET'S TURN IN EARLY, FOR TOMORROW!
STAND WATCH IN SHIFTS!
HOO HOO
I'LL TAKE THE FIRST ONE.

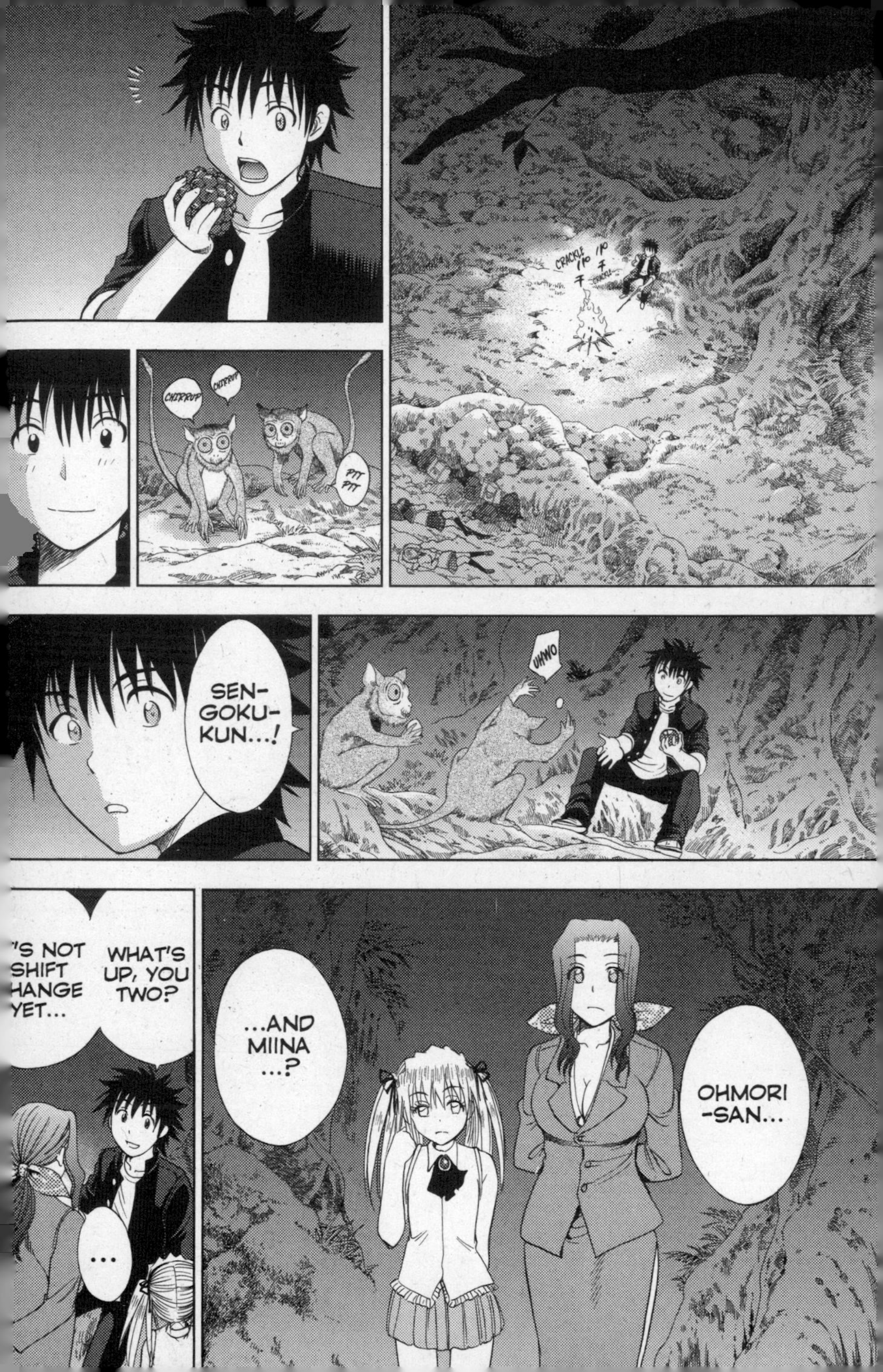
CRACKLE
パチ
パチ
CRACKLE
CHIRRUP
CHIRRUP
PIT PIT
UHWO
SEN-GOKU-KUN...!
OHMORI -SAN...
...AND MIINA ...?
WHAT'S UP, YOU TWO?
'S NOT SHIFT HANGE YET...
...

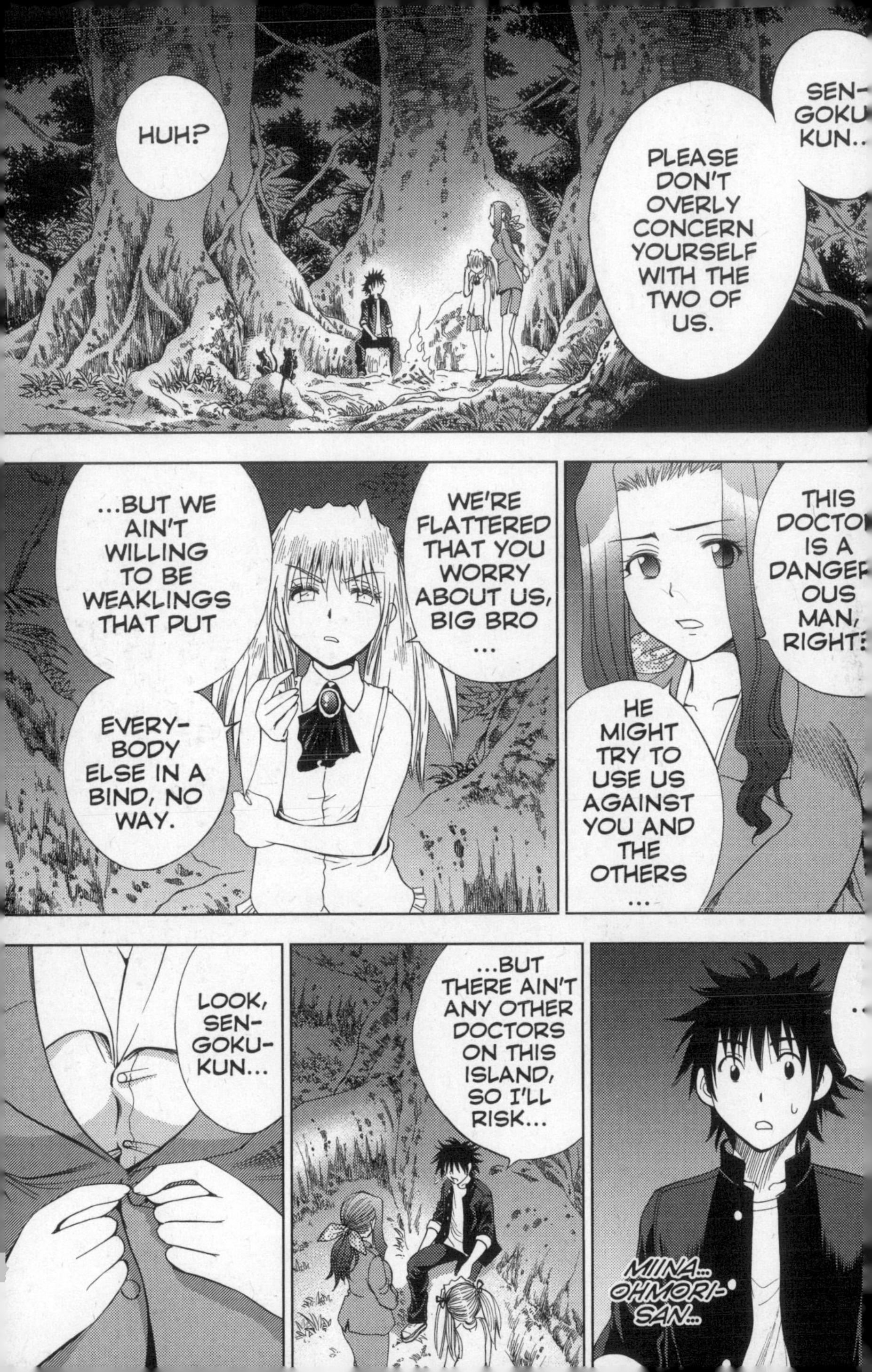
SEN-GOKU KUN..
PLEASE DON'T OVERLY CONCERN YOURSELF WITH THE TWO OF US.
HUH?
THIS DOCTOR IS A DANGER-OUS MAN, RIGHT?
HE MIGHT TRY TO USE US AGAINST YOU AND THE OTHERS ...
WE'RE FLATTERED THAT YOU WORRY ABOUT US, BIG BRO ...
...BUT WE AIN'T WILLING TO BE WEAKLINGS THAT PUT
EVERY-BODY ELSE IN A BIND, NO WAY.
MIINA... OHMORI-SAN...
...BUT THERE AIN'T ANY OTHER DOCTORS ON THIS ISLAND, SO I'LL RISK...
LOOK, SEN-GOKU-KUN...

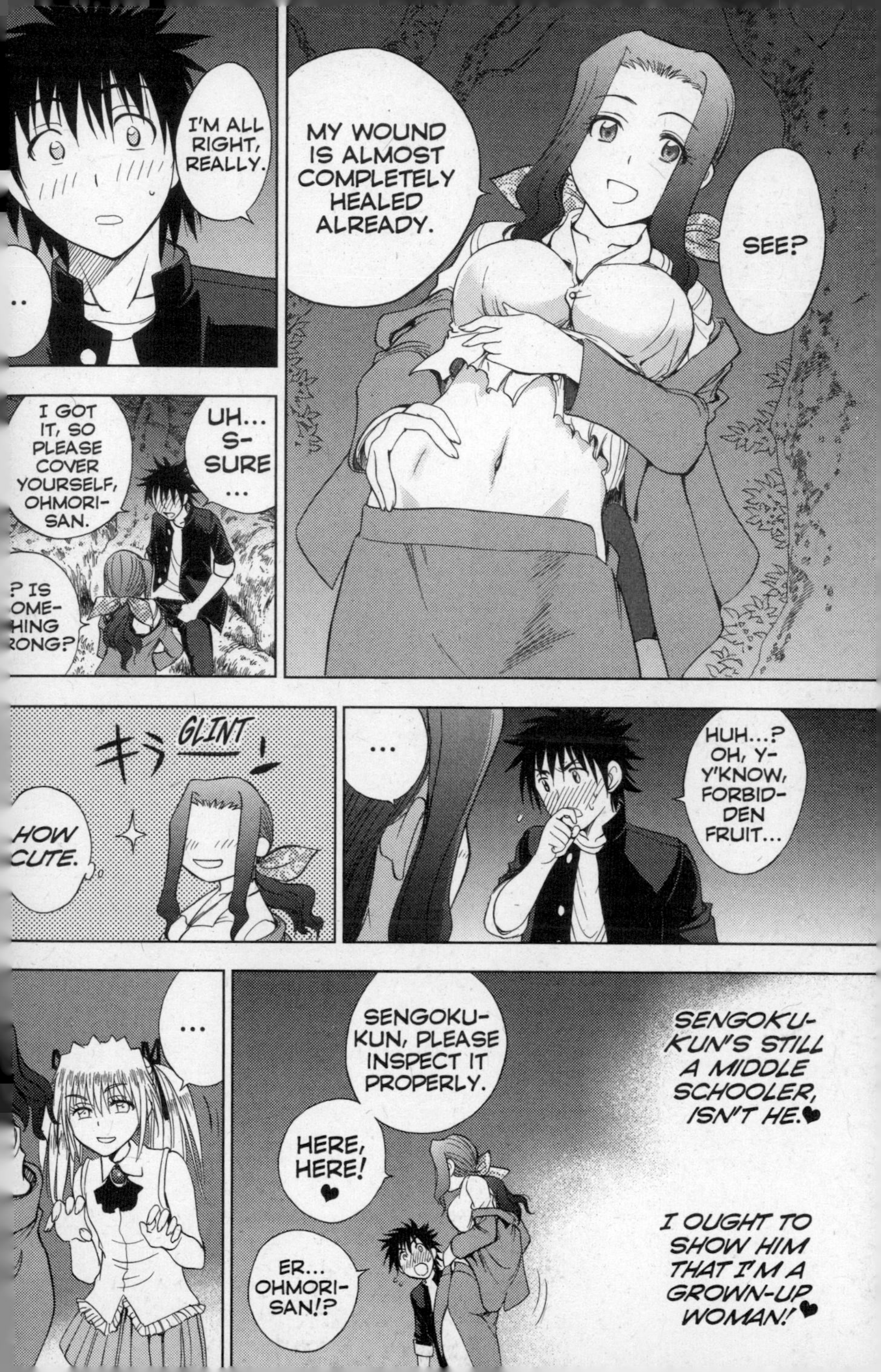
SEE?
MY WOUND IS ALMOST COMPLETELY HEALED ALREADY.
I'M ALL RIGHT, REALLY.
...
UH... S-SURE ...
I GOT IT, SO PLEASE COVER YOURSELF, OHMORI-SAN.
? IS OME-THING RONG?
HUH...? OH, Y-Y'KNOW, FORBID-DEN FRUIT...
...
GLINT
HOW CUTE.
SENGOKU-KUN'S STILL A MIDDLE SCHOOLER, ISN'T HE.♥
SENGOKU-KUN, PLEASE INSPECT IT PROPERLY.
I OUGHT TO SHOW HIM THAT I'M A GROWN-UP WOMAN!♥
HERE, HERE! ♥
ER... OHMORI-SAN!?
...

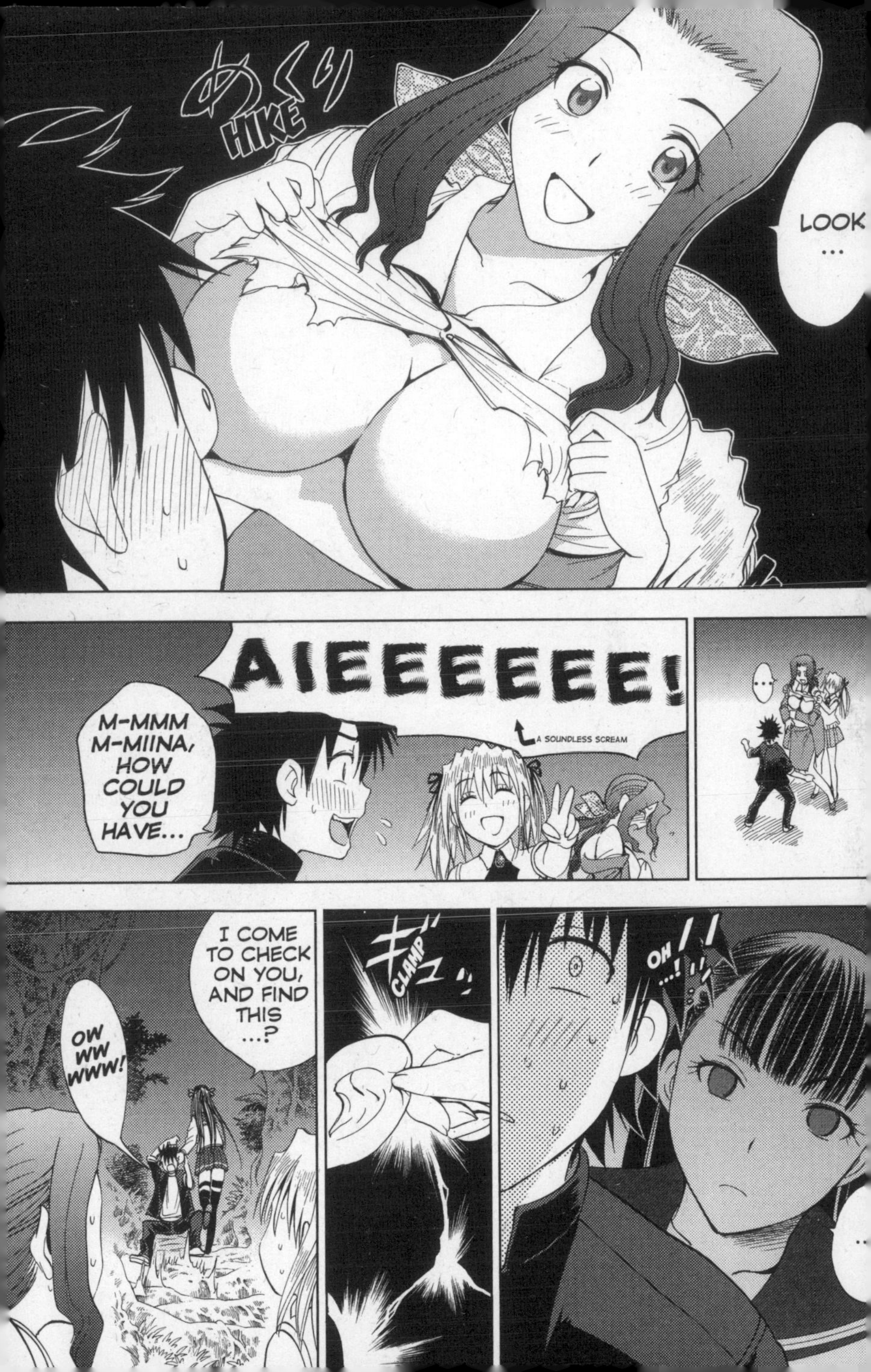
LOOK ...
めくり
HIKE
...
AIEEEEEEE!
M-MMM M-MIINA, HOW COULD YOU HAVE...
A SOUNDLESS SCREAM
OH ...!
...
ギュ
CLAMP
I COME TO CHECK ON YOU, AND FIND THIS ...?
OW WW WWW!

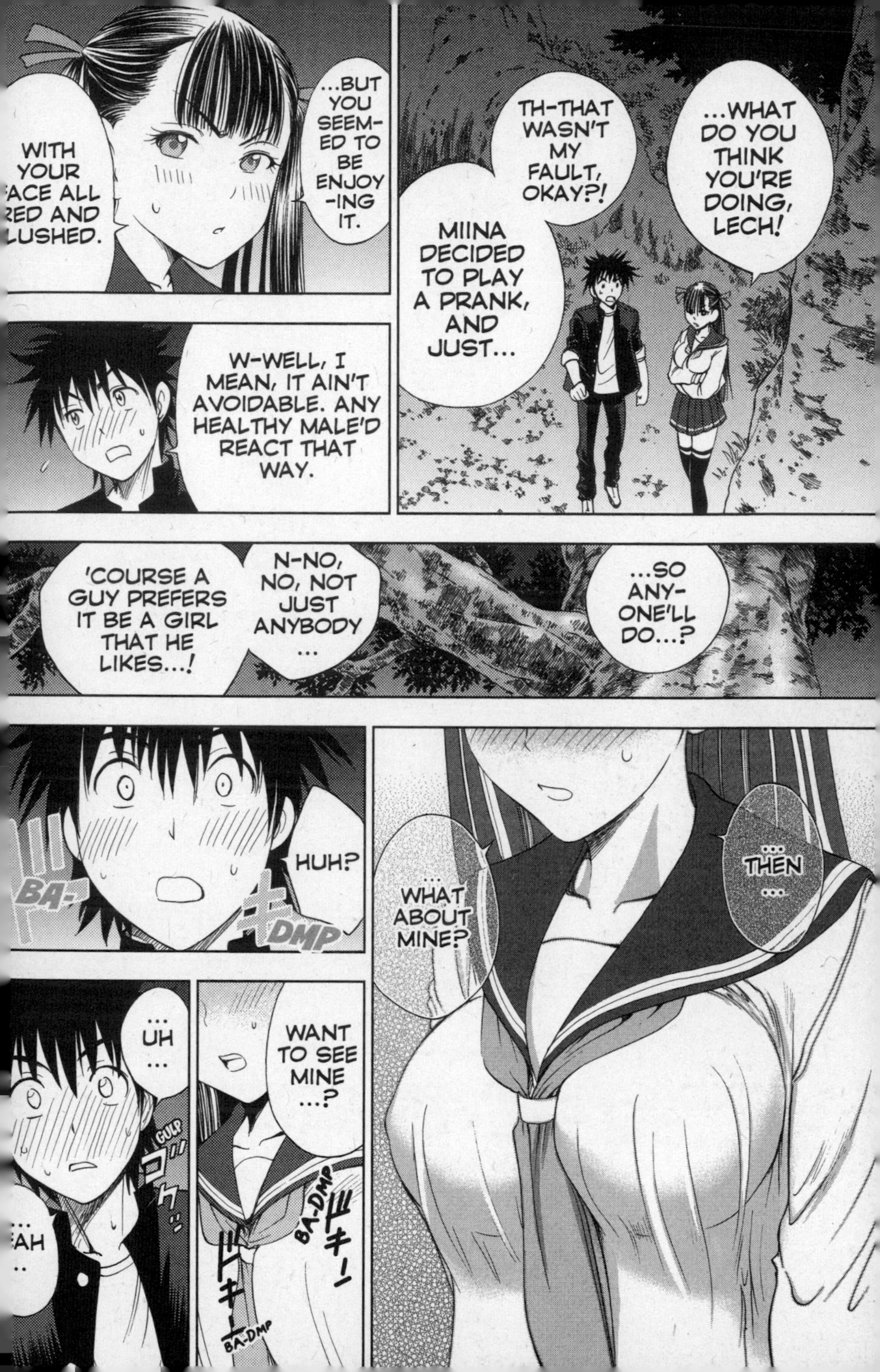
...WHAT DO YOU THINK YOU'RE DOING, LECH!
TH-THAT WASN'T MY FAULT, OKAY?!
MIINA DECIDED TO PLAY A PRANK, AND JUST...
...BUT YOU SEEMED TO BE ENJOY-ING IT.
WITH YOUR FACE ALL RED AND FLUSHED.
W-WELL, I MEAN, IT AIN'T AVOIDABLE. ANY HEALTHY MALE'D REACT THAT WAY.
...SO ANY-ONE'LL DO...?
N-NO, NO, NOT JUST ANYBODY...
'COURSE A GUY PREFERS IT BE A GIRL THAT HE LIKES...!
...THEN...
...WHAT ABOUT MINE?
HUH?
BA-DMP
WANT TO SEE MINE...?
BA-DMP
BA-DMP
...UH...
GULP
...EAH...

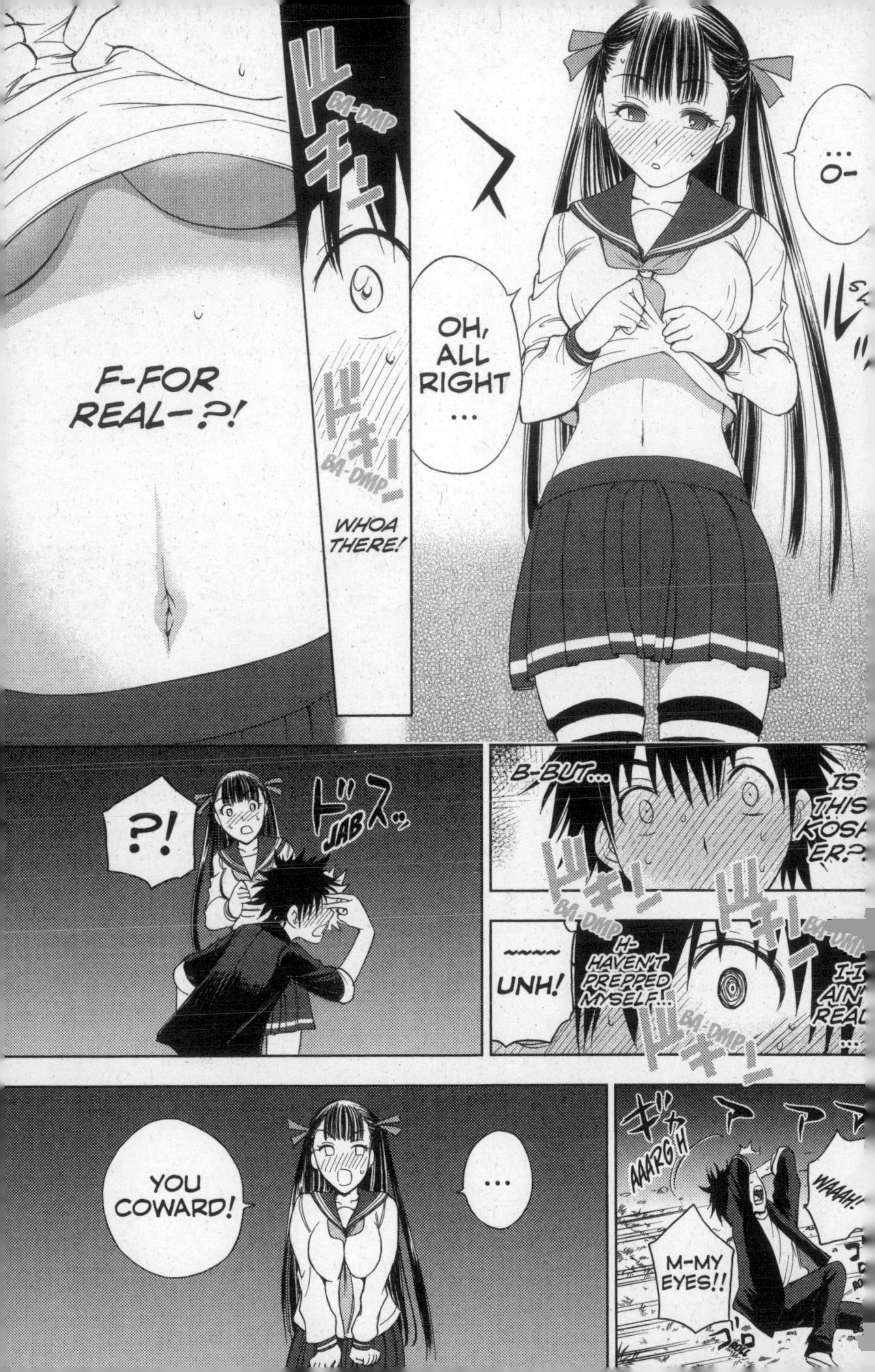
... O-
OH, ALL RIGHT ...
BA-DMP
BA-DMP
WHOA THERE!
F-FOR REAL-?!
IS THIS KOSHER?!
B-BUT...
BA-DMP
BA-DMP
H-HAVEN'T PREPPED MYSELF...
BA-DMP
~~~~~ UNH!
?!
JAB
AAARGH
WAAAH!
M-MY EYES!!
ROLL
...
YOU COWARD!
~~~~~

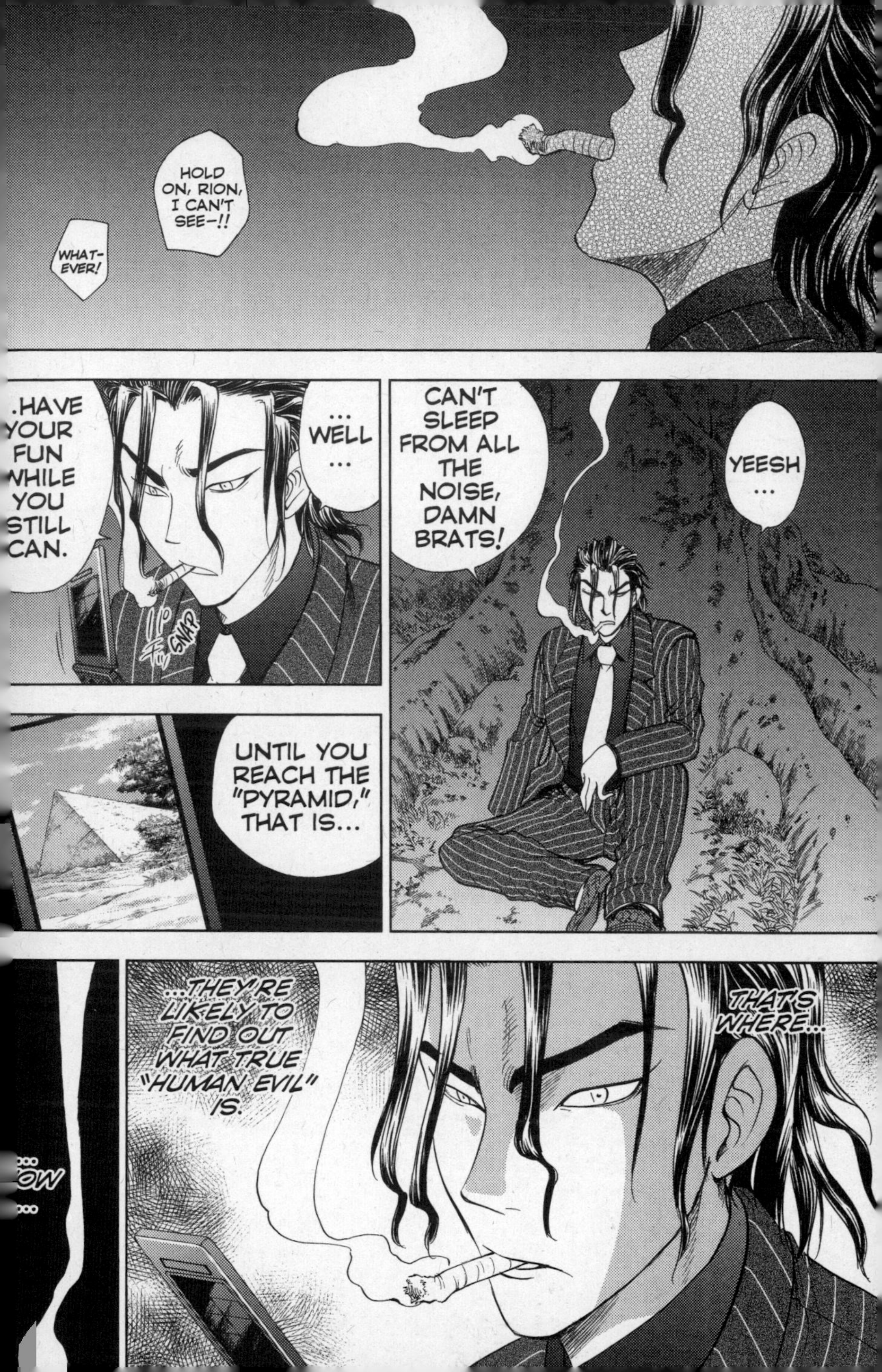
HOLD ON, RION, I CAN'T SEE-!!
WHAT-EVER!
YEESH...
CAN'T SLEEP FROM ALL THE NOISE, DAMN BRATS!
...WELL...
...HAVE YOUR FUN WHILE YOU STILL CAN.
UNTIL YOU REACH THE "PYRAMID," THAT IS...
THAT'S WHERE...
...THEY'RE LIKELY TO FIND OUT WHAT TRUE "HUMAN EVIL" IS.

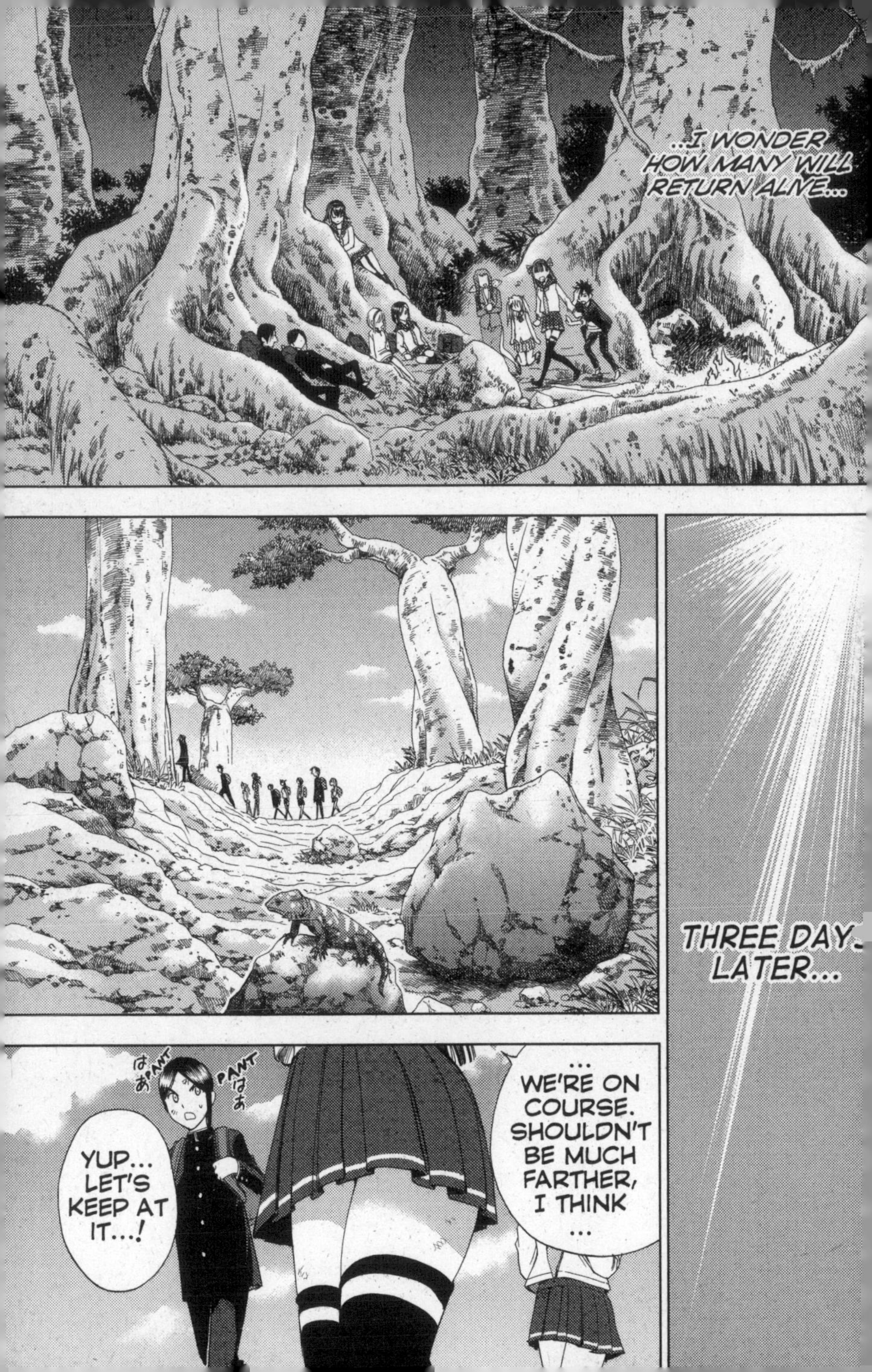
...I WONDER HOW MANY WILL RETURN ALIVE...
THREE DAYS LATER...
... WE'RE ON COURSE. SHOULDN'T BE MUCH FARTHER, I THINK ...
PANT はあ
はあ PANT
YUP... LET'S KEEP AT IT...!

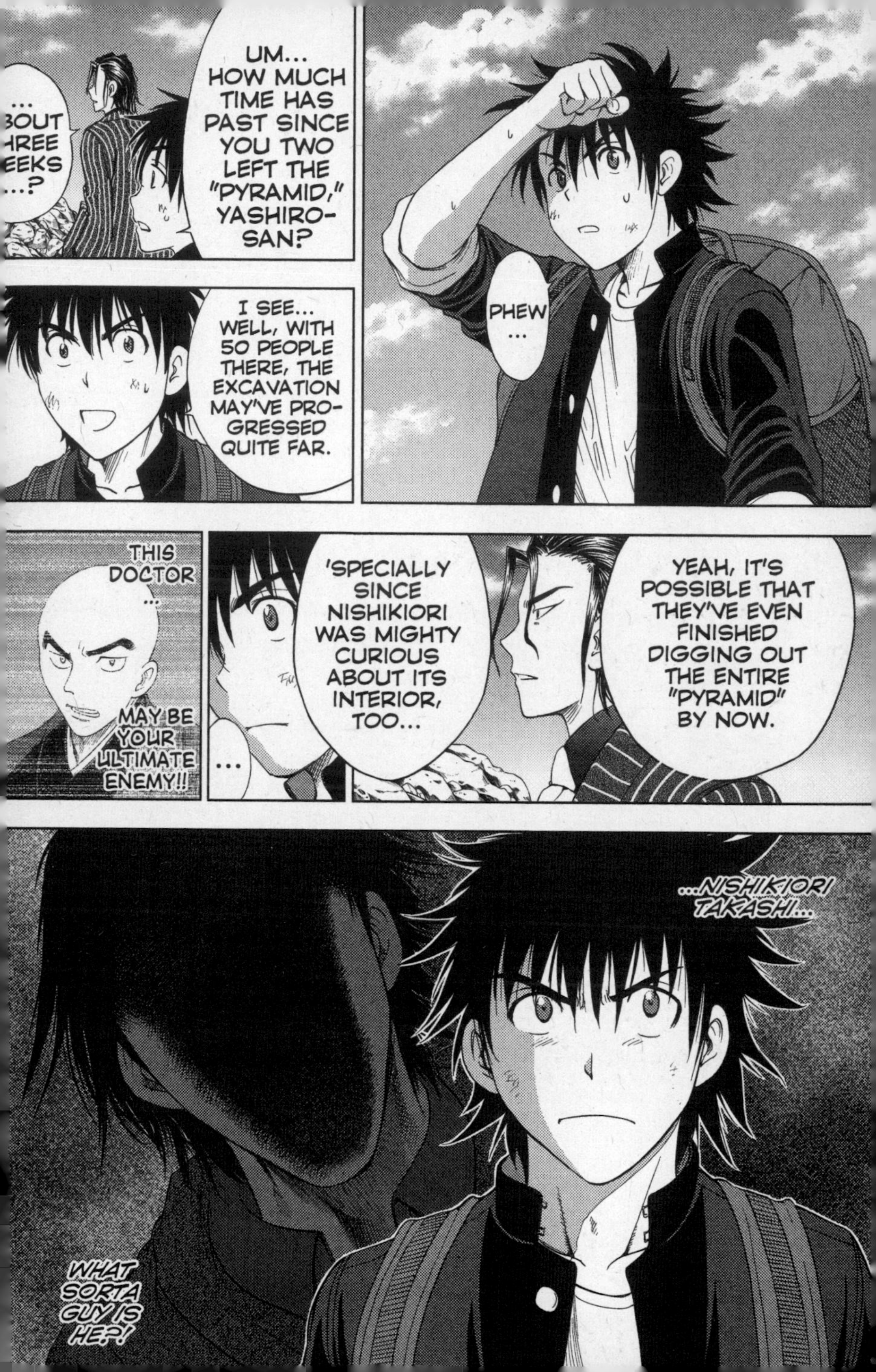
PHEW...
UM... HOW MUCH TIME HAS PAST SINCE YOU TWO LEFT THE "PYRAMID," YASHIRO-SAN?
... BOUT HREE EEKS ...?
I SEE... WELL, WITH 50 PEOPLE THERE, THE EXCAVATION MAY'VE PRO-GRESSED QUITE FAR.
YEAH, IT'S POSSIBLE THAT THEY'VE EVEN FINISHED DIGGING OUT THE ENTIRE "PYRAMID" BY NOW.
'SPECIALLY SINCE NISHIKIORI WAS MIGHTY CURIOUS ABOUT ITS INTERIOR, TOO...
...
THIS DOCTOR...
MAY BE YOUR ULTIMATE ENEMY!!
...NISHIKIORI TAKASHI...
WHAT SORTA GUY IS HE?!

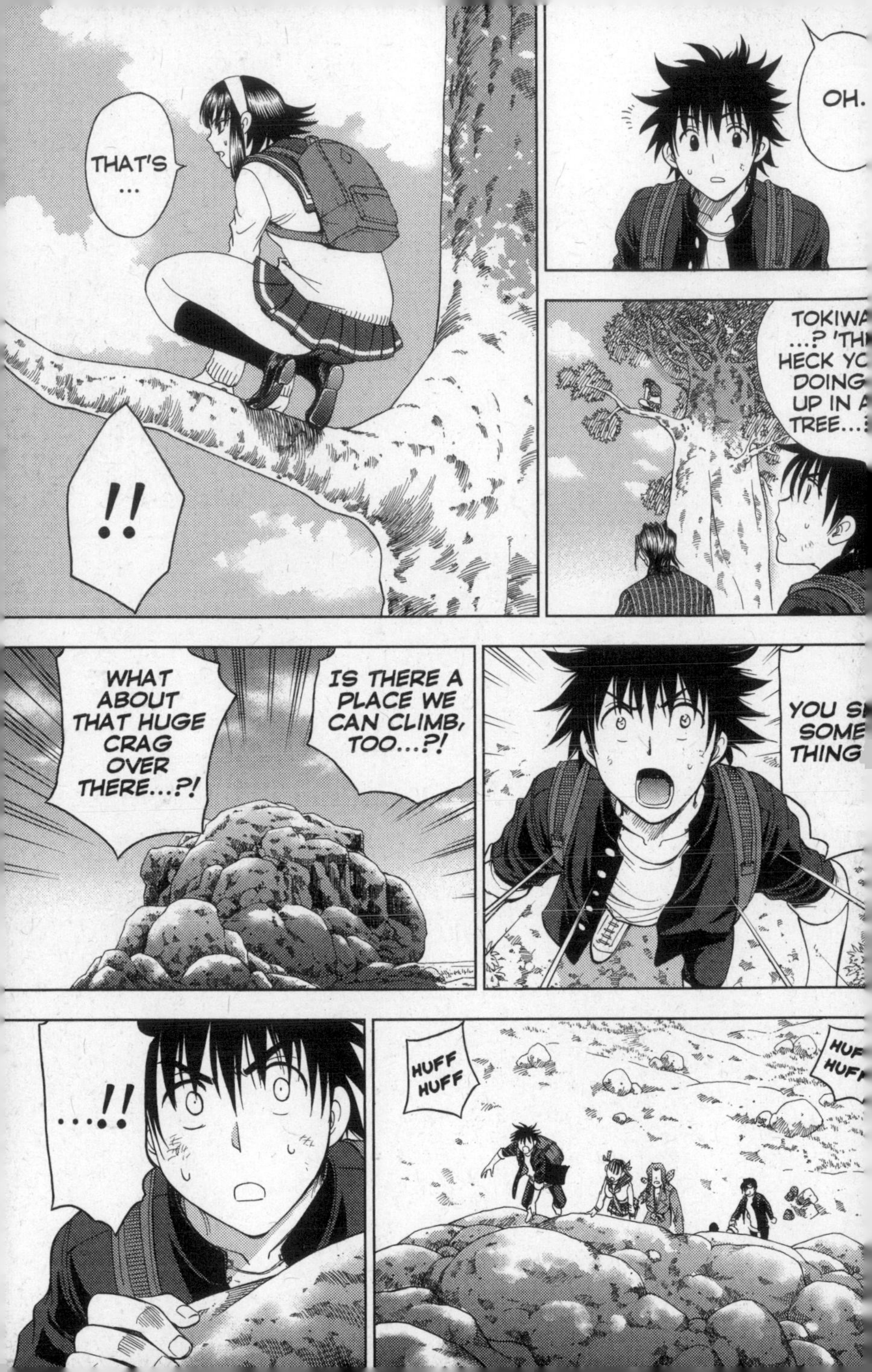
OH.
TOKIWA ...? 'TH HECK YO DOING UP IN A TREE...
THAT'S ...
!!
YOU S SOME THING
IS THERE A PLACE WE CAN CLIMB, TOO...?!
WHAT ABOUT THAT HUGE CRAG OVER THERE...?!
HUF HUF
HUFF HUFF
...!!

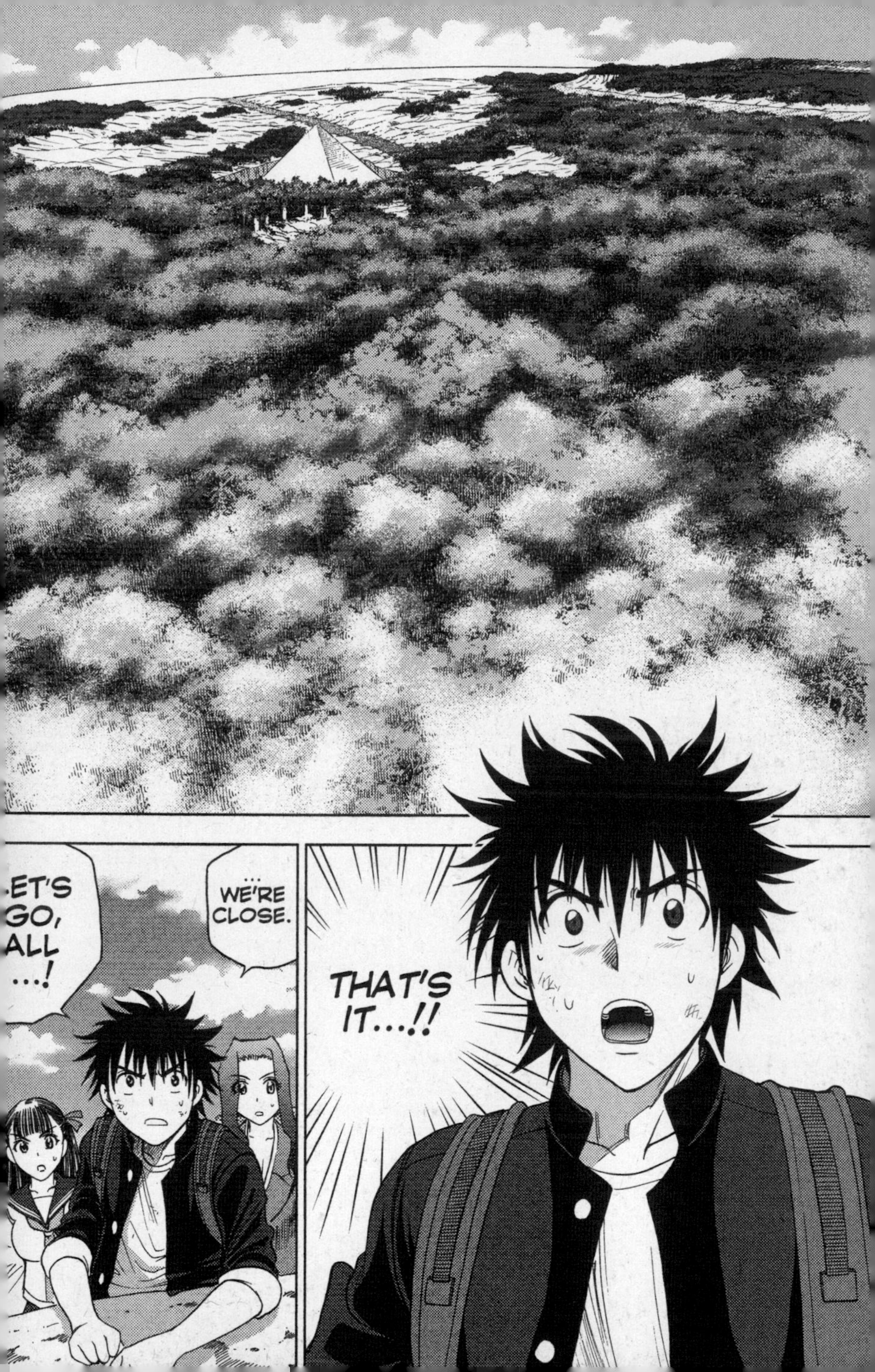
THAT'S IT...!!
...WE'RE CLOSE.
ET'S GO, ALL ...!

TO BE CONINTUED...

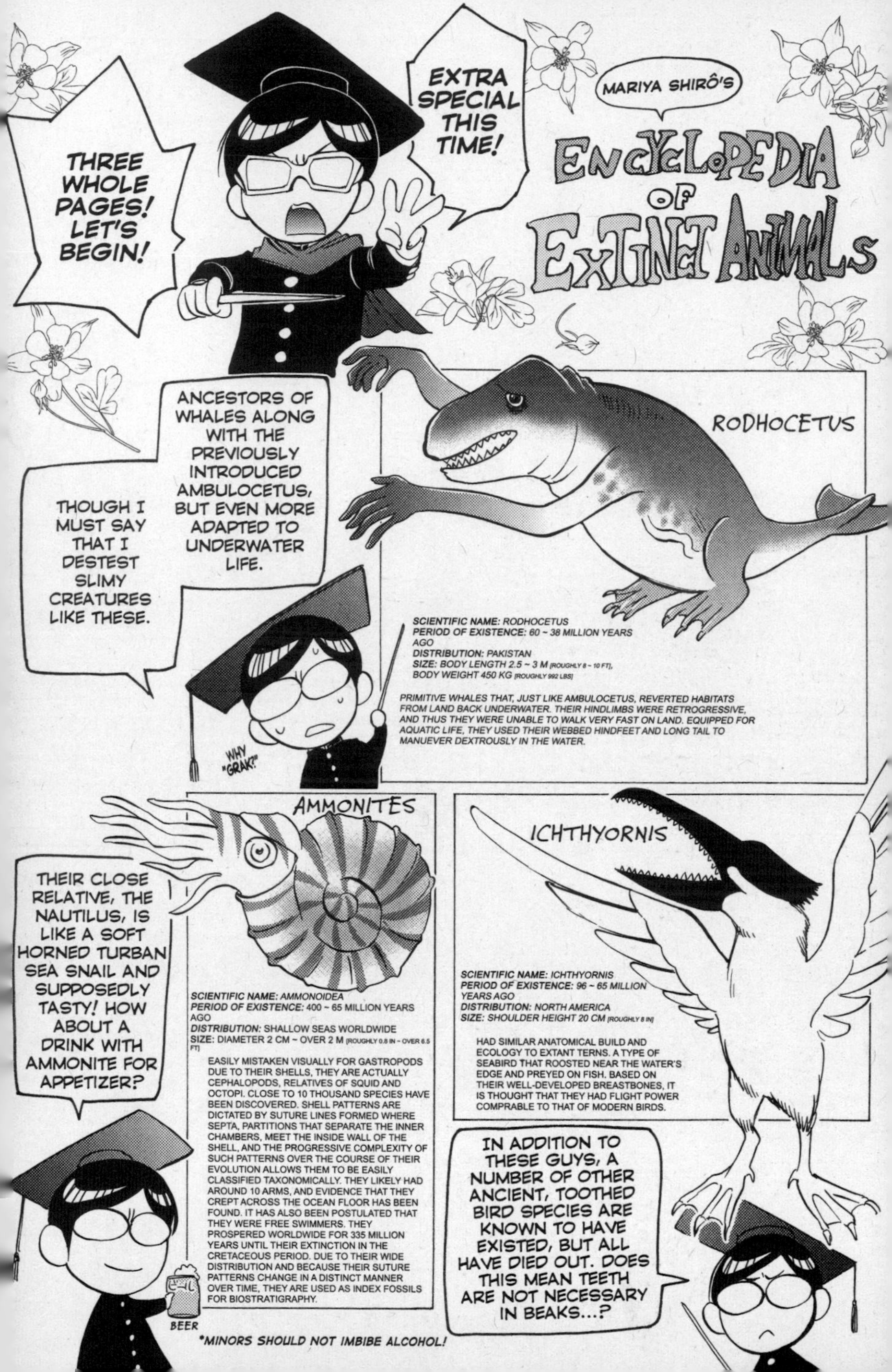
MARIYA SHIRÔ'S
ENCYCLOPEDIA OF EXTINCT ANIMALS
EXTRA SPECIAL THIS TIME!
THREE WHOLE PAGES! LET'S BEGIN!
RODHOCETUS
SCIENTIFIC NAME: RODHOCETUS
PERIOD OF EXISTENCE: 60 ~ 38 MILLION YEARS AGO
DISTRIBUTION: PAKISTAN
SIZE: BODY LENGTH 2.5 ~ 3 M [ROUGHLY 8 ~ 10 FT], BODY WEIGHT 450 KG [ROUGHLY 992 LBS]
PRIMITIVE WHALES THAT, JUST LIKE AMBULOCETUS, REVERTED HABITATS FROM LAND BACK UNDERWATER. THEIR HINDLIMBS WERE RETROGRESSIVE, AND THUS THEY WERE UNABLE TO WALK VERY FAST ON LAND. EQUIPPED FOR AQUATIC LIFE, THEY USED THEIR WEBBED HINDFEET AND LONG TAIL TO MANUEVER DEXTROUSLY IN THE WATER.
ANCESTORS OF WHALES ALONG WITH THE PREVIOUSLY INTRODUCED AMBULOCETUS, BUT EVEN MORE ADAPTED TO UNDERWATER LIFE.
THOUGH I MUST SAY THAT I DESTEST SLIMY CREATURES LIKE THESE.
WHY "GRAK?"
ICHTHYORNIS
SCIENTIFIC NAME: ICHTHYORNIS
PERIOD OF EXISTENCE: 96 ~ 65 MILLION YEARS AGO
DISTRIBUTION: NORTH AMERICA
SIZE: SHOULDER HEIGHT 20 CM [ROUGHLY 8 IN]
HAD SIMILAR ANATOMICAL BUILD AND ECOLOGY TO EXTANT TERNS. A TYPE OF SEABIRD THAT ROOSTED NEAR THE WATER'S EDGE AND PREYED ON FISH. BASED ON THEIR WELL-DEVELOPED BREASTBONES, IT IS THOUGHT THAT THEY HAD FLIGHT POWER COMPRABLE TO THAT OF MODERN BIRDS.
IN ADDITION TO THESE GUYS, A NUMBER OF OTHER ANCIENT, TOOTHED BIRD SPECIES ARE KNOWN TO HAVE EXISTED, BUT ALL HAVE DIED OUT. DOES THIS MEAN TEETH ARE NOT NECESSARY IN BEAKS...?
AMMONITES
SCIENTIFIC NAME: AMMONOIDEA
PERIOD OF EXISTENCE: 400 ~ 65 MILLION YEARS AGO
DISTRIBUTION: SHALLOW SEAS WORLDWIDE
SIZE: DIAMETER 2 CM ~ OVER 2 M [ROUGHLY 0.8 IN ~ OVER 6.5 FT]
EASILY MISTAKEN VISUALLY FOR GASTROPODS DUE TO THEIR SHELLS, THEY ARE ACTUALLY CEPHALOPODS, RELATIVES OF SQUID AND OCTOPI. CLOSE TO 10 THOUSAND SPECIES HAVE BEEN DISCOVERED. SHELL PATTERNS ARE DICTATED BY SUTURE LINES FORMED WHERE SEPTA, PARTITIONS THAT SEPARATE THE INNER CHAMBERS, MEET THE INSIDE WALL OF THE SHELL, AND THE PROGRESSIVE COMPLEXITY OF SUCH PATTERNS OVER THE COURSE OF THEIR EVOLUTION ALLOWS THEM TO BE EASILY CLASSIFIED TAXONOMICALLY. THEY LIKELY HAD AROUND 10 ARMS, AND EVIDENCE THAT THEY CREPT ACROSS THE OCEAN FLOOR HAS BEEN FOUND. IT HAS ALSO BEEN POSTULATED THAT THEY WERE FREE SWIMMERS. THEY PROSPERED WORLDWIDE FOR 335 MILLION YEARS UNTIL THEIR EXTINCTION IN THE CRETACEOUS PERIOD. DUE TO THEIR WIDE DISTRIBUTION AND BECAUSE THEIR SUTURE PATTERNS CHANGE IN A DISTINCT MANNER OVER TIME, THEY ARE USED AS INDEX FOSSILS FOR BIOSTRATIGRAPHY.
THEIR CLOSE RELATIVE, THE NAUTILUS, IS LIKE A SOFT HORNED TURBAN SEA SNAIL AND SUPPOSEDLY TASTY! HOW ABOUT A DRINK WITH AMMONITE FOR APPETIZER?
BEER
*MINORS SHOULD NOT IMBIBE ALCOHOL!

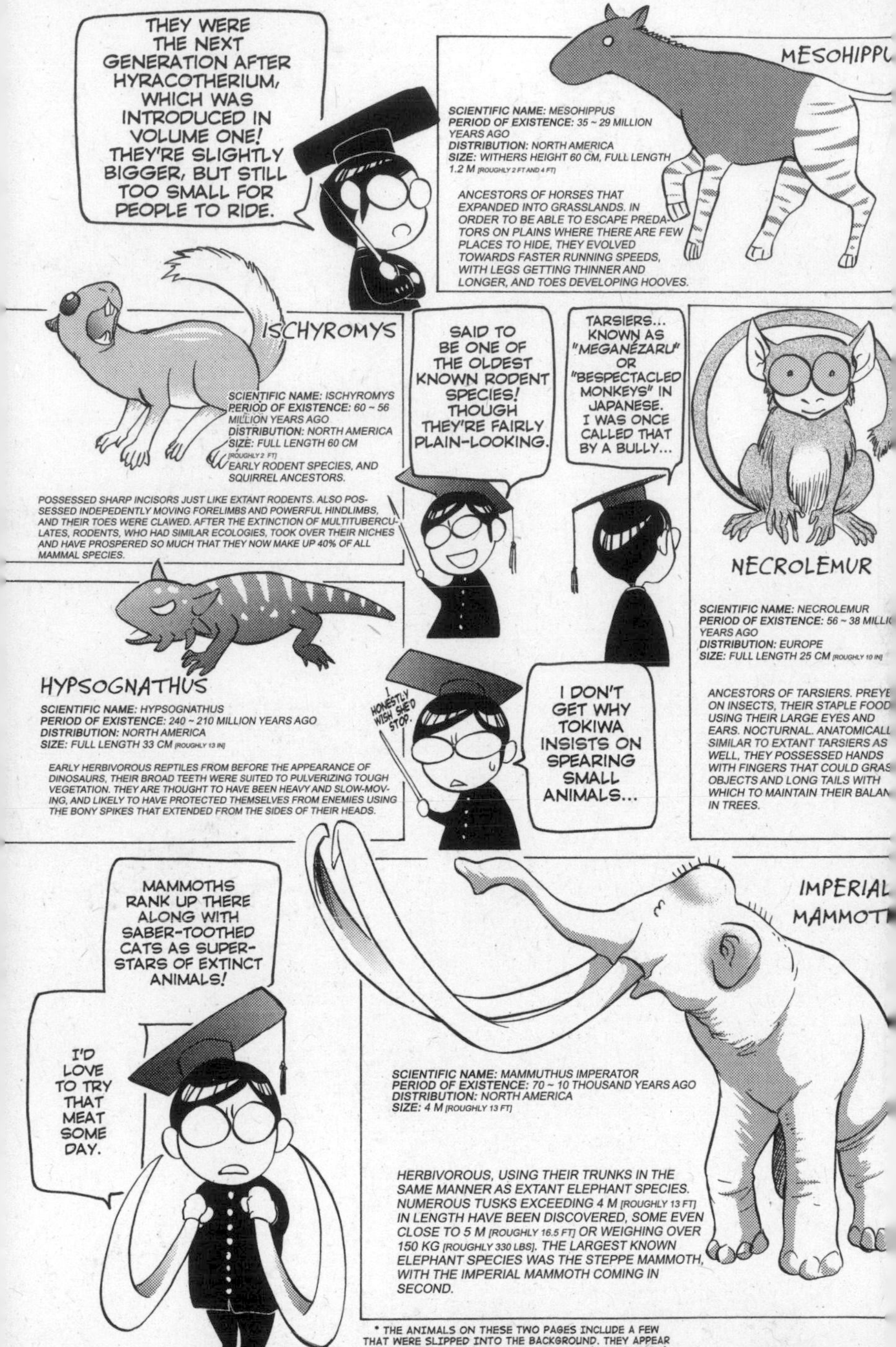

MESOHIPPU
SCIENTIFIC NAME: MESOHIPPUS
PERIOD OF EXISTENCE: 35 ~ 29 MILLION YEARS AGO
DISTRIBUTION: NORTH AMERICA
SIZE: WITHERS HEIGHT 60 CM, FULL LENGTH 1.2 M [ROUGHLY 2 FT AND 4 FT]
ANCESTORS OF HORSES THAT EXPANDED INTO GRASSLANDS. IN ORDER TO BE ABLE TO ESCAPE PREDATORS ON PLAINS WHERE THERE ARE FEW PLACES TO HIDE, THEY EVOLVED TOWARDS FASTER RUNNING SPEEDS, WITH LEGS GETTING THINNER AND LONGER, AND TOES DEVELOPING HOOVES.
THEY WERE THE NEXT GENERATION AFTER HYRACOTHERIUM, WHICH WAS INTRODUCED IN VOLUME ONE! THEY'RE SLIGHTLY BIGGER, BUT STILL TOO SMALL FOR PEOPLE TO RIDE.
NECROLEMUR
SCIENTIFIC NAME: NECROLEMUR
PERIOD OF EXISTENCE: 56 ~ 38 MILLIO
YEARS AGO
DISTRIBUTION: EUROPE
SIZE: FULL LENGTH 25 CM [ROUGHLY 10 IN]
ANCESTORS OF TARSIERS. PREYE ON INSECTS, THEIR STAPLE FOOD USING THEIR LARGE EYES AND EARS. NOCTURNAL. ANATOMICALL SIMILAR TO EXTANT TARSIERS AS WELL, THEY POSSESSED HANDS WITH FINGERS THAT COULD GRAS OBJECTS AND LONG TAILS WITH WHICH TO MAINTAIN THEIR BALAN IN TREES.
TARSIERS... KNOWN AS "MEGANÉZARU" OR "BESPECTACLED MONKEYS" IN JAPANESE. I WAS ONCE CALLED THAT BY A BULLY...
SAID TO BE ONE OF THE OLDEST KNOWN RODENT SPECIES! THOUGH THEY'RE FAIRLY PLAIN-LOOKING.
ISCHYROMYS
SCIENTIFIC NAME: ISCHYROMYS
PERIOD OF EXISTENCE: 60 ~ 56 MILLION YEARS AGO
DISTRIBUTION: NORTH AMERICA
SIZE: FULL LENGTH 60 CM [ROUGHLY 2 FT]
EARLY RODENT SPECIES, AND SQUIRREL ANCESTORS.
POSSESSED SHARP INCISORS JUST LIKE EXTANT RODENTS. ALSO POSSESSED INDEPEDENTLY MOVING FORELIMBS AND POWERFUL HINDLIMBS, AND THEIR TOES WERE CLAWED. AFTER THE EXTINCTION OF MULTITUBERCULATES, RODENTS, WHO HAD SIMILAR ECOLOGIES, TOOK OVER THEIR NICHES AND HAVE PROSPERED SO MUCH THAT THEY NOW MAKE UP 40% OF ALL MAMMAL SPECIES.
I DON'T GET WHY TOKIWA INSISTS ON SPEARING SMALL ANIMALS...
I HONESTLY WISH SHE'D STOP.
HYPSOGNATHUS
SCIENTIFIC NAME: HYPSOGNATHUS
PERIOD OF EXISTENCE: 240 ~ 210 MILLION YEARS AGO
DISTRIBUTION: NORTH AMERICA
SIZE: FULL LENGTH 33 CM [ROUGHLY 13 IN]
EARLY HERBIVOROUS REPTILES FROM BEFORE THE APPEARANCE OF DINOSAURS, THEIR BROAD TEETH WERE SUITED TO PULVERIZING TOUGH VEGETATION. THEY ARE THOUGHT TO HAVE BEEN HEAVY AND SLOW-MOVING, AND LIKELY TO HAVE PROTECTED THEMSELVES FROM ENEMIES USING THE BONY SPIKES THAT EXTENDED FROM THE SIDES OF THEIR HEADS.
IMPERIAL MAMMOT
SCIENTIFIC NAME: MAMMUTHUS IMPERATOR
PERIOD OF EXISTENCE: 70 ~ 10 THOUSAND YEARS AGO
DISTRIBUTION: NORTH AMERICA
SIZE: 4 M [ROUGHLY 13 FT]
HERBIVOROUS, USING THEIR TRUNKS IN THE SAME MANNER AS EXTANT ELEPHANT SPECIES. NUMEROUS TUSKS EXCEEDING 4 M [ROUGHLY 13 FT] IN LENGTH HAVE BEEN DISCOVERED, SOME EVEN CLOSE TO 5 M [ROUGHLY 16.5 FT] OR WEIGHING OVER 150 KG [ROUGHLY 330 LBS]. THE LARGEST KNOWN ELEPHANT SPECIES WAS THE STEPPE MAMMOTH, WITH THE IMPERIAL MAMMOTH COMING IN SECOND.
MAMMOTHS RANK UP THERE ALONG WITH SABER-TOOTHED CATS AS SUPER-STARS OF EXTINCT ANIMALS!
I'D LOVE TO TRY THAT MEAT SOME DAY.

* THE ANIMALS ON THESE TWO PAGES INCLUDE A FEW THAT WERE SLIPPED INTO THE BACKGROUND. THEY APPEAR SOMEWHERE IN THIS VOLUME. LET'S TRY FINDING THEM!

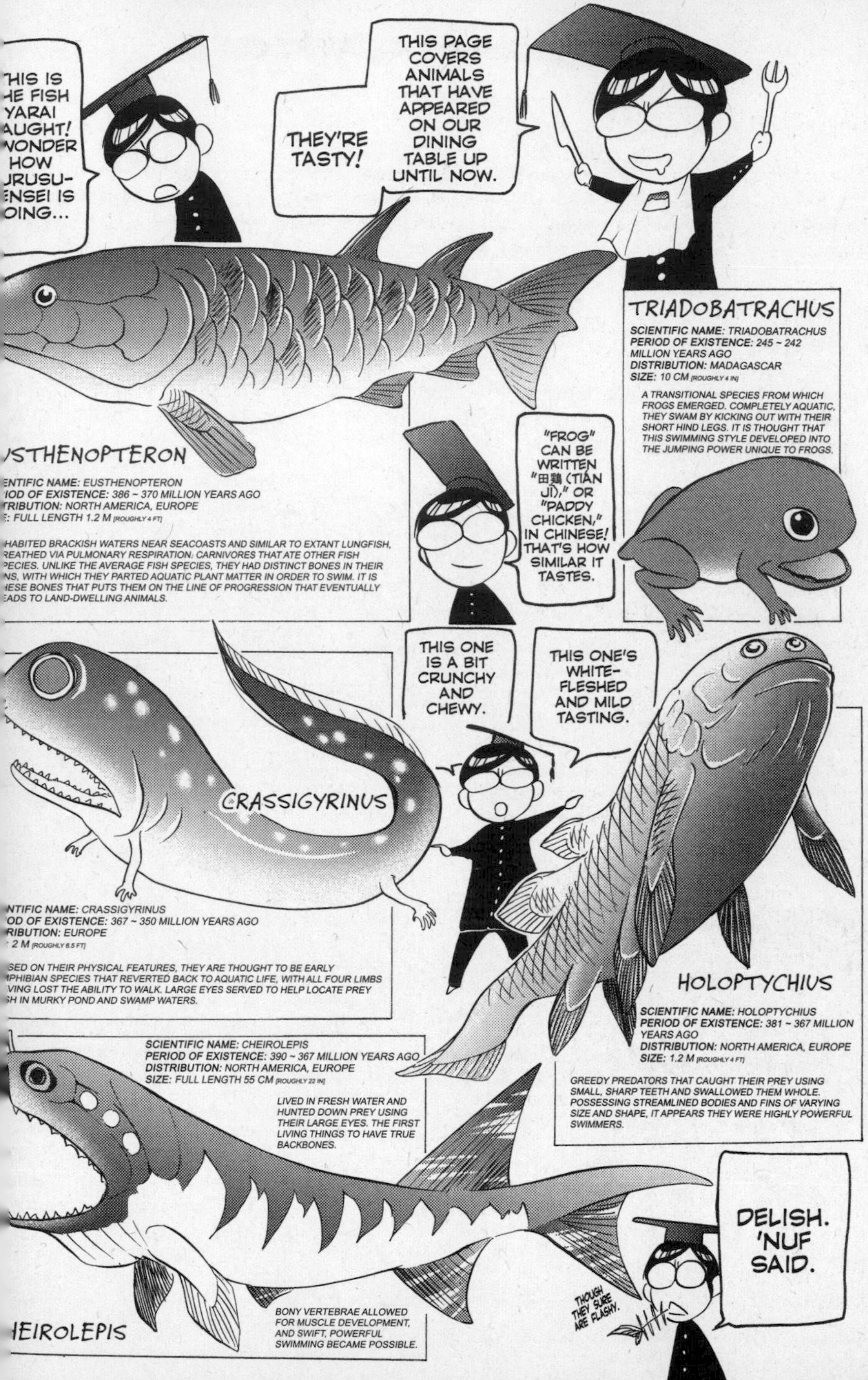
THIS PAGE COVERS ANIMALS THAT HAVE APPEARED ON OUR DINING TABLE UP UNTIL NOW.
THEY'RE TASTY!
HIS IS
HE FISH
YARAI
AUGHT!
WONDER
HOW
URUSU-
ENSEI IS
OING...
TRIADOBATRACHUS
SCIENTIFIC NAME: TRIADOBATRACHUS
PERIOD OF EXISTENCE: 245 ~ 242 MILLION YEARS AGO
DISTRIBUTION: MADAGASCAR
SIZE: 10 CM [ROUGHLY 4 IN]
A TRANSITIONAL SPECIES FROM WHICH FROGS EMERGED. COMPLETELY AQUATIC, THEY SWAM BY KICKING OUT WITH THEIR SHORT HIND LEGS. IT IS THOUGHT THAT THIS SWIMMING STYLE DEVELOPED INTO THE JUMPING POWER UNIQUE TO FROGS.
"FROG" CAN BE WRITTEN "田鶏 (TIAN JI)," OR "PADDY CHICKEN," IN CHINESE! THAT'S HOW SIMILAR IT TASTES.
USTHENOPTERON
ENTIFIC NAME: EUSTHENOPTERON
IOD OF EXISTENCE: 386 ~ 370 MILLION YEARS AGO
TRIBUTION: NORTH AMERICA, EUROPE
E: FULL LENGTH 1.2 M [ROUGHLY 4 FT]
HABITED BRACKISH WATERS NEAR SEACOASTS AND SIMILAR TO EXTANT LUNGFISH, REATHED VIA PULMONARY RESPIRATION. CARNIVORES THAT ATE OTHER FISH PECIES. UNLIKE THE AVERAGE FISH SPECIES, THEY HAD DISTINCT BONES IN THEIR NS, WITH WHICH THEY PARTED AQUATIC PLANT MATTER IN ORDER TO SWIM. IT IS HESE BONES THAT PUTS THEM ON THE LINE OF PROGRESSION THAT EVENTUALLY EADS TO LAND-DWELLING ANIMALS.
THIS ONE'S WHITE-FLESHED AND MILD TASTING.
THIS ONE IS A BIT CRUNCHY AND CHEWY.
HOLOPTYCHIUS
SCIENTIFIC NAME: HOLOPTYCHIUS
PERIOD OF EXISTENCE: 381 ~ 367 MILLION YEARS AGO
DISTRIBUTION: NORTH AMERICA, EUROPE
SIZE: 1.2 M [ROUGHLY 4 FT]
GREEDY PREDATORS THAT CAUGHT THEIR PREY USING SMALL, SHARP TEETH AND SWALLOWED THEM WHOLE. POSSESSING STREAMLINED BODIES AND FINS OF VARYING SIZE AND SHAPE, IT APPEARS THEY WERE HIGHLY POWERFUL SWIMMERS.
CRASSIGYRINUS
NTIFIC NAME: CRASSIGYRINUS
OD OF EXISTENCE: 367 ~ 350 MILLION YEARS AGO
RIBUTION: EUROPE
: 2 M [ROUGHLY 6.5 FT]
SED ON THEIR PHYSICAL FEATURES, THEY ARE THOUGHT TO BE EARLY PHIBIAN SPECIES THAT REVERTED BACK TO AQUATIC LIFE, WITH ALL FOUR LIMBS VING LOST THE ABILITY TO WALK. LARGE EYES SERVED TO HELP LOCATE PREY SH IN MURKY POND AND SWAMP WATERS.
DELISH. 'NUF SAID.
THOUGH THEY SURE ARE FLASHY.
SCIENTIFIC NAME: CHEIROLEPIS
PERIOD OF EXISTENCE: 390 ~ 367 MILLION YEARS AGO
DISTRIBUTION: NORTH AMERICA, EUROPE
SIZE: FULL LENGTH 55 CM [ROUGHLY 22 IN]
LIVED IN FRESH WATER AND HUNTED DOWN PREY USING THEIR LARGE EYES. THE FIRST LIVING THINGS TO HAVE TRUE BACKBONES.
BONY VERTEBRAE ALLOWED FOR MUSCLE DEVELOPMENT, AND SWIFT, POWERFUL SWIMMING BECAME POSSIBLE.
HEIROLEPIS

TRANSLATION NOTES

Rosalia Lombardo, page 20

Rosalia Lombardo, often referred to as the "Sleeping Beauty of the Capuchin Catacombs," was a Sicilia girl who died of pneumonia at age two. Her body is indeed remarkably preserved, though mostly due to a particular combination of chemicals and minerals that the embalmer her grief-stricken father commissioned, had used to intentionally mummify her.

Shisshi, page 20

There does not appear to be an exact equivalent English word or term, but "shisshi" is composed of the kanji for "moist" and "corpse."

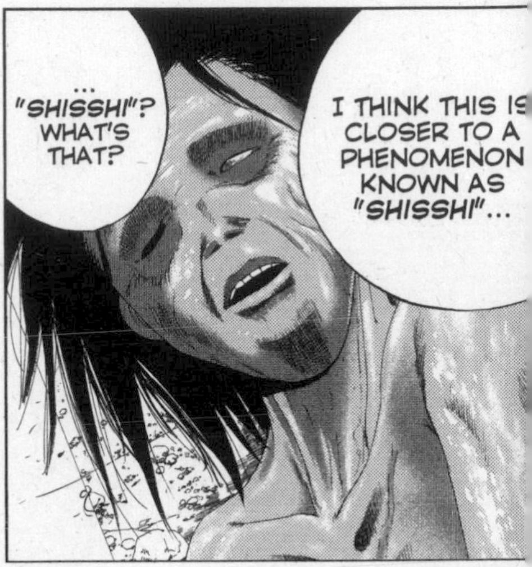
I THINK THIS IS CLOSER TO A PHENOMENON KNOWN AS "SHISSHI"...
... "SHISSHI"? WHAT'S THAT?

Sayonara home run, page 100

The Japanese term for a walk-off home run, a home run hit in the bottom of the ninth inning to break a tie or in the case where the home team is behind by one or more runs, to simultaneously tie and go ahead in points. The term "walk-off" is used because after that home run is hit and the point(s) scored, the players can "walk off" the field and go home, which is also why it is called "sayonara," or "good-bye," in Japanese.

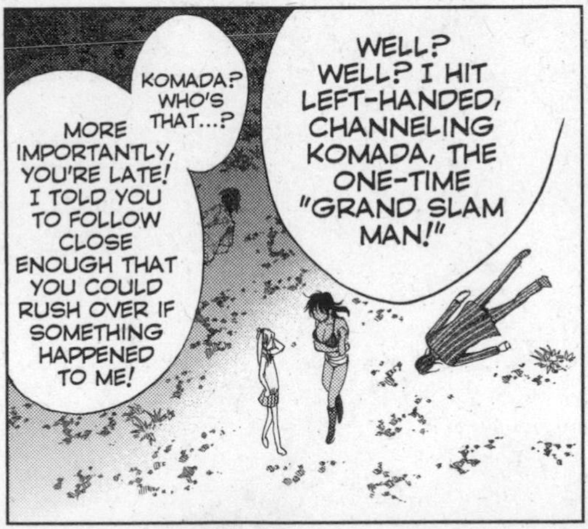
WELL? WELL? I HIT LEFT-HANDED, CHANNELING KOMADA, THE ONE-TIME "GRAND SLAM MAN!"
KOMADA? WHO'S THAT...?
MORE IMPORTANTLY, YOU'RE LATE! I TOLD YOU TO FOLLOW CLOSE ENOUGH THAT YOU COULD RUSH OVER IF SOMETHING HAPPENED TO ME!

Komada, page 100

Norihiro Komada is a former professional baseball player, coach, commentator, and tal personality originally from Nara prefecture. His nickname, the "Grand Slam Man," was well earned, having hit a grand slam in his first Nippon Pro Baseball at-bat and with hi 13 career grand slam home runs still placin him tied for fourth place among Japanese professional baseball players.

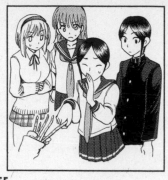

ting one's hand to one's lips, page
1

i is holding one hand up, sideways, to her lips as she's drawing
: stick. This is a gesture of prayer, although it is not clear
ether she's praying that she gets to be part of Akira's group or
.t she gets to stay behind.

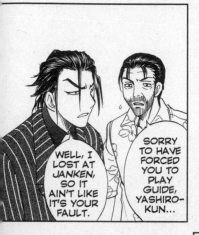

SORRY TO HAVE FORCED YOU TO PLAY GUIDE, YASHIRO-KUN...
WELL, I LOST AT JANKEN, SO IT AIN'T LIKE IT'S YOUR FAULT.

Janken, page 155

Janken or jankenpon is the Japanese term for the popular hand game "rock-paper-scissors", also known as "roshambo." In Japan, it is used much more common than flipping coins or throwing dice, and can involve any number of people to start.

to University of Science, page 167

ito" means "imperial capital," which is
v Edo/Tokyo was known from the Edo
iod to the end of the Second World
ır. Teito University of Science is likely an
nage to Tokyo University of Science.

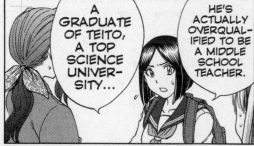

HE'S ACTUALLY OVERQUAL-IFIED TO BE A MIDDLE SCHOOL TEACHER.
A GRADUATE OF TEITO, A TOP SCIENCE UNIVER-SITY...

erial mammoth, page 187

re are some researchers who believe that imperial mammoths are merely large specimens of the
umbian mammoth (Mammuthus columbi) that have been misidentified and misnamed, instead of being
er a subspecies or an entirely distinct species. In addition to their size, another feature used by those
believe imperial mammoths are a different species is that the tips of their tusks cross, but since tusks
v throughout an individual's life, crossing tusk tips may just indicate older animals (which could also
unt for their taller height).

t true vertebrate, page 188

translator was unable to confirm the author's assertion that Cheirolepis were the first living things
ave a true backbone, though they do appear to be the first to have dermal cranial bones.

Cage of Eden volume 13 is a work of fiction. Names, characters, places, and incidents are the products of the author's imagination or are used fictitiously. Any resemblance to actual events, locales, or persons, living or dead, is entirely coincidental.

A Kodansha Comics Trade Paperback Original.

Published in the United States by Kodansha Comics, an imprint of Kodansha USA Publishing, LLC, New York.

Publication rights for this English edition arranged through Kodansha Ltd., Tokyo.

First published in Japan in 2011 by Kodansha Ltd., Tokyo, as *Eden no Ori* 13

ISBN 978-1-61262-262-0

Printed in the United States of America.

www.kodanshacomics.com

9 8 7 6 5 4 3 2 1

Translator: Mari Morimoto
Lettering: Rebecca Nelson

TOMARE!

[STOP!]

You are going the wrong way!

Manga is a completely different type of reading experience.

To start at the *beginning*, go to the *end*!

That's right! Authentic manga is read the traditional Japanese way—from right to left, exactly the *opposite* of how American books are read. It's easy to follow: Just go to the other end of the book, and read each page—and each panel—from the right side to the left side, starting at the top right. Now you're experiencing manga as it was meant to be.